THE
TUDOR COURT

THE
TUDOR COURT

David Loades

HEADSTART HISTORY

© David Loades 1992

First published by B. T. Batsford Ltd, London in 1986

Original typesetting: Latimer Trend & Company Ltd, Plymouth

Revised edition 1992

Published by
Headstart History
PO Box 41
Bangor
Gwynedd LL57 1SB
Great Britain

Printed by
Henry Ling Ltd
The Dorset Press
Dorchester

British Library Cataloguing in Publication Data
Loades, D. M.
    The Tudor court.
    1. Great Britain—Court and courtiers
    2. Great Britain—History—Tudors,
    1485–1603
    I. Title
942.05   DA315

ISBN 1 87 3041 38 1

Cover: The Family of Henry VIII (detail)
            Artist unknown

PUBLISHER'S FOREWORD

The Tudor court was at once the political and cultural focus of the state and the setting for the monarch, who there exercised his or her patronage and attracted and rewarded service of all kinds. David Loades has written the first general account of this important and glamorous institution, whose structure, operation and financing are of such fundamental importance in understanding how the Tudor monarchy worked.

The Tudors were personal rulers, who set great store by their honour and prestige. In this they competed directly, and successfully, with other and wealthier dynasties, notably the Valois and the Hapsburgs. Henry VIII and Elizabeth were particularly adept in creating powerful images for themselves, through court display and patronage, which contributed greatly to their authority at home and status abroad. In the sphere of domestic politics the role of the court was vital in providing a channel of access to the royal person. At the same time, the court's central position in the life of the nation ensured that it set the pace, not only socially and in the arts, but in religious and educational change.

Using extensive quotations from contemporary sources, Professor Loades builds up a vivid picture of this amorphous, constantly changing entity and its evolution over the period into the most stable and organised royal household in Europe after the papacy. The carefully chosen illustrations neatly complement the text, showing the process of image creation in practice.

The above description accompanied the original edition of this book published by Batsford in 1986. The Tudor court was a subject of general interest then and that interest has increased partly through the requirements of the education system at all levels and partly through the media who have frequently presented the sixteenth century court and its personalities to increasingly large and enthusiastic audiences.

It seemed to me that there was a need for this book to be made available again and like the *Oxford Martyrs* and *Two Tudor Conspiracies* I am able to publish *The Tudor Court* with comparative ease and the keen support of the author who is my husband! Every publisher hopes to produce books of quality and stature and I thank David for allowing me to add the titles to my growing list.

I must also thank Mike Heydon and Frank Hemming at Henry Ling Ltd, for their skill and support in production. The illustration on the cover is from the Royal Collection and reproduced by gracious permission of Her Majesty The Queen.

Judith Loades, 1992

CONTENTS

Publisher's Foreword   v
Contents   vii
  List of illustrations   ix
Preface to the Second Edition   x
Preface to the First Edition   xii

1 Introduction
  Maiestas   1
  Models and exempla   8
  The royal image   20

2 The institutions
  The structure of the court   38
  The *Domus Regie Magnificencie*   44
  The *Domus Providencie*   59
  Finance   73

3 Life at court
  Access, security and discipline   85
  Sports, entertainments and pastimes   96
  Scholarship and education   114
  Artists and others   127

4 Politics and religion
  The centre of patronage   133
  Faction and political strife   147
  Resident ambassadors   166
  Religion   172

5 Conclusion
  The impact of the court   184

Appendices

  I   The king's houses   193
  II   The principal officers of the court   204

CONTENTS

III   Illustrative documents   208
   1 Henry VIII's Privy Purse expenses
   2 Notes for the reform of the household
   3 On the ladies of Mary's Privy Chamber
IV   The structure of the court   210

Notes and references   215

Bibliography   240

Index   247

LIST OF ILLUSTRATIONS

between pages 90 and 91

1 Henry VIII as Solomon
2 Armour made for Henry VIII
3 Holbein's drawing for a fireplace at Bridewell Palace
4 A view of Richmond Palace
5 Henry VIII as *preux chevalier*
6 Henry VIII at the Field of Cloth of Gold
7 Whitehall stairs, from the Thames
8 Nonsuch in the late sixteenth century
9 Pen and ink design for a mural at Nonsuch
10 Henry VIII dining in his Privy Chamber
11 Title page of the Great Bible
12 Holbein's sketches of fashions in Henry VIII's court
13 Edward VI at the age of six

between pages 186 and 187

14 Alphonsus the Great enters Naples
15 *Allegory of Love*
16 Score check for the Accession Day tilts
17 The 'Ditchley Portrait' of Elizabeth I
18 The procession of the Knights of the Garter
19 Catherine Grey, Countess of Hertford
20 Mary I touching for the King's Evil
21 The 'Pelican Portrait' of Elizabeth I
22 William Fitzwilliam, Earl of Southampton
23 Sir Henry Lee
24 Henry Brandon
25 Edward VI and the Pope
26 Henry VIII
27 Mary I
28 Anne of Cleves
29 Mary I
30 Ground plan of Hampton Court
31 Ground plan of Nonsuch

PREFACE
to the Second Edition

The first edition of this book went out of print in 1989, but the subject continues to command considerable interest, and I am persuaded that a second edition is justified. In general I have seen little reason to revise either the structure of the original work, or the judgements which I made in 1985. However, scholarship moves on, and a substantial number of relevant articles and monographs have appeared, which are now listed in the supplementary bibliography. Two of these in particular have caused me to modify my own views, and have introduced new material into the discussion. The first is David Starkey's essay 'Intimacy and Innovation, the rise of the Privy Chamber, 1485-1547', in his own collection *The English Court from the Wars of the Roses to the Civil War*, published in 1987. Following Dr Starkey, I should point out with reference to the discussion on p. 39 (lines 7-12) that the attendance of councillors at court was far more than theoretical, and that in practice the council normally met there, often in the Privy apartments, although the monarch very seldom attended in person. Similarly, with reference to the Eltham Ordinances (p. 153, lines 30-35) of 1526, Wolsey's desire to reduce the Privy Chamber and remove Sir William Compton was matched by the king's own determination to increase the attendance of councillors, a move which was not to Wolsey's liking, and the implementation of which he managed to evade. It should also be added as a comment to the discussion of Sir William Compton's expenditure on p. 82, that the Privy Purse was theoretically limited to an expenditure of £10,000 per annum after the reforms of 1519-20, but that limit never seems to have been strictly adhered to. The second work of importance in this connection is Professor Dale Hoak's article 'The secret history of the Tudor court; the king's coffers and the king's purse, 1542-1553', which appeared in the *Journal of British Studies* for 1987 (vol. 26). Professor Hoak has demonstrated that there were two privy accounts after 1540, the Purse proper, which reverted to small scale activities, and the Coffers, which constituted a large spending department under the king's personal control, and was the operation for which Sir Anthony Denny was responsible (p. 82, lines 39-42). After Henry's death this distinction was maintained. Between January 1550 and January 1552 the Privy Purse proper handled only some £3988, and even that was probably not under the king's personal control. The account handled by Peter Osborne (p. 83, n. 173) which dispensed £40,000 over fifteen months in 1552-3, was clearly the Privy Coffers, not the Privy Purse. This is a point also discussed by J. A. Murphy in another essay in

Dr Starkey's *English Court*, 'The illusion of decline; the Privy Chamber 1547–1558'. Mr Murphy argues that plans were almost completed for Edward to take over the running of that account when his death supervened. The Privy Coffers were then discontinued. Neither Mary nor Elizabeth operated such a system. It is also worth noting that Denny was Keeper of the Palace of Westminster as well as Groom of the Stool in the latter years of Henry's reign, and it seems to have been in that capacity that he accounted for the Privy Coffers, rather than through his Privy Chamber appointment.

The reader will observe that not all the supplements relate to knowledge acquired since 1987. The opportunity has also been taken to repair one or two omissions, both bibliographical and otherwise. There are undoubtedly still other omissions, and some mistakes unremedied. For these I accept full responsibility, while acknowledging the kindness of those who from time to time point out the error of my ways. To all the scholars whose work has informed and improved my own I owe a debt of gratitude, and on this occasion particularly to my wife, Judith, and to Headstart History – the most companionable (if not the least demanding) of publishers.

Bangor   November 1992

PREFACE
to the First Edition

Nobody could describe the Tudor court as a neglected subject. Over the last twenty years the researches of Professor Sydney Anglo, Dr Penry Williams, Dr David Starkey, Dr Simon Adams and a number of other established scholars have illuminated many important aspects of its structure and functioning. At the same time, as Professor Geoffrey Elton pointed out in 1976, the court remains in some respects ill-defined and mysterious. In spite of the quantity of published research, and a large penumbra of doctoral dissertations, unpublished and in some cases unfinished, the only general description is still that provided by Sir Edmund Chambers in 1923 as an introduction to his work on the Elizabethan stage. This not only means that the hopeful student is without a manageable guide; it also encourages specialists in the politics of particular reigns, or the histories of particular families, to lose sight of the perspectives which they need in evaluating their own discoveries.

Consequently, I have endeavoured to create a portrait of the English court over the period of 140 years from the accession of Edward IV to the death of Elizabeth, its purpose, its structure, its funding and its way of life. It is, inevitably, a summary account, based partly upon my own investigations, but largely upon the researches of others. No doubt it will be found inadequate in some particulars, and mistaken in others, but I hope that it is not misleading, and that it will provide a framework for the large amount of work which still needs to be done. I have incurred many debts of gratitude, particularly to Dr David Starkey and Dr Robert Braddock for permission to cite from their unpublished theses, and to Dr Simon Adams, Dr William Tighe and Miss Elizabeth Culling for numerous helpful conversations. Thanks are also due to Mrs June Hughes for her indefatigable efforts with the typewriter and word processor, to Mr Neil Samman for compiling the index, and to my special subject students, both in Durham and in Bangor, with whom I have explored some of the recesses of the Tudor court over the last eight years to our mutual advantage.

David Loades

University College of North Wales
October 1985

1 INTRODUCTION

Maiestas

... hence I praise highly the magnificence and grandeur of the king's household, for within it is the supreme academy for the nobles of the realm, and a school of vigour, probity and manners by which the realm is honoured and will flourish.

(Fortescue, *De Laudibus Legum Angliae*, 111)

A medieval monarch was not simply, or even primarily, the head of an executive. His position was surrounded and upheld by a rich and multifarious symbolism which expressed the various aspects of his authority. He was expected to be, or to have been, an active leader in war, as the poet John Lydgate hopefully pointed out to the youthful Henry VI at the time of his coronation. Lydgate used the contemporary stereotype of Alexander, urging the infant king to emulate the physical courage and 'magnanymyte' of the most popular of the Nine Worthies.[1] The image of the king as warrior was one of great antiquity, and in England had still worn its stark Germanic face as late as the epics of *Havelok the Dane* and *Guy of Warwick* in the latter part of the thirteenth century, when the virtues portrayed had simply been those of strength and bravery in fighting. By the fifteenth century, chivalry and generosity had been added, to paint a hero of warmer colours, but the drive that sustained him was still victory in war. Such victory was as necessary to a king's honour in the sixteenth century as it had been in the thirteenth, which helps to explain why both Francis I and Henry VIII displayed such zeal in personal command, and why, half a century later, Philip II was so bitterly chagrined at his lack of opportunity to do the same.[2] Consistent with the importance of this priority, the symbolism of war was ubiquitous. Jousting remained a fashionable pastime long after it had ceased to bear any resemblance to real combat; 'coat armour' distinguished the gently born; and monarchs visiting the cities of their kingdoms were greeted with the ritual of conquest and submission.

Although it grew out of war, chivalry developed values of its own, frequently summed up in the word 'magnanimity', which represented the grafting of Christian virtues such as modesty and self-restraint onto the traditional heroic stock. Thus the Alexander of romance

... if alle he hade the victorye of his enemyes, he bare hym never the hiere therefore, ne empridede hym not thare-of.

1

and when all his army are tormented by thirst, refuses the one small supply of water in a gesture which must surely have provided the model for Sir Philip Sidney at Zutphen.[3] The chivalric *prud'homme* was a moral champion who far transcended the mere warrior; he was the image alike of courtesy, of piety, and of justice. Literary *exempla* abound: Chaucer's Knight; Lydgate's 'worthy Ector, of knyghthod spring and welle'; and numerous figures from the dream world of Malory's *Morte d'Arthur*. In real life the king was expected not only to pay lip-service to such ideals, but to signify his approval through the presentation of allegorical pageants, and through his own observation of the knightly code of honour. Although William Caxton might be scornful of the shortcomings of his contemporaries—'What do ye now but go to the baynes and playe at dyse?'[4]—chivalry was a potent force in the symbolism of monarchy, and in the intense competitiveness of the dynasties of western Europe.

However, the model king was not merely the knight writ large. His responsibilities as a 'good lord' and justiciar were not only more ancient than the chivalric code but also remained largely independent in practice. Chivalric justice was a generous sense of fair play, such as that displayed (on his own account) by De Joinville when he elected to fight on foot beside his soldiers on crusade, lest they should reproach him for his superior ability to escape.[5] Although royal justice included an element of equity, it was primarily the enforcement of a code of law. It was the king's business to interpret the laws of his realm, and to see that they were obeyed—a process which had long since developed its own formalities and rituals. By the fifteenth century these had largely become detached from the person of the monarch, or gone 'out of court' in the significant contemporary phrase. Edward IV, in the early part of his reign, still occasionally presided at formal sessions,[6] but the Tudors did not do so, and by the early seventeenth century Sir Edward Coke could deny that James I had any right to intervene personally in the administration of the common law.[7] Nevertheless, as Coke was to discover to his cost, the king personally appointed and dismissed the judges who acted in his name, and the Lord Chancellor, the formal head of the judicial system, was very much a royal servant. Similarly, the supreme legislative body, the High Court of Parliament, was not only convened, prorogued and dismissed at the will of the monarch, but was also graced by personal and ceremonial appearances at its opening, and when the royal assent to legislation preceded its close.

'Good lordship' was less formal, but equally essential to the proper functioning of authority. The monarch was expected to call his leading subjects to counsel, to arbitrate fairly in their quarrels, and to employ (and reward) their services. He was also expected to listen to their intercessions on behalf of their own clients, and, within limits, to recognise their rights of protection and promotion. For example, when the Prior of Durham sought redress from Edward IV in 1461, his cause was espoused by his own bishop, Laurence Booth, and by the Earl of Warwick. According to his own account

... my Lord of Durham took me in his hand, and sat down upon his knee before the king, and so did my Lord of Warwick, and I beside him; and they prayed the king to be my good lord; and the king answered and said 'Prior, I will be your good lord, and I will remember your bill' ...[8]

The Prior of Durham was well connected, and humbler suitors might have had to play a long and patient waiting game to receive similar consideration. Nevertheless, in a personal monarchy, promotion of this kind by those with normal or frequent rights of access to the king was an essential lubricant of the processes of government. The ritual of petition and response was a part of the liturgy of politics, the correct and frequent performance of which was much more important than the actual outcome of particular requests.

Another aspect of the same liturgy was the process of reward. In an age when regular fees and wages were small, or non-existent, except in the more menial grades of service, the process of reward was flexible, even gratuitous in its nature, giving maximum scope to a monarch's generosity. There was, of course, expected to be some relationship between service and reward, but it was very tolerantly perceived and only extreme factional bias (as in the case of Henry VI) or excessive whimsicality (dangerously approached by James I) might cause serious doubts to be cast upon the king's good lordship.[9] Many gifts were solicited, a procedure carrying no shadow of reproach, which brought together the functions of petition and reward. When Lord Lisle thought that he might be called upon to go to war in 1533, he asked the king to give him a 'hosting harness', or field armour. Typically, his request was 'moved' to Henry by his friend Sir Francis Bryan of the Privy Chamber, who wrote in January 1534

... his Grace sayeth ye shall not need to fight as yet ... Nevertheless at his Grace's next repair to Greenwich, which I suppose will be within these fourteen days, he will look out one for you himself ...[10]

Lisle duly received his armour in May 1534, although it seems unlikely that he ever used it. Generosity was no less appreciated as a virtue in the princes of the renaissance than it had been among the 'ring givers' and 'gold sharers' of the ancient northern epics. Baldesar Castiglione wrote of his ideal ruler

He should be a prince of great splendour and generosity, giving freely to everyone ... He should hold magnificent banquets, festivals, games and public shows ...[11]

This was a courtier's point of view—the view of a likely beneficiary. Those who had to find the money, such as the English House of Commons, might be less enthusiastic about largesse; but nobody denied that magnificence was inseparable from good lordship, and essential to the honour of a powerful king.

Reward, even at a modest level, also conferred the honour of the giver upon the receiver. Sir Robert Sidney, a man of considerable substance, rejoiced in the grant of the wardenship of the royal park at Otford in Kent, and esteemed it 'of great value, not for the profit but because it was of her Majesty's gift, and of reputation in his country'[12] To be the king's servant or 'fee'd man', and to wear his livery was both honourable and profitable at every social level. When Henry VIII wished to increase his direct influence in Wales and in the far north of England, he paid fees, or annuities, to prominent local gentlemen, effectively creating his own clientage system independent of those of local magnate families such as the Percies or the Herberts. Such gentlemen, or more commonly their sons, might also receive posts in the household, thus simultaneously increasing their access to the 'fount of honour' and binding their families more firmly to the Crown.[13] Similarly, only the king could create titles of honour, and the increasing formality of such creations in the later Middle Ages served to emphasise that fact. Earls had always been subject to formal creation, but as late as the end of the fourteenth century the distinction between the 'baronage' and the rest of the armigerous class was by no means clear. In 1383 Sir Thomas Camoys was both elected knight of the shire for Surrey, and received an individual writ of summons to the parliament.[14] The writ of summons, which was at the king's discretion, was the basis of the distinction which later emerged, but it was not used consistently and could be attributed to the 'natural' or territorial power of the man to whom it was directed. This situation began to change, however, after 1387 when a title was created for the first time by Letters Patent—the recipient being the Steward of the Household, Sir John Beauchamp. By the fifteenth century, creation by Letters Patent was normal, and the king's prerogative of ennobling blood had been significantly emphasised. At the same time, new ranks of nobility were created, giving the king greater scope for formal promotions. The first duke was the Black Prince in 1337;[15] the first marquis Robert de Vere in 1386; and the first viscountcy was created in 1440. It was also recognised that royal service enhanced social status without a formal grant. A king's messenger, for example, always ranked one degree above his proper status by virtue of his function, and close personal attendance upon the king was similarly regarded, quite apart from the opportunities it offered for more tangible reward.

The king carried out all his functions in the middle of a public stage, and, in an age accustomed to allegorical modes of thought, the symbolism of what was done was frequently more important than the action itself. The Evil May Day of 1517 was a turbulent and nasty little riot against Flemish and Italian merchants in London, potentially disruptive of England's relations with the rest of Christendom. Consequently the ritual punishment of the ringleaders was swift and severe, and the ceremonies of pardon were grand and exceedingly public. Firstly, Queen Catherine, on bended knee and with hair unbound, in the accepted pose of the female suppliant, obtained Henry's promise of grace for the 400 odd who remained in custody after the initial executions. Then, in a great ceremony at Westminster Hall, attended by numerous magnates and ambassadors, the prisoners were paraded in chains, crying out for mercy. This time Wolsey, who was clearly the stage manager, played the leading suppliant role, and after listening to his lengthy oration, the king at last ordered that the prisoners be released.[16] Many such scenes were enacted upon a smaller scale, designed to impress, and to reassure the spectators that the divine order was intact and functioning. In this respect the queen's role was particularly important. No doubt Catherine felt genuine sympathy for the offenders, but she also believed it to be her proper function to temper the edge of royal justice with mercy, just as it was the function of the Virgin Mary to awaken the mercy of God. The queen was an intercessor whose well known and public piety gave her a unique value in contemporary eyes. Her holiness of life and 'shamfastness' guaranteed that her voice would be heard, not only in Westminster but also in Heaven. For a similar reason the king's own piety required frequent public airing. Neither Henry VII nor Henry VIII appear to have been men of much religious sensibility, but both went through the motions diligently, and the latter's frequent attendance at mass, regular almsgiving and occasional, well-publicised pilgrimages attracted favourable comment early in his reign.[17] Edward VI's enthusiasm for godly sermons, and Elizabeth's histrionic touches with the English bible during her coronation entry in 1559, have to be seen in the same context, although in a different idiom.

The king was responsible to God for the well-being of his subjects, and the royal supremacy, in augmenting the authority, also augmented the responsibility. Edmund Brocke, an 'aged and wretched person' from Cowle in Worcestershire was unlucky to have been overheard and denounced to the authorities when he blamed the foul summer weather of 1535 upon the king's proceedings.[18] Shakespeare blamed foul weather upon the quarrels of Oberon and Titania, but an earlier generation found a more political explanation. The misbehaviour of kings disrupted the proper course of nature and deflected the goodness of God. The fact that Henry VIII did not have a son for so many years was not just a practical danger and inconvenience, it was an expression of divine disapprobation. Conversely the birth of princes conveyed God's blessing. The prompt fecundity of Elizabeth of York had greatly strengthened her husband's position, and the birth of Edward in 1537 appeared to justify the king's actions over the preceding years—a point celebrated by Hugh Latimer when he wrote to Cromwell

> ... verily God hath shewed himself God of England or rather an English God, if we consider and ponder well all his proceedings with us from time to time ...[19]

The symbolism of fertility was explicitly, and somewhat tastelessly, displayed in the pageantry at the coronation entry of Anne Boleyn (who was already five months pregnant) in 1533,[20] and more subtly in that which welcomed Catherine of Aragon in 1501. Even the existence of numerous royal bastards could be reassuring to the simple-minded.

The language of symbolism was universal. In a work of political theory and exhortation entitled *De Regimine Principum*, written in the 1440s and addressed to King Henry VI, the anonymous author anatomised the throne of Solomon as the symbolic structure of royal authority.[21] The six steps leading to the throne were the six qualities of royal virtue: the six material elements used in its construction represented good conscience, prudence, judgement, justice, mercy and counsel. Similarly the four gems inserted in the king's crown signified the four estates of the realm: jasper for the nobility, carbuncle for the prelates, sapphire for the other clergy, and onyx for the commons. 'Finaliter', he concluded, 'christianissime rex, per sceptrum regie maiestatis potest intelligi in decore regio supereminencia magnifice potestatis.'[22] ('Finally, most Christian King, by the sceptre of royal authority can be understood the full supremacy of sovereign power, as appropriate to that country.') Every implement used and gesture performed in the elaborate ceremonies of coronation symbolised some aspect of the king's authority and office. Such pageantry not only constituted easily comprehended treatises in political theory for the benefit of the illiterate; it could also present a sophisticated world view, intelligible only to the highly educated. As Professor Anglo has demonstrated, the pageants provided for Catherine and Arthur in 1501 expressed an entire and complex natural and political philosophy, expressly designed to demonstrate to the rest of Europe that the Tudor court was capable of challenging the highest standards of refinement, taste and erudition.[23]

In such a context the distinction between business and pleasure was extremely tenuous. A state banquet or a masque was almost certain to contain some expression of political intent, or to be used as a vehicle for conflict. For example, when Philip arrived in England in 1554 one of his gentlemen was swift to complain that the king was being served at table by Englishmen, and that the Duke of Alba was unable to bear his wand of office, as majordomo.[24] The English in turn complained of lack of access to the royal apartments, a situation which eventually provoked a rebuke from the emperor to his son, via his secretary, Eraso:

> You will tell the king that I beg him to be careful to please the English by summoning the foremost them at any rate to his levee . . .[25]

When Charles himself had visited England in the summer of 1522, he had been regaled with, among many other things, a play by William Cornish ridiculing his enemy Francis I of France, in the guise of a wild horse. Much of the constructive negotiation between Charles and Henry which characterised this visit had been conducted during a two day hunting trip to Windsor; and numerous other examples could be cited. The life of a king was a unity, and with rare and limited exceptions it was both public and political. Everything, from his coronation to the smallest detail of his domestic arrangements, was designed to contribute to his *maiestas*, that blend of dignity, magnificence and power which was necessary to ensure both the obedience of his own subjects and the respect of his fellow monarchs. His court was the vehicle through which this was accomplished. A vastly complex and expensive affair by the fifteenth century, it was both a stage and a forum; the centre of government, because the king was the centre of government; the machinery through which

6

patronage was sought and dispensed; and a cultural centre reflecting the tastes and ambitions of the ruler. John Paston, accompanying Margaret of York to Bruges for her marriage to Charles the Bold in 1468, recorded very much the kind of awed response which Charles must have been striving to achieve.

> ... as for the Dwkys coort, as of lordys, ladys, and gentlewomen, knytys, sqwyirs, and gentyllmen, I never herd of non lycck to it save Kyng Artourys cort. By my trowthe, I have no wyt nor remembrance to wryte to yow halfe the worchep that is her ...[26]

As we shall see, Burgundy was setting a hot pace in the mid-fifteenth century, and one which Edward IV of England strove in vain to equal. Nevertheless, he achieved much, and, contrary to what is sometimes argued, that achievement was sustained by Henry VII. The latter's reputation for parsimony was not altogether deserved, and the Milanese envoy, Raimondo de Sancino, could write in the summer of 1499 that the King of England was attending to nothing but amusements, and the enjoyment of his great wealth.[27] No doubt the king would have been well enough pleased to have created such an impression; and more so by the fact that de Sancino followed up his report by declaring that there were no commotions in England, and would be none as long as the king lived. Bearing in mind Henry's long struggle to achieve security, such a tribute is more impressive than the oft-quoted words of the Venetian Francesco Chieregato. Chieregato, writing in 1517, conferred the accolade of critical Italian approbation upon the court of Henry VIII.

> In short, the wealth and civilisation of the world are here; and those who call the English barbarians appear to me to render themselves such. I perceive here very elegant manners, extreme decorum, and very great politeness; and amongst other things there is this most invincible king whose acquirements and qualities are so many and excellent that I consider him to excell all who ever wore a crown ...[28]

It is to be hoped that Isabella d'Este, the recipient of this encomium, was equally impressed. In the next generation the Spaniards who accompanied the future Philip II for his marriage to Mary, and whose view of England was distinctly jaundiced, were reluctantly impressed by the sheer scale of the enterprise; wrote one:

> There are usually eighteen kitchens in full blast ... and they seem veritable hells, such is the stir and bustle in them. The palaces here are enormous, for the smallest of the four we have seen is certainly much bigger, and has more and larger apartments, than the Alcazar of Madrid, but the throng of people is such that they are full to bursting ...[29]

The court of Elizabeth, by contrast, became a work of art in its own right, which impressed curious Muscovites and sophisticated Frenchmen almost as much as it intrigued her narcissistic courtiers themselves. Sir John Davies, writing at the very end of the century, accurately summed up the achievement of the Tudor court at its highest level of development:

Since when all ceremonious mysteries,
All sacred orgies and religious rites,
All pomps, and triumphs and solemnities,
All funerals, nuptials and like public sights,
All parliaments of peace and warlike fights,
All learned arts and every great affair
A lively shape of dancing seems to bear.[30]

A dance of state, or the politics of appearances. Throughout the century the English court was out of proportion to the resources of the realm. At its most expensive it absorbed over a third of the Crown's ordinary revenue. Both Henry VIII and Elizabeth were larger than life, and their *maiestas* distorted the role of England in European diplomacy. This could have disastrous financial consequences, as was evident in the 1540s, but it was not simply the result of ambition or *hubris* on the part of the individual monarch. It was a necessary ingredient of order and discipline in an age when the coercive machinery of the state was primitive and ineffectual. *Maiestas* attracted service. This was not simply a question of mercenary employment but also one of loyalty and honour. Philip II's bid to outshine the French in the 1550s was an essential part of his campaign to increase his influence in the papal curia, and amongst those German princes who were opposed to his inclusion in the Imperial succession. Henry VIII tried a similar tactic with selected Irish chieftains, and created a short-lived affinity in Scotland while pursuing plans to marry Prince Edward to the infant Mary. The Tudors were not, with the possible exception of Henry VII, conspicuously successful in pursuing foreign policy objectives by these means, but they were successful at home. That slow process whereby the gentlemen of England became convinced that the king was a better lord than the Earl of Derby or the Duke of Norfolk, and that gentility itself consisted in a grant of arms from a royal herald, was mainly carried out in and through the court. The *maiestas* of the Tudors was essential both to the nature and success of their domestic policies, and to that developing sense of national identity which was the outward expression of the same success. In a sixteenth-century polity so much lay in the eye of the beholder, and it was the function of the court to attract and train that eye.

Models and exempla

What, then, was a court? And how had the typical late medieval court of western Europe come into existence? The division of the *Liber Niger*, or Household Book of Edward IV into two sections, *Domus Regie Magnificencie* and *Domus Providencie*, provides a convenient starting point.[31] The latter was the domestic household—that organisation which provided for the feeding of the king and his family, for cleaning, transportation and a host of other menial functions. As we shall see, it could be a large, complex and important institution, but neither its origin nor the stages of its growth are in any sense obscure. Apart from its size, and consequent sophistication of organisation, it was no different from the household of any important nobleman, as the surviving records of the Percy Earls of Northumberland or the Stafford Dukes of Buckingham make clear.[32]

The *Domus Regie Magnificencie*, on the other hand, presents many problems. Its function is clear enough: it was designed to sustain and focus the *maiestas* of the ruler; but its origin and development are not easy to trace. One of its roots clearly lay in the Germanic *comitatus* of the Anglo-Saxon king, those warriors who had been at the same time his companions in arms and his bodyguard. The successors of these thanes and huscarles are to be seen in the Household Knights of Henry II or Richard II, and in the Knights and Esquires of the Body who served Edward IV and Henry VII. Similarly the chaplains, scribes and scholars who gathered around Charlemagne or Alfred were succeeded by the Chancery and Exchequer clerks of a later generation, as well as by the royal secretaries, Masters of the Henchmen, and staff of the Chapel Royal. Nevertheless, early medieval rulers were 'saddle kings', conducting business on the move, and frequently in camp or in makeshift accommodation. We would look in vain for the strict concentric patterns, rigid protocol and elaborate ceremonies of later centuries in the court of Frederick Barbarossa, of Charles IV or Richard I. This did not mean that kings were indifferent to learning or the arts; Henry II, the most restless of them all, attracted the service of men as talented and diverse as Walter Map, Ralph de Diceto and John of Salisbury. It was rather that they provided no settled context for them to work in for any length of time, with the result that there was no court 'school' or style to attract imitation, and no carefully calculated *tableaux vivants* to enhance the authority of the ruler.

That aspect of the *Domus Magnificencie* came not from the north, but from the south, and particularly from the hierarchical and extremely formal courts of the Byzantine emperors, who seem to have invented elevated thrones, ritual costume, and special visual effects.[33] The theocratic pretensions of rulers such as Justinian brought together the secular pomp of the pagan emperors and the ecclesiastical ceremonial of the Christian church. Moreover, the Byzantine emperors, in spite of frequent military campaigns, were relatively static. They had a fixed capital, and built a vast urban palace to set off their dignity to best advantage. It was not the hard-riding Charlemagne, with his power base among the Frankish chieftains, who first transmitted this Imperial vision to the west, but the papacy. In spite of its vulnerability in an age of turbulent and extremely physical politics, the papacy had the immense advantages of fixed location and institutional continuity. By the eleventh century, when its Imperial ambitions were beginning to consolidate, the papacy had developed both a far-reaching political philosophy, and a sophisticated administrative machinery. This latter, the Curia, provided the most influential model for

9

royal imitation, and with the development of the electoral functions of the college of cardinals in the late eleventh century, a true papal court also began to emerge. This, the *Famiglia Pontifica*, grew more rapidly and significantly during the period of the 'exile' in Avignon during the fourteenth century.[34] the popes were major patrons of learning throughout the Middle Ages, but, unlike their renaissance successors, were not great builders and had little interest in ostentation for its own sake. On the other hand, their households did see the development of a liturgy of deference which was later to be widely imitated. These gestures—kneeling in the presence of the pontiff, kissing objects of common use, and so on—were transferred naturally from the rituals of the divine office, because successive popes placed great emphasis upon their role as Vicar of Christ and successor to St Peter. There was no trace of warrior-companionship among the *curiales* of a pope, but rather a deliberate emphasis upon the virtue of humility. In this civilian and bureaucratic atmosphere, a rigidly hierarchical and deferential protocol was to be expected.[35]

There was no single secular equivalent of the Curia, or the *Famiglia Pontifica*—certainly not the courts of the Ottonian or early Hohenstauffen emperors. Nevertheless, the households of the Norman rulers of Sicily provided a somewhat similar bridge between Byzantium and the west, and this was most obviously and significantly the case in the court of the Sicilian-bred emperor, Frederick II—the *Stupor Mundi* and one of the most remarkable men of the thirteenth century. Frederick was an intellectual, and a voracious reader, with a strong interest in antiquity and in natural history. In spite of his incessant travels, and almost equally incessant wars, he retained a base at Palermo where Greeks, Jews and Muslims were equally welcome; where jurists such as Pietro della Vigna and astrologers such as the notorious Michael Scott could meet, study, and discuss, and whither the noble youth of Italy and Germany flocked to improve their minds and social graces. Unlike most northern rulers, Frederick built extensively, and his elegant residences, such as Castel del Monte in Apulia, were characterised by lavish ornamental stone work and sculpture, efficient sanitation, numerous bathrooms, and lavish formal gardens of great intricacy and elegance. He lived in great magnificence, surrounded by scholars, poets and artists, as well as by the lawyers and soldiers who served him in the government of the Empire, and was probably the first secular ruler in the west to embrace the concept of *maiestas*, and to use it deliberately as a political weapon. It would be a mistake, however, to regard Frederick as an enlightened ruler in the modern sense, in spite of his rational scepticism and personal cleanliness. Not only was he capable of ferocious cruelties, his attitude towards women was distinctly oriental. In spite of, or perhaps because of, the fact that he encouraged Provençal troubadours, and himself composed love songs in the same idiom, the women of his court were kept in the strictest seclusion. His third wife, Isabella, the sister of Henry III of England, was discovered by her brother Richard during a visit, surrounded by luxury and amusements of every kind, but with no place at all in the life of the court.[36] Frederick, who fathered numerous illegitimate children, clearly regarded women simply as objects of pleasure and ornament, rather like the fine jewels and precious manuscripts with which he solaced himself in a life of conflict and movement. They were also, of course, useful diplomatic tools. He married three times himself—in Aragon, France and England—and his daughter Constance was wedded to the Emperor John Vatatzes, the Byzantine ruler of Trebizond. Frederick's Byzantine concept of his office brought him into incessant conflict with the papacy, and eventually did enormous damage to the Holy Roman Empire, but it also pointed the way to a sharp increase in the aspirations of other secular rulers, and those aspirations were to be reflected both in political theory and in the organisation of their courts.

There was nothing of the *prud'homme* about Frederick, neither the piety nor the gallantry. Chivalry was a distinctively western, and particularly French, invention. St Louis was one of its most earnest protagonists, but its literary and cultural origins go back much further, at least to the court of William IX of Aquitaine in the late eleventh century.[37] In its mature form it was a blend of many ingredients both Christian and pagan. Most important was the attempt, actively promoted by church leaders, to divert the warlike energies of Frankish warriors into morally constructive channels—the promotion of justice, the protection of the weak, and the defence of the faith. Second, and nothing at all to do with the church, was the cult of courtly love, a poetic fantasy invented by the troubadours, which seems to have had no obvious prototype in either classical or Germanic antiquity. Whatever modern feminists may think, courtly love was originally a means of protecting and enhancing the status of women, and of giving them a role in the normally male-dominated households of their husbands, sons and brothers. The ideal, set out most fully and explicitly in Andreas Capellanus' *De Arte Honeste Amandi*, written about 1190, was almost entirely one of service.[38] The lady was, almost by definition, unattainable, either because already married, or of superior social status. The knight, in consequence, devoted his life to a hopeless quest, performing feats of valour in his lady's honour, singing her praises, rescuing her (should she by any fortunate chance be in need of it), and indulging in frequent poetic fantasies of an erotic nature.

> Among eke, for thy lady sake,
> Songes and complayntes that thou make;
> For that will meven in hir herte,
> Whanne they reden of thy smerte.

—as Chaucer's translation of the ever-popular *Roman de la Rose* later expressed it.[39] Not surprisingly, the cult of courtly love was actively promoted by those ladies who were in a position to do so, notably Eleanor of Aquitaine and her daughter Marie de Champagne. Eleanor's own court, at Poitiers, saw a major flowering of romantic poetry in the middle of the twelfth century through the works of Benoit de Sainte Maure, Wace, and Bernart de Ventadorn. Such poetry, although sometimes far-fetched, was by no means frivolous, and

Eleanor herself also had serious intellectual interests which were facilitated and made more acceptable by her patronage of the poets. After her marriage to Henry II of England, who was also an active patron of scholars, the two strands naturally intermingled, and the two courts of Westminster and Poitiers should be seen as complementary rather than contrasting.

Marie de Champagne, for whose amusement the *De Arte Honeste Amandi* was written, presided along with her husband Henri, Count of Champagne, over a small but extremely civilised court, and was somewhat dubiously credited with having invented the 'court of love' in its formal guise.[40] Allegedly this was an all-female tribunal set up to adjudicate issues of correct romantic behaviour. More likely it was an occasional verbal game, such as that presided over by Elizabetta Gonzaga and portrayed by Castiglione. Given the hard-headed nature of feudal marriage arrangements and the depressed legal status of married women, to say nothing of the predatory nature of the warrior male, the social and psychological value of courtly love was considerable. For all its literary devices and absurdities, it provided a civilised code of conduct for a basically primitive game—rather like the Queensberry Rules. It obviously met a profound need, for it proved to be one of the most powerful and enduring cultural modes transmitted by the high Middle Ages to their early modern successors.

By the fourteenth century a handful of major courts had emerged as the leading centres of culture, learning and magnificence, but only that of the popes at Avignon could really be said to have developed a strong institutional structure. In keeping with the early development of financial and administrative institutions in England, the *Constitutio Domus Regis* of about 1135 shows an advanced structure of household departments,[41] but the *Domus Magnificencie* is embryonic. Nor do the establishment lists of 21 Edward III (1348) show very much advance in that direction. The list of the king's clerks, for example, runs

> ... the Kinges secretary, 2 receavers of the kinges chamber, the clerke of the kychen, the clerke marshall, 2 clarkes of the wardrobe, 5 clerkes of the prevey seals, 8 chappleyns, a surgeon, the clarke of the markett, and the kinges Procurator ...[42]

showing a fine disregard for the distinctions which would later emerge between the household below stairs and the king's Chamber. Nevertheless, after the papacy, it was probably England which had the most stable and best organised royal household, largely because it seems to have fluctuated less dramatically with the personality of the ruler. At the same time it was the Valois who set the pace in decorum, in splendour, and in the patronage of scholarship and the arts. The reign of Charles V, from 1364 to 1380, was the apogee of this achievement. In her *Livre des fais du Charles V*, Christine de Pisan described his orderly daily routine: his religious observances, formal audiences, council meetings, meals and cultivated relaxation. On summer evenings after supper, he would walk in his garden, and there receive 'merchants (who) came bringing velvet, cloth of gold or other things, and every kind of fine or curious thing, or jewels ...'[43] A connoisseur himself, the king also kept in his household servants whose business it was to advise him about such matters, and to them the would-be vendors were referred. Although intended as an encomium, Christine's work is nevertheless an impressive testimony to the quality of life achieved in the French court, and is supported by extensive evidence of the king's discriminating literary taste, enthusiasm as a book collector, and fluency in the Latin language. His brothers, the Dukes of Anjou, Burgundy and Berry were also distinguished patrons and collectors, and the *Tres Riches Heures*, commissioned by the latter, is one of the finest and most sophisticated examples of book illumination ever executed.

By the early fifteenth century, however, the French court was a spent force both culturally and politically, and faded into insignificance after 1413, largely on account of the mental deficiency of Charles VI. Meanwhile the English court had grown in stature, despite the violent change of dynasty in 1399. In the latter years of his reign, when he had succeeded in imposing his own personality, Richard II's court was an important centre of literary and artistic patronage.[44] His *curiales*, or Chamber knights, also played a major role in his attempts to bypass the limitations of feudal overlordship, and in his disagreements with the papacy. In the event, this political development of the Chamber turned out to be premature, and was not continued by his supplanter, Henry IV. Like Richard, Henry had clear reasons for wanting a magnificent and imposing court; in the early years of his reign he had an uphill task imposing his authority, and every additional scrap of prestige was precious. He attempted, unsuccessfully, to attract the service of Christine de Pisan, but his efforts in other directions were better rewarded, and by the time he died, his court, like his dynasty, was firmly settled and effective. Thereafter, following the fortunes of battle, the rise of England measured the eclipse of France. Henry V and Charles VI died within a few weeks of each other in 1422, but their legacies could hardly have been more different. While the latter's household officers were receiving a distribution of their late master's furs and silks, and the 'roi de Bourges' scarcely merited a court at all, the English Regent, John, Duke of Bedford, kept glittering state in Paris.[45] Living at the Hotel Saint-Pol, the private residence of the kings of France, John and his Duchess, Anne, the sister of Duke Philip of Burgundy, set the standards both in splendour and in protocol. Their only rival was Duke Philip himself, based at the Hotel d'Artois. Competition between the households of the two allies was incessant, in music, dancing, jousting, and the ostentatious display of jewels and furs; but English political and military power always ensured the regent the upper hand.

It was a shortlived ascendancy. By 1429, when Charles VII was crowned at Rheims and the Valois cause began to revive, Burgundy and England were already moving apart; the long minority of Henry VI was having its debilitating effect, and Duke Philip's court was emerging into that cultural supremacy which was to last for the remainder of his life—and well beyond. The death of the Duchess of Bedford in 1431 was almost as serious a blow to the English cause as military defeat.[46] By the time that the regent himself died in 1435, and the Duke of Burgundy changed sides, the confidence and vitality had long since gone out of the English presence in France, and the English court was in eclipse. Meanwhile, Duke Philip had signalled both his achievements and his ambitions by marking the occasion of his marriage to the Infanta Isabella of Portugal in 1430 with the establishment of the Order of the Golden Fleece. The *Toison d'Or* was set up, according to its article of foundation

> ... from the great love which we bear to the noble order of chivalry, whose honour and prosperity are our only concern, to the end that the true Catholic Faith ... as well as the peace and welfare of the realm may be defended, preserved and maintained to the Glory and Praise of Almighty God ...[47]

This was a shrewd, indeed a brilliant move on the duke's part. Pope Eugenius IV was delighted, hailing the knights as new Maccabeans, and it was very difficult for anyone to object to such laudable and honourable sentiments. The success of the new order was already apparent by the time the first Chapter was held on St Andrew's Day, 1431, and the pattern of strict formality and solemnity was established. The number of knights was limited to twenty-four, in addition to the Master, who was always to be the ruling Duke of Burgundy.[48] The strictest standards of orthodoxy and of aristocratic conduct were insisted upon, and the insignia was always to take precedence over every other.

Within a few years the *Toisin d'Or* had become both a symbol and a cause of Burgundian success. Although the Master himself was not a sovereign prince, he was by 1450 one of the wealthiest and most powerful rulers in Christendom, and rulers who were sovereigns were proud to wear his insignia. At the same time, one of the functions of the knights was to act as a ducal council—whose advice or reproach the duke was bound on oath to heed, as Charles the Bold did in 1468 and again in 1473.[49] The chivalry to which the order was devoted, and which became such a cult at the Burgundian court in consequence, was more a matter of form than of substance. Etiquette was extremely strict, and no deviation was tolerated; on the other hand Duke Philip's notorious sexual irregularities drove the Duchess Isabella away from the court into a nunnery, and populated the ducal service with acknowledged and unacknowledged bastards. This was not the kind of courtly love which Eleanor of Aquitaine had encouraged, and casts a curious light upon the knightly sense of honour of which so much was spoken, particularly because the duke's example seems to have been widely imitated, and to have attracted no reproach from the innumerable clergy who thronged the court, creating an atmosphere which must have been a curious mixture of the dévot and the licentious.[50] Otto Cartellieri probably identified the source of this paradox correctly when he wrote 'The guiding principle (of life at the Burgundian court) was that nothing was dishonourable if it was done in the service of the sovereign.'[51] Perhaps also the strictness with which the liturgy of deference and manners curbed other expressions of passion rendered such an outlet psychologically essential.

Partly because of its wealth, and partly because of the political opportunism of the dukes, the court of Burgundy had great attractions for political exiles from all over Europe, including (in 1456) the Dauphin of France, and (in 1470) the temporarily displaced Edward IV of England. This not only had the effect of spreading Burgundian influence; it also attracted diplomatic attention. Italian despots like the d'Este and Gonzaga kept agents there, not only to keep an eye upon their own dissidents, but also to exploit opportunities for trade and mutual support. It was no accident that Jan Van Eyck, the court painter of Philip the Good, was the one northern artist who was well known, and respected, by the masters of the Italian Renaissance.[52] Well-to-do Germans, such as Eberhart the younger of Würtemburg, or Ludwig of Zweibruken, came seeking political and financial advantages, and the duke's own aristocratic subjects were encouraged to dance attendance. The court in its wider sense was thus an important instrument of policy, and the general admiration which was attracted by its strict protocol and lavish entertainments brought a wide variety of useful and influential people within the reach of ducal management and influence. In spite of (or perhaps because of) its lax moral standards, it was an excellent marriage market, and Duke Philip took great pains in managing the matrimonial affairs of his more important subjects, an exercise which increased their dependence upon him, and encouraged others to seek his good lordship. Marriages such as that between Reinoud II of Brederode and Yolande de Lalaing also served to bring the diverse territories of the duchy closer together and to increase a sense of Burgundian identity.[53] Failure in this direction could also have serious consequences, and C. A. J. Armstrong has argued that if Charles the Bold had provided a suitable heiress for Philippe de Commynes, he would never have defected to Louis XI.[54]

Within this colourful and constantly changing throng of petitioners, fortune hunters, refugees and opportunists of all kinds, the duke's own household provided the core, the management and the discipline. Within the household, hierarchy and decorum were at their strictest. The service of the duke at table was explicitly modelled upon the celeberation of the mass, a kind of symbolic apotheosis which no one seems to have regarded as blasphemous, and which was actively encouraged by the church. Every detailed gesture was prescribed, and required an army of acolytes—*sommelier, panetier, fruitier, valet-servant* and so on—to carry out correctly.[55] The household establishment was headed by the Grand Pensioners. These were noblemen and knights of the highest family, the duke's chosen companions, a number of whom were constantly in attendance and appear upon the lists of daily expenditure. They were partly councillors of state, partly boon-companions, and partly *garde d'honneur*. The Chamber establishment was managed partly by the First Chamberlain (a position of great responsibility which also involved the custody of the Duke's Privy Seal) and partly by the *Grand Maitre d'Hotel*, who

15

was responsible for the liturgy of table service, and was particularly prominent at major feasts. For the rest, it consisted of five comptrollers, or under-chamberlains, sixteen esquires of good family who provided for the duke's daily entertainment, six physicians, and about forty *valets de chambre* who performed the domestic and menial services.[56] The Chamber was thus quite distinct, not only from the service departments such as the kitchen or the *sausserie*, but also from more honorific sections such as the Stables and the Heralds' office. In this respect it was notably more sophisticated than the English household, and provided a model for the latter to imitate. At the same time, Burgundy did not have the long tradition of settled bureaucracy which appertained in England, and the duke's household was much more closely involved in routine administration than was that of the Lancastrian kings. For example, the Council, presided over by the Chancellor, which was a routine court of justice staffed by *maîtres de requetes* and secretaries, appears in the account of Olivier de la Marche as a household department.[57] So, too, does the *Chambre aux deniers*, which was the equivalent of the Exchequer but which, in Burgundy, was presided over by the duke in person. There was a privy treasury, in the form of the Jewel House, but the duke's private expenditure seems to have been handled by the *Argentier*, who was one of the officers of the *Chambre aux deniers*.[58]

After 1471 the Burgundian household also overlapped to some extent with the standing army which Duke Charles then established. His four surgeons and two *epiciers* were constantly busy as he tended to have the aristocratic casualities of his numerous campaigns treated in one of his own residences at his own expense. They also supervised the work of another fifty physicians who catered for the wider needs of the army. The duke was attended at all times by a bodyguard of 126 esquires, assisted by a similar number of archers, which in time of war was merged in the army because the duke always commanded his forces in person. The inflated size of the *écurie*, which included fifty esquires, as well as numerous craftsmen, couriers and servants, can also be partly explained by its frequent and important place in warfare.[59] The camp also penetrated the court to some extent, particularly in the time of Charles the Bold, who endeavoured to impose a kind of paramilitary discipline upon his courtiers, and pronounced upon all sorts of relatively minor matters through formal edicts. There was some justification for this stiffness, just as there was for the formality of etiquette, in the tendency of courtiers to rowdy hooliganism, which resulted in trampled gardens, broken hedges and windows, and occasional arson.[60] Towns like St Omer tried very hard to limit the number of ducal visits, not only because of the official costs of the entertainment which was expected, but also on account of the trail of destruction which tended to result. The chamberlains, who had overall responsibility for discipline, and for the protection of visitors, envoys and ambassadors, were, and needed to be, formidable men in their own right. Their task was simplified, although hardly eased, by the fact that the duke's servants were exempt from the jurisdiction of any court other than that of the duke's commissioners. Such servants were also liable to dismissal without warning and without formal process *ad nutum principis*, and thereafter could be proceeded against in the normal way; so this danger of double jeopardy armed the chamberlains with powerful sanctions in their search for order and discipline.

Within this brilliant but insecure environment, an extraordinary culture flourished.[61] The code of chivalry was honoured with numerous jousts, and in a passionate concern with the minutiae of heraldry and genealogy. The names of Arthur, Lancelot and Tristan were household words, and 'antique' epics like *Le Geste des ducs* were popular. As we have seen, knightly honour was observed somewhat selectively, but in one respect it was taken very seriously. Courage in battle was imperative, and discretion was not accepted as the better part of valour. One reason for this was the tendency which warfare was showing by the mid-fifteenth century to become a commercial calculation. Nobles and knights raised troops as an investment, hoping thereby to take wealthy prisoners and to make a large profit in ransoms. One of the most successful and notorious practitioners of this art was the Englishman, Sir John Fastolf, who, in a skirmish at Patay in 1429, actually withdrew from a losing battle rather than run the risk of capture.[62] Clearly it was not in the interest of any ambitious commander to encourage such an attitude, and not only was Fastolf derided by the Burgundian chronicler Enguerrand de Monstrelet, but the ordinances of the Golden Fleece in 1430 specifically forbade a knight of the order to depart from any engagement in which banners had been displayed. The seriousness of this intention was actually tested within a few months, when a Burgundian force was defeated at Anthon, and both the commanders fled the field. Both had been designated for the *Toison d'Or*, but Count Louis of Orange was never admitted and Jean de Neufchatel (one of the duke's chamberlains) was compelled to return his collar to the duke.[63] Neufchatel was also required to undertake a pilgrimage in expiation of his offence, and died soon after in the Holy Land. Although chivalry may have been to some extent a courtly game, there was a tough practical streak in this concept of honour when it came to winning battles, and it was because they lacked honour in this sense that the highly skilled Italian *condottieri* were such easy meat for the French in the years after 1494.

A similar blend of the practical and the aesthetic can be seen in art, music and literature. In each there was a deliberate confusing and intermingling of the sacred and the profane, as there was in certain aspects of court ceremonial; and the objective was the same. Philip the Good, in defiance of ecclesiastical disapproval, not only went to great lengths to attract talented musicians of all kinds, but used them indiscriminately for court entertainments and the service of the chapel. Mass settings were based upon popular tunes, and royal musicians such as Gilles de Binche and Guillaume Dufay were rewarded with cathedral canonries.[64] The artist Jan van Eyck, on the other hand, who specialised in magnificent altarpieces such as that at Ghent, became a *valet de chambre* and undertook diplomatic missions on the duke's behalf. Van Eyck's position as a personal friend and confidant of Duke Philip was much resented by the Burgundian nobility, and was unusual in the courts of northern Europe, although common enough in Italy. Early in the following century, Albrecht Dürer was to write from Venice that in the republic he was treated as a gentleman, while at home (in Nuremburg) he was nothing.[65] Van Eyck was special, but not unique. Jean de Hennecart, the favourite miniaturist of Duke Charles, also became a *valet de chambre*, although Roger van der Weyden, to whose sensitive portraits we owe much of our knowledge of the appearance of Burgundian courtiers, seems always to have worked on commission. The main function of the poets and chroniclers was to celebrate the honour of the ruler, and to reflect the values which he desired to promote. Scholarship in the humanist sense was much less in evidence than romances and epics of chivalry, and the books with which the dukes were frequently presented by their authors seem to have been regarded more as costly works of craftsmanship than as stimulants to the intellect. Where these formal presentations are represented in art, as in the case of Duke Philip receiving the *Chroniques de Hainault* from the hands of Simon Nockart, they are very much set pieces of courtly etiquette. Formal piety, feats of arms and courtly love dominated the *mentalité* of this glittering but somewhat *fin de siècle* culture.

The dominance of the Burgundian court in the middle years of the fifteenth century was partly a consequence of the troubles which were afflicting its potential rivals. France had recovered its political strength by the 1450s, and the courts of Charles VII and Louis XI were important institutions, but it was not until the advent of Francis I in 1515 that the cultural ascendancy of the days of Charles V was recovered. Throughout the period the Imperial court was afflicted by dire poverty, and in England the prolonged minority of Henry VI was followed by a period of personal government characterised by a marked lack of worldly wisdom and mounting domestic disorders. In spite of its deficiencies in magnificence, however, the English court had undergone a marked organisational development since 1384. The household ordinance of 1445 shows a clear distinction between the *Domus Regie Magnificencie* and the *Domus Providencie*, with the king's Chamber establishment separated alike from the queen's Chamber, the Hall (*la Sale*), *le Countynghous*, and the various service departments.[66] The ordinances issued by the Great Council in 1454, during the king's illness, were even more explicit. The main object of these ordinances was to curb the soaring expense of the proliferating royal servants, but the order of the establishment list, with the Countinghouse standing between the honorific servants of the Chamber on the one hand, and the offices 'below stairs' on the other, shows a further conceptual advance in the direction of the *Liber Niger* of 1474.[47] So although Edward IV was right in believing that he had a great deal to learn from his brother-in-law Charles the Bold about how to conduct a splendid court, the structure of the institution over which he presided owed more to its English predecessors than it did to Burgundian influence. Olivier de la Marche, Duke Charles' master of ceremonies, was the greatest expert upon court protocol in Western Europe.

Edward sought his advice, and no doubt the king's servants read *L'Etat de la Maison* with profit, but the Burgundians did not have all that much to teach the English about formal deference, and although Edward remodelled the Garter ceremonies on the lines of the *Toison d'Or*,[68] the older English order had provided one of the models for the initiative which Philip the Good had taken in 1430.

Also, although it was the nearest and much the most important, the court of Burgundy was not the only influence operating upon English kings in the late fifteenth century. Despite constant commercial contacts, and the customary presence of cultivated Italian merchants in their midst, neither the Burgundian nobility nor their ducal masters showed much interest in classical humanism. Such humanist influence as reached England came direct, mostly through the visits of English scholars such as John Gunthorpe and William Grey to Italian universities. William Grey, who became Bishop of Ely, and Treasurer in 1469, had studied under Guarino da Verona, was himself a considerable patron of humanists, and bequeathed a substantial collection of philosophical and scholarly works to his former Oxford college, Balliol,[69] Italian scholars and diplomats also came to England. The Franciscan Lorenzo da Savona was teaching rhetoric at Oxford before 1478; Pietro Carmeliano addressed laudatory Latin verses to Edward IV; and other residents with court connections, such as Giovanni Gigli, the Papal Collector, and Filippo Alberico also tried their luck with literary offerings. It would be an exaggeration to suggest that Edward was an active patron of the humanists. His notions of education, which he took seriously enough to employ three pedagogues in his household—a 'master of Gramer', a 'master of song' and a 'master of henxmen'—seem to have been strictly traditional, and to have concentrated upon 'noriture', or the art of genteel behaviour.[70] The 'lettrure' which was the other side of traditional training, including the arts of reading and writing, French and basic Latin grammar, was certainly carried on within the court, but we have no means of knowing whether the more advanced manuals, such as that of John Anwykyll, were used.[71] Humanist learning seeped into the Yorkist court, and its influence is difficult to pinpoint; but some nobles, such as Earl Rivers, actively promoted it, and French romances of Burgundian origin were not the only reading matter to challenge the manuals of pious devotion for the attention of bored or curious courtiers. Nor was classical Latin the only Italian product to command attention in courtly circles. Although there is no evidence of direct influence, Edward IV's entry into London on 21 May 1471, after his victory at Tewkesbury, in the course of which he paraded the captive Queen Margaret through the city, has been fairly described as 'a Roman triumph'.[72] Such triumphs were frequently celebrated in contemporary Italy, usually by *Signori* such as the d'Este of Ferrara or the Gonzaga of Mantua, who used them as symbolic propaganda to support the absolutist theories which they were encouraging scholars such as Bartolomeo Sacchi and Diomede Carafa to produce.[73] English art showed no signs of renaissance influence before the end of the fifteenth century, but the constant comings and goings of prelates and other clergy to Rome inevitably alerted some Englishmen to the new standards of patronage being set by Pius II and Sixtus IV. The taste and discrimination of these pontiffs, as well as of secular pacemakers such as Lorenzo de Medici, presented a marked contrast to the somewhat vulgar opulence of Burgundy. It was to be a long time before Italian influences were to present a serious challenge to Burgundian supremacy in the culture of the English court, but they were present in some forms at an early date, and by the reign of Henry VII were sufficiently evident to merit serious consideration.

The royal image

Henry VI in his latter days was not a difficult act to follow. As late as 1445 enough of its former grandeur still clung to the English court to impress an Angevin envoy, Antoine de la Sale, who wrote that the English were '. . . the most ceremonious people in matters of decorum that I have ever seen'. However, by 1459, when the king in a characteristic gesture of generosity gave his best robe to the Prior of St Albans, the treasurer of the realm had to go behind the scenes afterwards and redeem it for 50 marks because it was the only decent one his master possessed.[74] No king could afford to be so careless of outward appearances, and it is significant that Henry's honour and reputation benefited relatively little either from his piety, his generosity to his courtiers, or his patronage of scholarship. The image which remained in the minds of his subjects was that recorded by the author of the Great Chronicle, describing Henry's appearance during his readeption in 1470:

> more lyker a play than the shewyng of a prynce to wynne mennys hertys, ffor by this mean he lost many and wan noon or Rygth ffewe, and envyr he was shewid in long blew goune of velvet as thowth he hadd noo moo to chaunge with . . .[75]

Edward had no intention of making the same mistake, but he could not afford to buy himself a reputation for magnificence by lavish expenditure. At first his image had to depend largely upon his energy, and upon the natural advantages of his physique. Contrary to the reputation transmitted to posterity by Commynes, Edward was an extremely hardworking king, not so much in conducting military campaigns in the far corners of his realm, but in council, in parliament, and in the enforcement of the law. A 'rightwise natural Sovereign Lord and very Justiciar', as he was described in 1479 after summoning a particularly difficult treason case from Bristol and dealing with it in council.[76] Neither his entry to London in 1461 nor his coronation were in any way remarkable, to judge from the surviving accounts, save for the impressive figure of the young king himself, who knew how to wear clothes, and how to speak eloquently in public. Early Yorkist propaganda was extremely conservative, concentrating upon genealogy and upon the defects of Lancastrian misgovernment. The 'Political Retrospect' of 1462 not only declared that the Lancastrians were usurpers—and the Yorkists consequently the true royal line—but also that the fall of Henry VI was the judgement of God upon the sin of his grandfather. Edward's victory was thus a direct work of providence:

> A great sign it is that God loveth that knight
> For all those that would have destroyed him utterly
> All they are mischieved and put to flight.[77]

No pageants or visual displays seem to have been used to reinforce this message, however, unlike the extremely pertinent spectacle provided for Henry VII's entry into Worcester in 1486, and the impression given is that Edward's court was visually unimaginative.

By 1466, when his finances had begun to improve somewhat, the standard of Edward's housekeeping was sufficient to dazzle the impressionable Bohemian Gabriel Tetzel. Tetzel visited England in the train of Leo of Rozmital and was invited to attend the ceremonies surrounding the churching of Queen Elizabeth after the birth of her first child by Edward. His description abounds with superlatives. Everything was supplied '. . . in such costly measure that it is unbelievable . . .' Lavish gifts were distributed among the minstrels and servants who had assisted at the feast; the queen herself ate in 'an unbelievably costly apartment'; and his overall impression was that Edward had 'the most splendid court that could be found in all Christendom'.[78] Considering that he and his master had just left the ducal court of Burgundy, this was no mean tribute. It need not be taken too seriously as a comparative judgement, but Edward was certainly giving the opulence of his court very high financial priority. When the 'Great Bastard', Anthony of Burgundy, visited England in 1467, lavish ceremonies were mounted for him, and this expenditure bore political fruit in the following year when the king's sister, Margaret, became the bride of Duke Charles. By the time that he had found £2500 for her trousseau and entourage, Edward was pawning the Crown jewels,[79] but his honour was suitably maintained under the searching gaze of the Burgundian nobility. After his brief and inadvertent sojourn as the guest of the Seigneur de Gruthuyse, Edward's addiction to the Burgundian lifestyle seems to have increased still further. This was most noticeable in the fact that he began to order illuminated manuscripts, mainly from the workshops of Bruges, and to have them bound and ornamented to his own taste with Yorkist devices, such as the rose 'en soleil'. His taste in literature was entirely conventional, and his collection consisted mainly of histories such as Raoul le Fevre's *Receuil des Histoires de Troyes*, moralising works like Alain Chartier's *Le Breviaire des Nobles*, and service books. French predominated over both Latin and English, but when he began to patronise William Caxton after 1474, he added a number of vernacular printed books to his collection, mostly of a moralising or religious nature.[80]

The Burgundian speciality of jousting also began to feature more prominently in the latter part of the reign, a particularly lavish tournament being mounted in January 1478 as part of the celebrations attending the marriage of Richard of York to Anne Mowbray. The 'many harneis of Milayn' which needed to be protected from the rain in 1480 were probably tilting armour; and generous gifts of crimson cloth and damask to two Knights of the Body 'for the covering of theire brygandyns' in the same year also suggest preparations for a tournament.[81] Edward was particularly proud of his membership of the *Toison d'Or*, and did his best to turn the Order of the Garter into a similar instrument of policy. The chapel of St George at Windsor was rebuilt on a magnificent scale, starting in 1473, and numerous diplomatically useful rulers, such as John II of Portugal and Federigo da Montefeltro, the papal commander in chief, were elected to the Order. In 1476 Pope Sixtus IV added to its prestige by granting an indulgence to all visitors to the Garter Chapel, and the king made a regular habit of keeping the feast of St George at Windsor. Edward's preoccupation with the forms of chivalry was not as obsessive as that of Charles the Bold, but seems to have been rather a calculated gesture of solidarity with his own nobility, whose service and loyalty he so badly needed to retain.

The sympathetic Croyland chronicler commented admiringly upon the magnificence of Edward's later years;

> ... for collecting vessels of gold and silver, tapestries, and decorations of the most precious nature, both for his palaces and for various churches, and for building castles, colleges and other distinguished places ... not one of his predecessors was at all able to equal his remarkable achievements.[82]

As we have seen, other observers had persistently struck the same note, and the manner in which he succeeded in creating this impression without damaging his financial position must be counted as one of the great successes of Edward's reign. Nevertheless, in other respects his image is hard to bring into focus. In spite of his obvious concern over his personal and dynastic position, his court seems to have been markedly less deferential and ceremonious than that of Richard II, or even his Lancastrian predecessors. Edward was noted for his affability and easy-going manners, and in this respect did not imitate the rigid protocol of his Burgundian *exemplum*. In his recent major analysis of the reign, Charles Ross observed that the king was inclined to treat England as a private lordship,[83] and, despite the conscientious discharge of his royal duties, showed little awareness of any theoretical responsibility towards the 'commonwealth'. The characteristic political theorist of the period was Sir John Fortescue, who, in spite of his Lancastrian antecedents, was a member of Edward's council from 1471 to 1473. Fortescue's advice, conveyed in *De Laudibus Legum Anglie*, with its emphasis upon financial independence and the supremacy of the common law, was largely reflected in Edward's practice. He was obviously anxious to be seen doing what a king should do, but the image he endeavoured to project was less that of a sovereign, aloof and hierarchical, than of a lord and *preux chevalier*, the hardworking captain of a noble team. His magnificence served two obvious and practical purposes: to win him friends and admirers abroad, and to discourage challengers and opponents at home. By the time he died it was an old-fashioned and limited image, about to be overtaken by the more imaginative and ambitious pretensions of renaissance monarchy.

The two years of crisis and upheaval which followed Edward's death in 1483 serve as a sharp reminder of the limitations of his achievement. In emphasising his own personal grandeur, and in relying heavily upon a small number of kinsmen and noble *curiales*, he had failed to recover the institutional strength and continuity which the English monarchy had so conspicuously displayed in the 1420s. Henry VII may have learned from these mistakes, or his sharply contrasting style of leadership may simply have been the result of a very different personality. He was insecure in the early years of his reign, but then so had Edward been; he was inexperienced in government, but no more so than the nineteen-year-old Earl of March, and nine years older, which may have been a more important consideration. Henry's early propaganda, like Edward's, was dictated by circumstances, but was different in every other respect. Although he did not neglect to vilify the memory of Richard III, he placed little emphasis upon his own immediate hereditary claim. This was partly because it was weak in itself, and partly because he was already contracted to marry Elizabeth of York, and had no wish to brand her father a usurper. Henry was very much king 'by the Grace of God', and by judgement of battle, although the judgement was against Richard personally, and not against his whole line. He was also the reconciler, and bringer of peace—an image which depended heavily upon his marriage.

> . . . whiche thyng not onely reioysed and comforted the hartes of the noble and gentelmen of the realme, but also gayned the favour & good myndes of all the comen people, much extollyng and praysyng the kynges constant fiddelyte and his polletique device, thynkyng surely that the daye was now come that the seede of tumulteous faccions . . . should be stopped . . .[84]

In pursuit of the same goal he was also willing, after a suitable lapse of time, to pardon and engage the sevices of many former Yorkists,

> . . . usyng the antique example of the Athenienses, whiche is to perdon and put out of memory all crymes and offences before tyme agaynst hym . . . perpetrated[85]

as a later chronicler was to write. Both Henry's marriage and his policy of conciliation were successful, so that it was as the healer of feuds and the bringer of domestic peace and stability that he entered into the pageantry and historiography of his successors.

Curiously enough for a king who claimed his throne partly by judgement of battle, Henry never seems to have placed any emphasis upon martial displays. Tournaments continued to be popular sporting contests, as they had been earlier in the century, but there is no suggestion that the king himself took part, and the trappings of Burgundian chivalry which had begun to appear in

1478 were not developed any further until the jousts which accompanied Prince Arthur's nuptials in 1501.[86] The rich symbolism which then began to flourish is sufficient proof that the king was not averse to such displays, but they never featured in his early image building. Even his progresses to York and the west country in 1486, which could well have taken the form of a parade of armed strength, were marked in fact by civic pageants whose principal themes reflected the king's own emphasis upon peace and reconciliation.[87] Instead there was an imperial thread in Henry's propaganda which had not been visible before. His Welsh ancestry, as Professor Chrimes has pointed out, was not much stronger than his Lancastrian claim, nor much more significant than Edward IV's descent from the Mortimers.[88] Nevertheless, many of the bards had hailed him as *y mab darogan*—the 'son of prophecy'—whose destiny it was to fulfil the words spoken by an angel to Cadwaladr the Blessed, and restore the sovereignty of the British race. It was largely for this reason that Henry had chosen to land in Wales, and the influence of the bards can be seen, both in his choice of route and in the support which he had gained on the way.[89] Having gained his crown, he could hardly afford to show too much concern for his Welsh roots, but the remote figure of Cadwaladr continued to figure in his thinking. The red dragon not only appeared on his standard at Bosworth, but was adopted as one of the supporters of the royal arms, and featured prominently on his coinage. Nor was it only the Welsh poets who drew attention to his supposed ancestry; the image of the heir of Cadwaladr appears also in works offered to the king by Pietro Carmeliano and Giovanni de' Gigli, as well as in those of the court poet Bernard Andre. So it is reasonable to assume that Henry welcomed such allusions, and sought to exploit them for his own purposes.

Apart from heraldry, the most obvious way in which he did this was to christen his eldest son Arthur. Such a name was not unprecedented, but it was exceedingly rare in the ruling family, and in choosing it the king was deliberately appealing not so much to Welsh sentiment as to the mythology of the *Historia Regum Britanniae*. Of course, the Welsh bards were delighted, and called upon the new hero to emulate the deeds of his forebear;[90] but that was not the main point. In alluding to these remote glories, Henry was both drawing attention away from his immediate ancestry and reinforcing his claim to transcend the conflicts of recent years. In the long run he was to be supremely successful. Because his dynasty survived, he continued to feature in pageant history and propaganda throughout the sixteenth century as the restorer of peace and justice to a land labouring under the judgement of God:

> Now civil wounds are stopt, peace lives again,
> That she may long live here, God say Amen.[91]

In the short term, it is very difficult to say how impressed his subjects were by such claims. With the exception of the Welsh bards, it is extremely unlikely that many of them saw him as the saviour of the realm in the first five years of his reign. It was the success of his government rather than the efforts of propaganda which created that image. Nevertheless, it is significant that Henry should have used such symbolism, and encouraged others to do so. Temperamentally he continued to be suspicious and insecure to the end of his reign, and never relaxed in his efforts at self-promotion. All observers agreed that his court was magnificant. Like Edward he spent lavishly on jewels, clothing and food. As Polydore Virgil recorded

> His hospitality was splendidly generous . . . He knew well how to maintain his royal
> majesty and all which appertains to kingship at every time and in every place . . .[92]

He was also alert to less conventional methods of expressing his honour. When he decided in 1497 to exploit the destruction by fire of the old palace at Sheen, he opened up a whole range of possibilities. Both the structure and the name of the new palace of Richmond were calculated gestures of grandeur. Costing over £15,000, it was dubbed the Rich Mount of England, and attracted the awestruck admiration of his subjects. It was an

> . . . earthly and second paradise of our region of England, and . . . of all the great
> part and circuit of the world, the lantern spectacle and beauteous exemplar of all
> lodgings . . .[93]

Nothing quite like it had been seen in England before. Designed and built as a single coherent whole, it had no military or defensive function, and was modelled on the palaces of Burgundy and France, particularly Bruges (see plate 4). The main building material was Flemish brick, which was not an innovation, but the long galleries, large bay windows and extensive formal gardens were all unfamiliar and impressive to English eyes. Inside, traditional decorations such as Arras tapestries were joined by panel portraits in the new Burgundian mode, and by extensive wall paintings celebrating the lineage and achievements of the English kings

> . . . pictures of the noble kings of this realm in their harness and robes of gold as
> Brute, Hengist, King William Rufus, King Arthur, King Henry . . . and kings of
> this royal realm, with their falchions and swords in their hands, visaged and
> appearing like bold and valiant knights. And so their deeds and acts in the
> chronicles right evidently both shown and declared.[94]

The culmination of this pageant, above the elevated throne at the end of the great hall, was the portrait of Henry himself:

> . . . the seemly picture and personage of our most excellent and high sovereign now
> reigning over us, his liege people, King Henry VII, as worthy room and place with
> those glorious princes as any king that ever reigned in this land . . .

These frescoes, like many of the panel portraits, were the work of a Flemish (or possibly French) artist known as Meynnart—or Maynard—who had entered the king's service in about 1496, and who had probably learned his craft from Roger van der Weyden.[95] Maynard became official 'King's

Painter' in 1503, and executed several other visual panegyrics of the Tudor dynasty.

Richmond was immensely important to Henry's image, because it signified not only wealth but permanence. In the words of a recent study, 'It attempted not only to define a new royal style, but to impose that style upon his descendants.'[96] It was inaugurated, obviously by design, during the magnificent ceremonial surrounding the marriage of Prince Arthur to Catherine of Aragon—which was in itself a symbol of the safe arrival of the Tudor dynasty upon the European scene. The ambitious sophistication of that pageantry is far too large a subject to enter into at this point, but it is worth noticing for its intellectual content. Unlike the sumptuous banalities of the tournament, the scenes presented to the young couple on their entry into London were expressive of a morality, cosmology and political theory which required a thorough grounding in contemporary learning to understand. They were not particularly 'humanist', but they were intended for a highly educated taste which Catherine certainly, and Arthur probably, possessed.[97] Like everything else, Henry's patronage of learning was put on show at Richmond, where a large room was devoted to his growing collection of books. These were regularly shown to admiring visitors, and Claude de Seyssel, the French ambassador, was sufficiently impressed to present the king with a beautifully illuminated copy of his translation of Xenophon's *Anabasis*.[98] It is doubtful whether Henry's lay subjects were much concerned about his patronage of learning, but his image among the more cultivated aristocracies of France and the Low Countries was much enhanced, as this episode serves to remind us. At the same time, learning and piety went hand in hand, and he was always scrupulously careful to appear as a dutiful son of the church, ever mindful of the tangible benefits of papal support. It was in this connection alone that the saintly shade of Henry VI was invoked, to confer his blessing upon a kinsman who, in every other respect, wished to be as remote as possible from such a disastrous example!

Henry VII was a man who knew how to enjoy himself, and who did so in a great variety of ways: hunting and gambling in the company of his courtiers, and employing musicians, jesters and entertainers of all kinds.[99] He was also, however, a very private man, unusually chaste among fifteenth-century princes, and not given to emotional display. The suspicious miser of popular folklore was a creation of the imagination of Francis Bacon, but contemporaries also perceived a cold and uncongenial streak in him. One reason for this was certainly the acquisitive fiscal policy of his latter years, which is sufficiently well authenticated, no matter what the justification for it may have been. Another was his reputation for omniscience. He was far more conscious of the need for good intelligence work than Edward had been, and chose extremely diligent servants. He also had an astute and patient mind. 'He is so wise and attentive to everything', wrote Hernan Duque de Estrade in 1504, 'nothing escapes his attention'.[100] At the same time he rebuilt much of the formal protocol and ceremoniousness which had characterised the English court from Richard II to Henry VI, but which had tended to fade away under the Yorkists, despite their Burgundian connections. Partly for political reasons, and partly because of his temperament, Henry was more aloof and dignified than the affable Edward. Although equally traditional, his style of kingship was more that of a sovereign, less that of a lord, more that of a dynast, and less that of an individual. Towards the end of his life poor health and melancholy added a sombre tone to his image; so although he remained a magnificent prince, it was his *gravitas*, the sober dignity and professional efficiency of his rule which remained in the minds of his subjects.

In this somewhat gloomy atmosphere, the young King Henry VIII exploded like a firecracker. The contrast is so familiar as to need no emphasis, but because it is so obvious, it is frequently misunderstood. The new king was, after all, in many respects what his father had made him. His athletic prowess was the result not only of a splendid physique, but of long and arduous hours of training under the best instructors. His intellectual and artistic tastes had similarly been shaped under the influence of tutors whom his father had appointed. Henry VII was a dynast, and his son was his masterpiece. The fact that he had performed no public duties prior to his accession, and seems to have been kept out of the public eye as much as possible, has never been satisfactorily explained. Perhaps the old king was concerned for his health and safety, or possibly distrustful of his abilities. But equally he may have feared that the rise of so spectacular a son would have kindled the affections of his subjects too warmly before he was safely in his grave. In the first flush of enthusiasm, the young king tried to be all things to all people—*uomo universae*—the complete renaissance prince. Lord Mountjoy, the patron of humanists and friend of Erasmus, was as enthusiastic as any:

> Heaven and earth rejoices; everything is full of milk and honey and nectar. Avarice has fled the country. Our king is not after gold, or gems, or precious stones, but virtue, glory, immortality . . .[101]

Niccolo Machiavelli, from a safe distance, was less flattering and more astute in describing the King of England as 'ricco, feroce et cupido di gloria'. The glory which both identified as being the main object of Henry's ambition was, of course, military. From the early weeks of his reign he took a positive initiative in encouraging gunfounders, armourers and ship builders—importing continental (mainly German) specialists to improve the quality of the native industries.[102] Chivalric tournaments rose to fresh levels of extravagance and ingenuity, and in January 1510 the king made his own debut in the lists. For the next fifteen years Henry's personal prowess in the joust was to be one of the main features of his image, and his success in that direction compensated somewhat for his indifferent performances in real warfare. Unfortunately for his romantic zeal, winning battles, let alone campaigns, had more to do with logistics, supplies and weather conditions than with knightly feats of arms.[103] A *prud'homme* like the Chevalier Bayard might still be a great ornament and encouragement to an army, but he was no substitute for an efficient siege train, let alone an effective commissariat. Henry's enthusiasm for war, expressed symbolically in jousting and politically in his attack on France in 1512, has been described as 'adolescent belligerence'—and so it was. It was also, however, a fundamantal characteristic of the aristocratic culture of the time, and one which needed outlets both in fantasy and fact.

The prolonged peace which Henry VII had so carefully, and so profitably, conserved had left his nobles restless and discontented, missing their traditional function. Consequently the young king's bellicosity not only provided a much needed safety valve for frustrated energies, but also enabled them to exploit his appetite for glory to their own honour and advancement.

> . . . on Sondaie the ii daye of October (1513) the kyng entered the cytee of Tournay at port Fountayne, and iiii of the chiefe of the cytee over him bare a cannapye with all the armes of England, every person was in his best apparrell . . . the kynge him selfe was rychely appereilled in ryche armure on a barded courser, his henxmen beryng his peces of warr . . . with his nobilitie, all richely apparelled with his sworde borne before him . . .[104]

The capture of Tournai was an isolated success in a not particularly glorious campaign, but one which earned the Dukedom of Suffolk for the king's companion in arms, Charles Brandon, and a significant increase in the influence of Thomas Wolsey, Henry's almoner.[105] At the same time the 'backdoor' campaign against Scotland resulted in the much more decisive victory of Flodden, and the promotion of the Earl of Surrey to the Dukedom of Norfolk. By the time that Wolsey had engineered the short-lived treaty of London in 1518, the King of England was already making a much larger figure in Europe than either his achievements or his resources justified. One of the reasons for this was the skilful diplomacy with which Wolsey exploited England's strategic importance in a confusion world of shifting alliances; the other was the extraordinary success of Henry's self-promotion. From 1509 until the accession of Francis I of France in January 1515, he was without a rival among the monarchs of western Europe. Louis XII and Ferdinand of Spain, who both had greater resources, were kings in the mould of his father. The Emperor Maximilian (who was also a gifted self-publicist), was ageing, and short of cash;[106] while the dashing James IV of Scotland, who met an early death at Flodden, had never been able to compete in the major league. This uniqueness was pure good fortune, but Henry exploited it very effectively. In October 1513 he jousted at Tournai before Margaret of Savoy, the Prince of Castile, and an international gathering of nobility; his prowess won acclaim on all sides. In 1517 a tournament in London drew awestruck comments from the Italian onlookers, both in respect of the spectacular costliness of the armour, and also of the combat between the king and the Duke of Suffolk, which one likened to the trial between Hector and Achilles.[107]

By the time that he met Francis I at the Field of Cloth of Gold in 1520 the world was changing. In the young King of France, the victor of Marignano, he had met his match in magnificence, and his superior in warlike accomplishment. At the same time the election of the even more youthful Charles I of Spain as Holy Roman Emperor in 1519 had created a new political pattern which was to dominate Europe for the next forty years. In that pattern, England's role could only be auxiliary, but it was important enough for both sides to flatter Henry with their attentions, and maintain his delusions of grandeur. Before that happened, however, he had brought to an honourable and successful conclusion the century-long search by English kings for some specific recognition of their standing in Christendom. In view of their well-nigh successful pursuit of their claim to the French crown, it had been particularly galling for the Lancastrians to be unable to match the Valois title of *Rex Christianissimus*. Consequently, when Henry VIII revived that claim in 1512, he also sought the transfer of the title. Julius II, who was a party to the alliance against France, was willing to comply, but he prudently made the transfer conditional upon a military conquest which Henry was quite unable to accomplish.[108] Nevertheless, his appetite whetted, he continued to pursue the matter through Wolsey and, ironically, in 1521 finally accomplished by letters what he had failed to achieve by arms. It was his tract against Luther, *Assertio Septem Sacramentorum* which finally won him the cherished designation *Defensor Fidei*, and parity with France and Spain.

No one could have been a more dutiful son of the Church than Henry VIII in 1521. Papal approval shone like a jewel in his crown as it had in his father's. However, there was a shadow over this triumph. As an astute Italian observer had noted in about 1500, although England was not subject to the rule of the emperor, it was subject to the pope; and he was not talking about spiritual jurisdiction but about that temporal suzerainty which had been acknowledged by King John. The kings of France had been recognised as 'Emperors in their own kingdom' since the Bull *Per Venerabilem* of 1202[109] not so the kings of England. How soon Henry's 'appetite for glory' began to reach out in this direction it is difficult to say, and, as is well known, he had many other reasons for repudiating papal jurisdiction in the years after 1530. Nevertheless, it is worth remembering that the well-known phrases of the preamble to the Act in Restraint of Appeals,

> Where by divers sundry old authentic histories and chronicles it is manifestly
> declared and expressed that this realm of England is an empire, and so hath been
> accepted in the world . . .

reflected an ambition of the kings of England which had nothing to do with Anne Boleyn—let alone Martin Luther. Although there was no break in the continuity of Henry's magnificence—his patronage of musicians, scholars, craftsmen and goldsmiths—there was a change of emphasis and direction after 1530. The king had retired from jousting by 1527, and his athleticism was beginning to diminish. At the same time he had a new and urgent need to rally and mobilise the support of his subjects. Threats of invasion by the emperor and the King of France helped to make the old image serve the new policies, but the royal supremacy created unprecedented problems of presentation. Sermons, and for the first time printed books and pamphlets, were used to argue the justice of the king's actions.[110] 'The king our master hath a special case', declared Stephen Gardiner in his *De Vera Obedientia Oratio*, 'because he is an Emperor in himself and hath no superior'. The need for obedience was urged *ad nauseam*, and the spectres of York and Lancaster invoked to add weight to the message; but the search for a new royal image was hesitant and confused. One of the reasons for this was Henry's continued aversion to doctrinal Protestantism, and consequent reluctance to be cast as a 'Godly Prince'. Another was the failure of Anne Boleyn to bear him a son, and set the seal of divine approval upon his actions.

The defeat of the Pilgrimage of Grace, and the birth of Prince Edward in 1537, gave the lie to the prophets of doom much more effectively than the noose or the stake. The king was again victorious and fortunate. He had also found an artist of genius to celebrate his greatness, in the person of Hans Holbein, whose great fresco at Whitehall (now lost) was painted in this year.[111] In the aggressive, self-confident pose of the splendid central figure, Holbein undoubtedly portrayed Henry as he wished to appear, and the image has endured to the present day (see plate 26). It did not, however, represent any new departure, or solve the particular problem of a king who was also Supreme Head of the Church. That could only be done by giving some visual or dramatic expression to the unfamiliar powers and responsibilities of such an office. Holbein was willing to make the attempt, and his miniature 'King Solomon receiving the Queen of Sheba' was a masterly adaptation of traditional imagery to new needs.[112] Henry VIII is shown as Solomon, enthroned and surrounded by inscriptions implying his direct dependence upon God (see plate 1). The Queen of Sheba, presenting her homage to Solomon, was a traditional type of the church. This small painting appears to have been presented to the king as a New Year gift, perhaps in 1535, and can never have been known to more than a small number of people. However, a similar image by the same artist was given much greater currency in the same year when he designed the title-page of Coverdale's translation of the bible, showing the king, enthroned, handing down the book to his kneeling bishops (see plate 11). When at last Henry was persuaded to authorise an official translation for general use in 1539, the title-page of the Great Bible bore a similar representation, which was thus given very wide currency. By that time, too, dramatic presentations were also supporting the king's position, following the advise of Richard Moryson, one of the publicists recruited by Thomas Cromwell, who suggested that plays could set forth

> ... lyvely before the peoples eies the abhomynacion and wickednes of the bisshop of Rome, monkes, ffreers, nonnes, and suche like, and to declare and open to them thobedience that your subiectes by goddes and mans lawes owe unto your magestie ...[113]

and he added

Into the commen people thynges sooner enter by the eies than by the eares, remembering more better what they see than what they heere . . .

Some such plays were presented between 1537 and 1540, perhaps including that by John Bale on the somewhat obvious subject of *King John*, attacking the claim to papal suzerainty at its root.[114] Also, in June 1539 a splendid water pageant was staged upon the Thames, in the course of which

. . . the Pope (and his cardinals) made their defyance against England and shot their ordinance at one another, and so had three courses up and down the water, and at the fourth course they joyned togither and fought sore; but at last the Pope and his cardinalles were overcome, and all his men cast over the borde into the Thames.

This was sufficiently explicit, and sufficiently public, to attract considerable attention and comment,[115] and to mark the full emergence of the royal supremacy as a part of the king's image.

The last years of the reign saw much less emphasis of this kind, although there was no retreat from the position taken up. These were years of renewed war, with Henry attempting to echo the image of his early days by appearing as a great and victorious commander.[116] Once again the achievement failed to match the pretension, but they were nevertheless years of success in another way. By the time of his death, Henry VIII, in spite of the obvious defects in his character and the controversial nature of many of his policies, had become the symbol and embodiment of England to a degree which none of his predecessors, not even Henry V, had attained. 'Remember good old King Henry the eighth' a bystander was to cry at Elizabeth's coronation in 1559. Partly because the break with Rome completed England's progress towards sovereignty, and partly because of the consummate skill of his image building, he ended his reign as a Great King in the eyes of his subjects. Another reason for this was the growth of national consciousness, which might have come about in any case, but whether intentionally or not, Henry VIII succeeded in harnessing that consciousness to the Tudor dynasty.

There could, of course, be no question of the infant Edward VI following literally in his father's footsteps, and in the event he did not live long enough to create any distinct image for himself. The image which his council endeavoured to create for him was that of 'England's Josias', and reflected the triumph of the Protestant party between January and June 1547. Josiah, king of Israel, coming to the throne as a boy, had restored the true worship of Yaweh after years of idolatrous backsliding, so the religious symbolism needed careful handling, and never seems to have had much appeal outside the court and the minority of Protestant congregations. More important from most people's point of view was to emphasise the legitimacy of his birth, and to express the hope that he would emulate the glory of his father. The dignified and resplendent baby of Holbein's 1539 portrait is supported by the inscription

Parvule patrissa, patriae virtutis et haeres
Esto, nihil maius maximus orbis habet.
Gnatum vix possunt coleum et natura dedisse,
Huius quem patris victus honoret honos
Aequato tantum, tanti tu facta parentis
Vota hominum, vix quo progrediantur, habent
Vincito vicisti quot reges priscus adorat
Orbis, nec te qui vincere possit, erit.[117]

After his accession a number of portraits show him in an unconvincing imitation of his father's classic pose: a somewhat gawky adolescent upon whom the magnificence of kingship as yet sat uneasily.[118] Edward himself was always intensely conscious of his royal dignity, and, given the opportunity, would probably have preferred the martial and athletic image of his father's youth. However, unlike Henry, he was assiduously protected from the dangers of the tiltyard. This was probably because of justified fears of an accident, but may also have reflected a realisation that the boy had no potential in that direction, and could not afford to make a fool of himself. So Edward, who seems to have had all the high spirits and slapstick tastes of normal youth, had to put up with being presented to the world as a paragon of learning and Protestant piety. As Nicholas Udall wrote,

> Howe happye are we Englishemen of suche a Kynge in whose chyldehood appereth as perfeict grace, virtue, godly zele, desire of literature, gravitie, prudence, justice and magnanimitie, as hath heretofore been found in Kinges of most mature age . . .[119]

Fortunately both the learning and the piety were genuine enough to stand reasonable scrutiny, and the official view of the young sovereign is probably best summed up in a somewhat crude panel painting, now in the National Portrait Gallery (see plate 25). Henry VIII, on his deathbed, gestures approvingly towards his heir, who sits enthroned, surrounded by his council. At his feet lies an open book, inscribed with the words 'The worde of the Lorde endureth for ever', and beneath the throne, in postures of subjection and dismay, cower the pope and two shaven friars labelled 'idolatry' and 'feigned holines'.[120] Such a representation would probably have appealed to Edward himself, who enjoyed the anti-papal charades and plays which were occasionally offered for his amusement, as at Shrovetide 1549, and Christmas 1549/50. He also enjoyed acrobatics, water tournaments, and spectacles of all kinds, as well as the sermons for which he is better known. His minority made the court, as we shall see, a very different affair from his father's, and in some respects its 'magnificence' faltered; but the main significance of this short reign in terms of the king's image was to demonstrate that the Supreme Headship of the Church was vested in the office of the king, and did not disappear with the awesome personality of Henry VIII.

Mary, coming to the throne at a mature age, and after years of involvement in public controversy, already had a clearly established reputation for loyalty to her mother's memory, and to the traditional ecclesiastical order.[121] That this was fully in accordance with her own wishes was demonstrated by her arrival in London on 15 March 1551, accompanied

> ... with fifty knights and gentlemen in velvet coats and chains of gold afore her and after her iii score gentlemen and ladies, every one havyng a peyre of bedes of black ...[122]

After her accession, her taste for traditional religious ceremonial was given full rein. The elaborate music of the Chapel Royal, curtailed by the Protestant liturgies of her predecessor, flourished again with the restoration of the mass. A woman ruler was an unprecedented experience, and the loyal greetings of her subjects conveyed personal affection and dynastic hope rather than any specific political message:

> Wee all (as one) do love her Grace
> That is our Queen, this Marigolde

The queen was fond of children, and was an assiduous godmother, but a domestic image accorded ill with the exercise of sovereign power, and the failure of her marriage left her poised uneasily between matron and monarch. She enjoyed sumptuous clothes and jewellery, but seems to have lacked both the skill and the physique to make an imposing figure. 'She is a perfect saint, and dresses badly ...' was one Spanish verdict,[124] and indeed the ageing housewife who looks sadly at the spectator from the lifelike portraits of Hans Eworth and Antonio Moro is much more human than impressive (see plates 27 and 29). No expense was spared to maintain the magnificence of the court, and, except at times when the queen was ill (a situation of increasing frequency and duration after 1555), dramatic entertainments and festivities continued to be offered. Their message, however, seems to have been confined to celebrating the traditional virtues of rulership, with piety playing a very large part.[125] As a younger woman, Mary had received hopeful dedications from humanist scholars, and had been well thought of for her Latinity, but as queen she showed few signs of intellectual interests, and although she was a substantial patron of schools her most active generosity was reserved for the restoration of religious houses.

Unfortunately, because of the painful experiences of her adolescence and early adulthood, Mary had no particular affection for her father's memory, and tended to look outside England for people to trust and confide in, particularly in matters of public policy. She also lacked political confidence, accepting the conventional view that her sex was a serious disability. Consequently, despite her courage, and her capacity for work, she failed to emerge as a national leader, being seen instead as a woman who was manipulated by unscrupulous foreigners for their own purposes. 'She is a Spaniard at heart ...' as they muttered in the London taverns, and Philip did nothing to ameliorate that situation. Although generous with gold chains and pensions, and unexpectedly gracious on his arrival in July 1554, he made no serious attempt to adjust either his policies or his image to the role of King of

England.[126] As far as he was concerned, the main advantage of marrying Mary was to augment his honour and reputation, which had been somewhat tarnished by the refusal of the German Diet to include him in the Imperial succession. There was also the question of useful strategic support against France. Philip's only major intervention in English affairs was his role in the reconciliation with Rome, which was negotiated between October and December 1554, and that was undertaken with a view at least as much to improving his image in Europe as discharging his responsibilities as king. In the second half of 1554 he enjoyed a 'triumph' in England, which was celebrated in a spate of Habsburg propaganda, such as *La Solenni e felice intrata delli serenisimi Re Philippo e Regina Maria d'Inghilterra nella Regal citta di Londra* and *Il Felicissimo ritorno del regno d'Inghilterra alla catholica unione*.[127] The organisers of the entry did their best to provide a suitable welcome:

O noble Prince, sole hope of Caesar's side,
By God apointed all the world to gyde,
Rightly hartely welcome art though to our land
The archer Britayne yeldeth the hir hand,
And noble England openeth her bosome . . .[128]

and the spectators of all persuasions were suitably impressed, but the reality was distressingly different, and was expressed in riots and murder over the months which followed. It is not surprising that Philip found England uncongenial, but he made his own situation worse by appearing little in public, and then always surrounded by his own nobles and servants. Frequently-expressed good intentions about employing English gentlemen and servants were never more than partly realised, and after his return to the Low Countries in August 1555, his influence in England dwindled away to nothing. Mary was left to redeem the situation as best she could, but with few options. As the neglected wife of a preoccupied and reputedly lecherous foreign potentate, she had as little honour as profit from her marriage.[129] Her subjects never lost their affection for her, but pity was more evident than respect, and the multiplying misfortunes of her later years—sickness, harvest failure and defeat in war—gave her the reputation of a ruler upon whom God had turned his back. Even her conspicuous piety seemed to be unavailing, and so encouraged the notion that it must be the wrong kind of piety to appeal to heaven.

Mary's enduring historical reputation, like that of Richard III, was created by her enemies after her death, and therefore does not properly belong to the story of the royal image. Nevertheless, it was partly the result of her failure to create anything more positive and appealing while she had the chance. Mary never found an effective propagandist—partly because she did not have long to try, and partly because she never seems to have appreciated the need. Although she never had the slightest doubt of her royal dignity and status, she remained confused and uncertain about how to project it. In her own lifetime she appeared most clearly as a loyal daughter of the church, but was unable

34

to give that image the flavour of Englishness which it needed and which, paradoxically, she actually possessed.[130]

By contrast, her half-sister and successor, Elizabeth, was one of the greatest image builders the world has ever seen: Eliza Triumphans in her own lifetime, and Good Queen Bess to every subsequent generation.

> ... some call her Pandora; some Gloriana, some Cynthia; some Belphoebe; some Astraea; all by several names to express several loves ...[131]

The existence of what Roy Strong has called the 'cult of Elizabeth' is so well known, and has been so frequently studied, that there is no need to examine it in detail here. To some extent it was the result of longevity, and a modest degree of substantial political success; to some extent also an accident of cultural development, which probably owed more to previous generations and to contemporary France than it did to the queen. Nevertheless, Elizabeth created the court in which it flourished, selected its ingredients, and shaped its growth by her responses. More practical and astute than Mary, Elizabeth was also a talented and enthusiastic public performer. According to one (unsympathetic) observer at the beginning of her reign, she 'gloried' in her father,[132] and that simple fact provides the key to much of her achievement. Her father had been a sovereign, and an Englishman. His *maiestas* had been of the conventional masculine kind—warrior, athlete and gallant; he had also symbolised his realm, and expressed its pride and pretensions. Elizabeth realised that she had to do the same, but could not, for obvious reasons, do it in the same way. Not only was she a woman, but also the reigns of her brother and sister had created a new situation. Whether she liked it or not, the royal supremacy had become an explicitly Protestant concept since his death, in a way which Henry himself had never countenanced. Either Elizabeth had to abide by the *status quo* in 1558, and rely upon the marriage market to provide her with an identity, or she had to seize the initiative, and follow her father as best she could.

In choosing the latter course, she eventually created an image in which there were three main ingredients: Protestantism, Englishness, and femininity. All these elements were presented in the opening months of her reign, although it is not easy to tell how far the queen herself was responsible for the form they took. Did she approve, or even suggest, the appearance of Deborah, Judge of Israel, among the pageant figures who greeted her entry to London?[133] Her favourable response to Protestant symbolism was certainly noticed on that occasion, and the religious settlement of the following summer provoked no surprise—except, perhaps, in Rome. However, having made her choice, restored her father's sovereignty, and obtained the loyal devotion of a serviceable bench of bishops, Elizabeth thereafter took her Protestantism very much for granted. When necessary, as during the Armada crisis, she could be very much the Godly Prince, but she had no desire to be cast as a crusader in Europe, and the ambiguity of some of her religious gestures worried the more zealous. Her Englishness, on the other hand, was always explicit and forceful, from the first time she described herself as the 'bride of England' until the 'Golden' speech of 1601.

> Here is my hand, my dear lover England,
> I am thine both with mind and heart

declared 'Bessy' in one of the ballads which greeted her accession,[134] and the fact that she was 'mere English' was a public and repeated boast. She had '...the heart and stomach of a king—yea and a king of England too!' as she declared to her dauntless, if ill-prepared, subjects at Tilbury.

The third element in her image, femininity, was both more complex and more original. There is no reason to suppose that Elizabeth set out to be a Virgin Queen; it was a condition eventually forced upon her by the hard choices of political reality, and although she made much in the early part of her reign of being wedded to her people, she would not have allowed that to stand in the way of an orthodox marriage. It was the impossibility, which Maitland of Lethington identified, of being both a wife and a sovereign which defeated her. In the normal course of events virginity is a perishable asset, and for that reason did not feature prominently in her early propaganda. However, as the prospects of marriage and dynastic security receded, Elizabeth began to make increasing use of the imagery of courtly love, turning the polite conventions of chivalric service into a hard reality of public life. The gallants who, for generations, had been swearing themselves to strive and labour for a lady's smile, were now taken at their word! Beauty, at first real enough, but latterly highly artificial, served Elizabeth in place of the athleticism and knightly skills which her father had displayed. Courtly love placed her beyond criticism, and beyond comprehension, as the 'Belle dame sans merci' had been answerable to none. It was in some ways a fragile pose, and her ministers and servants must often have wondered whether they were in council, or a courtly charade; but the game was so well adjusted to the courtly culture of the period that it enjoyed unparalleled success, gathering momentum as the reign advanced. The accession day tilts—the quintessential pageants of the cult, developed in the 1570s[135]—and most of the poetic and artistic celebrations of it, such as Spenser's *Faerie Queen* and the Procession portrait, date from the 1580s and 1590s. Elizabeth made her court, with its rituals, symbolism and courteous conventions, work as no other English sovereign had been able to do. It became an essential pillar of the state, because it maintained the realm in dutiful obedience to a woman, supposedly a weak and unfit creature to bear rule over men. This blend of mystique and *maiestas* was unique, and papered over with cloth of gold the innumerable cracks and strains which had developed in the body politic by 1603. The demotion of the Virgin Mary in a Protestant state had also left a large vacancy for a female deity, which Elizabeth set out to fill:

> She was and is, what can there more be said,
> In earth the first, in heaven the second maid.[136]

It was an impossible act to follow, as the Stuarts found to their cost.

Further reading

Full particulars of all works listed here and for subsequent chapters may be found in the Bibliography (p. 239)

S. Anglo   *Spectacle, Pageantry and Early Tudor Policy*

S. Anglo   *The Great Tournament Roll of Westminster*

C. A. J. Armstrong 'The Golden Age of Burgundy' in *The Courts of Europe*

Baldesar Castiglione   *The Book of the Courtier*

R. F. Green   *Poets and Princepleasers*

M. H. Keen   *Chivalry*

G. Kipling   *The Triumph of Honour*

J. W. McKenna 'How God became an Englishman' in *Tudor Rule and Revolution*

R. Strong   *Tudor and Jacobean Portraiture*

2 THE INSTITUTIONS

The structure of the court

In some respects 'the court' was a highly amorphous entity, and the succession of ordinances and household books which were issued between 1445 and 1604 bear witness to the constant struggle to impose order, definition, and above all economy upon an organism which was always threatening to get out of control. As we have seen, originally all the king's servants were a part of his *familia*, but by the fifteenth century certain departments had gone 'out of court', and the officers of the Chancery, Exchequer, and judicial benches were no longer members of the household establishment. At the same time, other offices, which were much more closely connected with the personal pleasures and 'magnificence' of the monarch, had also become detached. The most obvious was the Wardrobe, which in the fourteenth century had been the principal household treasury, and which had also handled the vast quantities of cloth and haberdashery of all kinds which the court distributed and consumed. By 1445, when Thomas Tudenham became Keeper, it had its own premises in the parish of St Andrew, Baynards Castle, with the status of a liberty, and accounted directly to the Exchequer.[1] By the sixteenth century it was known as the Great Wardrobe, to distinguish it from the Privy Wardrobes of the Robes and the Beds, and had also developed sub-departments of the Tents and the Revels. It continued to discharge its main function of purchasing, storing and issuing cloth, but also had custody of the tents and pavilions which were used for progresses and special festivals, and of scenery and properties, not only for masking and dramatic presentations, but also for pageants and entries. In January 1554 the then Keeper, Sir Edward Waldegrave, and his successors were granted the status of a 'body corporate and politic' with jurisdiction over all the mansions, tenements and other properties of the Great Wardrobe. Waldegrave then became wholly responsible for the properties and those employed in them, accounting once a year to the Crown, via the Exchequer.[2] By that time the personal involvement of the monarch with the affairs of the Great Wardrobe was very slight, but the same could not be said of the Stables, nor of the hunting departments, the Kennels and the 'Toyles'—or falcon. By the later sixteenth century the Kennels had three divisions—Hart Hounds, Buckhounds and Otter Hounds, and a total staff of a dozen or more; the 'Toyles' had a sergeant and five or six falconers, and the Stables formed a major department.[3] The Master of the Horse was an important appointment of high prestige and close proximity to the monarch, who kept his own table within the court, but who was neither paid nor controlled through the household offices. The Stables and the hunting departments were financed directly from the Exchequer, and answerable to no one except the monarch.[4]

There were a number of other offices which also appear to have been associated with the court, but which were not part of it, such as the Works, and the Royal Barge. At the same time, to emphasise the fact that the household was still a centre of government, royal councillors and secretaries, together with their servants, did enjoy 'bouge of court'—the right to be fed at the royal tables—because in theory they were in constant attendance upon the monarch. Others who came, no matter what their rank or business, did not enjoy the same right, and their constantly and unpredictably fluctuating numbers constituted a major problem of management throughout the period. One of the main points in having a court was to attract, dazzle and impress outsiders, but they could easily become an open-ended commitment for the commissariat. There seem to have been no clear cut rules relating to those who were not 'lodged within the court'. Respecting the service of meals in the king's Chamber, the *Liber Niger* says, rather uncertainly

> And if there be com such straugers that for certen causes must sett in the chambre, than as the ussher thinkith best according so to be sett and served by the assewer of the chambre . . .[5]

Presumably similar discretion had to be exercised by the appropriate official in respect of lesser mortals seeking meals in the Hall, and by the household officers in respect of the 'messes' which were served in their own quarters. The normal practice was for noblemen and gentlemen visiting the court to rent houses or lodgings in the vicinity, as they also did when sessions of parliament or other business called them to the capital, and to take the majority of their meals in their own lodgings. The great, or the fortunate, might also own property in or near London, and prefer the relative seclusion of their own homes even when entitled to reside at court. The Dukes of Buckingham, for example, tended to operate from Penshurst in Kent; while the Talbot Earls of Shrewsbury had a house in Chelsea, and later the former ecclesiastical mansion of Coldharbour.[6] There were several episcopal residences in London, most notably York Place and Durham Place, and, as the sixteenth century advanced, more and more aristocrats bought, or built, houses within easy reach of Westminster. Nevertheless, the court was always seething with people of every rank and status, and whether accommodation could be found for strangers that cometh but seldom' seems to have depended more upon chance than upon any rule or order of precedence. For example, when the Duchess of Alba arrived (somewhat unexpectedly) in 1554, she had to be lodged outside the court, much to the annoyance of her attendants and in spite of the fact that the duke was already in residence.[7] The task of the Lord Steward's officers in allocating accommodation must always have been difficult, and frequently invidious. In theory the number of servants allowed, both to residents and non-residents, was strictly controlled, but in practice such controls were constantly evaded or ignored; and there were also licensed delinquents, such as ambassadors. Accredited ambassadors were normally assigned lodging outside the court at the monarch's expense, but

> ... if it please the kinge to have them lie within the courte, they muste be in their owne chamber, and to have all manner of officers to attend them; and if they have manye menne, the steward or Treasurer must warne a man to wait on them and bringe them into the Halle ...[8]

The court in its wider sense was thus surprisingly ill-defined, and fluctuated greatly in size according to the season, even when it was settled in its commonest location, at Westminster. Since the court was also a jurisdictional liberty, and it was impossible to define membership in consistent personal terms, the jurisdiction of the Lord Steward's court had to be limited topographically. The traditional precinct of Westminster was enlarged by statute in 1537, and it seems likely that other established royal residences such as Richmond and Greenwich also had customary precincts, but when the court was on the move, or at lesser houses such as Oatlands, an approximate ten mile radius seems to have been used, which must have caused innumerable disputes and uncertainties. The Lord Steward had common law jurisdiction, *ex officio* without commission, and this was confirmed and elaborated by statute in 1542, when a coroner was also appointed for the household.[9] As we shall see, this court was supported by regular disciplinary officers, and also by occasional commissions, notably that issued to Sir Thomas Holcrofte and Brivesca de Muñatones to deal with Anglo-Spanish disputes in the court during the period of Philip's residence in 1554–5. This jurisdiction applied to anyone who happened to be within the verge at the time of their offence or misdemeanour, but its surviving records are minimal, and its effectiveness extremely hard to determine.

Even at the heart of the court, simple definitions are elusive. Some Chamber servants enjoyed bouge of court—which included provision for their own servants—some merely personal 'diets': some were paid wages or fees in addition, others not. Broadly speaking, however, it would be true to say that the two main divisions of the permanent court, the *Domus Regie Magnificencie* and the *Domus Providencie*, were distinguished from the outlying departments and from non-established attenders in three ways: by the enjoyment of bouge of court, by the receipt of fees, or wages, and by being subject to the authority of either the Lord Chamberlain or the Lord Steward (see Appendix IV). The first of these divisions was much the more volatile, being directly subject to the whims of the sovereign, his or her family circumstances, and political pressures generated outside the court. By the fourteenth century two main departments had emerged, the Hall and the Chamber, with the personal service of the king concentrating in the latter. In physical terms the Chamber was already a number of distinct rooms through which the monarch could retreat to the inner sanctuary of the Bedchamber, but this was not reflected in the organisation of the service, even as late as the *Liber Niger*, wherein it was ordered:

> The ussher of chambre ever to se and quikly to remedy every thing lacking or defautz as well in the kinges inner chambre as in the utter chambre . . .[10]

Although there were hints of such a development in the reign of Henry VII, the evolution of the Privy Chamber as a distinct department, or 'district', came only in the reign of Henry VIII, and probably as an imitation of French practice. By the middle of the sixteenth century, therefore, the Lord Chamberlain was responsible for two separate entities: the Privy Chamber, with a staff of Gentlemen, Ushers, Grooms and Pages; and the Great Chamber, with a similar staff, but also embracing the Privy Wardrobes, Cupbearers, Sewers, Carvers, Physicians, Chaplains, Yeoman of the Guard and Gentlemen Pensioners. Related to these departments, and counted as part of the *Domus Regie Magnificencie*, but not under the control of the Lord Chamberlain, were the Jewel House and the Chapel royal, the latter with a choristers' school attached. Also anomalous to some extent was the position of the king's secretaries. Originally Chamber servants of relatively humble status, by the 1530s they were among the monarch's principal men of business, and their subordination to the Lord Chamberlain was obsolete and largely forgotten. The Great Hall was by this time a twilight zone — more an occasional event than a regular department.[11] Its customary staff of Marshals, Surveyors, Harbingers and Messengers belonged to the *Domus Providencie* and were ruled by the Lord Steward, but semi-independent groups, such as the musicians of the 'King's Musik', Players, Artists and Artificers were sometimes grouped under this heading.[12] They were certainly members of the household, but were not accountable to the Board of Greencloth, and should therefore be assigned to the *DRM*, although they were not part of the Chamber nor, as far as I can tell, subject to the Lord Chamberlain. As we shall see, the household 'above stairs' went through a number of important modifications and changes of emphasis between 1509 and 1603, but its basic structure did not change. Except at times of crisis it was loosely controlled, not particularly hierarchical, and somewhat confused in its funding. It was also in certain respects highly politicised, and the Privy Chamber in particular was one of the main channels of access to the monarch.

For about half the Tudor period the upper household also included a consort's Chamber and Privy Chamber. These were physically and financially distinct from the 'King's side', were smaller, but similar in organisation, including Privy Wardrobes of the Robes and Beds, and were subject to the authority of the queen's Chamberlain.[13] The consort's Privy Chamber naturally contained a substantial proportion of women, the queen's maids and Chamberers, but the officers were always men. For a few years, from 1554 to 1558, there was actually a male consort's household, and, as we shall see, that created a number of problems by its very strangeness. Philip, either out of ignorance or from deliberate political calculation, brought a full Chamber staff with him from Spain, to find another awaiting him in England, complete with a guard of 100 archers. Both sides complained bitterly, and an uneasy compromise was reached, whereby many of the Spaniards went off to join the emperor's army in the Low Countries, and many of the English were 'stood down', theoretically on full pay.[14] The king was only in England for a matter of fifteen months, on two visits, but Mary's hopes, and the constant uncertainty about his intentions, caused his Chamber staff to be reconvened and dismissed several times in the intervals. Apart from a small group of young noblemen who accompanied him to Flanders in August 1555, and stayed for a few weeks, Philip never employed Englishmen in his household outside England. Finally, there were intermittently Chamber establishments for the royal children. These grew and changed with the children themselves, starting as nurseries, so that generalisations are difficult. Mary and Elizabeth, in the years prior to their accessions, had their own residences and their own revenues, and were independent magnates rather than members of the court,[15] but this was not the case with either Henry or Edward. Each of these princes had his own Chamber servants, as well as tutors and companions, and Edward certainly had his own officers, but they lived at court, and just how physically distinct their lives were is not very clear. Visitors to whom their precocious talents were proudly displayed, as was also the case with Mary in her younger days, clearly regarded them as ornaments of the *Domus Regie Magnificencie*.

The household 'below stairs', by contrast with these fluctuations and uncertainties, was bureaucratic and stable almost down to the last detail. The only major reorganisation was that attempted by Thomas Cromwell in 1539/40 when the office of Lord Steward was abolished by statute, and replaced with that of Lord Great Master.[16] The Lord Great Master enjoyed all the authority and privileges previously belonging to the Lord Steward, but in addition he was given authority over the Lord Chamberlain, so that the whole *Domus Regis* was placed under a single overall control—as had probably been the case before the emergence of the Chamber as a separate department. In addition, four new officers, the Masters of the Household, were established to work alongside the existing Treasurer, Controller and Cofferer in supervising the work of the various departments. The main object of these reforms was to impose tighter spending controls, and to increase the efficiency of the Countinghouse, to which the departments accounted, at the same time extending its function to cover the various 'districts' of the upper household. It turned out to be a shortlived experiment, partly because of the extreme conservatism of the household establishment, and partly because of the vested interests which would have been damaged by greater efficiency. By the end of Edward VI's reign, two of the Masterships were vacant, and Mary's first parliament in November 1553 repealed the earlier Act and restored the Lord Steward to his wonted functions.[17] The four Masterships were abolished. Under the Steward and the other 'head officers' the management of the household was vested in the Countinghouse, or 'Board of Greencloth' as it was normally called in the sixteenth century (see Appendix IV). At the time of the

Liber Niger all the officers were supposed to attend in the Countinghouse daily, but it seems unlikely that this strict regimen ever worked, and by the middle of the sixteenth century the Cofferer was the administrative head of the office. He was responsible not only for keeping a daily check upon the expenditure of the various departments, but also for making sure that they produced their budgets and estimates. As its name suggests, the Countinghouse was primarily a financial agency, but it also adjudicated disputes which arose within the *Domus Providencie*, and listened to the complaints from outsiders against those necessary but perpetual nuisances, the royal purveyors.

Answerable to the Countinghouse were the provision and service departments which obtained and prepared the food and drink consumed by the court in gargantuan quantities, and which provided and cleaned the utensils and table linen. All these departments showed an inexorable tendency to expand as the century went on, and their exact relationship to each other is not always easy to determine, but, with the exception of the Kitchen, all the 'head' departments were under the rule of Sergeants. From time to time attempts at economy led to the grouping of several departments under a single Sergeant, and some of the smaller units were really sub-divisions of the greater, performing specialised tasks.[18] An establishment list from the early part of Mary's reign, just after the middle of the century, gives as good a 'median' picture as can be obtained. In the order of this list the departments were: the Bakehouse, the Pantry, the Cellar, the Buttery (which distributed beer), the Pitcherhouse, the Spicery, the Chaundry (candles and tapers), the Confectionary (sweetmeats), the Ewery (table linen), the Laundry, the Wafery (biscuits), the Kitchen, the Larder, the Boilinghouse, the Acatry (meat and fish), the Poultry, the Scaldinghouse, the Pastry, the Scullery (pots and pans), the Woodyard, the Harbingers, the Almonry, the Porters, and the Carttakers. Of these the Bakehouse, Pantry, Cellar, Chaundry, Confectionary, Ewery, Kitchen, Larder, Acatry, Poultry, Pastry, Scullery, Woodyard, Harbingers, Almonry and Porters were 'head' departments. The Buttery, Pitcherhouse and Spicery were subordinate to the Cellar; the Laundry was under the Ewery; the Wafery and Boilinghouse under the Kitchen; the Scaldinghouse under the Poultry, and the Carttakers (probably) under the Porters.[19]

Of this sizeable list, only the Harbingers and the Almonry call for special comment at this stage, because each was headed by a court official of gentle rank, the only two in the lower household, below the Board of Greencloth itself. The explanation for this seems to have been purely functional. The Knight Harbinger was responsible for all accommodation when the court was on progress (which was a rare event except during Elizabeth's reign), and for organising the regular moves from palace to palace, which took place every few weeks, except in the depth of winter. He therefore needed to be in touch with the service departments, in case their well-established routines broke down, or were disrupted by royal whims. The Almoner was invariably a cleric of some standing, whose original task had been the distribution of the king's charity. In the early part of his career, Thomas Wolsey had been high in the king's confidence, and as 'Master Almoner' had organised much of the support for the Tournai campaign of 1513.[20] However, most Almoners did not aspire to such status, and with the development of the Privy Chamber the king's 'offerings' seem more often to have been made by the Chief Gentleman. This left the Almonry with the main task of distributing the 'broken meats' from the royal tables to the poor who (theoretically) clustered at the palace gate. In practice, many of the poor seem to have infiltrated the palace and helped themselves, while the Almoner's 'doles' were either sent to convenient charitable foundations or sold to other catering establishments and the money given to suitable causes. Nevertheless, the Almoner's department needed to be in close touch with the kitchens, and it is not surprising that the Counting-house wanted to keep track of the quantities of food disposed of under its auspices.[21]

At the end of this Marian establishment, and still answerable to the Countinghouse, comes a miscellaneous list of functionaries, not grouped together as a department—or at least not so described. On investigation, most of these turn out to be the officers and servants of the Great Hall—six Marshals, four Sewers, and so on down to the Dogkeeper, whose job it was to expel unwanted and insanitary curs. By the end of Elizabeth's reign the staff of the Hall had disappeared from the household lists altogether, which presumably means that service there had become so unimportant, or so infrequent, as not to justify the employment of specific servants.[22] The Marian list thus marks a halfay stage in the erosion of the Hall. In 1445 it had been a major department, headed by 'le chevalier mareschall'; by 1478 it had already shrunk by more than half, and was clearly under the Countinghouse. In the Eltham Ordinances of 1526 it was described in similar terms, and had acquired a Sergeant in addition to the Marshals; but by 1554 the departmental status had gone, and so had the Sergeant. Since cafeteria service had not been invented in the sixteenth century, it seems clear that the Great Hall was no longer being kept by 1600, and that the great communal focus of the medieval court had eventually disappeared after a long decline. In a story which is mainly one of proliferation and growth, the Hall is the major exception.

The Domus Regie Magnificencie

By the end of the fifteenth century, the Chamber had long since ceased to be the room behind the dais in the Great Hall. A complex set of royal lodgings existed at Windsor castle in the reign of Edward III, and it is unlikely that other royal residences in regular use would have failed to provide similar convenience. Edward IV's ordinance of 1471 appears to refer to three main rooms:

... our inner chamber doore be dailie kept with a gentleman usher, and in the second a yeoman usher, and the third doore with a yeoman of the chamber.[23]

However, the same section also uses the terms 'dyneing chamber' and 'upper chamber', so the geography is not very clear. Probably the dining chamber was the most accessible to the outside world, and the upper and inner chambers were the same. By the reign of Henry VII the terminology had changed somewhat, and we find reference to the 'Great Chamber', the 'Second Chamber' and the 'Secret Chamber'; Henry VIII called the latter two the 'Present Chamber' and the 'Privy Chamber', and those names remained in use until the appearance of the 'Bedchamber' and the 'Closet' in the early seventeenth century. It does not follow, of course, that each of these 'chambers' was a single room. If Hampton Court can be taken as typical, there were a number of ancillary rooms, particularly associated with the Privy Chamber — the king's tiring room, a 'withdrawing' room, and so on. There was also direct access to the queen's private apartments, and a back staircase giving directly onto the courtyard.[24] Older palaces may well have been less elaborate, but structural modifications seem to have been carried out in most of them as notions of splendour changed and the importance of comfort increased. In Henry VIII's new showpiece of Nonsuch, completed late in the reign, there was no Hall or Great Chamber; the royal apartments were on the first floor, both on the king's side and on the queen's side, and each contained some dozen distinct rooms. At the same time there was a Privy Gallery, and also a Privy Garden, on the south-eastern side (see plate 31).[25]

So the king's Chamber servants patrolled a sizeable territory, and meticulous attention had to be paid to everything that happened within it. There was constant tension between the king's honour, which required him to be accessible to his subjects (particularly the nobility), and common prudence and convenience, which dictated the tightest possible control of access. In spite of issuing some strict-seeming instructions, Edward IV does not seem to have solved this problem, and the only distinction made among the Chamber servants was that of rank. The Knights and Esquires of the Body were his closest personal servants, working, according to the ordinance of 1471, in two shifts, eight weeks on and eight weeks off.[26] The only man who was required to be in constant attendance at that level was Sir Roger Ray, at that point Deputy Chamberlain. The Sewers, Carvers and Cup-bearers were not body servants, but functioned in the semi-public context of the dining chamber, and the Gentlemen and Yeomen Ushers, the Grooms and the Pages, 'kept' the various doors and rooms without being admitted to any close personal contact with the monarch; all were equally subject to the Lord Chamberlain, and the notion of 'districts' within the Chamber had not yet emerged. The king could, of course, admit anyone whom he chose to intimacy, and his councillors, gambling companions and favourites were frequently present in the inner Chamber, but they were not normally part of the service establishment. The physicians and chaplains who, by virtue of their duties, enjoyed occasional intimacy, were members of the Chamber staff, and answerable to the Lord Chamberlain, but were not servants in the ordinary sense.

This situation seems to have changed significantly in the reign of Henry VII, who was a much more private person. The evidence is somewhat fragmentary, but by about 1494 the Knights of the Body had disappeared, and personal service was carried out by the Esquires and the Gentlemen Ushers, particularly the former. An ordinance of that year ran:

> As for Esquires of the bodie, they ought to array the King and unarray him, and noe man else to sett hand on the Kinge . . .[27]

Yeomen of the Beds and Robes were to be in attendance, assisted by Grooms, while the Ushers 'kept the door'. By 1501 these semi-formal *levees* seem to have been discontinued, and neither the Esquires of the Body nor the Gentlemen Ushers were admited to the 'Secret Chamber':

> the groom of the stoole, with a page with hym, or such as the kyng woll commande ought to wayte in the Kinges secrete Chamber especially and noone else . . .[28]

The evidence for this development has been carefully pieced together by Dr David Starkey, who has concluded that by the end of the reign the personal service of the king was almost entirely in the hands of a small group of Grooms of the Chamber, headed by the Groom of the Stool.[29] These men, who were not as yet differentiated from the remainder of the Chamber servants, handled the king's Privy Purse expenses, and some of them regularly undertook confidential missions both within the country and abroad. By 1509 there was consequently an official and an unofficial position. Officially there was a single, undifferentiated Chamber staff, as before, consisting of Esquires, Gentlemen Ushers, Yeoman Ushers, Grooms and Pages. Unofficially there was a 'Privy Chamber' staff of some half dozen Grooms and Pages, who virtually monopolised routine access to the king, and whose social status was noticeably higher than the humbled designations of their offices would suggest. Francis Marzen, who was actually described as 'oon of the groomes of our privie chambre' in 1501, undertook several diplomatic missions, and was knighted in 1506. Hugh Denys, who was Groom of the Stool for most of the reign, and Chief Groom of the Chamber by 1508, came from a well-established Gloucestershire gentry family.[30] By this time the main function of the Esquires of the Body was public rather than private, in that they represented the personal presence and authority of the king at times, and in places, where he could not be. In doing this they stood in an ancient tradition, but one which, in England, was increasingly turning the king into a public corporation.

One of the consequences of these concealed changes was that the function of the Secret Chamber was also subtly altered. It became the king's place of work, rather than simply a retreat, and this partly explains the contrasting images of Henry VII which both contemporaries and historians commented upon. The outer chambers were places of ceremony, and magnificence, where meals were served with pomp, entertainments offered, and public business transacted. Apart from the correct discharge of their duties, the staff of these chambers were expected to put on a show, and to behave with all the appropriate courtly graces. By contrast the Secret Chamber was a place of concentration and relative austerity, the staff of which were not on show, and where unobtrusive efficiency and discretion were the highest virtues. It was the most intimate of the public rooms, in the sense that public business was carried on there, but it was also an extension of the king's private apartments in the sense that he could put off his 'magnificence' and be unobserved by the outside world. It was thus very much a reflection of the king's personality, and could not be expected to continue in the same way under his very different successor.

Henry VIII reappointed the Earl of Worcester as Lord Chamberlain, a position which he had achieved in 1508, and resurrected the Knights of the Body.[31] He also introduced men from his previous establishment as prince into the service of the Chamber, notably four Grooms, William Compton, William Thomas, John Sharp and William Tyler. By November 1509 Compton had become Groom of the Stool, and these four names stood at the head of the list of Grooms of the Chamber. The implication seems to be that these, and possibly one or two others, constituted the staff of the Privy Chamber, displacing Denys and the others who had served Henry VII in that capacity. Compton, Sharp and Tyler were knighted in 1513, in the course of the Tournai campaign, and Compton was recognised as being one of the king's most influential favourites. Grooms and Pages of the king's Privy Chamber were specifically referred to in the Act of Apparel of 1516,[32] and indeed they had appeared as a group in the muster roll of the Tournai campaign, but they were as yet accorded no official recognition within the court. So far, it would appear that Henry VIII continued his father's practice with different personnel, but, unlike his father, the young king also admitted a second group of men to intimacy—the so-called 'minions'. These men, who varied from six to nine in number over a period of about eight years, were the king's cronies and jousting companions. Some of them were noblemen, like the Earl of Essex and the Marquis of Dorset; others had well-established pedigrees in the court and royal service, such as Henry Guildford and Charles Brandon.[33] The first group, who established themselves between 1509 and 1512, were mostly about ten years older than the king, and probably respresented his desire for the approbation and support of men whose personalities and physical skills were already fully developed. But between 1513 and 1516 a change occured: two of his early favourites, Sir Thomas Knyvett and Sir Edward Howard, were killed in France; one or two others lost favour, and younger men, such as Nicholas Carew and Francis Bryan, began to appear. They were a decade younger than the king, and twenty years younger than the older 'minions', reflecting a sharp change in Henry's perception of himself. By 1518 several, but not all, of these favourites had been given offices on the staff of the Chamber—Carew, for example, was Chief Cup-bearer—and the whole group, by virtue of their constant companionship with the king, constituted a *de facto* Privy Chamber.

So by that time there were two Privy Chamber groups, one of service and the other of *camaraderie* (although in the person of Compton the distinction was somewhat blurred), neither of which had any institutional definition.

This unsatisfactory situation was regularised between 1518 and 1520, as a direct result of the peace with France and renewed contacts between the two courts. In September 1518 a major embassy arrived, and the strictest protocol had to be observed, which appears to have involved pairing members of the embassy with members of the English court for a ceremonial entry into London. Francis I had recently created the new post of *Gentil homme de la Chambre*, and six of these gentlemen were present in the embassy. For the purposes of the entry they were paired with six of the 'minions', who were their exact equivalents in everything but title.[34] In the following month the English sent a similar embassy to France, headed by the Earl of Worcester, and four of the 'minions' were included in the party under the informal name of 'chamberlaynes'. A few months later the process of transition was disrupted by a political crisis. Ostensibly two of the 'minions', Carew and Bryan, had misbehaved themselves in France (rather in the manner of young men today after a football match), and this was used as an occasion for certain councillors to make representations to the king

> ... that certain young men in his private chamber not regarding his estate or degree, were so familiar and homely with hym, and plaied suche light touches with hym that they forgat themselfes ...[35]

No doubt there was truth in this, and it did not enhance the king's honour, but the real reason seems to have been that Cardinal Wolsey was becoming apprehensive of the increasing formality of the 'minions'' position about Henry. A fully developed Privy Chamber on the French model would inevitably form an alternative channel for patronage and political influence, and he would have been the main sufferer if the existing incumbents had managed to consolidate their positions. In the event four of them were ejected in May 1519, to their understandable rage and chagrin, and four Knights of the Body currently occupying offices outside the court were drafted in to take their place.[36] Although these men must have been acceptable to Henry, they were Wolsey's nominees, and were never admitted to the same terms of intimacy. For the time being they were known by the clumsy title Knights for the Body in the King's Privy Chamber. Perhaps because Wolsey was satisfied with having asserted himself in this manner, the institutional development of the Privy Chamber as a 'district' was then rapidly completed. The four Knights and two remaining Gentlemen of the Privy Chamber was 'put into wages' by being given life annuities of £100 and 50 marks respectively. Unlike the wages of the Chamber servants, which were paid out of the Exchequer at this point, these annuities were paid out of the Treasury of the Chamber, thus clearly distinguishing the holders from the remainder of the court. The wages of the Grooms and Pages were also transferred to the Treasury of the Chamber, and, as if to make the point, one man, Robert Knollys, held two positions, drawing £24 a year from the Exchequer as Chief Gentleman Usher of the Chamber, and £20 from the Treasury of the Chamber as Gentleman Usher of the Privy Chamber![37] By 1522 the last conservatism of terminology had been overcome, and the new department was fully recognised and acknowledged.

No sooner had this happened, however, than fresh problems began to arise. The king did not share Wolsey's concern with either stability or administrative neatness, and by 1525 the staff of the Privy Chamber had grown from fifteen to twenty-two. This had been achieved partly by transfers from the Outer Chamber (for which there was considerable pressure once the significance of the new development began to be appreciated), and partly by the creation of new positions, particularly of Gentlemen. To make matters worse, only three of these new appointments were 'put in wages', so that eight out of the twenty-two were technically supernumerary. Bryan and Carew had been reinstated before the end of 1519, and the whole situation was getting out of hand once more. Consequently, in the autumn of 1525, Wolsey returned to the charge, with a set of 'Ordenances devised by the Kinges highnes with thadvice of his counsail concerning the good order of suche persones as his grace hath deputed to be in his Privie Chamber.' These ordinances projected a Privy Chamber establishment of six Gentlemen (one of whom was to be the Groom of the Stool), 2 Gentlemen Ushers, 4 Grooms, a Barber and a Page—a total of fourteen.[38] To achieve this target, Wolsey had not only to persuade the king (again) to reduce the number of his intimates, but also to negotiate the removal of such as were in wages. Fees and annuities granted by Letters Patent could not simply be cancelled, as Richard Jerningham, Esquire of the Body, pointed out on another occasion. He had taken over his office from Sir William Parr in 1512, and a letter which he wrote to Wolsey when threatened with removal for non-attendance casts a shaft of light on the whole system:

> I and my frends payd CC marks to Sir William A parr, and not without the consent of the Kinges highnes, and at that time his grace gaff it me during my lyffe, and so I have it as strong as his lawes will mak it me.[39]

The Cardinal worked on this problem throughout the winter, and was unwise enough to keep his Christmas at Richmond with great pomp, while the king was at Eltham, evading the plague, 'with a small nombre'. By the end of January he had carried out all the necessary negotiations, and the Eltham Ordinances got rid of eight of the Privy Chamber staff, including the Groom of the Stool, Sir William Compton, who was by this time his particular *bête noir*. Only on one point did he not get his way: Henry Courtenay, Earl of Devon, remained as 'Nobleman of the Privy Chamber', without wages. In every other respect the programme of the previous year was implemented.

Although there were sound administrative arguments to support it, this purge of the Privy Chamber, like that of 1519, was mainly political in its inspiration. This was not, however, true of the remaining sections of the

Eltham Ordinances, which carried out some much needed reforms of the Chamber and household. The reason given in the Proheme, that

> ... many of the officers and ministers of his household being employed and appointed to the makeing of provisions and other thinges concerning the wars, the accustomed good order of his household hath been greatly hindred, and in a manner subverted ...[40]

was probably the real one, and most of the provisions are consistent with such a view. In respect of the household, the emphasis was upon discipline: strict accounting procedures, proper budgeting, and a tightening up of bouge allowances. The Lord Steward was required to inspect his staff, and to pension off anyone who was 'sicklie or unmete' for their position, but no structural reforms were attempted. The Chamber was more severely handled, because it was there that the main abuses had grown up. Large numbers of supernumeraries, particularly Gentlemen and Yeoman Ushers, were discharged, and taken out of the 'Ordinary', or establishment list. The Yeomen of the Guard, a band established early in Henry VII's reign and commanded by the Vice Chamberlain, was reduced to its original number of 100, sixty-four being discharged on a retainer of six pence a day.[41] Above all, the number of servants permitted to the officers of the Chamber was strictly defined, and orders given to the Sergeant Porter that no others were to be admitted to the 'verge'. How effective these measures were is, as always, uncertain; but to judge from the complaints recorded by Hall, in the short term they were strictly imposed:

> Wherefore first the officers servauntes, wer put oute of the courte, and many old officers were put to live in their countreys ... and young men were put in their romes ... Alas what sorowe and what lamentacion was made, when all these persones should depart the courte. Some saied that poore servauntes wer undone and must steale ...[42]

Hall's own comment, that many regarded the ordinances as 'more profitable than honourable', reflects not only his animus against Wolsey, but also the fundamentally intractable nature of the problem. Magnificence still required large numbers of servants and attendants; efficiency and economy required their reduction. In 1526 economy won a limited tactical victory.

In the Privy Chamber the struggle was soon resumed. In 1526 all but two of the staff had been put 'in wages', but overlap with the Outer Chamber was never quite eliminated; Sir Francis Bryan and Sir Edward Neville, both Gentlemen of the Privy Chamber, were also Chief Cup-bearer and Chief Sewer respectively, and it seems that the sharp distinction between the two 'districts' which appertained in theory by this time, was never so strictly observed in practice. Also, the inflation of numbers began again. By 1530 there were nine Gentlemen, and twenty overall; by 1532 eleven and twenty-four, and by 1539 sixteen and twenty-eight; and of these last nearly a third were supernumeraries.[43] In 1532 the household administration endeavoured to impose its own remedy, by decreeing that no more than five lodgings would be available for Gentlemen of the Privy Chamber at any one time, and drawing up a two shift system—six weeks on and six weeks off. This never seems to have worked, and indeed the problem was not the throng of Gentlemen at any given time, so much as their erratic comings and goings. This was largely the king's own fault since he continued to use them for confidential missions. Henry was perfectly capable of sending his Gentlemen off in all directions, and then complaining that there was no one to wait on him—which was another reason for the steady inflation of numbers.

Thomas Cromwell began to tackle this and several other problems connected with the household, in 1533. He appears to have had two main objectives: to cure the occasional shortage of attendance without adding to the cost, and to provide a bureaucratic structure which would make the whole court more efficient and easier to control. The first objective was achieved by reviving the supernumeraries whom Wolsey had tried so hard to eliminate, under the title 'Extraordinary'. Thus the ordinary establishment of the Privy Chamber by 1540 consisted of sixteen Gentlemen, two Gentlemen Ushers, three Grooms and two Barbers—all of whom were in wages. Extraordinary were two Noblemen (one of them Cromwell himself), two Gentlemen, and three Grooms.[44] The second, and much larger objective was partially achieved after a long battle in the Council, in the early part of 1540, but proved to be short-lived. Dr Starkey has analysed all the moves of this campaign, and argues convincingly that Cromwell's strategy was to eliminate the offices of both Lord Chamberlain and Lord Steward, replacing them with a single great officer on the lines of the French *Maitre d'hostel du roi*, to whom all the departments both of the upper and the lower household would be equally subject.[45] At the same time all departments, from the Woodyard to the Privy Chamber, would be funded through the Countinghouse, and equally accountable there.

As we have seen, the office of Lord Steward was abolished by statute later in the year, and replaced with a Lord Great Mastership, and from Christmas 1539 the wages of the Privy Chamber were transferred from the Treasurer of the Chamber to the Cofferer. However, the Lord Chamberlainship hung on, in spite of being kept vacant for two years after Lord Sandys' death in 1541. Sandys himself had been little at court in the latter part of his life, and the office was weak—which was one reason why the Privy Wardrobe of the Robes was transferred from the Chamber to the Privy Chamber at about this time— but with the appointment of the Earl of Arundel in 1546 it began to revive. The changed circumstances of Edward VI's reign, and the weakening of the Privy Chamber during a royal minority, completed the resurrection of the Lord Chamberlain, and spelt the defeat of Cromwell's grand design. The Lord Great Mastership had thus lost its point well before it was abolished by Mary. Similarly the four Masterships (again on the French model), which were offices of the Greencloth, served little purpose when the Chamberlain began to recover his authority. Two of them had been intended to oversee the queen's side of the Chamber, and these were probably the two which were vacant in 1554.

In one respect, however, the reforms of 1539/40 proved extremely enduring. Long before, in 1511, an attempt had been made to add an honorific bodyguard—the Spears—to the existing Yeomen. The experiment had proved abortive, but in 1537 the idea was revived, probably because of the example of Francis I. After considerable uncertainty, and a lot of rumours, in 1539 a band of fifty such gentlemen, with a Captain, Lieutenant and Standard-bearer, was created and called the Gentlemen Pensioners.[46] They formed a part of the staff of the Outer Chamber, and their function was largely ornamental, but places were so much sought after that a supplementary band of Gentlemen at Arms was created before the end of the reign, and positions began to be granted in reversion.[47] Like the Yeomen, the Pensioners formed part of the Ordinary, but they were not expected to be in constant attendance. Except on special occasions they served in shifts of about ten or a dozen at a time, and enjoyed bouge and lodgings only when they were on duty. This seems to have been the rule for the majority of Chamber servants by the end of Henry VIII's reign, and had been so for many years. By 1545 the Ordinary of the king's Chamber included several Privy Councillors who did not hold household office, such as Wriothesley, the Lord Chancellor, and Tunstall, Bishop of Durham, together with the three secretaries, and all the Chamber officers, including those of the Pensioners. The Chamber servants in this schedule consisted of three Cup-bearers, three Carvers, two Surveyors, four 'Gentlemen Ushers Daily Waiters', three Sewers, four Esquires of the Body, six Physicians and Surgeons, the Robes, the Beds, and the whole staff of the Privy Chamber.[48] A second part of the same schedule then goes on to list as Ordinary, with diet and wages, but without bouge, nine 'Gentlemen Ushers Quarterly Wayters', six Sewers and four Pages. A similar distinction was made for the queen's side, and it seems clear that those on the second schedules, whose wages were markedly lower, were not in regular attendance. Whether they served on a regular rota, or only when called upon, is not clear.

The indiscriminate mixing of groups of Chamber and Privy Chamber servants in these schedules may be the result of conservative drafting, but it would be a mistake to suppose that the Privy Chamber was in any sense isolated from the remainder of the court. With the drastic decline of the Great Hall, it was in the Chamber that the king took his formal meals, and there the chief officers of the household kept their tables, whether the king was present or not. In the Chamber, the Gentlemen of the Privy Chamber kept their own table, presided over by the Groom of the Stool, and were budgeted for like any other departmental group.[49] As we have seen, by the end of Henry VIII's reign the Wardrobe of the Robes was counted as part of the Privy Chamber, while its companion office, the Wardrobe of the Beds, remained part of the Great Chamber. The Groom of the Stool, who was also Chief Gentleman of the Privy Chamber and keeper of the Privy Purse, was the principal and most confidential officer of the Privy Chamber, but it is by no means clear that, even at the height of his power, he was recognised as the equal of the Lord Chamberlain and the Lord Steward—let alone the Lord Great Master. The relationship between the Lord Chamberlain and the Groom of the Stool was never clearly defined, and it is unlikely that the former had any effective control over the Privy Chamber between 1522 and 1547, but he retained his primacy as chief officer of the upper household. It was in the realm of politics, rather than of household management, that the Privy Chamber achieved its highest significance, as is indicated by the fact that Cromwell chose to purge it by political action in 1536 and 1538, where Wolsey had used administrative means in 1519 and 1526.[50]

Instead of diminishing its importance, the death of Henry VIII once more turned the Privy Chamber into a political battleground. The coming and going of individuals over the next five years does not concern us here, but the shape and definition of the institution was altered and blurred by the struggles in a manner which might have been of the greatest significance if Edward had not died so soon, and been succeeded by a woman. At the young king's coronation his princely household appeared for the last time, including the seven Gentlemen of his Privy Chamber, and five 'young lords and gentlemen' who were then his school fellows.[51] Within a few days of the ceremony this household had been disbanded, some, such as the last named group, being absorbed into the royal household proper, and others pensioned off.[52] At the same time some members of the existing Chamber staff were stood down to make way for the newcomers. The list of coronation liveries is headed, in the usual manner, by the Lord Chamberlain and Vice-Chamberlain, followed by the staff of the Outer Chamber, little changed in number or personnel from the list of 1545. The Privy Chamber list, however, is headed by no less a person than the Lord Protector, followed by five other peers only one of whom (the Earl of Warwick) had previously appeared on the Ordinary. The sixteen Ordinary Gentlemen who then follow show a number of changes, as might be expected; and Sir Thomas Henneage and Sir Francis Bryan are relegated to the category of Extraordinary Gentlemen, along with two others. It was natural that the Lord Protector, who was also Governor of the King's Person, should have required *ex officio* access to the Privy Chamber, but it also appears that he set out to dominate it with a posse of noble adherents. If such was his intention, it was probably not pursued because a more orthodox and effective method of control was devised instead. At some time before August 1548 his brother in law Sir Michael Stanhope, who had no previous connection with the department, was appointed Chief Gentleman and Groom of the Stool.[53] Unfortunately, Stanhope's control proved to be far from perfect, largely because the whole structure was based upon the assumption that the king himself was the dominant personality. Consequently, when the Protector's brother, Lord Thomas Seymour, began to intrigue against him, he was able to use his position in the Privy Chamber to manipulate Edward's confidence for his own purposes. With the aid of one of the Grooms, John Fowler, he began to pass small sums of money to the king, and to gain access at unorthodox hours. Eventually there was an unseemly and dangerous fracas, in which one of Edward's pet dogs was shot, and Seymour was arrested.[54]

For the remainder of Somerset's supremacy the changes of personnel appear to have been routine, but it was getting distinctly difficult to tell who was 'of the Privy Chamber' and who was not. The king's tutors, both regular and occasional, were ranked as gentlemen servants and were presumable on the Ordinary, but whether of the Privy Chamber or the Outer Chamber is not clear.[55] The same is true of his companions, although two of these, Lord Robert Dudley and Barnaby Fitzpatrick, did become Ordinary Gentlemen in the course of the reign. The fall of the Lord Protector in October 1549 brought more sweeping changes. Stanhope was removed and eventually executed, his office being replaced with no fewer than four Principal Gentlemen, three of whom were new to Privy Chamber service. At the same time the governorship of the king's person was 'put into commission' to six lords of the Privy Council

> ... it (being) requisite to have summe nobell men appointed to be ordynarely attendant about his Majesties person in his Prevey Chamber ...[56]

With the exception of the Earl of Arundel, who was soon replaced, all these 'heavies' were adherents of the ascendant Earl of Warwick, and their appointment has to be seen as part of a calculated plan to use the Privy Chamber as a machinery to dominate both the king and the court. The Ordinary of eighteen Gentlemen remained unchanged, but no fewer than ten of the earlier incumbents had been replaced by 1552.[57] So the plan which Somerset seems to have contemplated at the time of the coronation was carried out, and carried further, by his successor, who at the same time was encouraging the young king to appear more independent in affairs of state. By the same date the Privy Wardrobe of the Beds had joined its sister department under the aegis of the Privy Chamber, the number of Grooms had gone up from four in 1545 to twelve, and the number of Gentlemen Ushers from two to three.[58] Within the Privy Chamber itself, there are also signs that increasing numbers were leading to a new process of selection. It had always been customary for two Gentlemen of the Privy Chamber, in rotation, to sleep in the 'pallet chamber' adjoining the royal bedroom. In 1550 it was decided that one of these must always be one of the four Principal Gentlemen, and that one Groom should also be present—increasing the 'watch' from two to three. Edward himself seems to have been somewhat confused about the distinctions among his attendants, since he referred at one point in his journal to the 'outer' Privy Chamber. Whether he simply meant the Great Chamber, or whether an 'inner' Privy Chamber, consisting of the Noblemen, the Principal Gentlemen, and a selection of the other Gentlemen and Grooms, was beginning to emerge, is not at all clear.[59]

Given the Duke of Northumberland's acute concern about security, and the absolute necessity, from his point of view, of maintaining control over the person of the king, such a development is distinctly possible. At the same time, lack of clear reference to such precautions in the household records is not at all surprising. Northumberland's precarious position was also reflected in a number of alterations to the military establishment. The most important of these—the raising of a short-lived band of 850 'gens d'armes' in 1551, and the retaining of private bands by Privy Councillors and other trusted supporters—do not concern us here. Within the court, however, 207 Extraordinary Yeomen of the Guard were added to the 100 Ordinary Yeomen, and strenuous efforts were made to 'launder' the Gentlemen Pensioners.[60] In spite of removing Somerset's protégé, Sir Ralph Fane, from the Lieutenantship, and appointing his ally William Parr, Marquis of Northampton, as Captain, Northumberland's success in this latter direction was limited. The Pensioners held their positions by patent, and were not easy to remove. The solution adopted was to build up the band of Gentlemen at Arms, which already numbered over forty, and then to decree that

'. . . from hensfoorthe the Gentlemen at Armes shulde be placed successively in the pencioners roomes at every avoidaunce, and so give attendaunce on his Lordship as their Capitaine . . .'[61]

In fact little progress seems to have been made with this in the short period of the reign remaining, and the short-term practical solution was probably to call on the attendance only of those who were thought reliable, the rest continuing to draw their pay as a non-functioning reserve. When a succession crisis followed Edward's death in July 1553, the Gentlemen Pensioners split almost equally, twenty-one siding with Jane Grey and twenty-nine with Mary.[62]

The change of regime which then followed Mary's successful defence of her claim was peculiarly traumatic for the court. Not only were a large number of Gentlemen Pensioners under arrest, but virtually all the chief officers of the household had been implicated in Northumberland's attempted coup, along with several members of the Chamber and Privy Chamber. Rather surprisingly, only a handful of the Gentlemen Pensioners were deprived of their positions, either then or subsequently, for political misconduct,[63] but the Chamber was heavily affected, and the Privy Chamber totally transformed. There were other reasons for this, of course, apart from the succession crisis. Mary had a well-established household of her own, some of whom had been with her for many years, and had shared her hardships and misfortunes. Good places had to be, and were, found for men such as Robert Rochester and Edward Waldegrave. Also a ruling queen, married or unmarried, needed female body servants and had no use for an inflated team of Gentlemen of the Privy Chamber, let alone a Groom of the Stool! Consequently the staff of the Outer Chamber was largely replaced within the existing establishment; so that the number of Cup-bearers, Carvers, Sewers, Esquires of the Body and Gentlemen Ushers who attended Mary's funeral in 1558 was almost identical with the Ordinary of 1545.[64] The only significant changes were the appearance of nine 'Gentlemen Waiters'—a new category, who may have replaced the 'Sewers of the Chamber'—and a considerable inflation in the number of

Chaplains, from four to nine. Mary maintained both the Gentlemen Pensioners and the Yeomen of the Guard at their former numbers, but deliberately ran down the supporting group of Gentlemen at Arms by making no fresh appointments as the existing incumbents were absorbed into the Pensioners proper. There were only eleven left by 1558.

The Privy Chamber of 1553 was virtually a new creation. In place of the six Lords, four Principal Gentlemen and eighteen Gentlmen—many of whom were Privy Councillors and important officers of state—who had served Edward in the later part of his reign, appeared the purely domestic establishment of seven Ladies and thirteen Gentlewomen.[65] Mary seem to have had no favourites of high rank. For a short time in the autumn of 1553, Gertrude, the long-widowed Marchioness of Exeter, was high in favour and was described as the queen's 'bedfellow'; but favour did not survive her son's indiscretions, and she never seems to have been given any formal position.[66] The 'inner' and 'outer' Privy Chambers, hinted at in 1550, now became a reality for a quite different reason. Assuming that the Ladies and Gentlewomen performed the services previously supplied by the Gentlemen, it seems likely that the three 'Chamberers' took over the rather humbler role of the Grooms, and that these women alone were admitted to the private apartments which lay beyond the Privy Chamber proper. The male establishment was restricted to five Gentlemen and seven Grooms, with the Gentlemen apparently performing the functions previously discharged by the Gentlemen Ushers—that is 'to keep the door'. Thus John Norris, listed in the establishment as a Gentleman of the Privy Chamber, was explicitly described by Edward Underhill (who was in a good position to know) as 'Chief Usher to Queen Mary's Privy Chamber.'[67] The service of the Grooms was presumably confined to the main Chamber. There were also some other adjustments of a minor nature. Two Physicians appear on the Privy Chamber list for the first time; and also 'the two fools', Will Somers (who must have been of an advanced age by this time, and had never been so recognised in his prime) and a certain Jane, of whom Mary was particularly fond.[68] There was no acknowledged Chief Gentlewoman of the Privy Chamber, but the position was in fact filled by Susan Tonge, alias Clarencius, a women who had been in Mary's service for over twenty-five years, and was closer to her than anyone had been since Catherine of Aragon's death in 1536. Her official post was Mistress of the Robes—which had no exact equivalent in earlier establishments, being a sort of amalgam of Yeoman of the Robes and Groom of the Stool. Officially the Privy Purse was probably kept by George Brodyman, one of the Grooms, but unofficially Mrs Clarencius seems to have handled much of the business, and was a good deal more powerful than was ever publicly acknowledged.[69] Outside the Privy Chamber the fact that the sovereign was a woman made little difference, save that the Henchmen and their Master, who had vanished from the Chamber Ordinary in the early part of Henry VIII's reign, reappeared in the guise of the 'Queenes Maiesties Maids' and the 'Mother of the Maids'.[70] Like the Henchmen before them, their function in the court was largely ornamental, but the position enabled the queen to provide favours, and good marriages, for the daughters of well disposed gentlemen.

As we have seen, a complete Chamber establishment was provided for Philip before his arrival, including Gentlemen of the Privy Chamber (*gentil hombres de la boca*) drawn from the highest nobility in England.[71] In spite of his earlier expressed intentions, and the reproaches of his father, Philip could not, when it came to the point, bear to have these men in close attendance. Their strange language and suspect religion repulsed him; so although the English perfomed what might be called the Chamber service for him while he was in England, the Privy Chamber service was provided by a small number of trusted Spaniards—a situation which guaranteed that neither side would be satisfied. Within a few days of his arrival Philip dismissed his English Master of the Horse without any public explanation,[72] and he never employed the services of any of the queen's English clergy, having his own team of chaplains and confessors. But apart from that, he was generous in a distant way. Many of the English privy Council became his pensioners, and he faithfully, if somewhat belatedly, paid his English servants whether he used them or not. The last instalment, to the 100 archers of his English guard, was paid in 1562.[73] Philip's entourage certainly added both to the size and to the turbulence of the court during his months of residence, but it was no more significant to the establishment than the 'queen's side' had been under Henry VIII. If the English gentlemen and young noblemen who took service with the king expected that service to be the door to a richer and wider world, they must have been sadly disappointed. By the time that Mary died, her husband's English servants were no more than a complication in the accounts.

In many respects Elizabeth followed her sister's example. She changed virtually all the 'headofficers', only the Lord Steward, the Earl of Arundel, retaining his post. The structure of the Outer Chamber remained substantially unchanged; the Gentlemen Ushers (daily waiters) were reduced from five to three, and six Gentlemen Waiters Extraordinary were added; the Captaincy of the Guard was also detached from the Vice-Chamberlainship, the former office being given to Sir William St Low and the latter to Sir Francis Knollys. As in 1553, the personnel were extensively changed—only one Carver (Henry Carey), one Esquire of the Body (Roger Manners) and two Gentlemen Ushers continuing to serve.[74] In the more peaceful circumstances of 1558 there was no question of punishing political misdemeanours. Some of Mary's servants may well have withdrawn voluntarily as soon as the religious climate of the new court became apparent; others were displaced, not so much because they were uncongenial to Elizabeth as to make way for servants from her own former household, like Sir Thomas Parry and Bassingbourne Gawdy. Some may have sold their places to their successors, but most accepted pensions or annuities in lieu. The death of a sovereign always made it easier to deal with Life Patents. In the Privy Chamber the process was similar, except that there were no survivors at all from the earlier regime. Elizabeth did exactly what Mary had done, and surrounded herself with her own friends and confidants—and with the wives and daughters of her ministers and officers. It was only in this way that the connection between the Privy Chamber and the Privy Council, which had been so strong since the 1530s, could be tenuously maintained. The structure of the Ordinary staff was not greatly changed from Mary's pattern, but the terminology was·confusingly altered, and an extensive new Extraordinary establishment was created. In place of the seven Ladies and thirteen Gentlewomen, Elizabeth appointed four Gentlewomen of the Bedchamber (whose position seems to have been very like that of the four Principal Gentlemen of Edward's time) and seven Gentlewomen of the Privy Chamber, who are described in the coronation list as Maids.[75] Three Chamberers, as before, completed the Ordinary of the private apartments, the male Privy Chamber establishment being reduced drastically to one Gentleman, who was also Master of the Jewel House, one Gentleman Usher, and three Grooms. One of these Grooms, Henry Sackford, became the Keeper of the Privy Purse, and Catherine Ashley as Mistress of the Robes presided over the Inner Chamber, as Susan Clarencius had over Mary's.

In 1559 the Ordinary Privy Chamber staff was thus smaller than at any time since 1520, and the rota of service must have been very restricted. Indeed, Elizabeth seems to have expected all her Privy Chamber servants to attend continuously, unless they were excused for some specific reason. However, they could be supplemented from the Extraordinary list, which appears on the coronation schedule in two groups. The first of these, 'The Privy Chamber without wages', consisted of six noblewomen headed by the Duchess of Norfolk, who presumably occupied much the same position as the Noblemen of the Privy Chamber under Henry and Edward.[76] The second group, 'Extraordinary of the Privy Chamber', comprised eleven gentlewomen who could be called upon when required. Unlike the first group, they were not too grand to be paid but their attendance was too erratic to justify regular fees, especially in the eyes of a queen who was always very conscious of economy. Unlike Mary, Elizabeth also set up a second 'reserve' group outside the Privy Chamber. These were the 'Ladies and Gentlewomen of the Household'. Their function is nowhere specified, but since most of them were the wives of important royal servants, the category was probably invented to give them some official standing in court, without trespassing either upon established interests or the household revenues.[77]

This structure, outlined in the first three months of the reign, continued thereafter with little change, but even as late as 1589 the bureaucratic hands which drew up lists of offices and fees 'in her majesties gift' had not adjusted to a female ruler. As Dr Adams has recently pointed out, the so-called establishment list of 1576 is merely a copy of that of 1552, even referring to the 'Lord Great Master', a post abolished in 1554.[78] The 'Privie Chamber' list makes no mention of the queen's female attendants, although they were certainly in wages, and its list of officers could almost be a description of the Outer Chamber, as that had evolved by that time. The list of 1593 is almost identical, still budgeting for eighteen Gentlemen of the Privy Chamber, when there had never been more than two at any time in the previous thirty-five years. In reality, by the end of the century the Privy Chamber in the Henrician sense had withered away, or, more accurately, been reabsorbed into the Chamber. The attractive patronage for young gentlemen which these influential posts had provided between 1520 and 1553 now had to be provided in the main Chamber, which was no doubt one reason for creating the post of 'Gentleman waiter' in 1559. Also, if Dr Tighe is correct in his recent study, the band of Gentlemen Pensioners was increasingly used for this purpose, both the age and the social status of its members tending to rise as the reign progressed.[79] This band had been almost untouched by the extensive Chamber replacements of 1558, and nothing short of high treason could dislodge a Gentlemen Pensioner against his will; so by 1600 it had become totally stable and almost totally civilian. Long before Elizabeth's death, the Bedchamber, with its all-female staff, had absorbed the functions which the Privy Chamber of the Eltham Ordinances had been designed to discharge; and because of its nature, it stood alongside the power structure, rather than being part of it. Elizabeth's ladies, like those of Mary earlier, could be very influential in private matters, but, as was later recalled

> ... none of these (near and dear ladies) durst intermeddle so far in matters of commonwealth ...

They held no offices, and could not be sent on diplomatic missions. Nor, of course, did they pretend to any independence of the Lord Chamberlain, so that in this respect also the court of 1600 was closer to that of 1500 than to that of 1540. 'The court', declared Sir James Croft, Controller of the Household, in 1583, 'is divided into two governments, the Chamber and the Household'. *Plus ça change, plus c'est la même chose.*

The Domus Providencie

Domus COMPOTI CONSILII ET JUDICII, called also by the noble Edward thyrd 'le graunt garderobe du loistyel du roi' in which the worship and welfare of the hoole houshold is purposed, in wyche the correccions and jugementes be gevyn; in whom ys taken the audyte of all thinges of thys court, beyng of the thesaureres charge as princypall ...[80]

So the *Liber Niger* described the Countinghouse, and the description remained valid for the whole of the period with which we are concerned. As we shall see, the methods of funding the household varied from time to time, but the Countinghouse was always responsible for the money allocated to the service departments, no matter where it came from. Theoretically the three 'white sticks', or head officers of the household—the Lord Steward, the Treasurer and the Controller—were also the head officers of the Countinghouse, and the *Liber Niger* required them to be in daily attendance. However, by the time of the Eltham Ordinances, these officers were important men in the royal service, and daily appearances were neither expected nor required.[81] When the Board of Greencloth was sitting in judgement as a tribunal, the presence of at least one of the 'white sticks' was necessary, but the working head of the department was the fourth officer, the Cofferer, and this was the highest rank to which a household servant could expect to rise through the normal channels of promotion. In fact, successive Lord Stewards and Lord Great Masters were more interested in the day by day running of their domain than might have been expected, but this was rather to ensure that their extensive control over household appointments did not slip away than from any profound concern with efficient management. The Cofferer received such sums of money as were assigned to the household, issued 'prests' or advances to the purchasing departments, and paid the invoices issued by the purveyors. His own accounts had to be made up quarterly, in theory, but in fact always seem to have been presented and audited annually, upon the basis of weekly running totals of expenditure. These running totals in turn were based upon the daily accounts submitted to the Clerk of the Greencloth by the Clerks or Sergeants of the various departments. The Cofferer was supported in this onerous routine by a steadily expanding staff. In 1445 there had been two 'clerckes des accomptz'; one Clerk Controller, with an assistant; one Sergeant, one Messenger, one Groom and one Page.[82] By the end of Henry VIII's reign there were four Masters of the Household, three Clerks of the Greencloth, three Clerk Controllers, a Yeoman Usher, a Groom Usher, and the Cofferer's clerk—the last named originally a personal servant who had been taken on in the establishment very recently, in 1545.[83]

This expansion was largely the result of Thomas Cromwell's reforms of 1539/40, which took the existing supervisory and accounting role of the department and developed it in a series of meticulous regulations. In addition to the prests, budgets and daily accounts, the Cofferer was now made responsible for settling the purveyor's accounts on a monthly basis, and for paying the 'Wages, fees and Board wages' of all household servants. The Clerks of the Greencloth and Clerk Controllers became Inspectors General who were required to pay daily visits to the Larder to check the quality of the viands which had been purchased; to carry out similar inspections of the kitchens; and, once or twice a week, to

> ... view all the offices and chambers of the Household, to see if there be any Strangers eating in the said Offices or Chambers at the Meale times, or at any other time, contrary to the King's Ordinance; and in case they shall find any offending therein, to make relation therof to the Sovereigns of the House ...[84]

The Clerk Controllers were also made responsible for carrying out daily checks on the attendance of servants in the various Chamber offices, and making suitable arrangements to dock the wages of absentees and defaulters; for keeping the Ordinary or Check Roll up to date; and for expelling from the court all those superfluous servants of servants, who constituted one of the most intractable problems of the period. With this wide range of additional duties, it is not surprising that extra staff were required, and so the four Masterships of the Household were created. These Masters were intended to be the Cofferer's chief assistants, and their status was superior to that of the Clerks of the Greencloth. No specific brief for these officers survives, and even the exact date of their establishment is uncertain. However, an instruction from the Lord Great Master, issued in 1545, refers to two of them as being 'for the King's side' and two 'for the Queen's side', which suggests very strongly that they were intended to act as links between the Countinghouse and the Chamber.[85] Probably it was discovered that the Clerk Controllers lacked the status to deal firmly with defaulting Chamber servants, and the main function of the Masters was to give extra weight and authority to the checks and inspections which the clerks were supposed to carry out. This would also explain why two of the Masterships were allowed to lapse after Henry's death, and well before the decision was taken to abolish them and return to the old system. The 1545 instruction also makes it clear that Chamber supervision on each 'side' was entrusted to two teams, each consisting of two Masters, one Clerk of the Greencloth and one Clerk Controller, working a shift system of six weeks on and six weeks off. This was a Chamber pattern rather than a household pattern and was designed, partly at least, to minimise the amount of accommodation required. Since by 1545 there were, as we have seen, three Clerks at each level, it is reasonable to suppose that the third worked normally and continuously in the Countinghouse, dealing with the business of the service departments.

After the re-establishment of the Lord Steward, the staff of the Countinghouse was appropriately reduced, the Masterships not having had time to establish themselves as vested interests, and by the latter part of Elizabeth's reign there were two Clerks of the Greencloth, two Clerk Controllers, one Yeoman, one Groom and one Messenger. Elizabeth left the Lord Stewardship vacant for long periods, and this was recognised in the household book of 1601, where it was declared that the Treasurer

> . . . and Mr Comptrouler (there being no Lord Steward) have the government of the whole Household, and placing of all her Majesties servantes . . .[86]

The Cofferer continued to be the chief accountant 'receiving and disbursing all her Majesties moneys for Household affairs' and also controlling the activities of the purveyors, which by this time had become virtually a straightforward purchasing operation.[87] The same ordinances described the Clerks of the Greencloth concisely as 'the auditors of the Household', and the Clerk Controllers (rather less concisely) as

> . . . controllers of all Household affairs; that is to say of all her Majesties serfantes, if

they doe not their dutyes in their severall places. They have authority to check all expenses. They passe all billes for allowances, all brevements and rolles of expences, and turn back and refuse alle meates and drinkes unsavoury . . .[88]

Consequently the pattern of duties expressed in the *Liber Niger* continued substantially unchanged throughout the sixteenth century, apart from the dozen years or so when the Board of Greencloth extended its supervision to the Chamber. There was, as we shall see, considerable variation in the number and type of the 'foreign' accounts which passed through the Cofferer's hands, and also the development of a second set of Controller's accounts, as a check upon the Cofferer; but in terms of its responsibilities and of its structure the Countinghouse which Elizabeth bequeathed to James was very similar to that which Henry VII had inherited from Edward IV; its arms, of a crossed rod and key, signified 'that this office may close, open and punish other offices'.

All the service departments were labour intensive, and showed similar expansionist tendencies, because the pressure for places was intense, both from those who sought them and from those who wished to increase their influence by providing them. The Kitchen was both the most variable and by far the largest, because it always had two staffs—one for the sovereign and one for 'the Hall'—and when there was a royal consort it had three.[89] In 1553, before Mary's marriage, the total staff numbered forty, of whom twenty-eight were included in the Ordinary, the remainder being 'gallapins' or turnspits, who were unwaged and presumably lived off perquisites and gratuities of various kinds. The head officer was the Chief Clerk, who, with his two assistants, was responsible for checking the goods out of the Larder for the cooks' use, for determining the level of purchase, and for submitting daily statements and monthly accounts to the Board of Greencloth. This was a major responsibility because the quantity of food handled was so great. In one year the relatively frugal Elizabethan court consumed 1240 oxen, 8200 sheep, over 40 million eggs, and proportionate quantities of other commodities.[90] In 1445 there had been thirty-five servants in the Kitchen. A century later this had risen to fifty-nine, just before being sharply reduced by the disappearance of the 'queen's side'. Under Edward, and in the early part of Mary's reign, the number seems to have remained constant at about forty, but shot up to sixty-five when Philip's staff was added. Elizabeth reduced the Ordinary again to about thirty, and there was very little increase during her long reign. In 1601 there were three Clerks, three Master Cooks, six Yeomen, six Grooms, eight Pages and an unspecified number of 'gallapines'.[91]

The physical organisation of the Kitchen presents certain problems. As we have seen, a Spanish observer in 1554 referred to eighteen kitchens, all working at once. No Tudor palace contained anything remotely like that number of separate kitchens, so the bemused foreigner may have been the victim of a joke, or he may have been describing every separate cooking fire in the palace as a 'kitchen'; this would have included the Boilinghouse, the Scaldinghouse, the Pastry, and perhaps the Confectionary, in addition to the king's and queen's side. Even so, it would be extremely difficult to get anywhere near eighteen. By 1576, when William Cecil was having one of his periodic economy drives, he touched on this same problem

> Item, for that her majesties meate is dressed in two severall ketchins doth doble the expenses of wood and coles . . .[92]

and

> Item, meate dresses in divers places within the corte owte of her majesties owne ketchin, for divers and sondry persons, doth not only cawse greater expenses but also pestereth the corte with unfytt persons . . .

From this latter note it appears that food was actually cooked in 'privy chambers', on fires which were intended for room heating; and if that had been the practice twenty years before it may explain the visitor's estimate.

By 1601 the kitchen which prepared the queen's own food was known as the 'pryve kitchyn', and there seems to have been considerable manoeuvring and competition among the courtiers to obtain their rations from there, rather than from the 'Great ketchin', which clearly issued inferior provisions.[93] There was also a marked tendency to retreat into private quarters on fish days whereby . . . her majesties chamber is unfurnished . . .' and for much of the food provided to be borne away and consumed by the army of unauthorised hangers-on who depended upon the bounty of the Chamber servants. In earlier days the Hall had been the communal eating place of the household, and even when the Hall was no longer 'kept', in the sense that the monarch or one of the chief officers presided over it, regular service times were still stipulated. Both the Eltham Ordinances and Thomas Cromwell's reforms condemned the fact that

> . . . sundry noblemen, gentlemen and others, doe much delight and use to dyne in corners and secret places, not repairing to the King's chamber nor hall, nor to the head officers of the household when the hall is not kept . . .[94]

but the trend was irreversible by that time, and even Cromwell's attempt to forbid the provision of 'livery coles' to private chambers was ineffective. As we have seen, the palace of Nonsuch was built without a hall, and by the end of Henry VIII's reign the Chamber staff had finally and completely retreated. How long the regular service of hall meals for the menial servants continued is not clear, but this practice probably also disappeared in the early part of Elizabeth's reign, and thereafter it was normal for the household to collect their food from the Great Kitchen and consume it in their respective 'offices'. Communal meals in the Chamber continued, whether or not the monarch was present, and so did at least some of the officers' 'tables', but because these were also provided from the Great Kitchen, their popularity also declined. Consequently far more food was provided than was really needed for those who were entitled to consume it, and the same meal might be 'covered' three times over—by an ordinary 'diet' in the Chamber, by a 'room service' from the Privy Kitchen, and by uncooked rations 'dressed' in the recipient's own quarters. The confusion and waste must have been endless, and defied every attempt at tighter control and accounting.

Nor did the problem end with the unpredictable eating habits of the courtiers. Once food had been issued from either of the kitchens, it began to disappear. In the days when it had all been destined either for the Chamber or the Hall, there had been some chance that the Surveyors of the Dresser, whose task it was to 'check it in', might have noticed discrepancies. But as more and more was distributed in every direction to private rooms, theft and embezzlement became increasingly hard to detect. There was some compensation in private dining, in that once food had been delivered, it was likely to be consumed by those for whom it was intended, whereas food delivered to the Hall or Chamber and not consumed was legitimate prey. Dishes which had been broached but not finished were 'broken meats' and were technically at the disposal of the Almoner, but dishes which left the board untouched (of which there were a great many, owing to the nature of sixteenth-century meals) were the perquisite of the servants of the appropriate department. The Gentlemen Pensioners served the main course at Mary's marriage feast in Winchester in 1554, and Edward Underhill has left an amusing description of how he sent up to London the enormous venison pie which was his share of the loot.[95] On less formal occasions the principal beneficiaries were the Sewers, Ushers and Grooms of the Chamber, who no doubt made a handsome profit out of retailing what they obtained to those who were not otherwise provided for—either inside the court or outside it. In this manner an Ordinary of about 500 in the middle of the century was supporting a physical presence which has been estimated at three times that size.[96]

The ritual threats and lamentations about unauthorised servants could never result in effective action as long as they could be supported on such a generous and ill-regulated system of perquisites. These perquisites, or 'fees' as they were revealingly called, accompanied every aspect of life at court. The Sergeant of the Chaundry was entitled to all the clothes and bed linen which a newly created Knight of the Bath used during the ritual of his initiation—or a cash composition. More prosaically, he was also entitled to all the ends of spent candles, as the Sergeant of the Cellar could claim the lees of wine, or the Sergeant of the Bakehouse the crusts chipped off the loaves before they were served.[97] Obviously, such a system was open to abuse, and the Clerks of the Greencloth were supposed to check all commodities claimed as fees before they were removed from the court. In practice, close supervision was impossible, and it seems to have been quite common for some officers to make many times their official wage in this way. Stephen Darrell, for instance, surrendered the second Clerkship of the Kitchen, which was worth £44.6.9 a year in the middle of Elizabeth's reign, for the Clerkship of the Acatry, worth £6.13.4—and he certainly did not intend to lose by the transaction.[98] The Acatry, with large quantities of offal available for quick disposal, contained a number of plum jobs from this point of view, and so great was the abuse that the Board of Greencloth eventually abolished some of these 'waste part' fees altogether. Theoretically any fee could be stopped in this way, but in practice the resentment and disruption caused was more than the economy was worth, and it was seldom attempted.

After the Kitchen, the Bakehouse, the Cellar, the Acatry, the Pastry and the Scullery had the largest staffs—in 1533 twenty-one, nineteen, thirteen and eighteen respectively. The Bakehouse was the only one to imitate the Kitchen in having a privy department. This consisted of two Yeomen and two Grooms, whose job it was to produce the exceptionally fine bread which was supposed to be exclusively for the monarch's use. The other departments were undifferentiated, but several, notably the Spicery and the Pastry, accommodated craftsmen with special skills. Henry VII and Henry VIII also imported French cooks, who presumably worked alongside the normal staff, but who were differently paid and who did not count on the normal establishment.[99] Also, in spite of the enormous range of service departments, some work was still put out on contract. Henry VIII, who was exceptionally fastidious, employed a special fine laundress—a certain Anne Harris—who was not on the Ordinary, and Catherine Parr, his last queen, did the same.[100]

After Cromwell's reforms, in about 1540, there were some 230 recognised servants in the *Domus Providencie*. By the end of the reign that number had risen to 245 and by Mary's accession to 270. In 1560 the total was approaching 300, but thereafter it was slowly whittled down, and by 1600 was probably back to about 250.[101] The creation of additional recognised posts was nearly always the result of the sovereign's own initiative; Henry VIII, for example, is known to have added at least five between 1540 and 1545. The commonest time for this to happen on a significant scale was immediately after a monarch's accession, when his or her household as heir apparent was being absorbed. We do not know how many the young Henry VIII added in this way; but Edward brought in twenty-one of his own men, Mary thirty-three and Elizabeth thirty-eight—in addition to the extensive changes which each also made, as we have seen, to the Chamber.[102] Edward seems to have pensioned off some of the existing staff to make way for his nominees, and this operation may well have been carried out by the Paget/Hertford faction in their own interest. Mary displaced quite a number, including five departmental Sergeants, but upon what terms is not clear, and several of the original incumbents were back in their posts later in the reign, following either the death or the resignation of their supplanters.[103] Elizabeth displaced nobody, but resorted to widespread duplication, relying upon time and natural wastage to resolve the consequent problems. Each in turn showed considerable interest in the household below stairs, and allowed its officers much more access to their presence than has sometimes been supposed. It was not unusual for Clerks of the Greencloth, or of the Kitchen, to present petitions on behalf of their friends or 'countrymen', and Richard Hill, the Sergeant of the Cellar, was a frequent gambling companion of the king between 1527 and 1539. Hill was exceptional, and no doubt the servants of the Privy Chamber and Chamber had much superior opportunities for access, but there was no rigid distinction between the two parts of the household in this respect. Similarly, officers of the lower household were also used in royal service outside the court, particularly in time of war when the financial and management skills of the experienced Clerks were much in demand. If the king went to war in person, then his whole household was expected to accompany him in arms, but that was a different matter altogether, and happened only twice during the Tudor period.[104]

Although the monarch might occasionally intervene, routine replacements and promotions within the household were the responsibility of the Lord Steward (or Lord Great Master) who had '. . . the placing and displacing of all her Majesties servants' as the Ordinances of 1601 put it. As usual, however, the practice was much less straightforward than the theory, because the Sergeants and Clerks of the individual departments were directly concerned, and there were also well-established customs, the disruption of which might cause much bitterness and resentment. In general the expectation was that vacancies would be filled as they occurred by promotion from below, either within the same department or between departments; and that such promotions would be determined by the Board of Greencloth, after consultations both with the Lord Steward and with the appropriate Sergeants and Clerks. The higher the position, the more interested the Steward was likely to be; the more menial, the greater the influence of the Sergeants and Clerks. There were well-established household families, such as the Weldons, who made their careers in this way, introducing their young kinsmen as Pages and Grooms, who then worked their way up through the system. There was no formal training for household servants, and progress depended upon a mixture of competence and connection. The sale of household offices was technically illegal, but undoubtedly occurred, as we have already seen in respect of the Chamber. Periodically the Board of Greencloth endeavoured to enforce the law, but breaches were regularly connived at by the 'white sticks', and probably by the Clerks of the Greencloth themselves. When a vacancy did arise, it was essential to move fast, and at the appropriate level. On one occasion, when Sir Francis Knollys was Lord Steward, he found that a position for which he had a patronage candidate had already been filled by the Clerks of the Greencloth, and he was unable to overturn the *fait accompli*.[105] In fact the household was highly resistant to the pressures of ordinary court patronage, and even a man as important as Sir John Gage, who at different times was Controller, Vice-Chamberlain and Lord Chamberlain introduced his second son James as a Groom. James Gage advanced quickly, and was one of the Masters of the Household at Edward VI's coronation, but he had achieved that position without doing violence to household custom.[106] Sometimes, if the importunities of courtiers became particularly troublesome, or if powerful favourites or ministers could not be refused outright, supernumerary positions could be created, as they could in the Chamber. Such supernumeraries would not receive wages, or appear upon the Ordinary, but they did take the household oath, which was administered to all royal servants, and enjoyed a recognised status. Not only were they thus enabled to obtain a share of the perquisites, but they were also well placed to secure vacancies in the establishment, being, in effect, servants in reversion. Of course, servants who were appointed through the direct intervention of the sovereign were in a very different position, as Sir Henry Bedingfield noted.[107] They were fed and established from the start, and neither the Lord Stewart nor the Board of Greencloth could gainsay them. However, such people were always comparatively rare, and for long periods in the sixteenth century the prerogative was almost unexercised. The discrepancies which were regularly noticed between the size of the Ordinary and the number of bodies actually present, were partly the result of the supernumeraries, and partly of the wholly unauthorised 'servants' upon whom the disciplinary officers of the court waged constant war.

Once obtained, a place on the establishment was reasonably secure. Unlike the Dukes of Burgundy, the Tudors never 'stood down' their households, however acute the financial stringency, though individual servants might be dismissed for misconduct. Such a sanction appears in every set of Ordinances, but it does not seem to have been invoked very often. There was, of course, no normal retirement, and in 1526 the king ordered an investigation in order to determine the number and identity of those who were '. . . impotent, sicklie, unable and unmete' for the positions which they held.[108] A considerable number were pensioned off at this stage, but although the problem must have been a recurrent one, the operation does not seem to have been repeated. Most likely, regular informal pressure was brought to bear upon those who were no longer able to discharge their duties, and this may well have been the main reason why the sale of positions continued to be condoned, since the alternative would have been a potentially expensive pension scheme. Apart from any other considerations, the sovereign's honour required, and his safety dictated, that his servants should not be crippled or diseased. Nevertheless, by comparison with most occupations the members of the royal household were well off. During temporary sickness they were entitled to commute their allowances into 'boardwages', and when smitten with age could expect either to dispose of their positions by sale, or to obtain 'some convenient enterteynment' from the sovereign's bounty.[109]

The household of an heir or a consort was much more vulnerable. There must have been far more servants in wages for Edward as Prince of Wales than the twenty-one who were placed in his service as king. Similarly Catherine Parr had a Chamber staff of thirty-nine, headed by Sir Anthony Cope as Chamberlain, and a household of seventy under the rule of her Steward, Sir Thomas Tyrwhyt.[110] This continued after Henry's death, and also after her marriage to Sir Thomas Seymour in April 1547, but was brought to a sudden end by her death in September of the same year, when her servants were paid a quarter's wages and stood down. This must have been the normal situation when a consort died, and also occurred to Philip's English household when Mary died. The repudiated consorts, Catherine of Aragon and Anne of Cleves, were both allowed to retain diminished households, although in the latter case a settlement was made, and these servants were not paid directly by the king. It is not surprising, therefore, that positions in the royal household were much sought after. The material rewards and the opportunities for preferment were both good—Henry VIII paid his servants almost twice what the Earl of Northumberland was willing to afford—but above all they were 'civil service' posts. The Crown did not die, and the risk of being dispossessed by the accidents of mortality was minimal.

On the whole, the household below stairs did not work a shift system, but as the court moved about the number of servants required in the various departments must have changed. Nonsuch, for example, could not accommodate the same number as Whitehall or Hampton Court; and the small palaces like Oatlands and Woodstock were even more restricted. Skeleton staffs were maintained in unoccupied residences, but they were very small and did not belong to the main household.[111] The normal practice seems to have been for the head of the department to decide who would migrate, and who would draw their wages at home until their services were again required. There is no suggestion that this caused serious problems, and the regular pattern of movement no doubt meant that each department had its own established ways of coping with the idiosyncracies of each palace. Only the Harbingers were given a difficult time by these moves, and habit eased their burdens as well, since the same officers regularly used the same accommodation, whether in Westminster, Greenwich or Windsor. Progresses were a different matter, however. These were rare events in the early sixteenth century, because although Henry VIII was liable to take off at short notice, in order to go hunting or to flee the plague, he took few servants with him on these occasions, and the main court was not disrupted. Elizabeth, on the other hand, did not believe in 'riding households', and during the frequent summer progresses of her early and middle years, every department was sent trundling round the countryside on an assortment of wagons. One brief stay in Cambridge saw a different department billeted in every college of the university,[112] and a stay at a small residence like Sir William Petre's Ingatestone Hall was a nightmare, not only for the host, but also for the officers, who might find their establishments scattered across miles of countryside, in a dozen different towns and villages. Nor were the difficulties only logistic. In the best tradition of her medieval predecessors, Elizabeth was liable to change her mind about moving on, wasting her servants' time and her own resources in the most prodigal fashion. 'Item the alteration of removing' grumbled William Cecil to himself in one of his numerous memoranda for reform and economy, 'and daies not kept as they be appointed, doth not only cause great waste of provisions laid in divers places, but also in expenses of purveyors and others in removing the same again.'[113] There was no remedy. Cecil calculated that progresses added about £2000 a year to the cost of the household, but the queen was not to be diverted from these important exercises in self-display. Nor was she willing to be constrained, even by her own rules—insisting on having meat served in the Privy Chamber on public fish days, and encouraging her courtiers to demand the same 'room service' from the kitchens, again to Cecil's cautiously expressed disgust, because the public service of fish to the Chamber tables was largely sent away untouched.

The purveyors may have been kept exceptionally busy 'by reason of longer progresses and oftener removes', but they were always an important and contentious element in the life of the household. Purveyance was based upon the ancient right of the king to levy taxes in kind upon his people for the support of himself and his *familia*. By the fifteenth century this had developed into a right to make compulsory purchases at pre-determined rates. These rates were determined by the king's officers, and were always considerably below the going market rate, so it is not surprising that complaints and protests were incessant. The Ordinance of 1445 explicitly recognised the problem, and sought to provide a remedy by ensuring that only the right type of men were appointed as purveyors

> . . . sobre and peisible men, and men of good sufficeance and power, such as wyll se that the purveance and acate to be made by thayme be duely made for the kinges worship and profite, and in such wyse that the grete clamour had afore tymes upon purveances and acates made for the kynges household mowe cesse [114]

They were to be placed on oath, and to be made answerable to the officers of the *Domus Providencie* in the Countinghouse. Full returns were also to be made in writing '. . . describinge clerly all the parcels of his achates and purveiances, and the pris, and the persones names that the said parcels be taken of'. The complaints continued unabated. In 1478 the same orders were repeated almost verbatim, and equally without effect. Part of the trouble was that the burden fell very unevenly, because although in theory all counties were equally liable, in practice those closest to the royal residences were disporportionately affected. Highly perishable commodities, such as fresh fish and fruit, eggs and cream, were not subjected to purveyance, but rather such things as grain, cheese, bacon, salt fish, and animals on the hoof, which could reasonably be transported over long distances. Indeed sometimes cattle and sheep were driven from the remote north or west of the country, to await the attention of the Acatry at Tottenham or Highgate; but normally convenience dictated less extensive journeys, and the purveyors confined their attentions to the home counties. Another problem was that the purveyor's powers lacked clear definition. He was supposed to cause his commission to be read out 'before the people' every time he exercised his office, but this was a duty easily avoided, and apparently not very informative even when it was observed.[115] In 1449 a complaint was made in parliament against a certain William Gerveis, who held a commission to 'take up' horses for the king's use. The petitioners claimed that Gerveis was abusing his powers, and asked that his commission be withdrawn; but since their protest was rejected it must be presumed that the king's officers did not accept that any abuse had occurred.[116] Most of the complaints focused on two issues: either the purveyors were misrepresenting the prices which the Board of Greencloth was offering, and thus paying the vendors less than they should have received; or they were 'taking up' more than they declared, reselling the excess at the full market price for their own profit. The former complaint related mostly to small transactions, for which the purveyor was given a 'prest' out of which he paid cash for the commodities. Such transactions were extremely difficult to control, but were not supposed to exceed 40 shillings in value. For larger purchases the purveyor was supposed to give the vendor a receipt, which the latter then had to present to the Board of Greencloth for payment, and it was this system which was really open to abuse. A vendor living at any distance from the court was either put to great expense and inconvenience, or forced to make use of intermediaries who might claim a commission. At the same time an illiterate or careless vendor could easily be defrauded, and even if payment was eventually made in full, it might be inordinately delayed.[117]

The procedure laid down in 1445 required all debts of this kind to be discharged in plenary sessions of the Board of Greencloth held once a quarter, and strictly forbade *ad hoc* payments at other times.[118] From an accounting point of view this made good sense, but it added greatly to the sense of oppression which the system caused. Other grievances frequently voiced were that purveyors were taking bribes, and repeatedly requisitioning from those who did not pay—a form of 'protection money'; and that they took up good-quality produce, resold it at the full market price, and then purchased inferior and cheaper goods for the royal house.[119] The worst offenders were, or were thought to be, occasional purveyors; partly because they lacked the discipline of regular contact with the Countinghouse, and partly because they were inclined to go on using obsolete commissions for their own purposes after their connection with the household had ceased. *Ad hoc* commissions of this kind were generally used for victualling ships or fortresses in time of war, and sometimes to meet unexpected emergencies, like the special purveyance of empty wine casks, ordered in 1522.[120] In spite of the constant agitation, Wolsey's ordinances of 1526 did not advance very much beyond the fifteenth-century regulations, except that they did require the purveyors to render their own accounts directly to the Board of Greencloth '. . . by a certaine day then to be by them prefixed and limited', and ordered strict quality checks by the relevant departments upon all goods received. By 1545, however, Cromwell's reforms had sophisticated the system in a number of ways. Yeomen Purveyors were attached to the regular staff of all the main purchasing departments, and the careful instructions provided for the Purveyors of Ale and Poultry make clear that they were expected to deal with their main suppliers upon a regular, contractual basis.[121] In the case of poultry, the situation was complicated by the risk of over-provision because the demand was (apparently) particularly difficult to forecast and the birds could not be kept alive. So the London Poulterers were bound in recognisance to purchase the purveyor's surplus at the price which he had paid for it—a constraint which they obviously resented. There seem to have been about a dozen of these specialist purveyors employed on a regular basis by the middle of the century, extending into areas not hitherto subject to purveyance; the Yeoman Sea Fisher, Yeoman Purveyor of Fresh Water Fish, Yeoman Pigtaker, and so on. They still operated by virtue of commissions, but should have been subject to minute, almost daily, control by the officers of the household.[122]

Nevertheless, complaints of abuse continued, and even multiplied with the Cromwellian refinements, and a fresh attempt at resolution was made in Mary's third parliament, in 1555. The statute of 2 & 3 Philip and Mary c.6 did not introduce any procedural changes, but concentrated on tightening up the administration. All commissions were to be limited to six months' duration, and were to specify the county or counties for which they were valid. They were also to specify the type and quantity of the provisions for which the purveyor was authorised. When the purveyor arrived at any town or village within his jurisdiction, he was supposed to fill in a blank 'form', annexed to his commission, setting out the name of the place, and the precise commodities which he intended to 'take up' there. The form was then signed or marked by the Constable, or Headborough, as an indication that he knew what was going on. When the transaction was completed, the purveyor or his agent then made out a second 'docquet', listing what had actually been taken. This was delivered to the Constable, and passed on by him to the Justices of the Peace, who were supposed to 'certify' the content to the Board of Greencloth.[123] It is not at all clear when, in this elaborate bureaucratic process, the creditor actually got paid. According to the ancient rule they should have received their money at the first quarterly session of the Board following the certification of their docquet, but there is no reference in the statute to any such process, nor to any return of sums due by the purveyor. Cromwell's reforms had almost certainly abolished this slow and tiresome method of payment, and all bills—not just small ones—were settled on the spot in cash. The Ordinance of 1540 had decreed that the Cofferer should issue prest money to all purveyors weekly, on the basis of the estimated needs of the relevant departments, and should take monthly account from them within five days of each month's end.[124] The certification referred to in the statute was thus a cross check on the purveyor's accounts, and not a method of authorising payment. However, in the last analysis, and whatever the complainants may have claimed, the grievance was not abuse, but the system itself, and no matter how honestly or expeditiously administered, it would continue to rankle.

Cromwell had, in effect, made purveyance resemble as nearly as possible a normal commercial provisioning service, while retaining the differential price system which was the essence of the prerogative right. Before the end of Henry's reign a further logical step had been take in the same direction with the appearance of county composition agreements. These were basically contracts negotiated between the officers of the household and the Commissioners of the Peace for the county concerned, whereby the county agreed to supply annually a given quantity of specified produce at the 'king's price'. The produce was then purchased by the county's own agents at the normal market price, and resold to the household at a substantial discount.[125] The difference was made up by a county levy or tax, for which the county community assessed itself in the manner of a parliamentary subsidy. The great advantage of such an agreement from the county's point of view was that it was thereby freed from the attentions of any purveyor in respect of the commodities compounded for. Nevertheless, the idea made only slow progress, and was further disrupted by Protector Somerset's brief attempt to replace all purveyance with a general tax. The traditional system was almost universally restored in 1550—hence the need for the statute of 1555. By the end of Mary's reign about a dozen composition agreements were in existence, all relating to grain, and these proved to be sufficiently successful to pursuade Sir William Cecil of the desirability of going over to a composition system for all produce. It was uphill work, because taxation was no more popular than purveyance, and natural conservatism resisted change. Nevertheless, by 1561 it was considered worthwhile to draw up a book of 'rates, fees and compositions' to keep in the Countinghouse for the purpose of facilitating negotiations. By 1562 Lincolnshire, Leicestershire and Northamptonshire were compounding for sheep and oxen, but the evidence is very incomplete. A list for 1578 shows twelve counties as far apart as Essex and Cornwall compounding to varying degrees—Essex for twelve different commodities, Cornwall for oxen only.[126] Ten years later the picture was much more complex: nineteen counties were compounding, eight had compounded, but had defaulted, and ten had no composition agreement—including Cornwall. So the process appears to have been 'two steps forward and one step back'. At the same time the number of purveyors dealing with the uncompounded items and areas was increasing, reaching a peak in the 1570s when fifty-six purveyors held between them 111 commissions. Most, but not all, of these appear to have been regular household servants. It was not until the 1590s that compounding began to approach a complete system, and then only as a result of abandoning voluntary negotiation in favour of coercion. In 1591 a special commission was set up, of 'lords in commission for household causes', and they peremptorily ordered twenty-six shires to send delegations to London in October 1592 'for some composition to be made for her Majesty's household without offence by purveyors'. Even then, it took the full five years of the commission's existence to make composition agreements universal. In its mature form, by the end of the period, the system was a bureaucrat's dream, with long lists of commodities separately rated, constant slight changes of rate, and elaborate arrangements for getting the provisions to the appropriate department of the court in a fit state to be consumed. The purveyors did not disappear entirely; in 1603 they still conducted a small-scale operation for the queen's personal consumption. But the main, centuries-old grievance about large-scale purveyance had gone, to be replaced by new grievances about burdensome and inequitable compositions.

Finance

The Tudor court was never less than enormously expensive, but just how expensive it is very difficult to say. It was never the responsibility of a single accounting office, and many of the relevant accounts have not survived. Where the accounts are extant, they duplicate each other, overlap, and sometimes apparently conflict in the most baffling fashion. This is partly because some (usually summaries) are based on regnal years, and others on financial years. Periodically, too, the system of accounting changed. Wages which had been paid directly by the Exchequer were switched to the Treasury of the Chamber in the 1520s, then to the Cofferer in the 1530s, and eventually back to the Chamber or the Exchequer. Consequently it is very difficult to make comparisons between the account of the same officer in different reigns, or even to be sure whether summaries include the same range of subsidiary accounts over a period of a decade or so. To take a single example: in the financial year 1560–61 Thomas Weldon, Elizabeth's Cofferer, accounted for £50,912; in the same year her Treasurer of the Chamber, Sir John Mason, recorded payments of £11,389; yet according to 'A brief collection of the expenses of ye household', a summary compiled about twenty-five years later, the total expenditure for the third year of Elizabeth's reign was £44,828.[127] Was the compiler of the summary simply mistaken, or were Weldon and Mason handling accounts which were not strictly part of the household? Half a century earlier, such a question could not even be asked, because the Cofferer was dealing with little except diets; wages were paid out of the Exchequer without any consolidated account, and the Treasury of the Chamber was handling an enormous and undifferentiated range of expenditure, from binding the king's books to paying the garrison of Berwick. The confusion, however, is partly in the eye of the beholder; and despite constant alarms, recriminations, and abortive reforms, the debts never got out of control, and the royal servants never (well, hardly ever) went unpaid. There was certainly no repetition of the crisis of 1449, when the Sergeants, Gentlemen and Yeomen of the royal household had been constrained to petition parliament because the arrangement to pay their wages by Exchequer assignment had broken down. They had pleaded that the profits from the king's wards, and from vacant abbeys, should be granted to them on a temporary basis, and Henry VI had agreed.[128] Nor was Henry unique in getting his affairs into such a mess. As we have seen, nearly twenty years later a similar thing happened to the magnificent Duke Philip of Burgundy. The Tudors never suffered from cash-flow problems of such a dramatic nature.

In the early 1440s there were two main sets of bills to be met—wages and provisions. The former were supposed to be met directly by the Exchequer, and the latter by assignments on the Duchies of Cornwall and Lancaster, paid to the Treasurer of the Household by the respective Receivers General.

Neither system worked properly, and in 1442 the House of Commons claimed that there was a shortfall of 8000 marks (£5330) per annum in receipts from the Duchies.[129] They also alleged that nearly £4000 of direct taxation revenue had been allocated to the household, but never paid, with the result that there were many longstanding creditors. The solution proposed was that £4000 a year should be assigned out of the customs of the port of Southampton, with a further 5000 marks a year from the same source for three years, to clear off outstanding debts. Henry merely responded that he would consult his council.[130] Twelve years later, following more complaints about unpaid creditors, the parliament returned to the charge, proposing a list of specific assignments on various revenue sources, such as fee farms and customs, which amounted to £5500 per annum. This time the king accepted the proposal, but it can only have provided a partial solution.[131] The following year, in 1455, the problem of household wages arose again, when the Commons claimed, on behalf of the king's servants, that the profits of wardship were being granted away when they should be used for the upkeep of the household. Henry rejected the petition, presumably on the grounds that the arrangement of 1449 had only been intended to cover an emergency.

After the victory of Edward IV, the position improved substantially, in line with the general improvement which took place in the management of the king's revenues; but the exact relationship between the Exchequer, the Countinghouse and the Treasury of the Chamber is not easy to determine. By the time of the *Liber Niger* many household and Chamber wages were being paid in the Countinghouse, but there seems to have been no uniformity, and the rise of the Treasury of the Chamber to overall supremacy in financial administration may well have shifted the bulk of Chamber wages there by the end of the reign. At the same time the Exchequer continued to handle the household assignments, which were raised to £11,000 a year by statute in 1482, after another round of complaints from unpaid creditors.[132] In this respect Henry VII started exactly where Edward had left off, with another statute in the first year of his reign specifying a very long and detailed list of assignments totalling £14,000.[133] At the same time similar assignments of £2105 were made for the Great Wardrobe. Even Henry's well known efficiency, however, could not guarantee that such assignments would be met promptly, or at all, and every so often the list had to be altered to bring it into line with practical reality. Another assessment Act of 1495 reduced the overall total to £13,000, but both the principle and the approximate level were by then well established. In the financial year 13–14 Henry VII (1497/8) the Cofferer of the Household, William Cope, accounted for just over £15,000, of which all but £800 came from the Exchequer.[134] During this year the 'diets' of the household were running at about £200–£250 a week, peaking at Christmas to £580, and accounted overall for £12,159 of Cope's total expenditure of £13,009. The Cofferer's totals did not vary much during the remainder of the reign, and the Controller's accounts for the same period were virtually duplicates. Richard Guildford's accounts for 1500/01 do, however, reveal that the household received its money from the Exchequer in no fewer than eighteen irregular instalments, varying from £106 to over £9000.[135] The 'foreign' receipts arrived in even smaller doses: again eighteen, but totalling only £201.[136] By this time the household finances were apparently running very smoothly, but the appearance may be deceptive. In 1496 Cope had clearly got into difficulties, and had had to borrow £4000 from the Treasury of the Chamber, which he was bound to repay over four years.[137] Like all other officials who handled royal money, Cope would have been personally liable for any deficit at the end of his period of account, so this was a hazardous move. His own accounts for the relevant year do not show any sign of such a transaction, recording receipts from the Exchequer of £13,152, and expenditure of £12,211. It may be that the Exchequer 'receipts' represent what should have arrived rather than what actually did, but the episode casts some doubt upon the reliability of what appears to be a straightforward set of financial records.[138]

This doubt is increased by a warrant issued to the Barons of the Exchequer some time early in Henry VIII's reign, which confirms that the old problems of securing the honouring of assignments was still troublesome.

> It is shewed unto us that the great part of the said assignments ... payable at the tyme restethe uncontent. Wherfore our menial servantes and other persons be unpaid of their duties. Wherfor we wol and command you to make undelayed and sharp process agaynst theym that doo not ther dewties in paying the money assigned upon theym for the cause abovesaid so that they may be constrayned in al hast to bringe it in and to deliver unto the Treasurer of the said Household ...

This also demonstrates that the wages of the household, and possibly some of those in the Chamber, were still being paid in the Countinghouse at this point, although that is not clear from the accounts of the Cofferer or Controller.[139] Like his father, Henry VIII started off with a new statute of assignment, reshuffling the obligations, and raising the total to nearly £19,400. Since this was a period of negligible inflation, the scale of the king's housekeeping either had risen, or—more likely—was expected to rise in the near future. Apart from the fact that these payments were to be made to the Cofferer direct, rather than to the Treasurer of the Household, there seems to have been no change in the pattern of financial administration until 1523. In that year, however, the whole system was reorganised, and the role of the Exchequer greatly diminished. This was in line with Wolsey's general financial policy, and was no doubt partly intended to resolve the intransigent problem of unfulfilled assignments. By the statute of 14 Henry VIII c.19 the Treasurer of the Chamber was made responsible for collecting the household assignments, and since the Chamber was by this time handling the great bulk of the king's revenue, there was little danger of his not being able to meet his commitment to the Cofferer. The total allocated to the household remained the same, but the Cofferer no longer accounted to the Exchequer; like the Masters of the Jewel House, the Great Wardrobe and the Works, he became a 'foreign' accountant of the General Surveyors.[140] In other respects the scope and nature of his responsibilities appear to have remained the same.

In the event, however, this arrangement turned out to be an experiment which barely outlived Wolsey's supremacy. In 1531 the Act of 1523 was repealed and the household assignments were returned to the Exchequer. The reason for this reversal is not clear, but it may well have been found that conservative Receivers proved even more inefficient in delivering money to the Chamber than they had been through the wonted channels. By the time that Thomas Cromwell began to take a hand in the affairs of the household in 1533, the Cofferer's 'ordinary' account was regularly overspent. In 1529/30 he dispensed £25,812, and in 1531/2 £27,947.[141] The balance, between £6000 and £8000, was made up through special warrants drawn on the Treasury of the Chamber, just as a similar shortfall, when it had occurred earlier, had been made up by special 'foreign' receipts. Cromwell anticipated a debt of £13,000 on the year 1532/3, but the Cofferer's accounts show no sign of anything amiss, recording a surplus of £46. Obviously the accounts were 'doctored' to conceal the shifts and expedients necessary to cover the steadily mounting costs of '... provisionz ... with wages of household, lyvery costs and other necessary charges'. The problem was not so much that the assignments were unpaid, as that the money dribbled in months, or even years, late, and that £19,400 was nowhere near enough anyway. In addition, the situation was made worse by the fact that what the Cofferer actually received in the first instance was not cash, but Exchequer tallies, which then had to be redeemed. By 1539 there were tallies still outstanding from 1531, and consequently also advances from the Chamber unrepaid.[142] A chaotic situation thus lay beneath the smooth surface of the Cofferer's accounts, and Cromwell decided to abolish the whole system of assignments, and start again.

The Act by which this was accomplished, 32 Henry VIII c.52, did not reach the statute book until after his fall, but Professor Elton is certainly right in representing this as the culmination of a process of reform going back to the first investigations of 1533.[143] Although the Cofferer still accounted to the Exchequer, after 1540 he drew his revenues from the newly established revenue courts—Augmentations, First Fruits and Tenths, Wards and Liveries etc., by a series of warrants dormant, or as we would now describe them, standing orders. It was no longer realistic to expect the much diminished Treasury of the Chamber to provide 'back up', and warrants dormant were much easier to alter than assignments. In the event of such a warrant not being properly honoured because of shortages in a particular department, it was relatively easy to provide a supplement through an *ad hoc* warrant on a different source. The other major change which was brought about at the same time, as we have already seen, was to bring the payment of all fees and wages under the control of the Countinghouse. Hitherto, the wages of the *Domus Providencie* had been paid by the Cofferer, but the wages of the Chamber and Privy Chamber had followed no consistent pattern. Early in Henry VIII's reign most of the senior Chamber staff were paid direct by the

Exchequer, although some received fees of uncertain provenance 'by the king's commandment'. The lower Chamber staff were mostly paid in the Countinghouse, although some of them also drew on the Exchequer, while the Gentlemen of the Privy Chamber, when they were established, were paid from the Treasury of the Chamber, and the Grooms of the Privy Chamber from the Countinghouse. The new system came into operation on 25 March 1540, but was backdated to Christmas 1539, and added about £7300 to the household expenses—or rather to the Cofferer's account, which dispensed nearly £33,000 in the first year.[144] An estimate for the complex operation of the handover year judged that as much as £39,000 might be necessary to clear off accumulated debt, and, although this is not shown in the surviving accounts, it may well have taken place.

Like most things connected with household finance, this apparently neat and efficient system soon broke down. According to 'the declaration of the expenses of the household', the last half year of Henry VIII and the first half year of Edward VI cost £49,187—which is about what might be expected in a period of sharp inflation. But only £24,561 of that was accounted for by the Cofferer, Sir Edmund Peckham.[145] Some, at least, of the Chamber wages had already reverted to the Treasury of the Chamber, but nowhere near enough to account for such an enormous discrepancy. Clearly the £30,000 a year on warrants dormant, which had been provided in 1540, was no longer coming in regularly, and shifts and expedients had again become the order of the day. By 1552 both the Treasury of the Chamber and the Wardrobe were in great difficulties; the latter was running at a deficit of about £4000 a year, and had accumulated debts of £26,513.[146] Some of the Cofferer's normal charges may have been shifted in that direction on a temporary basis, but John Ryther's own account for 2/3 Edward VI showed a deficit of over £8000 on an expenditure of £38,804.[147] It seems unlikely that a clear picture can ever be distilled from these accounts, but a few points of significance emerge. The largest single provider of money for the household throughout Edward's reign was the Court of First Fruits and Tenths: £14,000 in 1547, £18,436 in 1553. In 1552 the annual expenditure on wages and fees in the Chamber and household was calculated at £16,867—and that did not include the Musicians and Players, who received another £1,728, let alone the other detached departments such as the Great Wardrobe, Tents, Revels, Hawking, Kennels, and the King's Barge.[148] In the last full year of Edward's reign the total spent was £65,923, and of that £55,791 passed through the hands of the Cofferer. When Mary's council took stock of the situation in the autumn of 1553, they calculated the debt of the household on the Cofferer's account at £21,021, of which about a third had been incurred within the last two years.[149]

The first thing that happened in the new reign was a review of the warrants dormant. Plans were already well advanced to reabsorb Augmentations and First Fruits and Tenths into the Exchequer; so the new warrants were drawn on Wards and Liveries (£12,000), the Duchy of Lancaster (£10,000) and the Exchequer (£8000)—thus somewhat unrealistically reverting to the £30,000 allocated in 1540.[150] Since then costs had risen by about 80 per cent, and the new warrants were obsolete before they had been implemented. In the second year of Mary's reign Richard Freston, her Cofferer, received £39,300 from Sir Edmund Peckham, the Treasurer of the Mint, who was temporarily handling all the main revenue accounts during the period of reorganisation, £6000 from the Duchy of Lancaster, and about £5000 from other sources.[151] He dispensed £59,353 out of a total expenditure of £75,043, and showed a deficit on the year of £10,170. Thereafter the situation was gradually brought under control. In the fourth year of the reign, when the 'charges of the household' were estimated by some anonymous optimist at £40,000, the Countinghouse received £11,737 from the Exchequer, £16,775 from Wards and Liveries, and £14,788 from the Duchy of Lancaster.[152] The deficit on the year was a little under £5000. By this time hardly any Chamber wages were passing through the Countinghouse, but a special arrangement seems to have been adopted for the wages of the Yeomen of the Guard, or 'Ordinary Yeomen of the Queen's Chamber', as they were described, whereby a special Privy Seal was issued to the Exchequer every three months. The Cofferer drew the money (about £660), and issued it to the men.[153] Why this clumsy, and probably temporary expedient should have been adopted is not clear, unless it was to conceal the distinction between the Yeomen of the queen's side and the Yeomen of the king's side. The latter were actually paid by Philip, and the Spanish money came either via the Jewel House or from the queen personally. Clearly, it did not always come, but since it was channelled through the Cofferer, this fact could be disguised and all the Yeomen were ostensibly paid at the same rate, and at the same time. Given the propensity of Englishmen to complain about the Spaniards, this small deception is perhaps understandable!

Early in 1559, when Elizabeth's council also estimated the outstanding debts, they assessed the household at £25,000, some of which could be traced back to Edward's reign. On this evidence the Lord Treasurer seems to have concluded that the system of warrants dormant had failed in its purpose, and in response to steady conservative pressure from the Exchequer, a new statute of assignment was passed in 1563. This was to a large extent modelled on its Henrician predecessors, but differed in two important respects. First, the total was £40,027—too little for an account which was by then averaging £50,000 a year, but not absurdly so. Second, the system of tallies was abolished— Receivers General paid direct to the Cofferer, and he was entitled to damages of £20 in respect of every default. In the event of assigned sources failing altogether, the Lord Treasurer was entitled to make alternative assignments without special authority, so some of the flexibility of the warrant system was retained, with the additional security of statutory backing. In practice, of course, the actual assignments were no better observed than before, and much of the Cofferer's income was derived from other sources, but it was not considered necessary to make any further formal provision for the funding of the household during the Tudor period. Throughout Elizabeth's long reign the Cofferer's and Controller's accounts show a remarkably consistent pattern.

In 1564/5 Thomas Weldon received £49,132 and spent £44,932; in 1582/3, Gregory Lovett received £48,102 and spent £54,904.[154] Deficits exceed surpluses by about two to one, and in a period of steadily rising prices such uniformity looks highly artificial. But there were repeated and prolonged economy drives, in spite of the progresses, and Cecil's perpetual grumbling had some effect. After the numerous changes which had taken place in the relationships between the different accounts over the years 1520–1560, the next forty years saw a period of great stability—almost ossification.

One indication of this, and a reason why expenditure declined in real terms, was the fact that fees and wages were hardly ever increased. The Cofferer's own £100, for example, was unchanged from 1552 to 1602. This was possibly because the real rewards of all these offices lay in their perquisites and opportunities for exploitation, rather than in their formal wages. In this they resembled all other positions in the royal service, but as the sixteenth century drew to a close, and inflation continued, the strains began to show. Courtiers complained of being unrewarded, and an apologetic queen encouraged them to exploit anti-social devices such as monopolies. Wages which did have to be increased, like those of the Artificers, Armourers and Musicians, were not paid by the Cofferer, and the effects were consequently concealed. As we have seen, there was a considerable number of separate departmental accounts connected with the court, which did not pass through either the Chamber or the Countinghouse, and some of these, such as the Revels, showed significant increases.[155]

Originally the other main financial department of the court, the Treasury of the Chamber, had been the king's private funds—almost literally the chest under the bed. However, by the middle of Edwards IV's reign it had become the most important revenue department in the kingdom; and as such it continued, with a brief intermission in the early part of Henry VII's reign, until after the fall of Wolsey. John Heron's accounts, from 1496 to 1505, are well known, and contain an enormous variety of entries, from major public expenditure, such as £4266 for troops going to Ireland, to minor casual rewards of a few shillings for unspecified services.[156] Offerings at the shrines of saints sit cheek by jowl with the king's gambling debts, substantial sums laid out for jousts and disguisings alongside the regular wages of minstrels, informers and chaplains. Altogether, in the fairly typical year 1503/4, £90,327 passed through Heron's hands.[157] Occasional payments, mostly small but on one occasion as much as £200, were made to household officers, but these were rewards, or to meet exceptional demands, and should not be seen as part of the regular financial provision. Some, but by no means all, Chamber wages were paid through this account, and the prevailing impression is one of informality. This was the money which the king spent as the spirit moved him, not the money which he used to meet his regular, recurrent commitments. It was also, as we have seen, the fund which was used to 'bail out' the Cofferer when his assignments were in arrears, but the king was understandably reluctant to tie up his free money in such a way, and repayment was strictly and promptly insisted upon. It was the logic of this situation which prompted Wolsey to make the Cofferer answerable to the Treasurer of the Chamber rather than the Exchequer in 1523; but the days of the Chamber as a national Treasury were numbered.

In 1531 the household account went back to the Exchequer, and the development of the new revenue courts over the following decade reduced both the size and the scope of the Treasurer's task. By about 1536, Sir Brian Tuke, who had taken over as Treasurer of the Chamber in 1528, was fighting a losing battle to keep his department solvent. The story of this decline is well known, and does not need to be repeated here;[158] in 1530 the Chamber handled over £55,000, ten years later this had fallen to £35,000, and by 1553 it was down to £16,563. Part of the trouble was an enormous burden of bad debt, which was credited to the Chamber, and which the Treasurer was supposed to collect as part of his funding. When Sir Thomas Moyle and Sir Walter Mildmay eventually investigated this situation in Mary's reign, they found 'obligations due' to the massive total of £396,155.[159] Some of this consisted of unpaid fines and recognisances going back to Henry VII's reign—and £60,000 of French pension—so that the commissioners concluded that no less than £346,158 should be written off as 'desperate'. By 1548 the Chamber was receiving only a minute proportion of its income direct, in the form of 'obligations'; the bulk was coming on warrants dormant from Wards and Liveries and the Duchy of Lancaster; and the Treasurer himself was accounting to the Chancellor of Augmentations. About 80 per cent of Chamber expenditure by this time was on wages: £2400 a year to Trumpeters, Minstrels, Singers, Falconers, Yeomen, Keepers of park and palaces, Artificers and Gunners; £5500 a year to Almain Armourers, the King's Watermen, Gentlemen Ushers, Sewers, Yeomen, and Grooms of the Privy Chamber; and £2400 to the Master of the Posts.[160] In addition the Chamber was still meeting the 'diets' of ambassadors, the expenses of 'making ready the king's houses', and the casual rewards to servants of the court at Christmas and Easter. In 1556, when presenting his accounts for the previous decade, Sir William Cavendish alleged that many wages 'which have heretofore ordynarily been made within the Office of the King's Majesties Treasury of the Chamber' had perforce been shifted to the Cofferer and other offices for lack of funds. He listed the Yeomen of the Guard, the Gentlemen of the Privy Chamber '... husshers, gromes and all other belongings to the Chamber', and the ambassadors' diets.[161]

As Cavendish correctly claimed, the Chamber was underfunded and 'much decaied'. He had paid the king £1000 for the Treasurership in 1546, and two years later was bitterly regretting a bad bargain. The office, he then declared, had been £12,000 in debt when he took it over, but this fact had been concealed from him by the fraud of one Thomas Knot, formerly Sir Brian Tuke's clerk. By 1548 the debt had risen to £14,000 and there was no money in hand.[162] In the autumn of 1553 Mary's councillors calculated the 'debts owing in th'offyce of the Chamber at midsomer last' at £17,968, and the situation became the subject of a special commission of enquiry.[163] Cavendish was eventually held personally responsible for £5237, and shortly before his death in 1557 submitted a lengthy and grovelling petition, claiming that the benefits of the office had been unjustly sequestered by Protector Somerset, and that he had spent hundreds of pounds of his own money in the service of Henry and Edward, without recompense. The Lord Treasurer laconically noted that the petition had been enrolled in the Exchequer, but Cavendish's executors do not appear to have been pursued.[164] The abolition of the Court of Augmentations in 1554 meant that Cavendish would normally have been accountable to the Exchequer, if it had not been for the special commission, and his successors accounted there for the remainder of the century, and beyond. For the last few months of Mary's reign the office was held, without patent, by Edmund Felton, who dispensed a mere £3136—almost all of which he received from the Exchequer. It was left to the next full incumbent, Sir John Mason, to get the office back on its feet again, and that process took about three years. The two years 1558–60 saw a turnover of £15,827, of which £7200 came from the Exchequer, and the balance from Wards and Liveries, the Hanaper, and the Duchies of Lancaster and Cornwall.[165] During this period, Mason paid out £8202 in wages, including the Yeomen of the Guard and some, at least, of the Chamber servants formerly paid. In 1562 he submitted a full breakdown of income and expenditure which shows that not only the Yeomen but the Musicians, 'Enterlude players', Huntsmen, officers of the Jewel House, and a few other court servants were on his payroll, but no Grooms, Ushers, Sewers or members of the Privy Chamber. The year's expenditure came to £11,689, and was met by warrants dormant of £3500 on the Exchequer, £4000 on the Duchy of Lancaster, £3000 on the Duchy of Cornwall, and £2000 on the Hanaper.[166] Thereafter a regular pattern of accounts was resumed—Mason (until 1565), Sir Francis Knollys (1566–68), and Sir Thomas Henneage (1568–1590) consistently spending between £11,000 and £16,000, with only a very slight tendency to increase as the reign advanced. The fluctuations are readily accounted for by the random element of special warrants, and the hard core of the Treasurer's wage bill and other court expenditure remained as constant as the Cofferer's similar expenditure on 'diets'.

The other main accounting department, the Great Wardrobe, stood outside the court, as we have seen, and always accounted direct to the Exchequer, even during the Chamber's highest ascendancy. Towards the end of Henry VII's reign it had expended about £1300, almost entirely on liveries and issues of cloth for special purposes—weddings, funerals, coronations and festivals. In 1510 a statutory assignment of £2,015 per annum was made to the Great Wardrobe. This was increased in 1513 to £4,015 but, like the main household assignment, was soon grossly inadequate. By the end of Henry VIII's reign the regular costs were running at about £8000, and there was a debt of nearly

£10,000.[167] Edward's ministers economised drastically, cutting expenditure to under £4000 by 1553. The first two years of Mary's reign, with both a coronation and a wedding, saw the costs soar to nearly £18,000, but by the end of the reign it was back to just over £6000, and Elizabeth held it at about that level, with occasional fluctuations.[168] All issues from the Great Wardrobe were in kind, and by warrant, and the money came, as usual, from a variety of sources by both dormant and occasional warrants. Although it was extremely important to the court as the provider of the finery which featured so prominently in public life and ceremonial, the Great Wardrobe was a world of its own, and neither its finances nor its personnel played a prominent part in the overall pattern of management.

If the Great Wardrobe was largely out of sight because it was physically separate, the last spending department to be considered was out of sight for the opposite reason—and that was the Privy Purse. Until the end of Henry VII's reign the king's personal requirements were met in the Treasury of the Chamber, and recorded in the Treasurer's accounts. Hugh Denys and other personal servants handled the king's money, but did not need to account for it as they were acting directly on the king's instructions and the sums involved were normally small. However, soon after Henry VIII's succession, substantial sums of £1000 and £2000 at a time began to be withdrawn from the Treasury of the Chamber, and placed at the disposal of Sir William Compton, the Groom of the Stool. In 1516 no less than £18,000 was withdrawn in this way, and Henry was clearly using Compton to pay major bills of a public nature.[169] Not even Henry spent that sort of money on his private pleasures! In 1526 Wolsey endeavoured to ensure that the keeper of the Privy Purse presented regular accounts, and his effort may well have borne fruit in the so-called 'Privy Purse expenses of Henry VIII' which run from 1529 to 1532. These accounts record the disbursement of £53,488 in the space of a little over three years.[170] They are very like the Chamber accounts in their scope and nature, but actually record substantial sums paid to Sir Brian Tuke, the Treasurer of the Chamber, as well as loans to the Cofferer and a host of personal expenses, including some very large gambling debts. They were audited by the king himself, and presumably presented by the Groom of the Stool. Consequently for most of his reign Henry VIII was running what amounted to two Chamber accounts, and the distinction between them in terms of function was not very clear. Nor is it clear where all the money came from. Some was certainly withdrawn from the Chamber, but since transfers were also made in the opposite direction, the Privy Purse may well have had independent resources. When Sir Anthony Denny, Henry's last Groom of the Stool, presented his accounts for audit after the king's death, he declared receipts of £243,387 between 1542 and 1547—nearly £50,000 a year—which he had dispensed on the king's oral commands.[171] Much of this money had been spent on jewels, plate, tapestries and building works. He was therefore a larger spending agent than the Treasurer of the Chamber, and one who was primarily concerned with the maintenance of the king's magnificence. Denny had not paid regular wages, or diets, and so in that sense was not a financial officer of the court; but the Privy Purse was certainly a major factor in the king's spending, and one which operated in the inner recesses of the Privy Chamber. Denny drew money from all the revenue courts, but primarily from the Court of Augmentations, which was operating at its maximum capacity during the early 1540s.

Henry's death brought an abrupt end to the Privy Purse as a major financial agency. Edward was kept extremely short of money by his watchful uncle, and his yearning to be able to distribute his own rewards made him vulnerable to the schemes of Sir Thomas Seymour. During a royal minority the Privy Purse was pocket money. Mary's personal transactions also seem to have been on a modest scale, and drawn from the main Chamber account, except that she acted as an intermediary for the payment of some, at least, of her husband's English servants. George Brodyman, one of the Grooms at the Privy Chamber, probably kept her Privy Purse, but no accounts have survived.[172] Money received by the queen for New Year gifts, which amounted to over £1400 in each of the last two years of the reign, remained in the Privy Purse, but we have no means of knowing what proportion of the overall receipts these sums represented. The situation in the early part of Elizabeth's reign is a good deal clearer, thanks to the survival of the accounts of John Tamworth, one of the Grooms of the Privy Chamber, and keeper of the Privy Purse from 1559 to 1569.[173] In that period Tamworth accounted for £26,701, of which £11,905 came from New Year gifts, £4000 from the Exchequer, and £3000 from the queen's agent in Antwerp, Sir Thomas Gresham. All but £26 of this income was spent, about half of it on public business, including a £5000 subsidy of the Earl of Murray. The remainder went on jewels, perfumes, horses, and 'provisions', at the modest rate of not much over £1000 a year. After 1569 the curtain descends again, but given Elizabeth's extreme conservatism, it is, perhaps, unlikely that this pattern, or level, of operations changed very much over the following thirty-five years. Nothing could highlight the contrast between the prodigal Henry and the frugal Elizabeth more sharply than the comparison of their Privy Purse expenses — a contrast in styles which the whole court inevitably reflected.

Further reading

E. Arber (ed.) 'The narrative of Edward Underhill' in *An English Garner*
E. K. Chambers *The Elizabethan Stage*, Vol. 1
H. M. Colvin *The History of the King's Works* Vol. IV, pt. 2
G. R. Elton *The Tudor Revolution in Government*

D. E. Hoak 'The King's Privy Chamber, 1547–1553' in *Tudor Rule and Revolution*

A. R. Myers *The Household of Edward IV*

W. C. Richardson *Tudor Chamber Administration*

J. G. Russell *The Field of the Cloth of Gold*

3 LIFE AT COURT

Access, security and discipline

There were many different kinds of access to the court. In one sense it was the
acid test of a nobleman's political status, and might require careful investigation. When in July 1554 the Earl of Rutland sent a servant to the Lord
Steward, the Earl of Arundel, to know the queen's pleasure 'touching my
access to the court', he was not just enquiring when there would be a vacant
chamber.[1] He needed to know whether his presence would be acceptable to
the sovereign. The notorious example of the Earl of Essex in 1601 demonstrates that not even the greatest could be sure of a welcome at all times and in
all circumstances. For anyone who was not on the Ordinary, formal permission was required, both to come and to go. Sudden withdrawal without
such leave was always regarded with suspicion, even when the cause was
illness, or some sudden domestic crisis. When the Earl of Pembroke went down
to one of his country residences in September 1554 there were rumours of his
disaffection;[2] and the Duke of Norfolk's precipitate departure in 1569 created
an atmosphere of near panic. At the same time, a summons to court might be
more ominous than the refusal of permission to attend. At times of crisis or
tension, it was the trusted nobility who were sent 'down to their countries', to
keep them in good order, whilst those who were regarded with suspicion were
kept under surveillance. Thus Mary summoned her half-sister in January
1554, and insisted upon being obeyed, despite all pleas and excuses.[3] It was
Elizabeth's summons to the Earls of Northumberland and Westmorland in
1569 which forced them into open rebellion; and an innocent-seeming
summons to the Duke of Buckingham in 1521 was the prelude to his arrest and
trial for treason. Major festivities, such as Christmas and New Year, always
saw a major influx, although how this was orchestrated is not clear. The
exchange of New Year gifts with the sovereign was a sure sign of being *persona
grata*, although whether it necessarily indicated physical presence at court is
less certain.[4] During the law terms, and more particularly during sessions of
parliament, there must have been a great deal of relatively informal coming
and going, rendered easier by the growing habit of maintaining houses or
regular lodgings in London; but to obtain access to the Chamber, or to
participate in any of the activities of the court, the consent of the monarch or
of one of the 'head officers' had to be obtained. Lawrence Stone's cautious
statement that the court 'was a place to which many (noblemen) came for
certain periods of the year' is probably as far as a generalisation can safely go.[5]

Elizabeth made it clear that she expected her peers, at least, to put in regular appearances, and did not excuse them, even when they feared for their own safety. The Earl of Sussex complained to the queen in 1565 that he was at court 'upon your highness' commandment and guard', and thereby exposed 'unarmed' to the hostility of the Earl of Leicester, who, he clearly implied, was not placed under similar constraints.[6] Between duty and opportunity, about two thirds of Elizabeth's peers were regular attenders in the early and middle years of the reign, and that was probably a larger proportion than at any other time during the century. Below that social level, access was nearly always related to specific business. If the initiative came from the court, it would be to participate in some particular function or ceremony; if from the would-be visitor, to present a petition or to supplicate a favour. The latter could be a protracted and dispiriting quest, as the guardians of successive doors had to be bribed or cajoled into allowing the petitioner to pass. It was possible to obtain access to the Great Chamber by such means, but the success of the quest was by no means assured, and the use of the good offices of a court servant, who could choose his opportunity, was probably both more efficient, and cheaper in the long run. There were no strict rules as to who might, or might not, be admitted to any palace or residence where the court was situated; a presentable appearance, a show of legitimate business, and a supply of ready cash, were all that was required. To obtain access to the Privy Chamber was a different matter; there the ushers were given the strictest instructions that no one should be allowed to pass who was not either a known officer or servant, or a person who had been specifically summoned to the royal presence.[7] The Privy Chamber was a sanctum, but the Outer Chamber and the passages of the court were constantly thronged with suitors. Mary, it was believed, was particularly amenable on her way to or from chapel, and was frequently intercepted; Henry, similarly, when setting off on hunting trips. Of security in the modern sense, there was, and could be, very little; and even when assassination began to be a serious risk, after 1570, the essential character of a renaissance monarchy precluded effective precautions.

The precautions which were taken were intended to confront threats of a rather different kind, particularly the related problems of superfluous servants and unauthorised hangers-on, 'rascals, boys and vagabonds' as they were usually classified. The Eltham Ordinances typically instructed that

> ... noe manner of persons, officers or others, have or entertaine a greater number of servants in the court than be appointed or assigned unto them

and ordered the porters on the gates to exclude all others.[8] Since the Porters could hardly have been expected to know every authorised servant by sight, they were presumably supplied with a list from the Countinghouse, which was brought up to date every so often, and were required to carry out periodic checks, but this is not made clear. All those servants who were to be admitted should be 'personages of good honestie, gesture, behaviour and conversation'. Pages of gentle birth were allowed to attend upon noblemen and women, and upon the chief officers of the court, but none other was to be admitted. These Ordinances were accompanied by an exhaustive schedule of service entitlement, whereby a Duke or Archbishop could be accompanied by twelve servants, the Lord Chamberlain by ten, a Gentleman of the Privy Chamber by four—and so on, down to the Sergeants and Clerks of the household at one each.[9] An indication of the kind of ostentation which made Wolsey so unpopular is given by the fact that he reserved to himself the right to be served by no fewer than forty men![10] In placing himself upon such a unique level, the Cardinal must have seriously undermined the credibility of his reform. If 'manred' and status supported each other, then masters and servants were bound to conspire to defeat a regulation which seemed designed only to feed Wolsey's pride. In any case, within a few years the nuisance was worse than ever, and a royal proclamation had to be issued, giving 'all vagabonds, masterless folk, rascals and other idle persons which have used to hang on, haunt and follow the court' twenty-four hours in which to depart.[11] Any lingering thereafter were to be whipped, pilloried or branded, in accordance with the laws against vagabondage. Similar proclamations in 1541 and 1555 indicate that little was achieved, and, given the prevalence of poverty and unemployment in and around London, that is not surprising. With its enormous scale and leaky control of provisioning, the court resembled a vast cornucopia, and was a standing invitation to the inhabitants of that twilight zone between service and vagabondage to which the lingering concept of manred continued to give a tinge of respectability. In addition to controlling entry, the Porters were supposed to ensure that no 'Victuails, Waxe-lights, Leather Potts, Vessells silver or pewter, Wood or Coles' were smuggled out, and to conduct a house search three or four times a day to expel any intruders who had hitherto eluded their vigilance.[12] Given the size and complexity of most Tudor palaces, and the fact that the Sergeant Porter had a team of only five Yeomen and two Grooms, the task was impossible. The Chamber premises, policed by a sizeable team of Gentlemen and Yeomen Ushers, could be kept clear of the obviously undesirable, but beyond that the problem was as intractable as the problem of waste and extravagance to which it was related.

In this situation, protecting the life and health of the sovereign amounted to little more than a series of hopeful gestures. Henry VIII was extremely fussy by contemporary standards about cleanliness, and acutely nervous of disease and infection, although whether he perceived any connection between them is not clear. Plague was particularly feared, and no one who was known to have had any contact with infected persons was allowed near the court. Sometimes the king would simply leave London if an outbreak was identified, as he did in 1528, when Hall noted that

> the kyng for a space removed almost every day, till at the least he came to Tytynhangar, a place of the Abbot of Saint Albones, & ther with a fewe determyned to byde the chaunce which God would send him.[13]

There the house was 'so purged with daily fyres and other preservatives' that no member of the royal party was infected, although several courtiers who had been left behind in London, notably Sir William Compton and William Carey—both members of the Privy Chamber—succumbed. During the same summer Henry also wrote to Wolsey, who could not afford the luxury of such isolation, urging him to 'keep out of the air, to have only a small and clean company about him', to eat and drink only in moderation, and to take some patent nostrum from the royal apothecary.[14] When the danger was less pressing, the precautions were less spectacular than those adopted in 1528. At Christmas 1526, as we have already seen, the court remained at Eltham, and admission was very tightly restricted. In 1535 and 1543 proclamations were issued forbidding the citizens of London to approach the court, and in the latter case, forbidding the servants of the court to go out into the city—which presumably meant that those who normally lived out had to sleep at their posts for the duration of the scare.[15] Understandably, very strict instructions were laid down in 1537 to protect the health of the infant Prince Edward, and at all times for the cleansing of the royal apartments. The Ordinances of 1526 not only carried out a purge of 'sicklie and unmete' persons, but also provided the Clerks of the Kitchin with extra funds to find 'honest and whole garments' for their scullions 'for the better avoiding of corruption and all uncleanesse out of the King's house'. At the same time waste food was not to 'lye abroad in the gallerys and courts', where it attracted the scavenging dogs which were supposed to be expelled on sight, but to be tidily committed to the scullery, whence the Almoner's staff were supposed to collect it.[16] Henry's courtiers clearly did not share his fastidious concerns, and a few months after his death it was even felt necessary to make public proclamation that

> no person, of what degree soever, shall make water or cast any annoyance within the precinct of the court ... whereby corruption may breed and tend to the prejudice of his royal person ...[17]

Mary and Elizabeth probably succeeded in improving this situation; at least there are no similarly obvious references to it in the second half of the century. Mary was every bit as sensitive to dirt and infection as her father had been, and had a long record of mild hypochondria. As queen, she moved frequently, and often complained of the effect of 'bad air' upon her health. She did not, however, make any attempt to restrict access to the court during the influenza epidemic of 1557–8, and that oversight may have contributed to her relatively early death. Elizabeth was less sensitive, but inherited Henry's concern with cleanliness, taking baths with a frequency which contemporaries considered to be debilitating. There were bad outbreaks of plague in 1569, 1592 and 1593, and during each of these epidemics elaborate proclamations were issued controlling the coming and going of all sorts of people to the court, in an endeavour to preserve normal working with the minimum risk of infection.[18] There was no repetition of the panic of 1528, but the queen can not be accused of failing to take reasonable care of herself. It would be a very long time before more genuinely effective measures were devised and implemented.

Apart from disease, the main hazard to royal life was violence, either accidental or deliberate. As we have already seen, protection against the 'privy assassin' was well nigh impossible, and was scarcely attempted. The elaborate ritual of making the royal bed had originally been devised to ensure that no poisoned weapon was concealed in the mattress, but this had faded from view by the time of the Eltham Ordinances, and the Tudors do not even seem to have employed a food taster. Nor could any protection be offered against the monarch's wilful self-exposure to physical risks. The most obvious of these was Henry VIII's penchant for jousting, a most dangerous sport which regularly resulted in fatal accidents, of which the most celebrated was that which befell Henri II of France in 1559. However, hunting could be almost equally hazardous. Henry suffered several heavy falls, one of which left him unconscious for hours, and in 1525 when 'folowing of his hauke' landed on his head in a ditch 'so that if one Edmond Mody, a foteman, had not lept into the water & lift up his hed, whiche was fast in the clay he had been drouned . . .'[19] It is not surprising that Edward VI was restrained from such activities by his minders, and was only allowed the relatively innocuous exercises of running at the ring and shooting with the longbow. Since he did not excel at either of these sports, however, it may not have been only the risk which prompted his council's attitude. Female rulers were not tempted or threatened by chivalric violence, and neither Mary nor Elizabeth endured the equally hazardous experience of childbirth, which carried off both Jane Seymour and Catherine Parr. All alike were put at risk, however, by the aristocratic code of honour, which required the violent expiation of insults, real or imagined, and which flourished exceedingly in the fiercely competitive atmosphere of the court. Gentlemen carried weapons and affrays were frequent, right up to the end of the sixteenth century. In 1573, in a typical incident in Fleet Street, John Fortescue was attacked by the Earl of Oxford with twelve retainers, and was badly beaten up before being rescued by his own servants.[20] It would appear that the increasing concentration of political activity at the court in the later sixteenth century actually made the immediate situation worse than it had been under the early Tudors, as brawls in and around London replaced larger scale acts of violence in the countryside. An excellent example of the violent consequences of a courtly feud can be seen in the conflict between Thomas Knyvett, a Gentleman of the Privy Chamber, and the Earl of Oxford. In 1580 Ann Vavasour, Knyvett's ward, gave birth to an illegitimate child of which Oxford was the father. Over the next three years a duel, three affrays and at least two murders resulted, while the queen made not the slightest attempt to restrain the parties.[21] Surrounded by such an atmosphere, the risks to the personal safety of the monarch were considerable, and attempts to insulate the court itself could never be entirely successful. As we have seen, the Earl of Leicester was accused of seeking to dominate the court by such means in 1565, and a few years later, when similarly threatened by Lord North, the Earl of Sussex declared that he would come 'in suche sort as I wyll not fere pertakers ageynst me'. Consequently the most strenuous efforts had to be made to police the verge, and to maintain peace and order within it.

Policing was the responsibility of the Knight Marshal and his staff, who also kept the Marshalsea prison and executed the decisions of the Lord Steward's court. For the most part the Knight Marshal's instructions resembled those of the Sergeant Porter, with whom his duties overlapped,[22] but it was he, and not the porters who had to cope with gentle offenders. Physical assault within the verge had always been regarded as a particularly grave offence, no matter who perpetrated it, and in 1542 parliament decreed the penalty of mutilation for anyone guilty of striking with bloodshed. Anyone so convicted by a jury of the household before the Lord Steward was to lose his right hand, and to suffer imprisonment and fine at will. The most elaborate ceremonial was prescribed for the process of amputation, which was to be attended by all the head officers and departmental Sergeants. However, the impact was somewhat blunted by the fact that noblemen could be differently punished at the discretion of the council, and were allowed to draw blood in the chastisement of their own servants without incurring any penalty at all.[23] As far as we know, these ferocious penalties were never exacted, although the ceremony was occasionally set up before a royal pardon supervened, and Lord Abergavenny had to be granted a special pardon in 1552 for striking the Earl of Oxford in the Presence Chamber. Even the shortest tempered gentleman did his best to restrain himself in the royal presence, and Charles Yelverton's response to an insult in the Privy Chamber in 1599 was merely a contemporary variant of 'come outside and say that'. The Italian and French fashion of channelling aristocratic violence into duelling made little impact in England until after 1580, and did not become a problem requiring royal intervention until the following century. The first fencing school in London was established in 1576, and the rapier was the original duelling weapon;[24] pistols were not at first considered to be gentlemanly weapons, although their dangerous nature had been recognised much earlier, and carrying them within three miles of the court had been forbidden in 1552.

Perhaps the most dangerous period, when tensions and animosities within the court were at their highest, was the twelve months from July 1554 to August 1555, when Philip's Spanish and Italian servants were literally at daggers drawn with their English equivalents. 'Not a day goes by', wrote one Spaniard, 'without knife work in the court', and another declared that only the special providence of God had prevented them from being massacred to a man.[25] There was an element of hysterical exaggeration about these complaints, but the records testify to a sufficient number of murders, robberies and affrays to justify exceptional concern. The major recorded incidents all occurred outside the court, and some were the result of unauthorised Spanish traders and artisans trying to set up their booths in defiance of London privileges;[26] but the atmosphere within the royal household was clearly explosive. Such a situation had been anticipated, and four months before Philip's arrival in England one of his father's councillors, Briviesca da

1 Henry VIII as Solomon, by Hans Holbein (Royal Collection)

2 A substantial figure: armour made for Henry VIII, *c.*1540 (Royal Collection)

3 Renaissance interior design: Holbein's drawing for a fireplace at Bridewell Palace, *c.*1540 (British Museum)

3

4

5

4 Anthony Van Wyngaerde: a view of Richmond Palace (Ashmolean Museum, Oxford)

5 Henry VIII as *preux chevalier*, jousting before Catherine of Aragon, February 1511; from the Great Tournament Roll (Royal College of Arms)

6 Imperial pageantry: Henry VIII at the Field of Cloth of Gold (Royal Collection)

6

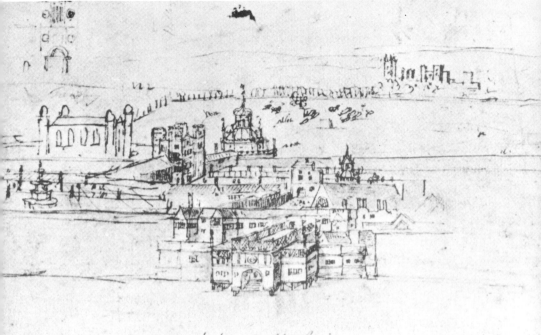

Whitehall Stairs

PALATIVM REGIVM IN ANGLIÆ REGNO APPELLATVM NONCIVI
Hoc est nusquam simile.

Whitehall stairs, from
the Thames, by Anthony
van Wyngaerde, c.1555
(Ashmolean Museum)

Henry VIII's
custom-built palace:
Nonsuch in the late
sixteenth century, by
Hofenagel (British
Museum)

Pen and ink design for a
mural at Nonsuch;
anonymous, c.1540 (British
Museum)

The inmost public
chamber: Henry VIII
dining in his Privy
Chamber, by Hans Holbein
(British Museum)

9

10

The Byble in
Englyshe, that is to saye the content of all the holy scrypture, bothe of ye olde and newe testament, truly translated after the veryte of the hebrue and Greke textes, by ye dylygent studye of dyuerse excellent learned men, expert in the forsayde tonges.

Prynted by Rychard Grafton & Edward Whitchurch.

Cum priuilegio ad imprimendum solum.
1539.

12

11 The king as Supreme Head: Henry
VIII hands down the Word of God;
from the title page of the Great Bible
(Mansell Collection)

12 Holbein's sketches of fashions in
Henry VIII's court, *c.*1540 (British
Museum)

13 The immature image: Edward VI at the age of six (Kunstmuseum, Basle)

Muñatones, had been sent over from Brussels to consult with the English council about the best methods of preventing and settling disputes. As a result a special commission was issued in May to himself and Sir Thomas Holcrofte

> ... to enquire and determine all criminal causes for all crimes and offences to be committed by any of the train of the Queen or Prince, that is to say either of the Spanish or any other strange nation amongst themselves or against any natural subject of the Queen, or of any such natural subject against any stranger being of the said train ...

The commissioners were required to confer daily, and were to be assisted by two provost marshals—one for the queen and one for the prince—who were required to 'use all diligence they possibly may to take away all occasions of contention between nation and nation ...' Capital offences were to be judged by the common law of England, and lesser crimes at the discretion of the commissioners, 'consideration (being) had to the usage of the nation of the offender'.[27] The jurisdiction of this commission was not confined to the court, but certainly included it, as is made clear by the fact that offending noblemen were to be dealt with only after consultation with the Lord Steward, and if necessary referred to the council, as was normal with offences committed by noblemen within the verge. There are no records for the operation of this *ad hoc* court, and it was not intended to supersede the normal jurisdiction of the Lord Steward, but it is possible that some of the Spaniards who were subsequently pardoned of capital offences had been tried in this way. As a means of coping with an extremely difficult situation, it was as equitable and expeditious as anything which could have been devised, but it seems to have done nothing to reduce the tension, which, if anything, became worse as the summer of 1555 advanced and the queen's pregnancy turned out to be a delusion.

Other periods of high political tension also produced security problems, although of a rather different kind. Henry VII seems to have been severely shaken by the treason of his Lord Chamberlain, Sir William Stanley, in 1495 and this may well have played a part in his decision to restrict access to his inner apartments to those menial servants who were later to develop into the staff of the Privy Chamber.[28] The establishment of the Yeomen of the Guard in the first year of his reign may also have been a sign of early insecurity, although the motive is just as likely to have been honorific as practical. During the unstable minority governments of Edward VI, however, the ordinary guard was substantially increased. In May 1550, 200 Extraordinary Yeomen were recruited, and deployed about the court under the command of Lord Clinton—a reflection of the fact that the Duke of Somerset had just been readmitted to the council.[29] The following February a continuing sense of insecurity prompted the Duke of Northumberland to raise twelve trained bands—about 850 cavalry—commanded by his friends and supporters, as a sort of additional palace guard. This may have been prompted by his relative failure to control the Gentlemen Pensioners, and was a short-lived experiment because of the cost. In addition, throughout the period of Northumberland's ascendancy, the Knight Marshal, Sir Ralph Hopton, kept forty of his own men under arms at the Tower of London, for which he was paid about £45 a month.[30] For about three years the court must have resembled an armed camp, not because of the need to protect the king from his enemies, but because of the need to maintain control over him in the face of jealous rivals. Once the young king was dead, the hollowness of this military display was quickly demonstrated. Northumberland managed to overawe the council and the City of London for about ten days in the name of Queen Jane, but his forces were quite inadequate to fight a civil war. Neither the Gentlemen Pensioners nor the Yeomen could be turned into a Praetorian Guard. Indeed, the usefulness of either for serious fighting may well be doubted, particularly in the light of the one and only time during the century when the court actually came under physical attack.

This was in February 1554, at the time of Sir Thomas Wyatt's rebellion, and early in Elizabeth's reign, Edward Underhill, one of the Gentlemen at Arms who had been present, wrote a vivid account of the incident.[31] When the first alarm was raised, on 3 February, the court was at Whitehall, and the Gentlemen Pensioners were mustered to watch through the night. Underhill, who was known to be a Protestant, was discharged as unreliable.

> . . . so departed I into the Hall, where our men were appointed to watch. I took my men with me, and a link, and went my ways . . .

He lived in London, and had considerable difficulty gaining admission to the city at that hour of the night, and with the rebel forces just across the river in Southwark. How many men he had with him is not stated, but apparently no more than two or three, because it was not the size of his company which caused the difficulties over his admission to London. On 6th February, when Wyatt had crossed the river and was advancing on the city, the summons was repeated, and on this occasion Underhill 'watched' with the rest. The Pensioners were again stationed in the Hall:

> Old Sir John Gage (the Lord Chamberlain) was appointed without the utter gate, with some of his Guard, and his servants and others with him. The rest of the Guard were in the Great Court, the gate standing open. Sir Richard Southwell had charge of the back sides, as the Wood Yard and that way, with 500 men.

However, the morale of the Guard was not good, many of them having been involved in the Duke of Norfolk's humilating defeat by the rebels a fortnight earlier,[32] and when a contingent of the Kentishmen under Thomas Cobham advanced on the court from Westminster, there was panic. Gage's men fled back into the courtyard, knocking him over in the rush, and shut the gate, whereupon

> By means of this great hurly burly . . . the guard that were in the Court made as great haste in at the Hall door; and would have come into the Hall amongst us,

which we would not suffer. They then went thronging towards the Water Gate, the kitchens, and those ways . . .

By this time, the courtyard was empty, and the Gentlemen Pensioners emerged determined to 'go upon' the queen's enemies; the gates were opened, and they sallied forth, only to discover that the rebels, having fired a volley of arrows at the gate, had retreated. When the Gentlemen had 'marched up and down the space of an hour', news arrived that Wyatt had surrendered, and all that remained was for them to be paraded in the queen's presence, and thanked for their gallantry. In spite of his involvement, Underhill was a somewhat unsympathetic and sardonic observer. Nevertheless, it seems clear that, even given reasonable warning, the royal household was in no condition to defend its sovereign against a determined attack. The entire household and Chamber staff were mustered on this occasion—a fact which Underhill does not make clear—and were issued with arms. It was presumably these servants whom Sir Richard Southwell was leading. Five years later the armoury was still trying to locate and recover the equipment which it had issued,[33] but whether this was the result of negligence, or of some unrecorded decision to leave the household in a state of armed preparedness, is not certain.

As Underhill's experience indicates, the appearance of religious differences within the court created an additional problem. Neither Mary nor Philip would entertain Chamber servants whom they did not consider to be sufficiently Catholic, but no serious attempt was made to purge either the Pensioners, the Guard, or the household below stairs, on such grounds. Indeed, as Underhill later testified, there was no better place to 'shift the Easter time', i.e. avoid taking the sacrament, than Queen Mary's court.[34] There were audible murmurings of discontent among the Yeomen of the Guard when Mary insisted upon celebrating a requiem mass for her brother, and although the overwhelming majority, like Underhill, placed loyalty to the queen above their religious sympathies, there was a degree of risk from the occasional Protestant enthusiast, just as there was under Elizabeth from the occasional committed recusant. William Oldenhall, Yeoman of the Guard, was committed to the Marshalsea in 1557, indicted for treasonable words against the queen, and subsequently died in prison.[35] Edward Lewkenor, one of the Groom Porters, was executed for involvement in the Dudley conspiracy in 1556, and there was a shadowy assassination plot against both Philip and Mary in November 1554, but the distrust was probably more tangible than any actual danger which resulted from these divisions.

Every royal servant, from the members of the Privy Council to the Grooms of the Scullery, swore an appropriate oath of loyalty to the sovereign, and Mary also exacted a second set of oaths to Philip as king. The form of words varied to some extent with the office—Councillors, household officers and Gentlemen Pensioners being specifically bound to reveal and denounce any treason or other practice against the monarch, while lesser servants were merely required to discharge their proper functions faithfully and diligently. All alike, however, were required to swear

> ... I shall be retained to no manner of persons or persons else of what degree or condition soever he be, by oath, livery badge, promise or otherwise, but only to his Grace without his special licence ...[36]

Multiple allegiance, which had been such a confusing characteristic of the bastard feudalism of the fifteenth century, was most rigorously excluded from the *Domus Regis*. Although in practice most Chamber and household servants had their own contacts and 'affinities', and many followed the fortunes of their greater colleagues, in principle the king was a jealous and exclusive master, as he was bound to be for his own protection. Loyalty and obedience, which the Tudors urged so persistently and effectively upon their subjects at large, had to begin—and to be seen to begin—at home. There was more than a physical risk to the monarch involved if treason and disaffection began to show its head within the household.

All kinds of indiscipline within the court reflected upon the sovereign's honour, whether or not there was any personal hazard involved; and it was not only aristocratic touchiness which produced disorders. Young gentlemen were as prone to fits of destructive high spirits in the sixteenth century as they were in Victorian Oxford. The escapade of Carew, Bryan and others, when they

> ... roade disguysed through Paris, throwyng Egges, stones and other foolishe trifles at the people

was not isolated.[37] Twenty years later the Earl of Surrey and his cronies did much the same thing in London, and there were many other incidents, usually resulting in brief spells of imprisonment or house arrest. Equally revealing is cap. 30 of the Eltham Ordinances, forbidding the 'Despoile of pleasures and commodities in noblemen's and gentlemen's houses'

> ... because it is often and in a manner dayly seene, that as well in the King's owne houses, as in the places of other noblemen and gentlemen, where the King's Grace doth fortune to lye or come unto, not onely lockes of doors, tables, formes, cupboards, tressels, and other ymplements of household, be carried purloyned and taken away, by such servants and others as be lodged in the same houses and places; but also suche pleasures and commodities as they have about their houses, that is to saye deer, fish, orchards, hay, corne, grasse, pasture and other store belonging to the same noblemen and gentlemen, or to others dwelling neere abouts, is by ravine taken, despoiled, wasted and spent ... to the King's greate dishonour ...[38]

Wolsey may have been oversensitive, but this long and highly specific ordinance suggests a problem of some seriousness. It was not so much that courtiers were thieves, but that they were destructive hooligans, who were treated with too much indulgence by their seniors. Perhaps it required a plebeian like Wolsey, who stood outside that aristocratic culture, to set it out in such a stark and unflattering light; because in spite of the carefully veiled language, menial servants did not treat noblemen's goods in such a cavalier fashion—they were too vulnerable to instant retribution. If undisciplined high spirits produced disorders at one end of the social spectrum, over-crowded and uncomfortable living quarters did the same at the other end, and too ready a supply of beer and wine contributed to both. It must also be remembered that the resident household was overwhelmingly young and male. Many older servants and officials lived in London or round about with their families, and only resided when the court moved out of range of their homes. There were few married quarters, except for the most favoured and distinguished, and few female servants, except for the queen's Privy Chamber.[39] Consequently there was a steady trade for the prostitutes of Westminster, and fights over women were of very frequent occurrence below stairs. The official reaction was simply one of rather half-hearted prohibition: the Knight Marshal was given instructions to exclude 'all such unthrift and common woeman as follow the court'; but one enterprising courtier suggested (perhaps not seriously) that he should be given a patent for procuring such services! It seems unlikely that his monopoly would have been respected.

On the whole doors were not locked; when it mattered they were guarded by servants, but cash, jewellery and weapons did tend to be kept under lock and key. There were even occasional robberies which must have been 'inside jobs', as when £600 disappeared from Edward VI's Privy Chamber. The court had its own locksmiths, and in the case of specific offices, the keys were clearly held by the appropriate officers. In the case of the monarch's private apartments—and presumably the consort's also—the room doors were fitted with locks, but how many keys there normally were, and who held them, is a matter for conjecture. In the time of both Henry VII and Henry VIII the Groom of the Stool held a set, but others may well have been issued at the king's discretion. In December 1557, when the court moved to Greenwich for Christmas, the Vice-Chamberlain, Sir Henry Bedingfield, noted that single keys to the queen's 'house', presumably the Privy apartments, had been issued to Susan Clarencius, Lord Hastings (the Lord Chamberlain), himself, Cardinal Pole, and Juan de Figueroa, Philip's personal envoy. He does not seem to have regarded this as in any way unusual, and it may well represent normal practice, but there is very little other evidence to go on. The Tudors did not often lock themselves away, and privacy was a rare luxury, not much sought after. Considering the openness of their lives, the crowded, turbulent, and often insanitary conditions which surrounded them, and the frequent unpopularity of their particular policies—to say nothing of what befell their fellow monarchs elsewhere—the English may perhaps be forgiven for believing that their rulers enjoyed a special dispensation of providence.

Sports, entertainments and pastimes

The court was the natural context of *homo ludens*, and the distinction between mere casual pastime and the serious business of magnificence was not always very clear. Music and dancing, or the antics of clowns, tumblers and jesters could be of either kind, according to the occasion, and much depended upon the role, or participation of the sovereign. There were, however, many amusements which were essentially informal and non-dramatic, and contributed only very indirectly to the royal image. One of the commonest of these was gambling—at dice, cards, or 'tables' (backgammon). All the Tudors were keen gamblers; even the frugal Henry VII drew regular sums of 60 or 100 shillings to finance his play, and Henry VIII appears to have lost upwards of £100 a year, mostly to the Gentlemen of his Privy Chamber.[43] This picture is a little deceptive, because only losses or advances were entered in the surviving accounts. We have no means of knowing how much the king won, so it does not follow that he was unlucky or unskilful; however, since individual stakes normally seem to have been small, it does follow that he played a lot. Mary had solaced an unhappy youth in the same way, and her accounts between 1536 and 1544 show her spending anything from 12/6 to 40/- a month.[44] The habit continued after her accession, and Sir William Petre, one of her Principal Secretaries, was taken by surprise in 1554 when he was suddenly required to play at 'passdice' with her. He had to borrow 13/4 from one of the Grooms of the Privy Chamber.[45] The young Edward was not encouraged to indulge himself in this fashion and was, as we have seen, kept short of pocket money. He would probably have learned the more familiar card games as a part of his general education, and may (like the six year old John Petre) have played for stakes of a few pennies, but if so nobody troubled to record the fact.

Elizabeth's courtiers were heavy gamblers, and there are a few references to her own participation, but the one surviving set of Privy Purse expenses is uninformative on the subject. All courtiers, by the nature of their occupation, had time on their hands, and gaming was one method of whiling it away. Even busy royal servants could be kept hanging about in ante-chambers for hours on end, and it must have been on such an occasion in 1553 that Sir William Petre lost 7/6 to the Earl of Arundel. Since Petre habitually played for very low stakes, they must have been at it for a long time. Petre's steward was unusually meticulous in recording these small sums, and they give us a valuable glimpse of one of the minor hazards of royal service. There was no regular pattern to Petre's gambling, which must have depended upon the vagaries of the queen's convenience. On one occasion he lost 4/- to Susan Clarencius, who must have been deputed to keep him amused.[46]

In spite of (or perhaps because of) the fact that it was so popular and fashionable, gambling attracted severe criticism from the moral reformers. Even Wolsey, who was not noticeably strait-laced, tried to introduce a measure of restraint. Chapter 65 of the Eltham Ordinances allowed that 'for some pastimes in the said (Privy) Chamber, in the absence of his Grace' the servants might 'use honest and moderate play', but condemned the 'immoderate and continuall play of dice, cards or tables' which was apparently going on even in the king's presence, and distracting his attendants from their duties.[47] The early Protestants were particularly censorious, and Edward Underhill— known as the 'Hot Gospeller'—recalled how, in Edward VI's court, there had been 'shifters and dicers' such as Ralph Bagnall and Miles Partidge, adding sanctimoniously

> With such companions I was conversant a while; until I fell to reading and following the preachers . . .[48]

In fact gambling was a part of that 'low moral tone' which had exposed the courts of Europe to charges of corruption and depravity time out of mind, and still produced literary attacks, such as Antonio de Guevara's *Menosprecio de Corte* (translated into English by Sir Francis Bryan in 1548) and Lorenzo Ducci's *Arte Aulica* (translated by Edward Blount in 1607). In England, gambling was actually prohibited to the lower orders by a statute of 1541, which was ostensibly designed to arrest the decline of archery practice, and presentations were occasionally made to the Justices of the Peace well into Elizabeth's reign.[49] Within the court, dicing and cards were at least as common below stairs as they were above, and seldom attracted attention unless a fight resulted.

Both cards and dice were also employed as adjuncts to the game of courtly love, for the purpose of telling fortunes, along the lines of 'he loves me . . . he loves me not'. So also was chess, which was always a popular pastime in its own right, and Froissart's *Chronicle* contains a long description of the game so used.[50] A king, being entertained in the house of a noble lady, plays chess with his hostess, delicately endeavouring to persuade her to wager her favour on the outcome. When he fails, he has equal difficulty in persuading her to accept the ring which was his own wager—the lady's deference and courtesy in subtle conflict with her unwillingness to be compromised. The imagery of chess was a frequent literary device, the queen being used as the symbol of the dominant mistress, but how much the game was actually played in the Tudor court is very difficult to ascertain. Henry VII on one occasion lost 13/4 in this way, and in 1539 Henry VIII paid 'John the hardewarman' for new boards and pieces,[51] but explicit references are infrequent. The commonest of all indoor games was courtly love itself, which embraced a whole range of activities, from formal courtesy and innocent banter to serious intrigue. On St Valentine's Eve (13th February) the ladies of the household chose their gallants— apparently on the basis of a lottery, since in 1537 the Lady Mary chose Thomas Cromwell! Apart from the joke, and perhaps some formal escort duties, the main substance of this convention lay in the present which the Valentine was supposed to make to his lady. On the occasion quoted, Cromwell's cost him £15.[52] This game was played with enthusiasm in the

Petre household, and again the Steward's careful accounts enable us to see gold trinkets and lengths of cloth being given as presents. On one occasion Sir William was 'drawn' by one of his own maids, who received an extra quarter's wages instead of a present. In the more august surroundings of the court, it seems unlikely that anyone outside the charmed circle of the Privy Chamber would have participated with the royal family. Earlier generations had played 'Ragman Roll', in which written divinations of a lover's fortune were drawn at random—rather like a modern game of consequences—but I have not found any references to its being played at the Tudor court. Games like battledore and shuttlecock, or blindman's buff, which have survived as children's amusements, were played by adults in the sixteenth century, again with allegorical meanings in terms of courtly love. However, fortune telling of this kind could be a hazardous business; and, if the king had a roving eye, could easily assume political overtones, as Sir Thomas Wyatt found to his cost. Also the advent of Protestant divines, with their sharp noses for 'superstitions' of all kinds, made the whole practice controversial, and ultimately unacceptable.

There was more to courtly love, however, than telling fortunes or exchanging courtesies on particular occasions. A lady expected to be woo'd, to see her gallant wear her favour in the lists, and to receive his homage in poetry and song. Henry VIII's formidable career as a jouster did not outlast his first marriage, and he always wore Catherine's favour down to his retirement in 1525. He also composed skilful little love songs for her, like his Christmas adaptation of the 'Holly and the Ivy':

> As the holy grouth grene
> And never chaungeth hew,
> So I am, ever hath bene,
> Unto my lady trew.[53]

Such verses and songs were so much a part of what was expected of a courtier that professionals like John Skelton conducted a flourishing business in supplying the needs of those whose ardour outran their talents. By the sixteenth century it was a deeply entrenched tradition, and the new generation of 'courtly makers', such as Thomas Wyatt and Henry Howard, Earl of Surrey, who appeared in the 1530s, added little to the convention. What they did do, by the exercise of their superior skills, was to give a misleading impression of depth and sincerity to their lyrics.[54] Wyatt may have been a passionate admirer of Anne Boleyn, and Henry was certainly suspicious of him, but the poems which he addressed to her do not prove it. If anything, they indicate the contrary: 'far from her nest the lapwing cries away ...'. Unless one actually knows the identities of both parties in these lyrical exercises, it is impossible to tell whether the emotions expressed are real or conventional, because genuine lovers used the same clichés. Lord Thomas Howard, who died in prison for daring to marry the king's niece (Lady Margaret Douglas) without permission, wrote in the usual courtly vein:

> ... My love truly shal not decay
> For thretnyng nor for punyshment;
> For let them thynke and let them say ... .[55]

and sealed these commonplace words with his life. Complex, allusive imagery and sophisticated banter were equally part of what was normally a light-hearted and ephemeral assault upon the lady's susceptibilities. Nor were the ladies themselves incapable of responding in the same vein; *Much Ado about Nothing* and *Love's Labour's Lost* have brilliantly captured for posterity the cut and thrust, the wit and humour, of this courtly game at its most highly developed. Three-quarters of a century earlier many of the same character-istics had been shown by the interjections of Castiglione's Emilia Pia into the somewhat pompous orations of the courtiers of Urbino.

Beyond this verbal play, but not much beyond it, lay the more physical play of 'dalliance'; chasing games, like 'post and pillar' and 'prisoner's base', and the whole ritual of the 'morn of May'.[56] Romantic make-believe was of the essence of Maying, and in 1510 the youthful Henry VIII celebrated the first May day of his married life by bursting into his wife's bedroom disguised as Robin Hood, and accompanied by his 'merry men'

> ... all appareled in shorte cotes of Kentishe Kendal, with hodes on their heddes, and hosen of the same, every one of them, his bowe and arroes, and a sworde and bucklar, like out lawes... whereof the Queene the ladies and al other there were abashed, as well for the straunge sight, as also for their sodain commyng, and after certayn daunces and pastime made, thei departed...[57]

As we shall see, 'disguising' was one of Henry's favourite pleasures, and this adaptation of it seems to have been unexpected, but dressing up and 'pastime' were essential parts of the Maying tradition. Usually an early morning expedition into the woods or fields to gather flowers and green branches to bedeck the house was the start of the 'observance'. The whole ritual was basically a fertility rite, and at the village level was often explicitly physical, but, as refined by the courtly love conventions, was more an occasion for showing off fine clothes and elegant manners than for indulging in the realities of courtship. By 1515 the king's Maying had become almost a state occasion, with an archery match, an allegorical procession of Flora, and a banquet built into the celebrations. Only the dancing provided any opportunity for the ladies to participate, and it was the only form of 'dalliance' which permitted physical contact between the sexes. As in so many other aspects of the game of courtly love, art and life had grown a long way apart.

Most of the other sports and recreations which took place were open-air activities. Some of them, notably jousting, running at the ring, tilting at the quintain, and shooting with long- or cross-bow, were basically military exercises, and jousting enjoyed a unique public and ceremonial status throughout the period. These were all participation sports, in which the courtiers competed with each other, or with their guests and visitors. Castiglione's warning that men of gentle birth should not compete against their social inferiors (unless they could be absolutely sure of winning) seems on the whole to have been heeded.[58] Jousting was an exclusively aristocratic sport, and few courtiers, except Henry VIII himself, were willing to challenge the well established skills of the yeomen archers. Of the peasant sports which Castiglione listed — lifting the stone, tossing the log, and so on — only wrestling featured in the English courtly repertoire. References to courtiers themselves wrestling are not numerous, but it clearly was done because Henry was tempted to try a fall with Francis at the Field of Cloth of Gold — although his lack of success perhaps suggests that he had had little practice.[59] Other athletic exercises with which the Italians were familiar, such as running and jumping, do not appear to have been used competitively in their own right, but only as adjuncts to some of the highly energetic dances in which the men indulged.

Ball games in the modern sense, with strict rules and consistent methods of scoring, were few, and the numerous rough and ready versions of football which were played on village greens and town commons did not attract the participation of the gentry. Two ball games of widely differing kinds were played at court, however. The first was bowls, for which alleys existed at Greenwich and Hampton Court, and after 1532 at Eltham, where one was installed at a cost of £4.4.8.[60] Both Henry VII and Henry VIII played, as we know from the records of their gambling losses. In 1540 Mary lost — of all things — a breakfast in a bowling match, and it seems likely that all the members of the royal family, men and women equally, played and gambled. Bowling must have been, along with cards and dice, one of the most consistently popular of pastimes, because it could be played on an open grass space if there was no alley available. The second game was tennis, which required a specially constructed court, and which was strictly for men only. Henry VII was something of a devotee, and retained several professional players at different times, as his Privy Purse expenses make clear:

To a Spaniard, the tennis player	£4.0.0....
To the tennis player, for balls	2.0....
To the new player at tennis	£4.0.0....

and even on one occasion

To Jack Haute for the tennis play	£10.0.0....[61]

which suggests some kind of an exhibition or tournament, since Haute was also regularly paid for organising plays and disguisings. It was presumably from these professionals that the young Duke of York acquired the skill for which he later became so famous. As king he played frequently, and continued to play long after he had given up the more demanding sport of jousting. As a young man he was reckoned to be among the finest players of his generation, but in later life lost money at it, as he did at every other pastime, and after his death the game lost a good deal of its popularity. In Elizabeth's reign tennis was used by athletic young men as a method of catching the queen's attention, and sometimes as a method of settling minor debts of honour, but it does not loom very large in the annals of the court. At the same time, lawn tennis seems to have been invented for Elizabeth's amusement, and the first recorded description of the game appears in an account of an entertainment offered to the queen at Elevetham in 1591.

> The same day after dinner, about three of the cloke, ten of the Earle of Hertford's servants, as Somersetshire men, in a square greene court before her Majesties windowe, did hang up lines, squaring out the forme of a tennis-court, and making a cross line in the middle. In this square, they (being stript out of their dublets) played, five to five, with the hand-ball, at bord and cord (as they tearme it) to so great liking of her Highnes, that she graciously deyned to beholde their pastime more than an houre and a halfe.

Despite the queen's interest, as far as we know this grass court version of the older game was not taken up, and remained an occasional curiosity.[62]

Like many of the more energetic women of the court, Elizabeth seems to have chafed somewhat under the conventional restraints imposed by the supposed limitations of her sex. We are told that she secretly performed the men's steps of the galliard (which involved extremely athletic leaps) as a means of keeping fit, and she was a tireless and expert horsewoman.[63] Like her father and grandfather, but unlike Mary, whose health seldom seems to have permitted such activity, she hunted and hawked enthusiastically. It was not only the attractions of her Master of the Horse which gave her a keen interest in the management of the Stables, and she paid a farrier for her own hackneys out of the Privy Purse.[64] Unlike many women who followed the chase, Elizabeth shot as well as rode, but the absence of reported accidents suggests a much more cautious approach than Henry's—and the self-conscious development of her image must also have restrained too hearty an approach to life, at least in public.

Animals featured in a number of ways in royal amusements. Not only were deer, hares and other creatures hunted, but Henry VIII seems to have kept special bears for baiting, and there was a mysterious and gruesome sounding entertainment called 'the killcalf'.[65] This is referred to a number of times, but the most explicit description is of a payment 'to one that killed the calf behind a cloth', so whether the butchery was literal or metaphorical is not certain. On a more pleasant note the menagerie at the Tower was kept up and augmented from time to time, the Keeper of the 'Lyons and other strange beastes' being paid the substantial fee of £36.14.6 at the end of the century.[66] Pet dogs, such as spaniels, are also frequently mentioned, and were exempted from the rules in the Eltham Ordinances which forbade the bringing of other dogs within the precinct of the court. These pets were normally referred to as 'ladies' dogs', but Henry VII himself kept a number of spaniels, because on one occasion he paid compensation for a sheep which they had killed.[67] The only other pets mentioned are singing birds, which were much favoured by royal and aristocratic women. Princess Mary received several as gifts, including a white lark, which was brought to her in January 1543.[68]

Thanks to the conventions of courtly love, women played a much more positive and essential (not to say dignified) role in the life of the *Domus Regie Magnificencie* than they did in the household below stairs; and nowhere is this better exemplified than in the quintessential aristocratic sport of jousting. Although in one sense the ladies were mere spectators at these feats of arms, the elaborate chivalric and romantic trappings with which Burgundian influence had draped them by the end of the fifteenth century ensured that they were also the focal point of the pageantry and drama. An excellent example of this is provided by the sumptuous tournament of February 1511, held to celebrate the birth of Prince Henry, and hence mainly in honour of Catherine: as Hall described it.

> . . . a solempne Iustes in the honor of the Quene the kynge being one, and with him three aydes; his grace being called Cure loial, ye lorde William erle of Devonshire, called Bon voloire, Sir Thomas Knevet named Bon espoir, Sir Edward Neville called Valiaunt desire, whose names were set upon a goodly table, and the table hanged in a tree curiously wrought, and they were called Les quarter Chivalers de la forrest salvigue . . .[69]

These four challengers entered the lists in a huge pageant car, appropriately designed like a forest, and adorned with allegorical beasts and other symbols. The following day the answerers appeared, led by Sir Charles Brandon with a hermit's robes over his armour, who petitioned the queen for her leave to respond to the challenge, and after another elaborate pageant entry, the actual tilting began. In June of the following year, on the eve of the French war, an even more explicitly romantic pageant preceded a similar, if less sumptuous combat.

> . . . first came in ladies all in White and Red silke, set upon Coursers trapped in the same suite . . . after whom followed a fountain curiously made of Russett Sattin, with eight Gargilles spoutyng Water, within the Fountain sat a knight armed at all peces. After this fountain folowed a Lady all in blacke silke dropped with fine silver, on a courser trapped with the same. After followed a knight in a horse litter . . . When the Fountain came to the tilt, the ladies rode rounde aboute, and so did the Fountain and the knight within the litter. And after theim wer brought twoo goodly Coursers apareled for the Iustes: and when thei came to the Tiltes ende, the twoo knightes mounted on the twoo Coursers abidying all commers. The king was in the Fountaine and Sir Charles Brandon was in the litter. Then sodainly with great noyse of Trompettes entered Sir Thomas Knevet in a Castle of Cole blacke, and over the castel was written, The dolorous Castle, and so he and the erle of Essex, the Lorde Haward and other ran their courses, with the King and Sir Charles Brandon, and ever the king brake moste speres . . .[70]

Jousting fashions changed, and this sort of elaborate pageantry, which had first appeared in England in 1501, was much less in evidence after Henry's campaign in France. The romantic imagery remained, however, and jousts continued to be essential accompaniments to any important diplomatic or ceremonial occasion, but the withering of the king's marriage, no less than the fading of his own physical energy, removed much of the panache of the earlier years. Henry's last major tournament, at Christmas 1524, centred on the 'Castle of Loyaltie', built at Greenwich, and showed a number of *fin de siècle* touches. Henry and Charles Brandon appeared before the queen in the guise of 'twoo ancient knights', whose chivalric courage she had to awaken to overcome their age and infirmities before the joust could commence.[71] The Castle of Loyalty, a conscious echo of the *Cure loial* of 1511, was also a final flourish of Henry's devotion to Catherine—to be made sadly ironic by the events of the following decade.

Henry's flamboyant personality, and the manner in which he used tournaments to advertise himself, sometimes conceals other important aspects of the sport. Henry VII, who, as far as we know, never participated himself, patronised and encouraged jousting as an outlet for the warlike energies of his younger nobles.[72] The most successful competitors also formed an informal elite within the court, rather like the cricket XI in a Victorian public school, and both military and political careers could be based on such success. Charles Brandon, Duke of Suffolk, is perhaps the most conspicuous example; another—and one post-dating the king's own heyday—is John Dudley, Viscount Lisle and Earl of Warwick. One of the reasons for this was that jousting was an international sport, and the honour of England, no less than that of the king, required creditable performances when ambassadors were to be entertained or dynastic marriages celebrated. The paradox of fighting each other in sport in order to encourage mutual understanding and goodwill was no greater in the sixteenth century than in the twentieth, and if emulation sometimes overcame good intentions, it could be forgotten in the banquetting and disguising which followed. While Philip was in England, during the winter of 1554/5, he organised a series of tournaments and other games in an effort to break down the animosity and distrust between the two nations.[73] His first attempt, in November 1554, was an almost total failure, because he chose the purely Spanish *juego de canas*, in which about eighty expensively attired gentlemen fought each other with sticks. The English spectators ridiculed the whole display, and even the king's own advisers admitted that it had been a mistake.[74] However, a month later he tried again, this time using a traditional style of combat, in which the participants fought on foot across a low barrier, and this seems to have been much more favourably received, partly because the king himself took part. In January 1555 a fully fledged joust followed, probably the first for some considerable time, and the list of defenders was headed by Ambrose and Robert Dudley, who only days earlier had been released from the Tower, where they had been expiating their role in their father's abortive *coup* of 1553. Not only was this an important gesture of reconciliation by Philip towards the English aristocracy, it also marked the beginning of the recovery of Dudley fortunes.[75] Apart from another foot tournament at Lord FitzWalter's wedding in March 1555, when the challenge was shared by Sir George Howard and a Spanish knight, there were few further opportunities to shine in this manner during Mary's reign. All the three surviving Dudley brothers served in Philip's St Quentin campaign of 1557, and Henry was killed, but there is no further record of their participating in jousts. The tournament of January 1555 is all the more remarkable because the Dudley brothers were in no sense members of the court, and were never *personae grata* with Mary. Indeed, she seems to have played no part in any of these conciliatory sports, and in such records as survive there is a marked absence of any romantic or chivalric overtones.

As Master of the Horse to the new queen, Dudley was admirably placed after 1558 to bring English jousting back to its former splendour, but if he had any such intention, he does not appear to have been particularly successful. It has recently been suggested that the book of rules and forms of jousting, which is now MS 6 at the College of Arms, and which contains the Spanish challenge of 1554, was written in Dudley's interest, as a part of the self-promotion in which he was vigorously engaged in 1559 and 1560. This may be so; the MS certainly contains a representation of Dudley's *impresa* shield, depicting an obelisk surrounded by a vine, and bearing the motto 'te stante virebo', which is sufficiently unsubtle to be authentic.[76] However, Dudley did not appear in the coronation tilts on 16th and 17th January 1559, nor at Greenwich in July, when the Gentlemen Pensioners were the main participants. He did joust in November 1559, but there is a marked lack of emphasis in the records, both on his achievements and upon the jousts themselves. Although the fourteenth-century rules were revived in 1562, it would be a mistake to assume that Elizabethan jousting immediately assumed that high romatic gloss which it was to achieve in the 1580s and 1590s, or that such a gloss was particularly connected with the person of Robert Dudley. The great period of the Elizabethan joust began in the early 1570s, as a part of the developing celebrations of the queen's accession day (17th November), and the Accession Day Tilts soon became the vehicle for an exotic outburst of chivalric fantasy, focusing upon the queen herself.[77] Spenser's *Faerie Queene* articulated the ideal version of the relationship between Elizabeth and her knights, through the mouth of Sir Guyon:

> She is the mighty Queen of Faerie,
> Whose fair retrait I on my shield do beare;
> She is the flowre of grace and chastitie,
> Throughout the world renowend far and neare,
> My life, my liege, my Souveraign, my deare . . .[78]

She was at once the sovereign mistress of all hearts, and the unattainable lady of the classic courtly love tradition. The tilts themselves were developed, and probably invented, by Sir Henry Lee.[79] As far as we know, Robert Dudley was never more than a spectator, since he would have been well past the jousting age by 1575, and the form which the jousts took may well not have appealed to the strict tournament etiquette of the older generation.

From 1584 onward, with the single exception of 1593, they were always held in the great Tiltyard at Westminster, and marked, as it were, the beginning of the winter season. The jousters were mainly drawn from the ranks of the Gentlemen Pensioners, although towards the end of the century some of the younger peers, such as the Earls of Cumberland, Bedford and Southampton, also took part. The jousters were selected, probably from a throng of volunteers, by the Master of the Horse and Garter King of Arms, who also paired them to produce good matches. It was then up to each participant to choose his entry theme, and stage his own entry, which could be a costly and competitive business. According to one observer, the German Lupold von Wedel, in 1584

> The combatants had their servants clad in different colours . . . Some of the servants were disguised like savages, or Irishmen, with the hair hanging down to the girdle like women, others had horses equipped like elephants, some carriages were drawn by men, others appeared to move by themselves . . . Some gentlemen had their horses with them, and mounted in full armour directly from the carriage . . .[80]

Von Wedel believed that the costs amounted to 'several thousand pounds each', but this was probably an exaggeration. Some entered in pageant cars, some on horseback; a servant of each then presented his *impresa* shield to the queen, with an oration which might be courtly and romantic or (apparently) burlesque.[81] The jousts were then run in strict accordance with the ancient rules, and the day concluded with the usual masking, and dances. It seems clear that these tilts were very much more public spectacles—the people were even charged for admission to specially constructed stands—and less courtly entertainments, then their Henrician or medieval predecessors. They also lacked the coherence of pageantry so noticeable in 1511 or 1524, when the whole show was staged, and paid for, at the king's instance. The Accession Day tilts were a traditional blend of the martial arts and courtly love, but also reflected Elizabeth's search for popular appeal and, like her progresses, belonged as much to the world of the theatre as the court.

Jousting was both a sport and an entertainment. Spectators added to the sense of occasion, but were not essential to it. Other forms of amusement or enjoyment in the court tended to fall into one or other of two categories: participatory, in which the courtiers sang, or danced, or mimed to please themselves; and performance, in which the main activity was left to professional specialists. Masks, or 'disguisings' belonged to the first category, and were extremely popular throughout the period. There were many variations of form, but the commonest was to begin with an 'entry', in which the maskers appeared, suitably clad and often mounted upon an elaborate pageant car. This was then followed by a 'presentation', in which a brief play or mime was performed, usually with some symbolic or allegorical meaning; and finally there was a general dance, or series of dances, in which the maskers and audience alike took part.[82] Each stage was accompanied by appropriate music: trumpets for the entry, singers and stringed instruments for the presentation, and tabors and rebecs for the dancing. The minstrels, unlike the other participants, were nearly always professionals, and the singers were often the Gentlemen and Children of the Chapel Royal.

The first major disguising for which a description survives is that which accompanied Prince Arthur's wedding celebrations in November 1501. On that occasion the maskers entered on cars devised like 'two marveylous mountes or mountaines', one planted with trees, shrubs and flowers, the other 'like unto a Rocke scorched and brent', but adorned with gold and other precious minerals.[83] On this barren hill sat 'xiii fresh Lordes Knights and men of honour most semely and straunge disguised', while on the other were a similar number of ladies, the two cars being joined by golden cords and chains. The presentation was purely musical, and provided by the lords and ladies themselves—the men on tabors, lutes and harps, and the women on clavi-chords, dusymer and claricimballs—at the conclusion of which they all descended and danced while the mountains were trundled away. Henry VII, as far as we know, never himself took part in these disguisings, but they were held regularly at festival seasons such as Christmas, as well as in honour of special occasions. The Privy Purse expenses record a number of payments to Jack (or Jaques) Haute for these entertainments. Haute was the Underkeeper at Kenilworth, and was probably responsible for the physical management rather than the choreography. A cost of £32.18.6 for the disguisings at Christmas 1503 does not suggest anything very lavish.[84]

Henry VIII, on the other hand, was almost as keen on masking as he was on jousting, and the two entertainments often tended to blend into one another. As we have seen, a great tournament was held to celebrate the birth of Prince Henry in 1511, and in the midst of the banquet and dance which followed, the king introduced a disguising of his own. Hall's description is worth quoting in full, because it conveys an excellent impression of the form and atmosphere of these events:

And in the midst of this pastyme, when all persones were moste attentyve to beholde the daunsing, the king was sodenly gone unknowen to the moste part of the people there . . . Within alittel while after his departing, the trompettes at the ende of the Hall began to blow. Then was there a devise or a pageant upon wheels brought in, out of which pageant issued oute a gentleman richeley appareilled, that shewed, howe in a garden of pleasure there was an arbor of golde, wherein were lordes and ladies, moche desirous to shew pleasure and pastime to the queene and ladies, if they might be licenced so to do, who was answered by the Queene, how she and all other there were very desirous to see theim and their pastime: then a great cloth of Arras that did hang before the same pageant was taken away, & the pageant brought more nere, it was curiously made and pleasaunt to beholde, it was solempne and riche, for every post or pillar thereof, was covered with frise golde, therin were trees . . . and other pleasant floures made of Satyn, damaske, silke, silver and golde ... In which arbor were vi ladies, all appareilled in whyte satyn and grene, set and embroidered full of H & K of golde ... in this garden also was the kinge and v with him appareilled in garments of purple satyn, all of cutted with H & K ... & every person had his name in like letters of massy golde. The fyrst was *Cuer loyall*, The seconde *Bone volure*, in the iii *Bone espoier*, The iiii *Valyaunt desyre*, The fyft *Bone foy*, The vi *Amoure loyall*, their hosen, capes and cotes were full of poyses & H & K ... when time was come ye saide pageant was brought forth into presence & then descended a lord & a lady by coples & then the mynstrels, which were disguised also daunced, and the lordes and ladies daunced, that it was a pleasure to beholde.[85]

The pageant thus picked up the romantic theme of the joust, with which it was clearly associated in the minds of the onlookers.

Not all Henry's efforts were on this lavish scale; sometimes disguisings were more like private charades, as when Henry and eleven of his cronies had appeared before Catherine in January 1510, in her chamber, disguised as Robin Hood and his merry men (clearly a favourite of his) with one Master Will, a page, as Maid Marion.[86] The Revels office provided the costumes and the props, and presumably made the pageant cars and other scenery. Sometimes the ideas came from the king himself, or from some member of the Privy Chamber, but the 'deviser' always seems to have been a recognised expert, who turned the ideas into action, music and (possibly) words. In the early part of Henry VIII's reign the great 'deviser' was William Cornish, Master of the Children of the Chapel Royal, and a whole series of elaborate disguisings can be attributed to him between 1510 and his death in 1523. His masterpiece, and perhaps his last effort, was the seige of 'Schatew Vert' at an entertainment provided by Wolsey for the Imperial ambassadors in 1522.[87] Imprisoned in the fortress were eight beautiful ladies with allegorical names: Beauty, Constance, Mercy, Pity, and so on; guarded by eight evil dames (Disdain, Jealously, Scorn etc.) played by the Children of the Chapel Royal. The rescuers were the king and his companions, wearing their usual *nommes de guerre*, who, after a furious exchange of fruit and baubles, duly raised the siege and led forth the imprisoned damsels (who included the king's sister Mary, and Anne Boleyn) to the dance.

Cornish was succeeded by John Rightwise, and the tradition of court entertainment continued without disruption down to the end of the decade, including a major effort in 1527 for the French ambassadors.[88] After that, however, the political climate turned sour, and the old team began to die off—Rightwise in 1532, Sir Henry Guildford in the same year, and the long-serving Yeoman of the Revels, Richard Gibson, in 1534. John Browne, the Sergeant painter who had executed many of the 'devices', also died in 1532, and John Rastell, who had written and directed a number of entertainments in the late 1520s, joined Thomas Cromwell's propaganda team.[89] There were plenty of court entertainments in later years, particularly in Elizabeth's reign, as we shall see, but they tended to be increasingly professional performances of one sort or another, and the Henrician tradition of masking and 'disguising' was not revived until the great work of Ben Jonson and Inigo Jones in the following century.

All the Tudors, with the possible exception of Edward, were musical, and not only employed large numbers of professional musicians, but also sang and played themselves, encouraging their courtiers to do the same. Henry VIII not only wrote music, but also played upon the organ, virginals, lute and recorder, performing well enough 'in company' to attract complimentary comments from Italian visitors in letters which were only intended for their recipients.[90] As a child, Mary was regarded as something of a prodigy as a virginal player, and was paraded by her proud father; in later life she continued to play frequently and well, and also practised regularly upon the lute, as her steady consumption of new strings testifies. Elizabeth also played the lute, and probably the virginals, but more surprising is the note in her Privy Purse expenses recording the provision of 'one great Sagbutte for the Queen's use' at the enormous cost of £15.0.0.[91] It is therefore safe to assume that most members of the royal family played regularly upon a variety of instruments, and it is highly unlikely that they played alone, although whether they were accompanied by their friends or by their professional servants is not very clear. As we have seen, ladies and gentlemen of the court did, on occasion, perform in public and since music was an essential part of a courtly education for both sexes, the great majority were probably quite competent. When Princess Margaret met her future husband James IV of Scotland in 1503, he 'begonne before hyr to play of the clarycordes, and after of the lute', while on another occasion, she provided the same entertainment for him.[92] From references of this kind it seems certain that 'chamber music' of an entirely amateur sort must have been a regular feature of the 'pastime' of the aristocracy, both in the court and out of it. In 1538 the Marquis of Exeter's servants included a group of half a dozen, some of gentle birth, who were specifically noted for their instrumental skills.

However, instrumental music may well have been less common in this connection than singing. As John Stevens has noted 'vocal chamber music was the real metier of the noble amateur'.[93] Part singing was a favourite recreation of Henry VIII, and he occasionally chose his Gentlemen of the Privy Chamber for the quality of their voices, and skill in this connection. A song book belonging to one of them survived into the eighteenth century, when it was transcribed; and the collection known as Henry VIII's MS consists of simple songs, straightforwardly annotated, which would have been suitable for amateur performances.[94] One of John Skelton's characters, perhaps intended to be a social climber, begged to be taught the same art:

> Wolde to God, it wolde please you some daye
> A balade boke before me to laye,
> And lerne me to singe Re-my-fa-so!
> And whan I fayle, bobbe me on the noll.[95]

Apart from Henry himself, English courtly amateurs do not appear to have been well thought of by outsiders, and a Frenchman describing Anne Boleyn's musical accomplishments in 1536 (including her singing), declared that she was so good that it was hard to believe that she was English! In spite of her known enthusiasm, Mary's brief reign has left few records of amateur music, although the restoration of full Catholic ceremonial to the Chapel Royal must have given the musical of life of the court as a whole a considerable lift.[96]

The flowering of English court music came during the long reign of Elizabeth, when the presence of such distinguished composers as Thomas Tallis and William Byrd, and skilled instrument makers like George Langdale and William Treasorer, not only reflected the keen interest of the queen, but encouraged an altogether more sophisticated level of general accomplishment. New instruments, such as the viol, began to appear, and many technical developments were adopted from France and Italy. This was a great period for household music in general, and every person of gentle birth and education was expected to be able to 'bear a part' in singing, and to accompany him (or her) self upon an appropriate instrument. From this period many song books and collections of lute and keyboard music survive. William Byrd, in dedicating one such collection of his own composition to Sir Christopher Hatton, expressed the hope that

> ... these poor Songes of mine might happily yield some sweetness, respose and recreation unto your Lordship's mind, after your daily pains and cares taken in the high affairs of the common wealth ...[97]

and in his Epistle to the Reader,

> If thou desire songs of small compass and fit for the reach of most voices; here are most in number of that sort.

There was music for all occasions, observed Francis Meres in 1598, and music subdued all hearts. As she grew older, Elizabeth seems to have played less, and she never had a very remarkable singing voice, but music and dancing remained among her favourite recreations, and all those who shared any part of her leisure time might find themselves called upon to participate.

Although the courtiers entertained themselves to some extent, in all these activities the main performances were provided, and the standards set, by professionals who were either retained on the staff of the household, or imported upon an occasional basis to meet particular needs. Edward IV kept no more than five musicians on a permanent basis, and nine others are recorded who come in 'at the five festes of the yere ...'[99] By 1502 Henry VII was paying regular wages to nine trumpeters, four sackbuts and three 'string mynstrels', while a bagpiper and a Welsh harper received 'rewards' on several occasions.[99] Many noblemen, prelates, and town corporations maintained minstrel bands at the end of the fifteenth century, and while the Duchess of York's minstrels were being rewarded for performing at court, the king's musicians might be appearing at Canterbury or New Romney. There are references to groups maintained by the queen and Prince Arthur, as well as by the king during these years. They appear to have played mainly at banquets, masques, jousts, and other ceremonial occasions, often in collaboration with the 'players of interludes', or with the Gentlemen and Children of the Chapel Royal, who formed the other half of the professional musical establishment. Concerts, in the modern sense of free-standing musical entertainments provided by groups of varied instrumentalists, do not seem to have appeared until much later.

Henry VIII built substantially upon the base which his father had created. The number of trumpeters was increased from nine to sixteen within a few months of his accession, and by the middle of his reign, upwards of fifty men and women were receiving regular wages in the household for playing a great variety of instruments: flutes, shawms, rebecs, tabarets, sackbuts, lutes and viols.[100] The King's Musik was (and was designed to be) the finest royal orchestra in Europe, and appears to have compared very favourably with that of France, where Francis I lacked Henry's keen musical appreciation. How this very large and varied group actually worked is a matter of some speculation, and probably varied with the occasion. Trumpets, pipes and tabors were much in demand at jousts, and a mixed ensemble of about half a dozen functioned as 'the minstrels of the Queen's chamber', providing not only entertainment but support and accompaniment to aristocratic vocalists and instrumentalists. Some also played outside the court, although whether on a regular or a casual basis is not clear.

Many of these instrumentalists were recruited abroad, and Henry used his minor diplomatic agents, particularly in Italy, as 'talent scouts'. His first star catch was Dionisius Memo, the organist of St Mark's, Venice, who came in 1516, bringing a large organ with him.[101] The king was hugely delighted with Memo's talent, and used him extensively to entertain and impress visitors to the court. One such recital in July 1517 lasted over four hours. At the same time Benedictus de Opitiis, another organist, from Antwerp, was appointed 'to waite opon the king in his chamber' at a salary of 33s 4d a month.[102] This was far more than the regular musicians were paid, and indicates that these imported talents often occupied a special place. Zuan Piero, another Venetian, was a favoured lute player, and there are also references to more than one harpsichordist. Attracting the services of such virtuosi was a part of the general competitiveness of European courts, and Henry soon acquired the reputation of a generous patron. Not all the foreigners enjoyed such status, of course; most of them were ordinary musicians, like the eighteen German, Italian and French minstrels who were on the establishment in 1547 at 4d a day—the same pay as the messengers.[103] Nevertheless, most of them seem to have been satisfied with their entertainment, and some families, such as the Van Wilders and the Bassanos, stayed for several generations. The select 'Chamber musicians' were never very numerous, and varied considerably in function and status. Philip Van Wilder acted as a music tutor to the royal family in the 1530s, supervised the other Chamber entertainers, including Mark Smeaton the virginal player, and looked after all the king's musical instruments; but he did not occupy an established post, and no one replaced him.[104] As the appearance of Smeaton in this context indicates, not all the favoured musicians were foreigners, and there were also social duties attached to entertaining the royal family which might have political implications—and even disastrous consequences.

By 1552 the musical establishment of the court numbered sixty-three, including two instrument makers, but excluding the Gentlemen and Children of the Chapel Royal. Their wages varied from £40 a year for the Sergeant Trumpeter to £18 5s for undifferentiated 'mynstrells', and the annual bill amounted to some £1908.[105] The economies of Mary's and Elizabeth's reigns reduced these numbers somewhat, removing two harpers, one flautist and twelve general minstrels. By 1593 the cost was down to about £1100,[106] a large saving in real terms brought about partly by the fact that none of the wages had been increased. Elizabeth's known interest in music, and her patronage of such distinguished composers as Christopher Tye, Thomas Tallis and William Byrd, did not induce in her a generosity on the scale of her father or brother. Nevertheless, every entertainment offered to the queen required its appropriate accompaniment, and when the Earl of Hertford received his royal mistress at Elvetham in 1591, he almost certainly borrowed the queen's own musicians to provide the

> ... exquisite consort; wherein was the lute, bandora, base violl, citterne treble violl and flute

which 'so delighted her Majestie that shee commaunded to hear it ... three times over'.[107] The King's (or Queen's) Musik provided well regarded, and well paid, employment at a time when there were few other opportunities for professional musicians. Noble households still supported small groups, but the 'town waits' of an earlier generation disappeared as the advance of the reformation removed so many of the occasions for their services. The Musik also provided one of the very few chances for suitably talented women to earn an independent livelihood. They never formed more than a small minority of the minstrels, and are hard to identify as individuals—for example the woman sackbut player who, with her colleagues, presented a New Year gift to Mary in 1557 is simply called 'Mary'[108]—but they formed the only significant group of women at court, apart from the ladies of the Privy Chamber.

Another type of professional entertainer much in evidence at court was the 'player', or presenter of interludes. In a few weeks in 1502 rewards were given to 'Four players of Essex', the 'French players', 'my lord of Northumberland's players' and 'the king's players'.[109] Over thirty years later the pattern was much the same. Between February 1537 and February 1538 seven different groups performed, bearing the names of the king, the queen, the Lord Chamberlain, the Lord Chancellor, the Duke of Suffolk, the Marquis of Exeter, and the Lord Warden of the Cinq Ports.[110] The King's Players, and possibly the Queen's also, were regular household servants, who appeared in the Ordinary as yeomen servants of the Chamber, and who performed normal duties when their acting services were not required. The others probably belonged to the households of the lords whose names they bore, although the connection may have been one of livery and protection rather than regular service. The plays which these groups performed seem to have been specially written or adapted English dramas, such as Henry Medwell's *Fulgens and Lucres* or John Heywood's *The Pardonere and the Frere*—sometimes moralising, sometimes comic. Medwell modelled his drama on an Italian original, the *De vera nobilitate* of Bonaccorso of Pistoia; it was a tale of love and civic virtue in the high days of the Roman republic, and was a reflection of that humanist influence which was already becoming significant at court before 1509.[111] Medwell was not a member of the royal household, being a chaplain of Cardinal Morton's, but his plays seem to have been performed on a number of occasions, and to have shown an advanced level of technical development. Heywood was the court's resident dramatist, being employed primarily as a singing man, but his salary of £5 a quarter provided recognition of his additional duties, and some indication of the regard in which he was held. William Cornish who, as we have seen, devised many masques, does not appear to have been a dramatist in the same sense.

During the 1520s, contemporary political comment began to filter into drama. Sometimes it was disguised as ancient history, as in John Rastell's *Four Elements*, and sometimes as an old-fashioned morality play, as in Skelton's *Magnyfycence*. Wolsey was usually the target, and it is therefore unlikely that such plays were performed at court until 1529. At the same time, the Cardinal made his own use of drama, commissioning plays (which were performed at court) in 1527 to celebrate the alliance with France and the triumph of the church over heresy. The latter was performed in Latin by 'clarkes'— presumably of the Chapel Royal—and is described at some length in the Revels accounts.[112] Such a play, in which appearances were made by 'the heretyke Lewtar lyke a party frer in rosset damaske and blake taffata (and) Lewtars wif lyke a frowe of spyers . . .' was rather too overt to be classed as ordinary entertainment. A more subtle approach was tried in the following year, when an orthodox performance of Terence's *Phormio* by the children of St Paul's was followed by a brief 'interlude' of political allegory.[113] Children were much appreciated as entertainers, and frequently rewarded; sometimes, as on this occasion, being specially imported; at other times the choristers of the chapel were used, both for orthodox drama and for allegorical presentations at jousts and feasts.

In the 1530s Thomas Cromwell was an active patron of polemical drama outside the court, and some of the plays which were performed before the king were explicitly anti-papal, but extreme caution was necessary in this connection. Conservative churchmen were deeply (and justifiably) suspicious of 'players of interludes', and the kind of anti-clerical ribaldry which flourished in inn courtyards and the homes of sympathetic gentlemen could not be tolerated at Westminster or Greenwich. By 1552 there were eight 'players' on the household list, but the fact that they were paid only £3 6s 8d a year each suggests that they were still part-timers.[114] This establishment remained unchanged through the reigns of Mary and Elizabeth, and was unaffected by the queen's decision in 1583 to grant her patronage and title to a professional company performing in the public theatres, which by then were beginning to appear. Performances at court by professional companies of plays which had been written for a normal commercial market was quite normal by the early part of Elizabeth's reign. Specially commissioned plays were probably becoming less common by then, quite possibly because the court could no longer compete with the standards being set outside. John Heywood, Nicholas Udall and William Baldwin were the favourite presenters during the middle years of the century, Heywood having narrowly escaped execution for treason in 1544—allegedly because the king had such a high regard for him as an entertainer.[115] Udall's *Ralph Roister Doister* was specifically written to try and revive the ailing Edward VI in 1552, and, despite his Protestant sympathies, his plays continued to be in demand at court under Mary. *Respublica*, a celebration of her accession—though not of her Catholicism—was probably performed there in 1554. In September 1556 William Baldwin wrote to Sir Thomas Cawarden, the Master of the Revels, offering him an idiosyncratic play called 'love and lyfe' in which all the characters' names began with 'l'— as 'Leonard Lustyguts, an Epicure', 'Syr lewes lewdlyfe, a chaplayn', etc. Since it needed a cast of over sixty, and was 'iii howres long', it was probably never performed.[116]

By the reign of Henry VIII the Master of the Revels was in charge of all court entertainments, and his original subordination to the Great Wardrobe had been replaced by virtual independence. The Revels department not only manufactured and stored (out of court), the props, costumes and scenery,[117] but also provided the funds for hiring additional help, and ultimately vetted the suitability of what was on offer. Apart from plays, masques and jousts, this also included the occasional incursion of a Lord of Misrule, whose function was effectively that of a carnival king.[118] Normally associated with Christmas and twelfth night, these 'lords' kept state with a train of followers, who might include heralds, magicians, 'cardinals' and burlesque characters. George Ferrer's expenses as Lord of Misrule at Christmas 1551 amounted to £299, and his own 'sute of carnacyon satten all over striped with silver . . .' alone cost 40s 10d.[119] This was exceptional, and in the latter part of Mary's reign, with reduced activity, the Revels office was costing between £200 and £250 a year, exclusive of fees. Casual entertainments may well have escaped the Revels office and certainly do not appear in its accounts: the dancing girls and jugglers to whom Henry VII paid many rewards, the acrobats and wire walkers who so delighted Edward VI, and the owners of enterprising hounds or monkeys, which showed off their tricks. Finally, there were those resident comedians whose presence we have already noted, but whose status was highly uncertain—the jesters. Patch, Will Somers and Jane the Fool spanned over half a century between them, but their activities can be glimpsed only occasionally. Somers performed in the masques and plays of Christmas 1551,[120] but his normal role seems to have been more private, and after his retirement Elizabeth discontinued the tradition. The last Tudor, who loved music and plays, to say nothing of jousts and pageants, seems to have lacked the 'music hall' tastes of her predecessors, and the entertainments of her court must have presented a striking contrast to those of her grandfather in that respect.

Scholarship and education

Unlike the princes and *signori* of Renaissance Italy, the monarchs of northern Europe in the fifteenth century made little attempt to attract distinguished scholars to their courts. The household of Lorenzo de' Medici included not only Politian, one of the greatest classical linguists of his generation, but also the rhetorician Christoforo Landino, and the neo-Platonist philosopher Marsilio Ficino.[121] Ficino had at one time been Lorenzo's tutor, but he remained a member of the court after that appointment came to an end, and the principal service which each of these scholars performed for their patron was to gratify his intellect and enhance his reputation by publishing the fruits of their scholarship. By contrast, the courtiers of the Dukes of Burgundy, who were by no means unlettered or indifferent to education, produced mainly chronicles, romances, and manuals of aristocratic courtesy. Jean de Wavrin's *Anciennes Chroniques d'Angleterre* and Guillebert de Lannoy's *L'Instruction d'un jeune prince* may be taken as typical of their output.[122]

The main reason for this contrast was not a lack of communication, but the absence from the north of any tradition of secular scholarship. Ecclesiastical scholars had not been lacking in the courts of the fourteenth century, but their energies had waned notably after about 1420, and they were contributing little to the intellectual life of the laity by the later decades. Both Henry V and Henry VI of England had been interested in contemporary theology, but the scholarly tastes of the latter had achieved nothing to commend themselves to his supplanter, and Edward never showed any sensitivity to intellectual pursuits. His court included noblemen like John Tiptoft, Earl of Worcester, and Anthony, Earl Rivers, who were interested in Italian humanism and proficient in classical Latin, but their presence owed nothing to those accomplishments. As we have seen a number of the senior clergy were similarly skilled, and were considerable benefactors of education; but none of this touched the king, except very indirectly. He collected books and fine manuscripts, probably in conscious imitation of Philip the Good, and patronised William Caxton's press in its early days; but the description of him by the Croyland Chronicler as 'a most loving encourager of wise and learned men' is little more than flattery.[123]

Edward's own education had not been neglected, but, like that of most young aristocrats, it had concentrated upon skill in arms and social graces. In 1454, when he was about twelve, he had written to his father from Ludlow

> Plaese hit your hieghnesse to witte that we have attended our lernyng syth we come heder . . .[124]

As king, his skill in French was frequently commented upon, and he probably had a basic knowledge of Latin in its traditional form. This was also the type of education which he provided within his own household. The Master of the

Henchmen, who was the most prestigious of the three tutors listed in the *Liber Niger*, was required to

> ... show the scoolez of urbanitie and nourture of Inglond, to lern them to ride clenly and surely, to drawe them also to justes, to lerne hem were theyre harneys; to have all curtesy in wordez, dedes and degrees.[125]

The master of grammer taught not only the Henchmen and the Children of the Chapel, but also anyone else, child or adult 'disposed to lern in this science'. However, his brief also reveals that only a very limited kind of technical instruction was on offer

> ... in poetica atque regulis positionis gramaticae expeditum fore quibus audientium animos cum diligentia instruet ac informet.[126]

This was very much the kind of curriculum against which later humanist teachers were to revolt, and was clearly not designed to stimulate a serious interest in classical scholarship. The third tutor was the master of song, whose duties were confined to the Chapel, of which he was expected to be a member. Not very much is known about the education which Edward provided for his own sons, and they did not survive to show the benefits of it, but it seems probable that it was entirely conventional, and that Edward V, had he lived, would have been vastly more interested in Froissart or Commynes than in Tacitus or Livy—let alone Origen or Plotinus. The culture in which he grew up, and in which his mother was at least as influential as his father, was predominantly French in inspiration, and took what Italian works it did receive at second hand through French translations.

In spite of the troubled years during which he grew up, Henry Tudor's education does not seem to have been very different from that which Richard, Duke of York, had provided for the young Edward IV. He was already fourteen, and his formal schooling would have been virtually completed, when his uncle Jasper removed him to Brittany in 1471. Before that, his most formative years, from 1461 to 1469, had been spent in the household of William, Lord Herbert, where he was 'well and honourably educated in all kind of civility brought up', along with Herbert's own children.[127] Although he passed the whole of his childhood in Wales, and as an infant had a Welsh nurse, it is not certain that he ever learned Welsh. The Herberts, and most of their upper servants, were English speaking, and French was the language of courtesy and chivalry. Given the interest which the Welsh bards took, both in the Herberts and in the young Henry, he must have acquired some familiarity with their work, and consequently some understanding of the Welsh language, but it was not sufficient to survive the years of exile, or to make any appearance after his accession.[128] Many years later, in a judicious and probably candid assessment of Henry VII's character, Polydore Vergil described him as 'not devoid of scholarship', which would have meant rather more than at first appears because Vergil, writing after Henry VIII's accession, had high standards in such matters and would not have regarded a conventional grounding in Latin grammar as 'scholarship' at all.[129] However, such evidence as there is for Henry's intellectual tastes is sparse and circumstantial. The fact that he appointed an Italian, Pietro Carmeliano, as his Latin secretary in 1495 is a small straw in the wind. Bernard Andre, his Poet Laureate and a tutor to Prince Henry, was also a scholar, although scarcely in the humanist mould; and Henry's other tutor, John Skelton, was an original and eccentric character who wrote books of 'courtesy' in the Burgundian tradition. When Erasmus visited Henry's court in 1499, in the company of Thomas More, he made polite comments about a number of things, but the flourishing state of humanist learning was not among them.[130] The prevailing cultural influence was, as we have seen, Burgundian; and that meant that total ignorance of letters was regarded as a disgrace, while a knowledge of the works of Cicero and Julius Caesar provided useful support to the established skills of knighthood. This was not, however, what Petrarch had understood by good learning, as his question 'where do we learn that Cicero or Scipio jousted?' makes plain.

Henry VII's courtiers, like their Burgundian prototypes, took their classical literature in translation, and copies of Jean du Chesne's *Les Commentaires de Caesar*, Pierre Bersuire's *Livy, Lucane, Suetoine et Saluste en françois*, and Simon de Hesdin's version of Valerius Maximum among the Royal MSS now in the British Library indicate that the king did the same.[131] Nevertheless, somebody made the future Henry VIII into a competent Latinist, good enough, indeed, to provoke the surprised and somewhat sceptical Erasmus into considered praise soon after his accession. Perhaps it was Bernard Andre who claimed to have enjoyed a similar success with Prince Arthur, or perhaps William Hone, about whom little is known beyond his name and the fact that he was for a time tutor to the Duke of York. Skelton is the most likely candidate, and was probably the ablest of the three tutors, but there is no clear evidence, and like many things about Henry VIII's upbringing, it will probably remain a mystery. A few years ago, in his authoritative study of the king, Professor Scarisbrick suggested that his grandmother, Margaret Beaufort, might have been responsible for organising his education, and that Skelton and Hone could have been imported from Cambridge on the advice of her friend and adviser, John Fisher.[132] Both Margaret and Fisher were considerable patrons of education outside the court, and Fisher was deeply interested in humanist scholarship. If he was involved in any way with Henry's upbringing it would certainly help to explain why the young prince developed academic skills and interests which his father had never shown, but there is not enough evidence to be sure. There were, of course, distinguished humanist scholars in England by 1500—men such as Linacre and Colet—and well-regarded patrons like Lord Mountjoy, so Henry VII's court was not setting any kind of pace in the promotion of learning. This was quite in keeping with English tradition, and with the kind of chivalric magnificence which Henry was so concerned to promote; but it was becoming old-fashioned by the time he died because the French invasion of Italy, and the subsequent upsurge of Italian influence in France, had begun to set new standards of intellectual ambition. If Henry VIII wanted to compete on the European stage, a library full of French romances and translations of the classics would no longer be adequate for the purpose.

This European dimension has to be constantly borne in mind, because, whereas Henry VII had adopted an essentially defensive attitude to the outside world, and concentrated his ambitions at home, his son immediately took up a more extrovert stance, and was quite intelligent enough to perceive what was expected of him. In this he was also greatly assisted by his marriage. Catherine had been carefully educated by her mother, Isabella of Castile, who had, understandably, not paid much attention to contemporary views about the inferiority of women. Her taste for books was quickly appreciated, and when she was feeling homesick, shortly after her arrival in England, Henry VII

> ... curtesly lete desyre and call unto him the Princes and her ladies, wt dyvers ladies of Englond, and brough them to a lybary of his, wherein he shewed unto her many goodly plesaunt boks of werks full delitful, sage, merry and also right cunning, bothe in Laten and in Englesse.[133]

She was a skilled Latinist in the humanist tradition, probably better than Henry, widely read in theology and history, and fluent in Italian and French as well as her native Spanish.[134] Henry's relations with his queen in the early days of their marriage were close and affectionate, and it is not surprising that the young man who aspired to be *uomo universale* should have become aware of the relative provincialism of his own upbringing. He wished, he told Lord Mountjoy, that he was more learned, thus gladdening the heart of Erasmus's friend, and awakening the expectations of his wide circle of humanist correspondents. There are a few signs that Henry took this personal aspiration seriously. In 1519 he made a short-lived attempt to learn Greek under the tuition of Richard Croke, and made some progress in Spanish and Italian, probably instructed by Catherine herself.[135] His interest in theology was genuine, and his attainment remarkable for a monarch who was not noted for his powers of diligent application. He was also 'well seen' in mathematics, astronomy and cosmography. However, it would not be wise to exaggerate Henry's intellectual accomplishments; he had a retentive memory, was quick witted, and conceited. A desire to impress was always uppermost in his mind, and he succeeded because so many of those with whom he was dealing were willing—indeed anxious—to be impressed. He could not compete with his brother-in-law James IV of Scotland, who spoke six languages in addition to Latin, but James played in the 'second division', and in any case was killed in 1513. By comparison with most European monarchs, and particularly with his arch-rival Francis I of France, Henry's personal learning stood up pretty well, and that was what mattered to him.

It was, however, less than half the battle. Patronage was a far more important field of competition, and the main incentive to personal learning for a monarch of the renaissance was to acquire honour as a discriminating and well-informed patron. Here, too, Henry did well, particularly after 1514, with the capable assistance of Thomas Wolsey—himself a man more noted for patronage than for his own scholarship. Writing to a friend in 1519 Erasmus declared

> Learning would triumph had we such a prince at home (in the Low Countries) as England hath . . . He openly shows himself a patron of good letters. He silenceth all brawling contenders. All studies are restored for the better by the Cardinal of York; and by his kindness to many, inviteth every body to the love of studies . . . And even the king's court abounds with greater numbers of the learned than any university . . .[136]

In fact Erasmus's enthusiasm was only partly justified. John Colet, perhaps the leading English humanist of his generation, certainly enjoyed royal favour, gaining the preferment of the Deanery of St Paul's and encouragement to found his celebrated school; but he was not a member of the court. Nor was Richard Pace, who spent most of his time on diplomatic missions; and Thomas More was a valued but occasional visitor rather than a regular courtier. The two men who did establish the humanist presence at court in the early years of the reign were Thomas Linacre and William Blount, Lord Mountjoy. Linacre, who had made a brief appearance in Prince Arthur's household in 1501, was appointed as a royal physician shortly after Henry's accession, and was subsequently tutor to Princess Mary, born in 1516.[137] Lord Mountjoy, who, as we have already seen, was a well known and well connected patron of scholarship, became Catherine's Chamberlain in 1509, and subsequently married one of her Spanish maids of honour, Iñez de Venegas.[138] Henry's attitude was more than a little schizophrenic, because although he aspired to scholarship, and even more to the applause of the influential humanist connection, fundamentally he had little sympathy with their pacifist and enlightened ideals. The new style of education produced skilful diplomats, whose ability to exchange Latin epigrams and notes on Greek syntax with sophisticated Italians advanced the king's business; it produced good civil servants, and learned and pious churchmen. However, it also produced contempt for the traditional chivalric and warlike *mores* which Henry continued to accept and uphold to the end of his life. No one who could describe the *Morte d'Arthur* as 'open manslaughter and bold bawdry' could ever earn the king's unequivocal approval.

Consequently Henry's reputation as a patron always owed more to Wolsey and to Catherine than was openly acknowledged. It was she who first encouraged her countryman Juan Luis Vives, while he was living in obscurity in Bruges, and caused him to dedicate his *Commentaries upon St. Augustine* to the king in 1522. The following year Wolsey appointed him to lecture at his new college in Oxford, and Catherine engaged him to tutor the seven year old Mary.[139] For the next five years he was a regular visitor to the court, and wrote his influential *De institutio Christiana feminae* for Mary's guidance, prescribing a biblical and classical education of great strictness. Meanwhile, Henry had given hostages to fortune by writing the *Assertio Septem Sacramentorum* against Luther. How much of this modest tract was actually the king's work is less important than the fact that he wanted to claim the credit for it. Both its theology and its Latinity fell short of the highest standards, but it served its purpose—enhancing his reputation for literacy, and also earning him the coveted title of *Fidei Defensor*, which he had failed to win with his sword a decade earlier.[140] In 1525 Mary was despatched to Ludlow, and although her schooling continued, it made little impact upon the remainder of the court; as the political skies darkened during the later 1520s, learning assumed a new and more sombre role. Scholars were mobilised and pressurised by both sides over the king's 'Great Matter', and fine points of theology or canon law became the raw material of an increasingly fierce and purposeful polemic. The peaceful world of humanist scholarship—already beginning to be troubled by the implications of Luther's challenge—was further disrupted by conflicts of political philosophy.

The main issues of the 'Great Matter' lie outside the scope of this study, but for the first time the court in the 1530s began to be a prey to ideological conflicts, and the intellectual interests of the courtiers influenced their political alignments. This was not a question of humanists versus scholastics; under the intense pressure, the humanists split—older men such as Fisher and More siding with Catherine, and younger men such as Stephen Gardiner and Richard Morrison with the king.[141] The catalyst in the complex chemistry of these years was Thomas Cromwell, not a scholar himself, but a man with a keen appreciation of the value of intellectual skills. Under his management a party of the 'new learning' emerged, at court, in the universities, and eventually in the political nation at large.

Characterised by men like Thomas Cranmer and Thomas Starkey, the 'new learning' was dedicated to reform in church and state.[142] It was not Protestant at this stage, seeking rather to promote a simplified, scriptural piety, not very different from that advocated by Erasmus in his younger days. Placing their faith in the royal supremacy, these writers and preachers advocated the diversion of ecclesiastical resources into education, the promotion of the vernacular bible, and an energetic programme of social legislation. Their first major patron at court was Anne Boleyn, who not only drew the king's attention to such radical works as William Tyndale's *Obedience of a Christian Man*, but also drew scholars like Cranmer from the universities into the royal service. From the beginning the 'new learning' was compromised by its association with religious radicalism, towards which the king continued to be implacably hostile, with the result that much of its most constructive writing concentrated on secular themes, and its protagonists were also sometimes known as the 'commonwealth men'. After Anne Boleyn's fall they continued to be patronised by the family of his next queen, Jane Seymour, and, of course, by Cromwell. Most of the authors and translators who worked in this interest were not themselves members of the court, although Richard Taverner, who translated a number of humanist works from Latin into

English, was a clerk of the Privy Seal. The only active scholar who could be described as a courtier was Henry Parker, Lord Morley. Morley had begun his career in the circle of Catherine of Aragon, and continued to be friendly towards Mary, but he also enjoyed good relations with Cromwell, and seems to have struggled vainly to preserve the disintegrating humanist consensus.[143] In 1539 he sent Cromwell his own translations of Machiavelli's *Prince* and *History of Florence*, as well as presenting the king with a whole series of treatises rendered into English from the Latin of Plutarch, Lapo Birago and Donatus Acciaiuoli.[144] Altogether seven of his works were eventually dedicated to Mary, and their orthodox piety became more pronounced as the years passed. By the time he died in 1556 he was clearly in the conservative camp of Gardiner and Pole.

The fall of Thomas Cromwell in 1540 sent the more radical scholars of the 'new learning' scurrying for cover, and signalled a sharp attempt to apply the brakes to religious change. It did not, however, reverse the underlying tendency of the previous decade towards reforming humanism in the culture of the court. In 1539, when Cromwell and Cranmer were working together to establish new cathedral chapters furnished with Readers in Divinity, Greek and Hebrew, and new royal foundations were taking shape in both universities, they also set up a *domus scholarum* for the young Prince Edward.[145] This was a project very close to the king's heart, and he kept a vigilant eye on it, which may help to explain why it was unaffected by the 'reaction' of 1540–43. The Chamberlain was Sir William Sidney, a cousin of the Duke of Suffolk, the Vice-Chamberlain Sir Richard Page, and the Lady Mistress Margaret Bryan, sister of Lord Berners and wife of Sir Thomas Bryan. The Almoner was Dr Richard Coxe, imported from Cambridge.[146] Since the prince was less than two years old when this establishment was created, it did not at first have any educational function, but the views of its members, insofar as we know them, might be described in the modern idiom as 'broad left'—in other words sympathetic to the 'new learning', but not exposed to charges of either radicalism or heresy. In 1544, when Edward's serious education began, conservative influence was on the wane, and the king's last marriage, to Catherine Parr, had brought to prominence another court family in the Boleyn/Seymour tradition. It now appears that Catherine's influence upon the young prince's upbringing was much less decisive than used to be supposed,[147] and that she was a follower rather than a leader of intellectual fashion. Nevertheless, her commitment to the 'new learning' is well attested by the sequence of her own pietistic writings: *Prayers styrring the mynd*, *Prayers or medytacions*, and above all *The lamentacion of a sinner*. Nicholas Udal, whom we have already noted as an author of entertainments for the court, in 1548 dedicated to Catherine his translation of Erasmus's Paraphrases on the Gospel of St. John, and his preface is an illuminating comment upon the queen and her circle.

When I consider, most gracious Quene Katerine, the great noumber of noble weomen in this our time and countreye of England, not onelye geuen to the studie of humaine sciences and of straunge tongues, but also so throughlye experte in holy scriptures, that they are hable to compare wyth the beste wryters as well in endictynge and pennynge of godlye and fruitfull treatises to the enstruccion and edifynges of whole realmes in the knowledge of god, as also in translating good bokes oute of Latine or Greek into Englishe . . . I cannot but thynke and esteem the famous learned Antquitee . . . ferre behynde these tymes . . .[148]

However, none of this would have been possible without the king's active connivance, as the fate of several conservative plots against both the queen and Cranmer during these years makes plain. If anyone was exercising a decisive influence over Henry during these years, it was certainly not Catherine, as she was the first to acknowledge.[149]

Consequently, although it corresponded very happily with her activities, and may have taken account of her views, the provision for Edward's academic training which began to be made in 1544 was the king's work and not the queen's. Richard Coxe was advanced from Almoner to Dean, and with that title became the prince's chief tutor.[150] At the same time another outstanding humanist scholar, John Cheke, was brought in from Cambridge as his assistant, to be supplemented within a year by William Grindal, described as 'the best Grecian among them'. By 1545, therefore, for the first time a distinguished group of professional scholars was resident within the court on a regular basis, not as royal secretaries or councillors but as pedagogues. Their responsibility embraced not only Edward himself but that small, aristocratic nursery school which was built up round him, in the usual manner of the time. Similar provision had been made in the early 1520s for Mary, and also for Henry Fitzroy later Duke of Richmond— although not at court.[151] The identity of some of the young prince's companions is well attested: Henry Brandon (Duke of Suffolk on the death of his father in 1545), Barnaby Fitzpatrick (a cousin of the Earl of Ormonde), Henry, Lord Hastings, and Robert Dudley. There were about fourteen of them in all, enough to be a demanding class, and the names of most are little more than guesswork, but they may well have included Lord Thomas Howard, the son of the Earl of Surrey, Lord Lumley and Lord Mountjoy.[152] It is not even certain that all were boys, because there is a persistent tradition that Lady Jane Grey, the ill-fated daughter of the Marquis of Dorset, also shared the prince's lessons. The regimen imposed upon these children, the oldest of whom cannot have been more than seven or eight, was strict, and very much in the tradition of Vives and Erasmus. An up-to-date Latin grammar, based on William Lily's authorised text, seems to have been especially prepared, and this was followed by substantial doses of Cato and Aesop.[153] Scripture was also read, and the official catechisms learned; but there is not a shred of direct evidence that Edward and his companions were taught any explicitly Protestant doctrine until after Henry VIII's death. The view that he was given a Protestant schooling, while understandable in the light of what was to happen after his accession, cannot be substantiated. Nor can it be proved that any of his tutors, with the possible exception of Jean Belmain, had actually embraced such doctrine before 1547. Belmain was his French tutor, but did not take up his duties until October 1546. Coxe was an enlightened teacher, who did his best to make learning a game, and the curriculum was enlivened with music, dancing and fencing, but Edward's precocity may well have been exaggerated by his anxious mentors. Not only did they wish to enhance their own reputations, but over the whole operation hung the looming cloud of Henry's waning health. In a sense the prince's education was a race against time.

The king's own intellectual tastes in the last years of his life remain something of an enigma. That he considered himself to be a competent judge of theological disputes, and the ultimate arbiter of orthodoxy, is clear. He appears to have remained loyal to the traditional doctrine of trans-substantiation, and the sacrifice of the mass. On the other hand, his sympathy with the 'new learning' is amply attested, not only by the arrangements for Edward's education, but also by his willingness to receive the dedications of such works as Cheke's *Homilies on Chrysostom,* and Sir Anthony Cooke's translation of St Cyprian—offered as a corrective to 'superstition'.[154] In the last months of his life particularly, he was surrounded by men and women of this persuasion, highly educated and deeply committed to humanist values: Catherine herself, Catherine Willoughby, Duchess of Suffolk, Sir Anthony Denny, Sir Anthony Cooke, Thomas Cranmer, the Earl and Countess of Hertford, and many others. It was something of a cultural *coup d'etat,* and, as we shall see, had profound political significance.[155] By the latter part of 1546 Henry was no longer in control, and was only fitfully aware of what was going on, but long before he had reached that state he had made a deliberate decision to commit the future to the 'new learning'.

Edward's formal education continued until the summer of 1551, when he was approaching fourteen. By then his personal commitment to Protestant doctrine, his facility in Latin and French, and his basic knowledge of Greek, had all been attested by his own writings. According to some observers who had no need or desire to flatter him, he was also well seen in some more secular disciplines, particularly mathematics and cosmography, and was beginning to take an active and intelligent interest in affairs of state.[156] The decision to bring the *domus scholarum* to an end must have been taken by John Dudley, Duke of Northumberland and Lord President of the Council, who was Regent in all but name, and is consistent with his known desire to involve the young king more directly in the processes of government. Northumberland was primarily a soldier , and was much less sympathetic to intellectuals and their values than had been Lord Protector Somerset, whom he had overthrown in the autumn of 1549. Consequently, although the king's Protestant zeal continued to inflict many sermons on his courtiers, and royal patronage was generously extended to the numerous continental divines who came to England in the wake of the Imperial interim, the court itself became less and less a centre of learning. Even the cautious Cranmer did not conceal his dissatisfaction and disquiet that education benefited so little from the dissolution of the chantries, and the subsequent commission for church goods. Others, such as Hooper and Knox, were more outspoken.[157] By 1553 Northumberland was at loggerheads with his ecclesiastical allies, and conducting a regime the priorities of which were openly secular and philistine. The triumph of the 'new learning' had rapidly turned sour—or perhaps, more accurately, its sour, iconoclastic side had come out on top—because the desire for reform, and particularly for simpler and more scriptural worship, had already wrought havoc with England's artistic and literary heritage. Henry VIII, despite his conservatism and patronage of learning, had taken no initiative to preserve the monastic libraries, and had shown only a passing interest in the activities of the antiquarian John Leland, whose efforts eventually salvaged something from the wreckage.[158] Leland was far better appreciated by his fellow scholar, the radical Protestant John Bale, who was not a humanist. The bleak Erastianism in which Edward VI's reign ended was an ironic comment on the hopes which Coxe and Cheke had raised in the royal schoolroom.

After 1551 there were no more royal tutors, and consequently no academic establishment within the court, apart from the succession of Masters who taught grammar to the Children of the Chapel. Mary was no enemy to scholarship, whatever her Protestant critics might think, but she had no personal commitment to it either, and her priorities were elsewhere. As befitted the daughter of Catherine of Aragon, and a pupil of Vives, she had wrestled dutifully and competently with humanist Latin, but her surviving Privy Purse expenses indicate that the only books which she bought, and used regularly, were liturgical.[159] During the 1530s she had understandably acquired an acute distaste for the 'new learning', and conservative humanists, such as Morley, later dedicated their works to her, in the hope that her patronage might revive the tradition of Linacre and More. It was not to be; even the great collected edition of More's works, which William Rastell published during her reign, attracted no support from the queen.[160] Somewhat ironically, her own piety seems to have been very much in the tradition of More, and of Richard Whitford, the monk of Syon, who had published a number of pious works in the Erasmian vein during the 1540s. Mary was a respectable patron of education, encouraging her courtiers and bishops to establish schools and colleges, but had she fulfilled her ambition to restore all monastic property to the church, a great many of her father's and brother's educational foundations would have disappeared.

Some notable scholars came to England with King Philip, but for a number of reasons they kept a low profile, and their influence is hard to assess. Alonso a Castro and Bartolomé Carranza were both at court, and Carranza remained behind when Philip departed in August 1555.[161] However, there is no sign that the presence of these distinguished Spaniards made either Mary or her court more aware of contemporary Catholic scholarship in the rest of Europe, and Mary made no attempt upon her own initiative to attract into her service men who could have remedied the insularity of her own subjects. In other respects the queen seems to have preferred foreign advisers, but in theology her protégés were almost entirely English. One reason for this was probably the early influence of Stephen Gardiner, who was keenly aware of the xenophobic streak in his fellow countrymen, and anxious to make the restored Catholic church appear as English as possible.[162] Another was the disillusionment of Cardinal Reginald Pole with controversial theology altogether. Pole was a man with a distinguished record as a patron of humanism, although never more than an indifferent scholar himself. However, with the triumph of the *Zelanti* at the Council of Trent, even conservative Erasmianism began to be looked upon as heretical, and Pope Paul IV used Pole's humanist past as an excuse to launch charges of heresy against him.[163] Consequently, although he worked hard to combat the influence of the 'new learning' in the universities, and helped to bring on a younger generation of Catholic scholars, Pole never established a scholarly circle in his own household in England, as he had done in Viterbo. Nor did it occur to any observer, however sympathetic, to compare Mary's court to the house of the muses. In one very important respect the English did benefit from Spanish learning during this period: in 1558 the English mariner and cosmographer Stephen Borough was allowed to visit the *Casa de Contratacion* in Seville, and he returned with Martin Cortes' *Breve Compendio*, which Richard Eden translated into English and published in 1561.[164] This achievement owed much to Philip, but nothing at all to Mary, who, unlike all the other rulers of her family, seems to have shown no interest in navigation, ship building, or any other art of the sea.

Elizabeth had, of course, been very much closer in age to Edward than to Mary, and this was reflected in the nature of her education. After a somewhat chequered infancy, at the age of about eleven or twelve she was placed under the tutorship of Roger Ascham, at the same time as her brother was being taught by Coxe and Cheke.[165] She was probably rather too old to have shared any of Edward's lessons, but the regimen, and the spirit which informed it, was very much the same. By the age of thirteen she was proficient in Italian and Greek, as well as Latin and French, and had presented the king and queen with a number of her own translations: the *Mirrour of a Sinfull Soul* from French into English; *Prayer or Medytacions* from English into Latin, French and Italian; and the *Dialogus fidei* from Latin into French.[166] Unlike many of her brother's schoolfellows, she was an apt and diligent pupil, and absorbed all the aspects of the 'new learning' with enthusiasm and commitment. After Edward's accession she continued her studies under Ascham, Jean Belmain, and Baptiste Castiglione, probably until she was put in possession of a substantial independent estate in the early part of 1550.[167] Katherine Ashley, who had acted as her surrogate mother from an early age, continued in her household, and probably exercised a stronger personal influence than any of her tutors. Ascham's return to his studies in Cambridge in 1550 marked the end of any kind of regular schooling. By then the princess was seventeen, an important figure in her brother's court and, like him, a committed Protestant. From 1553 to 1558 Elizabeth studied the arts of survival, and mastered them with her customary efficiency. She visited her sister's court only when invited—or summoned—and played little or no part in its social or intellectual life. Mary disliked and distrusted her for a number of reasons—not least because, in spite of her professions of religious conformity, she personified the 'new learning', and the prospect of her succession signalled the triumphant return of its banished professors.

Contrary to what is sometimes thought, there was nothing very new or adventurous about Elizabeth's choice of servants and advisers in the winter of 1558/9. She got rid of all her sister's confidants, but the men and women who took their places were either her Boleyn and Howard kinsfolk, or they were experienced Edwardian councillors and civil servants, such as Sir William Cecil and Sir Francis Knollys. Just as her religious settlement was based on the Edwardian church of about 1550, so her courtiers shared her commitment to the 'new learning', without the radical and philistine tinge which that had acquired between 1550 and 1553. It was, as Professor MacCaffrey has pointed out, an exceptionally intellectual and well educated regime.[168] It was also exclusively lay. Elizabeth's bishops and archbishops, although men of learning and probity, were not admitted to her inner councils, and were not among her favourite companions. The anti-clericalism which had lurked beneath the surface of the 'new learning', even when most of its active practitioners were themselves clergy, became institutionalised after 1559. Elizabeth's personal piety remained very much where her tutors had left it. She still composed Latin prayers, and elegant meditations in Italian after her accession;[169] but she had little taste for theology, and the courtly humanism which she encouraged became increasingly secular and poetic. Elizabeth seems to have made no particular efforts to attract scholars to her court, because she had no direct use for them. Her bishops and university clergy wrote anti-Catholic polemic, some of it extremely learned, encouraged and patronised by Cecil and Walsingham, but the queen did her best to keep religious controversy away from the court. Not only did she wish to be free to use conservative servants and to entertain Catholic ambassadors, but she remembered the alarms and stresses of the days of Catherine Parr. On the other hand the younger generation of courtiers who grew up in Elizabeth's household—men like Philip Sidney and Francis Bacon, were expected to show an intellectual gloss and accomplishment which would have astounded their grandfathers. Elizabeth was also the only Tudor to share wholeheartedly the humanist horror of war and warlike displays. As we have seen, humanist values sat uneasily upon Henry VIII, with his natural bellicosity and love of Burgundian chivalry. Not so Elizabeth. As a woman she naturally had no desire to be a knight-errant, but unlike Isabella of Castile, she had no desire to be a crusader either. The knights who jousted before her were closer to the world of the *Faerie Queen* than they were to the real battlefields of the 1580s.[170]

Partly because of this pervasive climate of renaissance humanism, it is not very easy to pin down Elizabeth's role as a patron. She kept scholars at the universities, as her father and grandfather had done,[171] and maintained the Readerships which her father had founded, but she was not a major patron of formal education. She received the dedications of many works in all branches of learning, and gave the cartographer Christopher Saxton an official status and commission. But most of the scholarly and scientific work of the period, like most of the poetry, drama and music, came about without her direct encouragement or participation. On the other hand, it was her courtiers, nobles and officials who provided the effective patronage, and they knew that such activity was expected of them, not only by their clients but also by the queen. For example, Archbishop Matthew Parker, in patronising historians and antiquaries, was deliberately building up the historical defence of the English reformation, and justifying the royal supremacy.[172] Robert Dudley, Earl of Leicester (a man whose failure to master the classics aroused the despair of Roger Ascham), was a keen student of mathematics, and the patron of Dr John Dee, whose *General and Rare Memorials Pertaining to the Perfect art of Navigation*, published in 1577, enlisted both cosmography and astronomy in the service of Eliza Triumphans.[173] Elizabeth's court deserved, far more than did that of Henry VIII upon which it was bestowed, the accolade of Erasmus. Lord Burleigh, in caring for his wards, transformed the out of court education of the English nobility, and helped to send the sons of the gentry flocking to the universities by the end of the century.

> Alasse, you will be ungentle gentlemen, if you bee no schollers; you will do your prince but simple service, you will stand your countrie but in slender stead, you will bring yourselves but to small preferment, if you bee no schollers

wrote an author in 1586, expressing what by then was conventional wisdom.[174] How Ascham and Pace—to say nothing of Erasmus—would have been cheered by this advance of *litterae humaniores*!

> ... noble men borne
> To lerne they have scorne,
> But hunt and blowe an horne,
> Lepe over lakes and dykes
> Set nothyng by polytykes ...

John Skelton had written early in the century,[175] and as we have seen, Henry VIII had not been averse to jumping dykes. However, in bringing up his younger children in the 'new learning', he had shifted the balance decisively in favour of academic training, and the cultivated court of Elizabeth was the result.

Artists and others

Like so many other things in the early Tudor court, the arts of limning came from Burgundy, and were imported by Henry VII, firstly in connection with the establishment of his library in 1498, and secondly to service the building of Richmond palace from 1498 to 1501. Edward IV had employed a court painter, a certain John Serle, but little is known of his work, and he may well have been principally an illuminator of manuscripts.[176] If so, he was not a patch on the men from the Ghent-Bruges school who followed Quentin Poulet to England after his appointment as royal librarian. A sudden improvement in the quality of illumination accompanied their arrival, and some of their work, such as the illustrations to Bernard Andres' *Grace entiere sur le fait du gouvernement d'un prince*, is as fine as anything produced in their school of origin.[177] They do not, however, appear to have been capable of working on a large scale—or perhaps it never occurred to the king to ask them—because when ambassadors arrived from Spain in 1496 to negotiate the *Magnus Intercursus*, Henry found himself in an unexpected embarrassment. The ambassadors brought with them full-sized portraits of Philip the Fair and Juanna of Castile, and the king was unable to reciprocate. Henry's response was to engage the services of that 'Meynnart' whose work we have already had occasion to notice. He it was who produced the portrait sequence at Richmond in 1501, and the wedding portraits for Margaret and James IV of Scotland in the following year. In 1503 he became 'King's Painter', and retained that position down to the end of the reign.[178] Thereafter, although no longer retained in royal service, he is known to have collaborated with Torrigiano on Henry VII's tomb, and to have painted the memorial portrait of Margaret Beaufort in about 1512.[179] Henry employed a number of other craftsmen, such as Piers Enghein the tapissier, who was a Fleming, and the anonymous French plaster worker to whom he gave 40/- in reward, establishing on a small scale those royal workshops which his son was to expand and develop.[180]

The most important of these continued to be the *atelier* of illuminators established at Richmond, and managed after 1509 by a second Flemish librarian, Giles Duwes. The advent of printing had not reduced the demand for fine manuscripts at this level, but humanist influences had affected their style, and it was again from the Low Countries—this time from Brabant— that a suitably skilled scribe named Peter Meghen was imported to bring the others up to date.[181] In 1517 Henry VIII opened a new workshop by bringing in a Dutch glasier called Gaylon Hone, and establishing him in Southwark with the title of 'King's Glasier'. It was Hone who a few years later produced the windows for the royal pavilion at the Field of Cloth of Gold, which attracted universal admiration.[182]

However, Henry's major patronage *coup* in this area came in 1525, when Duwes persuaded virtually the whole Horenbout family to leave the service of

Margaret of Austria, the Regent of the Netherlands, and join the Tudor court. Gerard Horenbout, the head of the family, was a famous illuminator, and the most distinguished living member of the Bruges-Ghent school. His son Lucas and daughter Susanna were almost equally talented, and each was an established, independent artist. Gerard's initial salary was £20 a year—a gentleman's income in 1525—and in 1528 Lucas was promoted to be King's Painter with the princely remuneration of £66.13.4d.[183] The Horenbouts transformed the artistic horizons of the Tudor court. Although basically illuminators, they could turn their hands to many kinds of work, and virtually invented the portait miniature. In the words of Sir Roy Strong

> They were artist-craftsmen who could paint panel portraits, design and often make jewels and plate, execute designs for tapestries and stained glass, supervise the decor and costumes for court fêtes, provide drawings for engravers or illuminate official documents.[184]

It is possible that Cardinal Wolsey, who was himself a considerable patron of artists and scuptors, had some hand in the importation of the Horenbouts, but more likely that the initiative came from the king, because Henry was acutely sensitive to the achievements of Francis I of France, and seized this opportunity to steal a march on his rival in an area where neither court was particularly distinguished in the early 1520s.

Jean Clouet was beginning his celebrated career at about the same time, and in 1526 Madame d'Alençon, Francis's sister, sent to Henry a pair of jewelled lockets containing miniatures which may well have been by him. These were much admired, and Strong suggests that Henry immediately called upon Lucas Horenbout, who was known to be accomplished in the same field, to portray himself and his queen in the same manner.[185] Several miniatures by Horenbout survive from the period, and this interpretation may well be correct, but the evidence is circumstantial, and Horenbout may equally have painted some of them before the arrival of the French challenge. Lucas was the dominant member of the family. Gerard remained primarily an illuminator, and some superb work is attributed to him, but he disappears from the records in 1532, and may well have died about then. Lucas and Susanna continued to run the family workshop, producing not only miniatures and manuscript illuminations, but full-size portraits, woodcut illustrations, and designs for seals, furniture and jewellery. Lucas's miniatures, of which about two dozen survive, were the most notable products of the workshop in artistic terms, and set a courtly fashion which was to continue beyond the end of the century. He died in 1544, but the workshop may have continued longer, because the date of Susanna's death is not known, and as late as 1547 a payment was recorded to 'Lucas wyfe for makynge of the Queens pycture & the Kynges ... 40/-'.[186] Whether this means that Horenbout's widow continued to paint royal portraits after his death, or whether it was the settlement of a long outstanding debt, is not certain.

Although the Horenbouts were the first to be established, they were by no means the only artists working in and around the court in the latter part of Henry's reign. There were the Sergeant Painters, who did mostly what we would now call 'interior decorating', although much routine illuminating work on plea rolls and other official documents also came their way. There was the so-called 'Cast shadow master', who executed a number of historical portraits;[187] and there was Hans Holbein the younger. Holbein had been born in Augsburg in about 1498, and trained in the workshop of his father. He visited Italy and France, and had worked in both Lucerne and Basle before arriving in Antwerp in 1526. There, probably through the Flemish artist Quentin Metsys, he established contact with the humanist circle, and in December of the same year arrived in London bearing a letter of introduction from Erasmus to Sir Thomas More. He stayed for about eighteen months, during which time he executed portraits of Archbishop Warham, Sir Henry Guildford, and other courtiers, including the famous group of the More family, now lost; but he does not appear to have received any commissions from the king. In 1532, alienated by the iconoclasm of the reformation in Basle, which had destroyed many of his earlier religious paintings, he returned to England and set up his workshop in London. At first he worked mainly for his fellow countrymen in the Steelyard, decorating their banqueting hall, and designing the elaborate allegorical arch which they contributed to the coronation entry of Anne Boleyn in May 1533.[188] It may well have been the possibilities suggested by this which brought him to the attention of Henry's master of propaganda, Thomas Cromwell. Familiarity with the More circle was certainly no passport to court favour by this time, but Holbein began to receive royal and court commissions, and was soon in receipt of an annuity of £30. This was generous, but less than half what Lucas Horenbout was getting at the same time, and helps to account for the fact that Holbein continued to do a great deal more private work than the Flemish master. In spite of this, it was Holbein who created the enduring image of Henry VIII, in the great wall paintings at Whitehall which we have already noticed, and who designed most of the masking and pageant scenery which played such an important part in projecting the king's magnificence.

Holbein was at least the equal of Clouet as a portraitist—which Horenbout was not—and it is for his portraits of Henry's courtiers that he is particularly remembered (see plate 22). His services were eagerly sought, for in this respect the English court had hitherto been backward, and gentlemen like Sir Thomas Elyot, who had travelled to France and Italy, were anxious to take this opportunity to get abreast of European fashion.[189] Two or three sittings were probably necessary to produce the lifelike drawings of which so many survive, and it is unlikely that any of his non-royal subjects would have sat before. When he died suddenly of the plague in 1543, Holbein left behind a great many unfulfilled commissions, and the books of drawings which represented them were acquired on behalf of King Edward VI for £6 by his Master of the Revels, Sir Thomas Cawarden.[190] He appears to have learned the art of painting miniatures from Lucas Horenbout, and surpassed his teacher in skill, as the exquisite respresentations of Henry and Charles Brandon demonstrate (see plate 24). Fourteen of Holbein's miniatures now survive, but there is no means of knowing what proportion of his output that represents. The deaths of Horenbout and Holbein within less than a year left the English court for some time without the regular services of a first class artist, but not without a considerable amount of artistic activity. A highly skilled group of foreign craftsmen were employed almost full time at Nonsuch from about 1541 until the end of the reign: Nicholas Bellin of Modena, who had worked with Primaticcio at Fontainebleau, Bartolomeo Penni, and above all Antonio Toto.[191] While working at Nonsuch they were part of the king's Works rather than the court, but they were by no means merely artificers. Penni was a portrait painter of some skill, and Toto, who had come to England in 1511 with Torrigiano, became Sergeant Painter in 1543 and executed several wall paintings at Hampton Court. There were also some lesser English artists who received occasional royal commissions, such as John Shute and John Bettes, who seem to have done their best to fill the gap left by Holbein, and to have painted a number of courtiers and their wives.

It was to be many years, however, before another painter of Holbein's stature held a court appointment in England. His direct successor, in so far as he had one, was another product of the Ghent-Bruges school. Levina Teerlinc (or Terling) was the daughter of Simon Benninck, a contemporary of Lucas Horenbout, who had also been his equal in skill and reputation. She came to England in 1546 with her husband, a certain George Teerlinc, probably by invitation, since they both seem to have entered the royal service at once.[192] George became a Gentleman Pensioner, and Levina painted on occasional court commissions, such as that which earned her the large sum of £10 in 1551 for a portrait of Princess Elizabeth.[193] Her fortunes were much improved by the accession of Mary, who appointed her to an unspecified post in the Privy Chamber with an annuity of £40.[194] Since this was more than the Ladies of the Privy Chamber received, and Levina does not appear in any of the regular Privy Chamber lists, she was presumably in fact, if not in name, the queen's official painter. She presented her mistress with specimens of her work as New Year gifts, but little of it now survives, and Sir Roy Strong had considerable difficulty in assembling even a putative *corpus*.[195] Perhaps because she was a gentlewoman and had other duties of a social nature around the palace, her output was small. It was certainly not very distinguished by comparison with either Horenbout or Holbein (see plate 19), so presumably she had other qualities which commended her to two successive queens, because Elizabeth retained her in post, explicitly as *pictrix dominae reginae*, until her death in 1576. In spite of the uncertain ascription and poor quality of much of her painting, Levina Teerlinc occupies an important 'link' position in the history of court painting, because she learned her art in the same school which had trained Horenbout, and transmitted that style to a younger generation of miniaturists in England—notably to Nicholas Hilliard.[196]

If Levina Teerlinc should be considered Holbein's successor, then the formal successor to Lucas Horenbout was William Scrots, poached from the Regent of the Netherlands like Gerard Horenbout twenty years earlier, and paid, like Lucas, at the high rate of £62 10s a year. Although his appointment dated from 1545, it is mainly as court painter to Edward VI that he is remembered, and most of his surviving portraits represent the king.[197] He was an accomplished artist in the latest continental style, and the fact that he left England on Mary's accession suggests that he may have had some sympathy with the reformation. Several other artists were active in England during these years, and painted occasional portraits of statesmen and ecclesiastics— Gerlach Flicke, the German who executed the best known likeness of Cranmer, is a case in point—but they had no official connections with the court, and did not receive royal commissions. Mary seems to have patronised only one portrait painter apart from Levina Teerlinc—Hans Eworth, whom Strong describes as 'virtually' her court painter.[198] He painted the queen several times, and probably a number of her courtiers as well, although most of his surviving work is of a later period. As we have seen, Mary made no attempt to create a dramatic image for herself, and the contrast between Eworth's best known portrait, that of 1554 (see plate 27), and the later iconography of Elizabeth, is instructive. Antonio Moro, who also painted Mary in 1554, came to England with Philip, and although he received rewards from Mary he did not stay, and is not known to have executed any other work here at that time. Eworth did not secure Elizabeth's favour, and received no more royal commissions, although whether on aesthetic or religious grounds is not clear. The fact that his later clientele consisted mainly of the conservative nobility points in the direction of the latter.[199]

It took Elizabeth some time to appreciate the value of visual propaganda, and although her attack of smallpox in 1562 made her sensitive on the subject of her appearance, the official portrait promised in 1563 was never commissioned. Four years later the Earl of Sussex was apologising to Margaret of Parma for his inability to produce a satisfactory likeness of his mistress; and such portraits of the queen as survive from that period confirm his judgement.[200] Without a first-class artist in regular employment, it was impossible to control the royal image, and it was only after 1572 that this problem began to be solved. Typically, however, Elizabeth made no clear-cut decision. The man who was later described as her 'normal' portrait painter during the 1570s was the rising and brilliant young miniaturist, Nicholas Hilliard, but Hilliard held no court post, and was actually in France from 1576 to 1579.[201] The Sergeant Painter appointed in 1572, William Herne, was no more than a decorator, and when Levina Teerlinc died in 1576 after a long period of inactivity, she was not replaced. The queen's policy, if she had one, was hand to mouth. After his return from France, Hilliard did much of the diverse art-work which, fifty years earlier, had been done by the atelier of the Horenbouts, but he was commissioned and paid piecemeal, thus having neither the standing nor the financial security of a royal painter. It was not until 1599, when his work was flagging and old-fashioned, that he was finally employed on a regular basis—

and then at £40 a year,[202] which was worth less than half its 1553 value, when Levina Teerlinc had first received it. Hilliard was not the only sufferer in this situation, and at least he had the consolation of knowing that no one else was receiving what was withheld from him. Only George Gower, who succeeded Herne as Sergeant Painter in 1580, could be described as a respectable artist in regular court employment, and he posed no threat as a competitor for the highest quality commissions.

As was the case with scholarship and learning, Elizabeth expected her courtiers' and ministers' patronage to do her work for her, and to a large extent it did. Portraits of the queen had become symbols of loyalty by the 1580s, and the demand for them rose dramatically. Elizabeth sat to Federigo Zuccaro and the Marcus Gheeraerts, father and son, as well as to Hilliard, and possibly others between 1580 and 1593 (see plates 17 and 21),[203] and innumerable studio copies were made from their studies. No doubt it was a profitable business, but neither Zuccaro nor the Gheeraerts were court painters in the proper sense. Zuccaro had been imported by the Earl of Leicester, and the Gheeraerts were patronised chiefly by the Cecils and their friends. The whole situation was paradoxical, because the queen was commissioning a lot of work, and it would probably have been just as cheap to maintain a proper *atelier* as to pay for everthing *ad hoc*. However, Elizabeth liked to keep her options open, and to avoid commitment, so the most brilliant period of courtly art which the Tudor dynasty saw was led from behind, like the Duke of Plaza Toro's army. Hilliard and his pupil Isaac Oliver at the height of their powers created a royal iconography of dazzling splendour, which Holbein himself had never matched, and obviously in conformity with the queen's wishes, but with only a fraction of the royal patronage which Henry VIII had bestowed.

Further reading

E. Auerbach   *Tudor Artists*
F. E. Emmison   *Tudor Food and Pastimes*
J. K. McConica   *English Humanists and Reformation Politics*
A. W. Reed   *Early Tudor Drama*
J. Stevens   *Music and Poetry in the Early Tudor Court*
Lawrence Stone   *Family and Fortune*
Lawrence Stone   *The Crisis of the Aristocracy, 1560–1640*
R. Strong   *The Cult of Elizabeth*
R. Strong   *The English Renaissance Miniature*
Neville Williams   *Henry VIII and his Court*
J. Wilson   *Entertainments for Elizabeth I*

4   POLITICS AND RELIGION

The centre of patronage

England was governed from the court, because the monarch governed and the court was the monarch's immediate context. At the centre of this process lay the twin functions of patronage and petition, like the two sides of the same coin. When John Paston wanted a favour from Edward IV, he decided to invoke the good will of 'Sir George Brown, Sir James Ratcliff and others of my acquaintance which wait most upon the king and lie nightly in his Chamber ...'.[1] John Bedell, imprisoned for his role in Henry Dudley's conspiracy in 1556, and facing torture and death, wrote desperately to his wife 'move mistress Clarenceau for me'; and in 1566 even the Earl of Leicester was urged, during a period of absence from the court, to press his petition for a grant through Blanche Parry, one of the most trusted members of the queen's Privy Chamber.[2] Grants of office and land, annuities, commercial privileges, profitable wardships, and pardons for all kinds of offences—these were the raw materials of the political system, the bricks out of which loyal service, and consequently a reliable administration, were constructed. Henry IV may have received as many as 3000 petitions a year in the early fifteenth century, and some idea of the enormous range and variety of such requests can be gained from the list of June 1552, which included relief for the children of the Earl of Surrey (attainted and executed five years earlier), fee farms for five officials and members of the Privy Chamber, an annuity of £200 for Sir Nicholas le Strange, and a pardon to one John Smallwood for inadvertent manslaughter.[3] To put it another way:

> All such as aspire and thirst after offices and honours run thither with emulation and disdaine of others; thither are the revenewes brought that appertain unto the state & there they are disposed out againe.[4]

Attendance at court, or at least a reliable channel of communication to the court, was essential, not only for those with high political ambitions, but for such as sought the rangership of a forest, the lease of a royal manor, or an improvement of their ranking on the Commission of the Peace. At the same time, absence or exclusion from the royal presence could be a fatal handicap. Stephen Gardiner's despatch on embassy to the emperor in 1545 signalled his defeat by the Earl of Hertford and his allies, just as Wolsey's embassy to France in 1527 had given his enemies at court an opportunity to influence the king's mind against him. In 1537 Ralph Sadler protested to Cromwell that enforced absence would mar his fortunes forever, while sixty years later a perceptive friend warned the Earl of Essex that his hold upon the queen's affections was not to be presumed upon. 'Let nothing draw thee from the court; sit in every council . . .'.[5]

In spite of this warning, and of the dire consequences which followed its neglect, Elizabeth was not the fickle mistress of romantic legend. Except to the Earl of Leicester in the early days of her favour, she dealt out her patronage sparingly, but with an even hand. Nor did she build up and destroy her chief servants, in the manner of Henry VIII with Cromwell and Wolsey; and if her fancy lighted upon many men in the course of her longish life, their fortunes were much less drastically affected than those of her father's mistresses and queens. In spite of the unpredictability of her tactics, Elizabeth's patronage strategy was consistent and conservative, like that of her grandfather. 'Study to serve me', he is alleged to have told Sir Henry Wyatt, 'and I will study to enrich you'[6]—a cautious 'step by step' policy of matching reward to service which lay at the very heart of Henry VII's successful method of kingship.

By contrast with these two, both Edward IV and Henry VIII were prodigal with their favour, although in rather different ways. Edward tended to trust a small number of men on a large scale, such as Lord Hastings and his own brother, Richard, giving them great wealth and widespread authority. Unfortunately, he sowed the seeds of disaster by building up his brother and his wife's kindred, the Woodvilles, at the same time, as though oblivious of their mutual hostility. When his own restraining hand was withdrawn, they fell upon each other, and destroyed his heir and the stability of the kingdom in the process. Henry VIII's generosity was much less concentrated, and for much of his reign appeared to be controlled by his chief ministers. However, appearances were deceptive, and Henry never ceased to reward those who pleased him, from Charles Brandon to Edward Seymour, quite independently of the wishes of Wolsey or Cromwell.[7] When courtiers complained of the former that 'nought might be had at the king their master's hands, save by his means', their frustration was only partly justified. The Cardinal carried on an extensive brokerage business, but he knew better than to suppose that Henry had surrendered his prerogative. Like Sir Thomas More, he had no illusions about the nature of the king's favour, or the security of his own position. Henry was the most fickle and suggestible, as well as the most ruthless of the Tudors, but also, thanks to the dissolution of the monasteries, he had the largest resources to dispense. His patronage, unlike that of any other English king since William I, brought about a major and enduring shift in the distribution of landed wealth.[8] This time, Thomas Cromwell was the initial broker, but control lay with the king, and the pattern of distribution enhanced his authority. Many noblemen and gentlemen increased their fortunes, but no new principalities were created to challenge the Crown in the next generation, and the dependence of the beneficiaries upon the court was intensified rather than diminished. Only during the minority of Edward VI did the patronage of the Crown pass out of the personal control of the monarch, and those few years in consequence saw a revival of unrestrained aristocratic competition of a kind which posed a real danger to political stability. Mary, although easily led in some ways, knew her own mind in this respect. She used her patronage to restore much that her father had destroyed, both secular and ecclesiastical. In time, such a policy might well have created problems of its own, but Mary did not live long enough to re-establish more than a handful of noble families—the Howards, the Courtenays and the Percies—and her short reign made little impact upon the situation which her father had created.

The judicious use of patronage, and accessibility to petition, constituted the essence of 'good lordship', but medieval kings were not entirely free agents in the distribution of their favours. Just as the king's honour consisted of magnificence and manred, so the honour of his aristocratic subjects consisted in part in a proper relationship with their overlord. As we have seen, royal favour conferred honour on the recipient, even when the result was financially disadvantageous, as could easily be the case with an embassy or military command. The Duke of Suffolk got heavily into debt through leading an army royal to France in 1523, and the Earl of Leicester had a similar experience in the Netherlands in 1585.[9] Lord Hunsdon was even advised against accepting the prestigious office of Lord Chamberlain on the grounds of the enormous expenses involved—but chose the honour rather than the profit. As Mervyn James has explained, the concept of honour was deeply rooted and many faceted.[10] Some aspects, such as lineage and noble birth, were not within the control of the individual, but the pursuit of virtue and the code of honourable conduct were powerful influences upon political behaviour. Faithfulness to kindred and friends was required, as well as to one's lord, and 'chamber companionship' among young men serving together in a court or household could reinforce the bonds of loyalty which already existed. This can be seen very clearly in the case of Henry VIII's *mignons*, and was both the basis of their familiarity with the king and the main reason why Wolsey broke them up in 1519. The nobility expected to be admitted to the circle of the king's friends. There were never more than about fifty adult peers at any one time,[11] and they varied considerably in talent and ambition, but when their expectations were disappointed, and a relationship of trust did not exist, the possibility of disaffection was always present. It was partly because they believed that the king himself had breached the code of honour that Lord Darcy and Lord Hussey took up arms in 1536,[12] and despair of the queen's favour was a major contributory factor in the almost accidental defiance of the Earls of Westmorland and Northumberland in 1569. Consequently, although no monarch could allow his patronage to be constrained by expectation, or admit to office all those who aspired to it, political prudence dictated a policy of equity and vigilance. Patronage, like political theory, could outrage conventional opinion, and create serious stresses within the structure which it was designed to support.

Henry VI had provided the direst possible warning of what could happen when a king, either through ineptitude or lack of interest, lost control of his patronage. Not only had this meant that certain powerful nobles—De la Pole and the Beauforts particularly—had been able to take enormous profits for themselves, and exclude anyone who was not of their affinity; it had also meant that grants were duplicated, revenues doubly and even trebly assigned, and pardons distributed with a lavishness which undermined the whole judicial system.[13] These fundamental mistakes were not repeated, and Edward IV certainly never relinquished his prerogative, but his own policy was of questionable wisdom in a number of ways. Not only did he celebrate his triumph in 1460 with the creation of seven barons and two earls, plus the elevation of his brothers George and Richard to the Dukedoms of Clarence and Gloucester, but he continued this policy down to 1471, with a further duke (George Neville), eight earls and six barons. By the end of his reign he had created thirty-two new peers, including four dukes, two marquises and ten earls. This was not the result of weakness—a mere yielding to importunity—but of a particular style of government which placed heavy reliance upon noble support. In spite of the experience of 1470–71, which markedly cooled his enthusiasm for new creations, Edward persisted with this style to the end. His creations were accompanied by generous grants of land and office which turned middle ranking knights like Sir William Herbert and Sir William Hastings into peers and powerful magnates, and already powerful noblemen like Richard Neville, Earl of Warwick, into satraps who believed that they could dominate the Crown at will. The lesson eventually administered to Warwick was a costly one, and very ill-learned by the king who, having recovered his authority, proceeded to make the same mistake again, creating what was virtually a provincial governorship in the north for his brother Richard, and an almost equally dominant position in Wales and the Marches for his wife's brother, Anthony, Earl Rivers.[14] This highly selective patronage prevented him from mobilising the support of the aristocracy as a whole, because the majority, even of the peerage, received very little at his hands. It also had the effect of strengthening the control of his favoured magnates over the gentry in their spheres of influence, and thus of reducing the political importance of his *curiales*. In a sense he mortgaged his patronage in expectation of service, and thus made his court a place where powerful men gathered, rather than a place where men came constantly seeking the bricks and mortar to build their fortunes.

After 1485 the situation was dramatically different, although an interested observer could be forgiven for not noticing this at first, since within a few weeks of his accession Henry had created one duke (his uncle Jasper) and two earls (Thomas Stanley and Philibert de Chandee), while restoring another duke (Buckingham), one marquis (Dorset) and two further earls (Oxford and Devon). Thereafter, however, his bounty in this respect was sharply curtailed: two barons in 1486, and another one twenty years later; the restoration of the Marquisate of Berkeley and the Earldoms of Rivers and Surrey; and multiple honours for his own sons, constituted the full extent of his patronage in that direction.[15] It has been said that Henry regarded the Order of the Garter as the most honourable reward in his gift, and he certainly created far more knights than he did peers—thirty-seven in all.[16] The Garter carried no expectation of additional endowment, and was not hereditary, thus being both cheaper and easier to control. It is perhaps not surprising that the king did his best to match its reputation to that of the *Toison d'Or*, and to encourage his lay servants to regard it as the summit of their ambitions. Henry VII was not, in fact, particularly mean with grants of office, land and other tangible benefits, but his priorities were consistently different from those of Edward. He was perfectly willing to reward loyalty and good service, but not in advance of performance, and not usually all in one go. Those rewarded at the beginning of his reign had shared his exile, or risked their lives and fortunes to bring him to the throne. No further probation was applied to them, and in any case many of them were ecclesiastics—such as John Morton, Richard Fox and Christopher Urswick—who could be rewarded with benefices. Others were his close kindred–his uncle, his stepfather, and above all his mother. By 1490 Margaret Beaufort, Countess of Richmond and Derby, was one of the greatest magnates in the kingdom, and was certainly the most influential. She controlled the wardship of the young Duke of Buckingham and his brother, Henry Stafford, and was endowed with numerous manors and lordships giving her an income probably in excess of £3000 a year.[17] Her influence throughout the reign is incalculable, and by no means confined to pious works and education.

Once his authority was established, that is after the battle of Stoke, Henry's patronage settled into a consistent pattern. There were no more major endowments or great titles, but numerous small grants and favours, widely dispersed among courtiers and officials. Hardly any of these were gratuitous, or made on impulse. Most were in return for services which can be either positively identified or readily surmised; a few were in the nature of retainers. Some of the recipients were peers or prelates, but the majority were knights and gentlemen; those men whose work upon innumerable judicial and investigatory commissions steadily advanced the effectiveness of the king's government. It is now recognised that Henry's distrust of the nobility was largely a subsequent invention. In fact forty-three peers (about two-thirds of the whole body) were called at one time or another to serve on the king's council, and the nobility remained, until long after 1509, the predominant force in provincial politics.[18] The Duke of Buckingham was to complain with some justice in 1515 that his estates had been plundered during his minority, and that he had been unfairly burdened with debts and costs of over £10,000 as a result of receiving seizin of his lands in 1498.[19] However, it seems clear that neither his revenues nor his lifestyle were much affected by this 'disfavour', and as a great magnate of the royal blood he was bound to be watched with some vigilance. More typically, George Talbot, fourth Earl of Shrewsbury, served the king with consistent loyalty at Stoke in 1487, on the brief French campaign of 1492, and in controlling the Midlands during the various alarms connected with Perkin Warbeck. His rewards included the

Garter in 1487, and the Lord Stewardship of the household in 1502.[20] Although he was closer to the king than many peers, and a frequent attender at court even before 1502, he was not greatly rewarded in material terms, and probably did not expect to be. The borderline between peers and greater gentry was in any case a thin one, and the king used the threat of debt exaction against all those whose resources made it useful, whatever their social rank.[21] Henry VII was suspicious of anyone who was powerful enough to do him harm or obstruct his will, but he expected his peers to serve him in court and council, and they did so. He could not, after all, have it both ways; if he wanted them to be effective agents in their 'countries', they could not be constantly dancing attendance in the Chamber. The fact that most of them seem to have appeared only briefly and for special occasions would thus suggest a high degree of trust, rather than the reverse. It remains true that Henry did not admit any of his aristrocratic subjects to a high degree of intimacy; he had no *mignons*, and no princely favourites. This was partly because his own family life appears to have been happy, partly the shock of Sir William Stanley's treason in 1495, and partly a simple desire for privacy. He may also have been unwilling to permit the appearance of patronage brokers, preferring to keep his bounty firmly under his own control, even at a comparatively humble level. The evidence is sketchy, and more work needs to be done, but it would be quite consistent with his general style of government to discourage intermediaries in order to ensure that the benefits accrued only to himself.

As we have seen, his son took a much more relaxed and self-confident view. No sudden outburst of *largesse* followed his accession, because he had no personal following to reward, but the warlike noises which he immediately began to make promised a return to the profitable continental campaigning of almost a century before, and a recognition of the fact that a nobleman's honour—no less than a king's—was based upon martial prowess. Major peerage creations flowed steadily throughout the reign, starting with the elevation of the Duke of Buckingham's brother, Henry Stafford, to the Earldom of Wiltshire in 1510. William Courtenay was restored to the Earldom of Devon a few months before his death in 1511, and Lady Margaret Pole to the Earldom of Salisbury in 1513.[22] These early moves should probably be seen along with the cancellation of many recognisances and obligations, and the executions of Empson and Dudley, as designed to reassure the aristocracy of the king's good lordship, and to indicate a more generous style of government.

In 1514 came the first major rewards of war: the Dukedom of Norfolk to Thomas Howard, Earl of Surrey, the victor of Flodden; the Dukedom of Suffolk to the king's favoured companion in arms, Charles Brandon, and the Earldom of Worcester to Charles Somerset, Lord Herbert. In 1525 another flurry of peerages accompanied the creation of the king's illegitimate son, Henry Fitzroy, as Duke of Richmond; Henry Courtenay, Earl of Devon, became Marquis of Exeter; Henry Clifford, Earl of Cumberland; Henry

Brandon, the Duke of Suffolk's nine year old son, Earl of Lincoln; and Thomas Manners, Earl of Rutland. Thereafter, most creations followed the twists and turns of royal policy: the Earldom of Wiltshire for Sir Thomas Boleyn in 1529, and the Marquisate of Pembroke for his daughter three years later; the Earldom of Hertford for Edward Seymour in 1537; and the Earldom of Essex successively to Thomas Cromwell (1540) and William Parr (1543).[23] Altogether, excluding his son, Henry created or restored two dukes, two marquises and sixteen earls, and each of these creations was accompanied by grants of land, although not all were equally generous. However, as is well known, there was another side to this story; two marquises and two earls of the king's creation died on the scaffold, as well as the Duke of Buckingham, the Earl of Surrey, and Edmund de la Pole, the rightful but unrecognised Duke of Suffolk.[24] The close connection between the fortunes of his peers and their attitude towards his controversial policies is an obvious feature of Henry VIII's reign. Several major families were destroyed for arousing his suspicion, without any overt acts of disloyalty: the Staffords, the Courtenays, the Percies, and finally the Howards. Conversely, several climbed to fame and fortune through his various marriages: the Boleyns, the Seymours and the Parrs. The risks involved in not knowing the king's mind, or guessing wrongly about his intentions, kept even the most distant noble alert for tidings from the court, and the politically ambitious maintained an assiduous correspondence with the king's secretaries and other well-placed officials.[25]

The crisis over the king's 'Great Matter' thus increased the political importance of the court in a number of ways. As long as Wolsey was in power, and Catherine was Henry's queen, he could pass for a very traditional kind of king, but after 1530 the familiar landmarks began to disappear. The king became so preoccupied with enforcing obedience to his will that he did not hesitate to do violence to other loyalties, most particularly to that knightly code of honour and obligation which the courtly spectacles of his reign had seemed to uphold as late as 1527. When Lord Darcy stood by his promise, publicly given to Robert Aske in 1536, he became a traitor to his king, and eventually paid with his life.[26] In a similar manner Sir Thomas More died, not for his loyalty to the Catholic faith, but for his refusal to betray an allegiance to the papacy which was fundamental to his own concept of honour. When the Pilgrimage of Grace and the so-called 'Exeter Conspiracy' of 1538 failed to deter Henry from his chosen course, they also revealed the political weakness of traditional values when assaulted by the twin weapons of attainder and patronage. This game was not exclusively played out upon the chessboard of the court, but it was there that the moves were plotted and the forfeitures demanded. 'We will not be bound of a necessity to be served with lords', commented Henry in appointing Sir William Eure as Warden of the East March in 1537, 'but we will be served with such men of what degree soever as we shall appoint to the same.' Such a boast was not entirely justified, and without the loyalty of such families as the Talbots, Stanleys and Cliffords, with their powerful regional affinities, the outcome of the Pilgrimage might well have been very different.[27] Nevertheless, the messgae was clear. Office under the Crown was the key to security and fortune, while power without office would be attacked and undermined at every opportunity. The same message was conveyed by the reorganisation of the council between 1535 and 1540, which turned that body almost exclusively into a panel of office holders. Henry had no aversion to nobles, and used titles of honour and grants of arms naturally as marks of favour and recognition; but he did expect his servants, noble and non-noble alike, to seek favour and preferment at his own hands, and not to presume to bargain with him from positions of strength.

The key man in establishing this pattern of behaviour was Thomas Cromwell, who, both as Secretary and as Lord Privy Seal between 1533 and 1540, exercised enormous influence over the distribution of offices in the gift of the Crown, and was the principal agent for the sale of monastic property.[28] His surviving correspondence is littered with begging letters, like that from John Lucas, who sought the post of King's Solicitor, and offered £10 worth of wine as an inducement. There was, of course, nothing new about this kind of petition, but the decision to sell monastic property in large quantities did create unprecedented opportunities. Writing to Cromwell in July 1539, Sir Richard Grenville, the Marshal of Calais, declared

> ... I have bethought me that if I have not some piece of this suppressed land by purchase or gift of the king's majesty I should stand out of the case of few men of worship in the realm ... And because my heirs shall be in the same mind for their own profit, I will gladly, if it might stand with the king's majesty's pleasure, buy certain parcels of this suppressed land in these parts (Cornwall). ...[29]

There is a hint of the 'hard sell' about this letter—the desire to 'do as others do', and the suggestion that the king might take such an overture as a gesture of loyalty, as well as the desire for gain. Not all would-be purchasers made their approach through Cromwell. Well-placed courtiers such as the Duke of Suffolk or the Earl of Hertford had no need of his mediation, but the whole operation was controlled through the court, and courtiers and officals were the chief beneficiaries. This continued to be the case after Cromwell's fall, when the officers of the Court of Augmentations, and particularly Sir Richard Rich, began to take an important hand. By 1547 land to a capital value of about £800,000 had been disposed of, most at a standard twenty years' purchase. One of the consequences of this was to recreate the situation at the end of Henry VII's reign, when a large proportion of the artistocracy had been in debt to the Crown; another was to create a major vested interest in the royal supremacy.[30] A few major new estates resulted, such as those of the Russells and the Thynnes, but for the most part the existing artistocracy were the beneficiaries. Despite the financial difficulties under which the Crown was labouring by 1547, the capacity of the king to reward his servants was vastly greater than that of any other lord. With the death of the Duke of Suffolk in 1545, and the fall of the Howards at the end of the following year, there were no magnates of the old style left, and the distance between the monarch and his peers in terms of power and resources had never been greater. Subsequent wisdom was to declare that the rapid sale of monastic land deprived the king of a golden opportunity to be financially independent, and mortgaged the future to a politically conscious aristocracy; but it did not look like that in 1547. When Henry VIII died, leaving his heir a minor, there was no mobilisation of retinues, or summoning of noble councils to remote castles. Instead there was intense lobbying and intrigue in the palace of Westminster. By then the court dominated the world of English patronage, rather as the Bourse at Antwerp dominated the world of European finance.

However, unlike the Bourse, the court depended for its proper functioning upon a single figure. Without an adult king, or even a regent of the royal blood, a 'spoils' system quickly made its appearance. Within a few weeks the Earl of Hertford and his friends had rewarded themselves liberally for their successful *coup*. Hertford himself became Duke of Somerset; William Parr, Earl of Essex, became Marquis of Northampton; and John Dudley, Lord Lisle, became Earl of Warwick. [31] There was also a generous hand-out of lesser grants, allegedly in accordance with the express, but unwritten, wishes of the late king. At the same time Thomas, Lord Wriothesley, the only important conservative to survive the coup, was created Earl of Southampton, which might suggest the purchase of his compliance, but for the fact that he was dismissed from office and disgraced soon after. We are not concerned here with the complicated political battles of the next five years, but they dominated the distribution of patronage during that period. From 1547 to 1549 Somerset distributed officers and grants of land or annuities to strengthen his own position, and that of his followers, such as Sir Michael Stanhope. After his overthrow in October 1549, the Earl of Warwick did the same. John, Lord Russell and William Paulet, Lord St John, were advanced to the Earldoms of Bedford and Winchester respectively in January 1550, when Warwick's victory was finally secure. Finally, in October 1551, Warwick himself became Duke of Northumberland, Paulet was advanced again to the Marquisate of Winchester, and Henry Grey, Marquis of Dorset, became Duke of Suffolk. Like Somerset, Northumberland was an ambitious man who used political power to enrich his family and friends, extend their estates and increase their power. [32] As we have seen, these new magnates imposed themselves upon the Privy Chamber, and sought to dominate both the court and the council. Inevitably, much regular patronage continued to be exercised by entrenched officials independently of their influence, and much was subject to reversion or purchase which made it unavailable; but it is impossible to speak of any royal policy between 1550 and 1553, apart from the interests of the Dudleys, the Greys, the Parrs, and those who adhered to them.

The danger which this situation posed for the Crown was great, but should not be exaggerated. Had Edward attained his majority, it seems likely that he would have continued his father's policy, and the Dudleys would soon have been cut down to size, although not in the drastic fashion which eventually occurred. The real danger was that, after Edward's early death, Northumberland should have turned queenmaker, and successfully set his puppet, Jane Grey, upon the throne.[33] His failure to achieve that ruthlessly exposed the limitations of the new magnates. Had Henry VIII been confronted with the united forces of the Duke of Norfolk, the Earl of Derby and the Earl of Shrewsbury in 1536, he would hardly have prevailed. Yet Mary succeeded in shrugging off the power of Northumberland, Suffolk and Northampton in a matter of days. Their power, with the exception of the traditional lands of the Marquisate of Dorset, was court-based, and, despite their imposing revenues and estates, had little root in manred or local affinities. Five years was too short a time to turn a court magnate into a genuine overmighty subject, and the shift of political emphasis from the provinces to the court over the previous half century was, paradoxically, the salvation of the Tudors in this most dangerous crisis.

Mary, preoccupied with thoughts of divine providence, does not appear to have grasped this point at all. Her patronage was directed at first to the restoration of the Howards and Courtenays.[34] The aged third Duke of Norfolk was rescued from the Tower and restored to his lands and dignities, whereupon his grandson, later to be the fourth Duke, became Earl of Surrey. Edward Courtenay, the long-imprisoned son of the Marquis of Exeter, was also released, and created Earl of Devon; while his mother Gertrude, the dowager Marchioness, enjoyed a brief familiarity with the queen, and received a generous grant in her own right.[35] Four years later Sir Thomas Percy was created Earl of Northumberland, and received the whole of the vast estates which his uncle had surrendered to the Crown in 1537, along with the Marcher offices traditionally held by the earls. These were Mary's only major peerage creations, and, with the exception of the last, appear to have been prompted more by conscience and nostalgia than by political purpose. The resurrection of the Percy earldom has to be seen in the context of the Anglo-French war, and of relations with Scotland,[36] but it remains an isolated and eccentric action. Percy was not a courtier, and had few court connections, so that his promotion represents a brief return to that dependence upon 'natural' lords from which Henry VIII had gradually emancipated himself. The same thing might have happened with the Courtenays in the south-west if the Earl of Devon had not behaved like an idiot, and died abroad, unmarried, in 1556.

Whether Mary really had a reactionary policy in respect of the nobility is not clear. She made no particular use of the young Duke of Norfolk after his grandfather's death in 1554, and made no attempt to restore the fortunes of the Staffords. Apart from the three families already mentioned, her largest single benefaction was to the new Abbey of Westminster, which received lands to the value of £1460 per annum.[37] In other respects, Mary's patronage was also curiously indeterminate. She was reasonably generous with small grants, annuities, and release of debts, particularly to those who supported her in the crisis of 1553. Her most trusted courtiers and officials, men such as Sir Robert Rochester, Sir Francis Englefield and Sir Thomas Cornwallis, collected numerous offices, grants and privileges—Cornwallis augmenting his income from £300 to £2300 a year in the course of the reign, which placed him on a level with many major peers.[38] At the same time the Earl of Westmorland, who was seldom at court and who held no major office, received lands to the value of £1258 per annum, in a number of grants spread over five years. Several important office holders, such as the Earl of Arundel and the Marquis of Winchester, received virtually no bounty, and none of her favourtites were granted titles of nobility, or permitted to accumulate large estates. Cornwallis's large revenue was derived primarily from the fruits of office, and disappeared when he went out of favour at the end of the reign.

Philip was given no control over English patronage, but was generous with his own pensions, and with gold chains worth several hundred crowns each, which were standard presents, rather like the pieces of plate which the queen gave out at New Year. Little can be deduced from the pension lists, except that the king was anxious to provide some inducement to every courtier or royal servant who might be of use to him, and his grants were graded in accordance with their perceived importance—1000 crowns a year to the Marquis of Winchester, 1500 to Lord Paget, 300 to Colonel Edward Randolf, and so on.[39] The total was considerable, but no single pension was large enough to make a significant difference to the wealth of the recipient, and hardly any were dispensed outside the court. The king took no Englishmen of standing into his service, apart from the household officers who were provided for him, and the only major promotion which was secured by his influence was that of Lord Paget as Lord Privy Seal in 1555. A handful of Spaniards were given ecclesiastical benefices or other minor rewards in England, but none was a person of any consequence, and there seems to have been virtually no exchange of patronage between the two monarchs.

Between 1547 and 1553 an attempt had been made to build up a powerful court nobility committed to Protestantism and backed by gentry affinities also centred upon the court and royal service. This had been frustrated, partly by the internecine strife which had destroyed the Seymours, and partly by Mary's victory in 1553, which had destroyed the Greys, Parrs and Dudleys. Mary made no attempt to create a Catholic courtier nobility of the same kind. Of the peers who served on her council, only Viscount Montague was sufficiently committed to the papacy to get into major trouble under Elizabeth, although Lord Hastings should also be counted as a stout Catholic. The Marquis of Winchester, and the Earls of Shrewsbury, Derby and Pembroke continued to serve in the following reign.[40] Perhaps significantly, the three major beneficiaries of Mary's patronage who survived into the reign of Elizabeth were all attainted in 1571, but of them only the Duke of Norfolk played any significant role at court. Beyond a general benevolence to those of a conservative religious persuasion, and moderate generosity to a few middle-ranking courtiers, it is hard to discern a deliberate policy in Mary's patronage. Office holding clearly mattered less to her than to her father in the latter part of his reign—or to Elizabeth. No fewer than seventeen of her councillors held no identifiable office, and no office holder received the kind of major bounty which resulted in the establishment of a family of lasting importance.[41] Mary seems to have seen herself as a restorer of normality, but the main effect of her reign was the eclipse of the Protestant magnates, followed by a sharp decline in the political importance of court-centred patronage.

At first sight it appears that the accession of Elizabeth simply represented a fresh rotation of the turntable, as the Englefields, Waldegraves and Cornwallises retired into obscurity, to be replaced by the re-emerging Seymours, Dudleys and Parrs. William Parr was again elevated to the Marquisate of Northampton in 1559, and Sir Edward Seymour to his father's Earldom of Hertford. Moreover the men who swiftly rose in the new queen's favour, such as Sir William Cecil and Lord Robert Dudley, had all been associated with one or other of the Edwardian regimes. However, it soon became apparent that there was to be no revival of the Protestant magnates, and that Elizabeth intended to keep a close control over her own patronage. Like Mary, she made few direct grants of any size, even to Lord Robert when her affection for him was at its warmest.[42] The Duke of Norfolk was constrained to borrow £2000 from her in 1560 to equip himself as Lieutenant of the North, and was grateful to be allowed to discharge the debt two years later by making an exchange of lands with the Crown.[43] From the beginning Elizabeth favoured indirect rewards for her servants: customs concessions or farms, wardships, leases in reversion, and a variety of licences. These could be extremely profitable. Dudley sold his licence for transporting finished cloths to the Merchant Adventurers in 1564 for £6266, and received £2500 a year from Thomas Smith, Customer of the Port of London, who leased his sweet wine monopoly.[44] Such rewards were not a drain on the exchequer, save in the sense that they reduced the yield of the customs revenues, and after 1570 were increasingly supplemented by manufacturing monopolies, for a wide variety of commodities from soap to playing cards. As is well known, these became intensely controversial towards the end of the reign. Dudley (Earl of Leicester from 1564) was the outstanding Elizabethan courtier. By 1575 his income from offices, licences and other court perquisites was approaching £4000 a year, considerably in excess of his landed revenues, which probably stood at about £3000. He was a pluralist on a considerable scale: Master of the Horse, Constable of Windsor Castle, Constable and Steward of Warwick, Chamberlain of the County Palatine of Chester, Warden of the New Forest, and many others.[45] Most were sinecures, or exercised through deputies, and were conferred as sources of honour and profit rather than as opportunities for service. Dudley was also seriously in debt, which is not surprising considering that, even in the first year of the reign, he had spent upwards of £2500 on jewels, clothes and entertainments. At one point he owed the queen £15,000, and in December 1576 a consortium of friends tried to bail him out to the tune of £10,000. He eventually survived that crisis without calling upon their aid, but subsequently mortgaged his Lordship of Denbigh for £16,000, and frankly confessed to living beyond his means.[46]

Elizabeth was less forgiving than her father, who had once written off over

£20,000 when his friend Charles Brandon was in a similar mess, but she was more generous to Dudley than to anyone else. Usually her courtiers and officials had to serve long and faithfully before any major grant or preferment came their way. Important offices, both in the court and in the administration, were doubled up, or kept vacant for years on end—as was the case with both the Lord Stewardship and the office of Principal Secretary. Peerages and other titles of honour were hard to come by; apart from the creations already noticed, Elizabeth promoted only four earls—Ambrose Dudley (Warwick, 1561), Walter Devereux (Essex, 1572), Edward, Lord Clinton (Lincoln, 1572) and Charles Howard (Nottingham, 1597)—a total of one marquis and six earls in forty-four years. A handful of young men caught her fancy, and were rewarded without significant service, or in advance of it—Christopher Hatton, Walter Raleigh, Robert Devereux, second Earl of Essex—but these exceptions hardly affect the main pattern. Great fortunes were not made in Elizabeth's service, but a small number of other men, apart from Dudley, did well enough. William Cecil, Lord Burleigh, laid the foundations of two noble families, and his younger son Robert probably succeeded in milking the system more efficiently in the last five years of the reign than anyone else had done, including Dudley.[47] Sir Christopher Hatton, Sir Thomas Heneage and Sir Henry Sidney were also major beneficiaries, while the Earls of Warwick, Sussex and Essex found the court reasonably profitable. One of the reasons for this was that the queen distributed her limited bounty, if not fairly, at least with some regard to equity and the legitimate expectations of different parties. There were no great patronage brokers during her reign, as the Earl of Essex discovered to his cost when he staked his credit on obtaining the Attorney Generalship for Francis Bacon. But there was always an inner ring, who were listened to in the making of appointments, and allowed to reward their own clients within reasonable limits. In the first decade this ring consisted of Dudley, Cecil, Winchester, Pembroke and Nicholas Bacon. After about 1575, Leicester and Burleigh were joined by Walsingham, Hatton and Sussex, and in the 1590s the scene was dominated by Robert Cecil, Essex, Buckhurst and Nottingham.[48] Only at the very end of the reign was there real strife (as opposed to rivalry and emulation) within that inner ring.

Altogether, including Irish titles and the earldoms which we have already noticed, Elizabeth created twenty-one peers. At her accession, there had been fifty-seven, of whom thirty-eight were barons; at her death there were fifty-five, of whom thirty-six were barons. The average noble income from land had risen during the reign from £1780 per annum to £2410, which represented a decline in real terms of about 30 per cent.[49] The equivalent average for Henry VIII's reign had been £1200, so the overall decline since the 1530s must have been something like 50 per cent. This did not necessarily mean that all Elizabethan peers were poorer than their predecessors, but it did mean that the inroads of inflation upon their estates had to be compensated by other means, and of these means (which included improved estate management and commercial speculation) the proceeds of office and royal favour were by far the most important. In spite of her relative meanness, Elizabeth's patronage was as important to her peers and other courtiers as that of her father had been in the last decade of his reign. In 1521 the estates of the Duke of Buckingham had been worth about £5000 a year; in 1602 the lands of the richest peer (the Earl of Shrewsbury) realised £7500.[50] After an inflation of nearly 500 per cent Shrewsbury's real income was approximately one third that of Buckingham. Inflation hit the Crown hard in many ways, but it had one immense advantage; the licences, customs concessions and commercial privileges with which Elizabeth rewarded her servants were 'index linked', and did not lose their value like annuities, or lands encumbered with long leases. The same was true of the profits of office—not the derisory official fees, but the real profits derived from selling services, or commodities obtained at concessionary rates. The great fortunes from this source were not made until the following century, when Robert Cecil could receive nearly £7000 from political office alone in the year 1608-9. Nevertheless, the rewards were great enough to consolidate the position of the court as the heart and focus of the patronage network. As aristocratic lifestyles changed, and the size of noble retinues and households declined, royal service became the only career option for an ambitious gentleman. Knighthoods might still be earned at the hands of a royal commander on the field of battle, but increasingly they were the rewards of industrious bureaucrats, successful lawyers, and the heads of serviceable county families. As with peerages, Elizabeth was not generous— fewer than 900 were dubbed in the reign (and these included some regrettable aberations by the Earl of Essex)[51]—but scarcity kept the value high, and made honour do some of the work of more tangible benefits. The same was true with grants of arms, over which the royal heralds had gradually established monopolistic control between 1484 and 1540.[52] These heralds did a flourishing business in the second half of the century, and social ambition made the lesser gentry amenable to royal service through this means, no less than their more exalted neighbours were made amenable by office and dignity.

Royal patronage advanced, not steadily but somewhat jerkily, throughout the period. The great magnates of Edward IV's reign, mortgagees of royal power with their own princely courts, did not disappear overnight, but steadily declined in number, wealth and independence. As they went they were replaced by courtiers and office-holding nobles, like Charles Brandon, Thomas Boleyn, and William Paulet—men whose dignities and wealth were rewards, and who had neither the will nor the manred for independent action. Before the end of Henry VIII's reign, such men were clearly in the ascendency, and the older type of provincial magnate, such as the Earls of Shrewsbury, Derby and Arundel, were drawn into a similar dependence by the lures of office and monastic land. Briefly, during the reign of Edward VI, the whole situation threatened to get out of control, but Mary reduced the new magnates before they could establish themselves—much as her father and grandfather had reduced the old ones. Elizabeth thus inherited a re-established royal control, and, with the aid of economic circumstances, completed the ascendency of the court. The so-called 'rebellion' of the Earl of Essex in 1601 strikingly illustrates the nature of the change. Driven desperate by his exclusion from royal favour, his finances ruined by the loss of his sweet wine monopoly, and backed by a group of disappointed patronage seekers, he attempted a *coup* against the court.[53] A hundred years before he would have retired to his estates in North Wales and summoned his friends and affinity, but in 1601 his only chance of success was to seize control of the nerve centre. In a sense the Tudors had succeeded too well, because the integrity of the court deteriorated under the fierce pressures and demands which became concentrated upon it, and James I found himself operating a market place in which his patronage once again got out of control and undermined the political edifice which it was designed to support.[54]

Faction and political strife

During the latter part of Henry VI's reign, and certainly by the time that William de la Pole was created Duke of Suffolk in 1448, the court was itself a faction, and the main axis of political conflict was between those who controlled it, and those who were excluded from office and the fruits of patronage. In 1451 the House of Commons, alarmed by the strife which this situation was causing, petitioned for the removal of Edmund Beaufort, Duke of Somerset, and twenty-three of his adherents from the king's presence as evil influences and inimical to the common weal.[55] Neither this, nor the Duke of York's abortive *coup* in 1452 succeeded in persuading the king to change his policy, but in August 1453 he suffered a mental breakdown, and the political situation was briefly transformed. Without the king's support, Somerset lost control of the council, and was imprisoned in the Tower. His place was taken by York, abetted by the Neville Earls of Salisbury and Warwick, while Somerset's adherents up and down the country were exposed to the revenge of their enemies. In terms of good government, York's Protectorate was not much of an improvement, although it was more broadly based, and as soon as the king recovered at the end of 1454, he restored the *status quo*. The result was the first battle of St Albans, at which the Yorkists recovered control of the king by force of arms, and Somerset was slain. There is no need to pursue the story of this strife over the next five years. The king's impartiality had been exposed as a fiction, and the Yorkists had been constrained to invent the dubious concept of the 'councillor born' in order to justify their action in forcing their presence upon his court. After Somerset's death the 'court party' was effectively led by Queen Margaret, who pursued her enemies with such vindictiveness that they were left with no option but to depose Henry if their own lives and properties were to be preserved.[56]

The lesson of these years was not wasted upon the young Earl of March, whose accession as Edward IV in 1460 was the direct result. From the first he took great pains to conciliate those Lancastrians who sought his peace; and within a few years several of them, notably his future father and brother-in-law, Lords Rivers and Scales, were prominent members of his court. In spite of the participation of a number of potentially powerful magnates, Lancastrian opposition had been suppressed by 1464, and the king was so far from pursuing partisan policies that some of his own former followers were accusing him of ingratitude, and of failure to reward their sacrifices. There was, consequently, little conflict between 'court' and 'country' interests, or between 'in' and 'out' parties as there had been formerly. Instead, there began to develop personal and family quarrels within the court, which were to prove every bit as dangerous to the stability of the regime. For these, the king himself was very largely to blame–and most particularly in the manner of his marriage. In marrying clandestinely a widow of minor peerage rank with a large kindred to provide for, Edward laid up for himself a store of trouble. In fact the Woodvilles were not as grasping as they were represented to be, and apart from arranging a large number of advantageous marriages for Elizabeth's female kin, the king did not bestow extravagant bounty upon them.[57] But he did promote Lord Rivers to an earldom, and give him the lucrative and prestigious offices of Treasurer and Constable of England; and he did frustrate the plans which the powerful Earl of Warwick was promoting for the marriages of his own daughters. Edward fell out badly with Warwick over the Woodvilles, not so much because of his excessive promotion of their interests as because of the brusque and disparaging way in which he treated the Earl's honour and advice. By 1469, despite the generous patronage which he had received, Warwick was thoroughly alienated from the king, and had found an ally in Edward's disgruntled younger brother, George, Duke of Clarence.[58] Having failed in an attempted *coup* in that year, the malcontents then made common cause with the exiled Lancastrians, and briefly restored the discredited Henry VI in 1470. Edward's victory in the following year, with Burgundian help, recovered his kingdom and destroyed Warwick, but it did not cure the problem of internecine strife within the court. However unjustified it may have been, suspicion and jealousy of Woodville power was just as rife after the readeption as it had been before. They were certainly capable of acting in a high-handed and tyrannical manner, and were hard to gain redress against, as Sir Thomas Cook found to his cost.[59] Moreover, their influence was concentrated at the court, close about the king's person, and they loomed larger as the reign progressed and other powerful magnates fell—the Nevilles in 1471, Clarence (eventually) in 1478. In a revealing episode in 1479, the London Mercers and Merchant Adventurers had fallen into the king's displeasure through defaulting on a subsidy. Industriously, they petitioned the queen, her son the Marquis of Dorset, the Earl of Essex and Lord Hastings to intercede on their behalf. Hastings, who was himself a man of great influence, and one of Edward's most trusted servants, promised to be 'their very good and especial lord', but advised them to make their principal suit 'unto the Queen's grace and the Lord Marquis', and it was eventually Elizabeth who secured their relief.[60]

It would be an exaggeration to describe the queen as the leader of a faction in Edward's court, but the Woodvilles continued throughout to be a closely knit interest group, and there was thus a tendency for those who feared or distrusted them to come together. This was particularly true in the last years of the reign of Hastings, Richard of Gloucester, and Henry Stafford, Duke of Buckingham—all men of immense power and resources. Consequently, when Edward died suddenly in 1483, leaving his heir a minor, he also left a most dangerous political situation, with the Woodvilles entrenched at court, and Earl Rivers as Governor of the Prince of Wales, confronting the senior Prince of the Blood, Richard of Gloucester, backed by most of the other magnates upon whom the king had relied. Since Edward also left two contradictory sets of instructions for his son's minority, one naming the queen as Regent, and the other Richard of Gloucester, it is not surprising that a tragic crisis resulted.[61]

By contrast with the high drama of the Yorkist court, that of Henry VII was peaceful, and its politics for the most part extremely restrained. Henry never allowed the surviving Woodvilles to gather around his wife as they had gathered around her mother, and indeed the elder Elizabeth was quietly consigned to a nunnery in Bermondsey in 1487 to prevent any revival of her promotional activities.[62] Like Edward, Henry began his reign with the intention of conciliation, and accepted the services of many former Yorkists. Like Edward also, he had mixed fortunes with that policy. John de la Pole, Earl of Lincoln, was still sitting in council in early February 1487, when he was already deeply involved in the plot based upon Lambert Simnel's impersonation. His flight shortly after, followed by his leadership of the invasion in late May, and subsequent death at Stoke, intensified Henry's caution in dealing with former opponents.[63] The major traitor of the reign, however, was not a former opponent, but a man who had been one of his staunchest supporters, and who held high office close to his person, his Lord Chamberlain Sir William Stanley. Why Stanley chose to get embroiled with Perkin Warbeck has never been satisfactorily explained, but it does not seem to have been the result of any feud or rivalry touching the court. If Stanley was, as has been suggested, dissatisfied with the rewards which he had received at Henry's hands, that did not persuade the king to raise the stakes at court. If anything, the Lord Chamberlain's crime reduced the Great Chamber as a channel of access to the king, and consequently the opportunities of its staff for daily contact. Rodrigo de Puebla, the Spanish ambassador, who knew Henry reasonably well, wrote in 1507 that he had no confidential advisers, and that may well explain why there seems to have been so little political in-fighting at his court. He was not capricious, did not discard servants lightly, and was extremely reluctant to believe the worst, even of proven offenders.[64] Many of his trusted agents, particularly Edmund Dudley and Richard Empson, became extremely unpopular towards the end of the reign, but if there was any organised court lobby against them, it has left no trace in the records. Henry was much influenced by his mother, but although she was a great promoter of religious and educational causes, she does not seem to have maintained any political clientage at court. Perhaps she did not need to, when the king could write to her (as he did in 1501):

> ... I shall be glad to please you as your heart can desire it, and I know well that I am as much bounden so to do, as any creature living for the great and singular motherly love and affection that it hath pleased you at all times to bear me ...[65]

Jasper Tudor, Duke of Bedford, the only magnate of royal blood, served his nephew faithfully, and died without lawful issue in 1495. Edward Stafford, Duke of Buckingham, with much more distant royal connections, was a minor who did not obtain livery of his lands until 1498. When he did, he found them encumbered with debts which took several years to pay off, and although this undoubtedly gave him a sense of grievance, it reduced his level of political activity. Buckingham was never excluded from the court, but his influence there was slight and he did not make any serious attempt to increase it.[66] Henry Percy, the fourth Earl of Northumberland, was a man whose power in the north the king was bound to recognise, but he was killed in a riot at Cocklodge in 1489, when his son and heir was only eleven, and Henry was able to control the great Percy interest through the wardship.

The dominant figures in Henry VII's court were his family and his officials rather than his nobles. This was not so much because he distrusted nobles as because he kept most of them busy on his behalf in their countries. Their function at court was to grace major occasions, not to compete for power in the council. The only power in the council was the king himself, and no member of his family was given an opportunity to bid for independent political influence. Neither Arthur nor the younger Henry grew to maturity during their father's lifetime, or had any chance to create their own clientage. Elizabeth of York was given neither the opportunity nor the resources to promote her kinsfolk, and seems to have been genuinely devoted to her husband, while Margaret Beaufort was far too discreet to cause any problems. At the same time, by curbing magnate power in general, and by having a consistent patronage policy, Henry reduced the incentives for nobles to maintain lobbies at court, either through personal attendance or through representatives.

There were, of course, disagreements between Henry VII's advisers, but their consequences are hard to determine. Henry VIII, on the other hand, as a young and inexperienced king, was much more open to pressure and manipulation. At first the tension was mainly between the impetuous young king and the cautious councillors he had inherited from his father. His nobles were for the most part neither young nor impetuous,[67] but they were more than ready to welcome a renewal of the French war, and the promotion of Henry Stafford, which we have already noticed, probably signalled a revival of their influence at court. Whatever problems it was to cause him later,

Henry's marriage to Catherine of Aragon in 1509 was entirely innocuous in terms of domestic politics. Although she tended to foreclose his options in foreign policy, Catherine had neither a fortune nor a following of her own to cause her husband embarrassment. She was a princess of the highest blood in Europe, gifted, beautiful, and intensely pious. Despite the discrepancy of their ages, she appeared to be an ideal bride for Henry, and the court glittered and sparkled with revelry and celebration. For the first two or three years of the reign the king's servants and his chosen companions were entirely distinct. While the council was still dominated by Warham, Foxe and Fisher (who were all middle-aged ecclesiastical bureaucrats), the *mignons* were coming into their own: Henry Stafford, the Earl of Essex, Edward Neville, Edward Howard, Charles Knevett, Henry Guildford, William Compton and a number of others.[68] These were young noblemen and gentlemen, without much political weight themselves but often representing powerful families, who were a constant source of anxiety to the king's men of business, without ever posing a serious challenge to them. It was the emergence of Wolsey as the king's chief adviser between 1512 and 1514 which imposed a pattern upon this somewhat unstable situation. Like the *mignons*, Wolsey was very much Henry's own man, and although he was eighteen years older than the king, he knew better than to lecture him about his royal responsibilities. For the next fifteen years Wolsey dominated the politics of the court, and effectively prevented any other powerful interest groups from forming. As we have seen, he twice purged the Privy Chamber when its Gentlemen appeared to be establishing too much independent influence, and played an important part in the crucial fall of the Duke of Buckingham in 1521.

Buckingham had become a member of the council in 1509, and his relations with the king had appeared to be good. He cut a splendid figure at court, and played a prominent part in the numerous ceremonies and revels of these years. There was a minor ruffle in 1510, when the king's roving eye alit briefly on the duke's sister, and a potentially much more serious one a few years later when it was discovered that Buckingham was illegally retaining Sir William Bulmer, who was a Knight of the King's Body. However, neither of these circumstances led to a real estrangement, and as late as 1519 the duke's position appeared to be under no threat. However, Buckingham could not escape from the fact that some people regarded him as the heir to the throne, a circumstance which consistently excluded him from Henry's full confidence, and increased insidiously in importance as the king became more worried about his lack of a son. Also the duke had a strong hereditary claim to the Constableship of England, which he pursued tenaciously in council and through the courts, ignoring the clear signs of Henry's mounting displeasure.[70] The fact that Buckingham's case was good in law did not alter the king's determination to have no Constable. The office was, as Justice Neville declared 'very hault et dangerous & auxy very chargeable al Roy in fees'; in fact it was a standing reminder of the duke's royal blood and possible pretensions. Nor was Henry likely to be reassured by contemplating Buckingham's extensive affinity. His wife's brother was the fifth Earl of Northumberland, his younger sister was Countess of Huntingdon, and his daughters were married to Thomas Howard, Earl of Surrey (Duke of Norfolk in 1514), Ralph Neville, Earl of Westmorland, and George Neville, Lord Burgavenny. Belligerently anti-French, he bitterly condemned Wolsey's peace policy in 1518, and conducted a small-scale foreign policy of his own. Constrained by his honour to accompany the king to the Field of Cloth of Gold, he became sardonic at the Cardinal's expense, and withdrew from the court to his new castle of Thornbury in October 1520. The danger signals were multiplying, and neither Wolsey nor the king could afford to ignore them, especially when Buckingham began, in November, 1520, to mobilise an armed bodyguard for the purpose of touring his Welsh estates. In fact the duke seems to have been genuinely afraid of his Welsh tenants, and to have had no sinister purpose in mind, but he must have been extremely unintelligent not to have perceived the effect which his words and actions would have.

In the event, Wolsey had no difficulty in constructing a case of a sort against the duke, by exploiting the grievances of some of the latter's ex-servants; but it was mere hearsay, and should have been given no credence in a court of law. However, Henry had decided that Buckingham was a traitor, summoned him to court, and when he duly appeared, had him arraigned and executed. The ease with which the duke's destruction was accomplished is sufficient proof that there was no conspiracy about to issue in armed rebellion. Apart from a demonstration in London, there were no disturbances.[72] His noble affinity did not stir, and do not seem to have allowed the event to disrupt their own careers or interests to any great extent. In the words of his latest biographer, Carole Rawcliffe, 'Buckingham died because his pride and ambition made it impossible for him to accept the passive role of satellite and courtier which had been forced on so many of his peers'.[73] He could also be described as something of a political dinosaur, lacking the sharp ears and nimble feet which were necessary to retain his balance in a renaissance court. After ten years of chivalry and diplomacy, Henry VIII was becoming dangerous and unpredictable, suspecting even those who were ostensibly his closest friends. In 1519 he had actually written to Wolsey (a thing he very seldom troubled to do) instructing him to

> ... make good wache on the duke of Suffolke, on the duke of Bukyngham, on my lord off Northecomberland, on my lord off Darby, on my lord off Wylshere and on others whyche yow thynke suspecte ...[74]

Contrary to what is often said, the Cardinal's own relations with the English nobility were by no means consistently bad, or even distant. Wolsey's appearances at court were frequent, but usually of short duration; servants seem to have moved regularly and easily from the Cardinal's household to the king's and vice versa; and the matrimonial and political alliances which were formed at court were subject to his constant scrutiny. His good offices were frequently solicited, even by the greatest, and Suffolk, particularly, had many occasions to be grateful to him. On the other hand, one of the results of Wolsey's ascendency was that a division grew up between those who were prepared to work with him and support his policies, and those who were not. Norfolk and Suffolk tended to be in the former camp; Buckingham, Northumberland and Shrewsbury in the latter.[75] Shrewsbury's position was particularly difficult. As Lord Steward his presence at court was needed and expected; as an opponent of Wolsey he found the court distasteful, and stayed away as much as possible—and more than was wise.

After 1521 the position began to change. The financial situation deteriorated, Wolsey began to make mistakes—particularly in the parliament of 1523 and over the Amicable Grant—and the king's anxiety about the succession became chronic. War with France from 1523 to 1525 kept many of the nobility busy with military responsibilities; and the treaty of the More, which brought that war to an end, was no more universally popular than the treaty of London had been in 1518. There was a flurry of political activity in the summer of 1525, as the king's illegitimate son, the six year old Henry FitzRoy, was created Duke of Richmond and endowed with great estates in the north of England. In one sense, FitzRoy was no more than an excuse to revive conciliar government in the north, and his entourage was a vehicle for Wolsey's influence.[76] However, the peerage creations which accompanied his elevation, particularly those of Henry Courtenay as Marquis of Exeter and Henry Brandon as Earl of Lincoln, indicate that the king was following his own priorities, and serve as a reminder that there were always powerful courtiers who owed little to the Cardinal, and who dealt with him as independent agents, not as clients. It was at this time that the king released his brother-in-law the Duke of Suffolk from his enormous burden of debt, and thereby surrendered a weapon which Wolsey would probably have preferred to retain. The Cardinal's sensitivity to challenges at court was revealed again in January 1526, in the Eltham Ordinances. As we have seen, there was a strong case for reform,[77] but the main thrust of the scheme lay in the reduction of the Privy Chamber, and particularly in the removal of Sir William Compton, the Groom of the Stool. However, this was to be Wolsey's last significant victory. By 1527 he was losing the king's confidence, and Henry's developing relationship with Anne Boleyn presaged a complete change in the political situation. The progress of the king's 'Great Matter' is too well known to need discussion here, but its impact upon the court was profound.

In its early stages, while Wolsey was still upon the scene, it produced an alliance between Anne, her father Lord Rochford, her kinsman the Duke of Norfolk, and the Duke of Suffolk, against the Cardinal. He was accused of ousting the aristocracy from their rightful places about the king, of 'accroaching' the king's authority, and even of supplanting the 'councillors born'.[78] At first much of this bile seeped out through the writings of John Skelton, who, in spite of (or perhaps because of) his court connections, was a Howard client. The instigators of this campaign knew little about Henry if they thought that he would submit to the imposition of 'councillors born', but they rightly judged that his mind was ready to be poisoned against Wolsey. Ironically, because this was largely a court matter, those peers who had kept their distance, and who in many ways were the Cardinal's most thoroughgoing enemies, such as the Earls of Shrewsbury and Northumberland, played no part in it. Wolsey was trapped, because if he failed to secure an annulment of Henry's marriage, the king would clearly lose patience with him, while if he succeeded, he would face the bitter hostility of the new queen and her kindred. His eventual fall in 1529, and death in the following year, did not resolve the crisis, but it did produce a revival of noble influence at the centre of government—and a fresh crop of peerages. Lord Rochford became Earl of Wiltshire, George Hastings, Earl of Huntingdon, and Robert Radcliffe, Earl of Sussex. None of these men, however, had the courage or imagination to cut the Gordian knot of Henry's marriage, and it was more humble advisers, such as the authors of the 'collectanea satis copiosa', and eventually Thomas Cromwell, who succeeded where they had failed.[79] This produced a fresh alignment of forces in 1532–3. As the Boleyns gained the ascendency they became less dependent upon Norfolk and Suffolk, who lost political influence, particularly after the rise of Cromwell and Archbishop Thomas Cranmer in 1533. At the same time the nature of the solution which was found—no less than the repudiation of papal authority—introduced for the first time an ideological element into court politics.

Anne Boleyn herself was openly sympathetic to religious reform, more so, probably, than the nature of her position demanded.[80] In that she was not followed by the two dukes, but was in close sympathy with Cranmer and Cromwell, the latter of whom had become the king's chief adviser by 1534, and had attracted a numerous clientage of his own. At the same time Catherine's determined resistance, and the shabby treatment which she and Mary received at the king's hands after their formal repudiation, attracted the loyalty and sympathy of religious conservatives. Such sentiment was strong in the court, where Catherine in particular had been popular, although to call it the 'Aragonese faction' is to give an impression of definition, even organisation, which is most misleading.[81] Eustace Chapuys, the Imperial ambassador, talked with many discontented noblemen, and formed a vague impression of powerful opposition to the king's proceedings—but that was what he wanted to believe, and although several peers, notably the Earl of Shrewsbury, carefully absented themselves from Anne's coronation, their opposition was exceedingly reticent and restrained.[82] At this stage only Sir Thomas More, the former Lord Chancellor, objected openly and on principle to the king's ecclesiastical jurisdiction; and his execution in 1535 effectively deterred anyone else of importance from following his lead. It also destroyed a minor, but once influential, court affinity. The politics of the court in the tense years from 1533 to 1536 were more a question of degree than of clear-cut divisions. Religious reformers, like the young Lord Thomas Wentworth, were among Anne's most enthusiastic partisans, but conservatives such as Stephen Gardiner could be equally committed to the royal supremacy. Similarly not all those who sympathised with Catherine regretted the exclusion of the pope, or had any clear conviction that the king had acted *ultra vires*. Also, the brooding presence of Thomas Cromwell, and his exceedingly efficient intelligence work, prevented parties or factions from developing any kind of identity or momentum.[83]

The factor which disrupted this precarious stability was the death of Catherine of Aragon in January 1536. Henry, who had been tiring of Anne for some months, and seeking consolation with a young lady of modest birth called Jane Seymour, could now remove his queen and start afresh. A divorce was prepared, based upon the consanguinity resulting from the king's liaison with Mary Boleyn, but events soon swept this moderate solution aside. One reason for this was that Anne was a fighter, and her affinity was strong in the court, even when it was no longer supported by the Howards or Suffolk. Another was that Thomas Cromwell had begun to find the reforming proclivities of the Boleyns more of a hindrance than a help in promoting his cherished plans;[84] and the third was that Mary's supporters believed that a mere divorce would not be sufficient to bring about the princess's reinstatement. 'Stone dead hath no fellow', as was later said of Strafford. The alliance which formed against the Boleyns in March and April 1536 was thus as opportunist in its nature as it was overwhelming in strength. Cromwell's involvement removed the inhibitions which had earlier frustrated the growth of faction, and gave the campaign a ruthlessness and efficiency which it might otherwise have lacked. At the end of April the queen was framed on charges of treasonable adultery which even her arch-enemy Eustace Chapuys found unconvincing.[85] Also involved were her brother George, Lord Rochford, three prominent members of the Privy Chamber, Sir Francis Weston, Henry Norris, and William Brereton, and one of the musicians, Mark Smeaton. The Earl of Wiltshire was left, isolated and powerless, to die three years later without surviving issue. Inevitably, no sooner was this victory achieved than the alliance fell apart. Mary herself seems to have been convinced that as soon as 'the concubine' was removed, she would be restored to her father's favour. It therefore came as a most unpleasant shock when the king himself insisted upon submission to his ecclesiastical supremacy. Mary resisted, Henry became enraged, and Cromwell rapidly detached himself from his conservative allies. The Marquis of Exeter and Sir William Fitzwilliam were excluded from the court, and several others, including Sir Nicholas Carew, Sir Anthony Browne and Sir Thomas Cheney were questioned about expressions of support for 'the Princess'—a title which Lady Hussey was sent to the Tower for using.[87] Cromwell had not only side-stepped adroitly, leaving the Marians to collide with the full force of the king's wrath; he also succeeded in compelling her submission. This not only strengthened his own position in Henry's favour, but also cut the ground from under the feet of those who seem to have been preparing to use Mary as a figurehead for belated resistance to the king's policies. Within a few days her household had been reconstituted, and partly through the good offices of the new queen, Mary was able to return to court.

Within the court, Cromwell's victory during the summer of 1536 had been complete, and he was able to build up his own affinity within the Privy Chamber, temporarily detaching the offices of Chief Gentleman and Groom of the Stool.[88] Outside the court the situation was much more threatening. In early October rebellion broke out in Lincolnshire, followed a few weeks later by the Pilgrimage of Grace, which spread right across the north of England. How far these risings were the result of the defeat of the Marians at court, and how far of widespread and spontaneous discontent is a matter of controversy.[89] Disaffected courtiers such as Lord Darcy and Lord Hussey were certainly prominent; and the involvement of a large part of the Percy affinity (although not of the Earl of Northumberland himself) probably arose also from court-centred grievances. However, Mary's cause did not feature very prominently in the Pilgrims' Articles, and none of her most powerful sympathisers, such as the Earl of Shrewsbury or the Marquis of Exeter, became involved. Little as they may have liked Cromwell, the magnates were not convinced by Lord Darcy's appeal to ancient chivalric honour, and rallied to the Crown—Derby and Cumberland, no less than Norfolk or Suffolk. At Christmas 1536 Mary played a prominent role in the festivities of the court, as though to demonstrate that her political importance had been neutralised. Nevertheless, faction was more easily stimulated than quelled, and the passing of real danger to the regime (which the Pilgrimage had certainly been) did not see a return of peace to the court.

The struggles of the next few years are obscure in many details, but clear enough in outline. In 1538 Cromwell defeated the remaining conservatives, exploiting Henry's fear of the residual dynastic challenge of the 'White Rose'. The Marquis of Exeter and Lord Montague went to the block, and the aged Countess of Salisbury to the Tower, to be executed in 1541. In 1540 an alliance of religious conservatives, led by Stephen Gardiner, with the Howards and other court nobles, succeeded at last in poisoning the king's mind against Cromwell, and he was also hustled unceremoniously to his death. However, Cromwell's fall turned out to be only a very partial victory for his enemies. Not only did his secular affinity—men such as Audley, Rich and Paget—continue in office and authority, but his powerful ecclesiastical ally Cranmer also retained the king's confidence.[90] In fact the reform movement had grown, even within the court, into something much wider than a mere 'Cromwellian faction', and although the destruction of the great minister was a major setback, it was not a final defeat. Queen Jane had not survived the birth of Prince Edward in 1537, but her kindred had; Edward Seymour became Earl of Hertford in that year, and his brother Sir Thomas was shortly after appointed to the Privy Chamber. Both were members of the 'reform party', and both retained their places in 1540. It is probably more accurate to see the years 1540–43 as a Howard ascendency, rather than a religious reaction, and the fall of Catherine Howard, Henry's fifth wife, in the latter year brought that phase to an end. From then until the end of the reign the reform party continued to grow in size and influence. Henry's last queen, Catherine Parr, supported it, and so did her kin, notably her brother William who was given Cromwell's former Earldom of Essex in 1543. Together with the Seymours and the surviving Cromwellians, they formed a formidable alliance, and dominated the Privy Chamber by 1545. Against them, the Howards became increasingly isolated. Shrewsbury died in 1538, Southampton in 1542, and Suffolk in 1545. Stephen Gardiner tried hard to exploit the king's horror of radical heresy, and turn his mind against the reformers as he had against Cromwell; but he was defeated both over the so-called 'prebends plot' aimed at Cranmer in 1543, and also in his attack on the queen in the Anne Askew case three years later.[91] In the last months of the reign, Hertford, Paget and Sir Anthony Denny, the Groom of the Stool, enjoyed complete ascendency at court—and they achieved that position with Henry's full knowledge and consent.

Whether the king either knew of, or consented to, what happened in the last weeks of his life is, however, another matter. Gardiner's fall from favour was a direct consequence of his defeat by Catherine over the Anne Askew affair, and was certainly Henry's own doing,[92] but the use of a dry stamp in place of the royal sign manual to authenticate documents makes it hard to be certain of the king's effectiveness in the latter part of 1546—especially since the stamp was controlled by Denny. By the beginning of December the Privy Council was not meeting at court but at the Earl of Hertford's town house, and on the twelfth of that month the Howards were suddenly struck down. The Earl of Surrey's arrogant and indiscreet behaviour had given his enemies the opening which they had long been seeking, and he and his father were both arrested on charges of treasonable conspiracy. Henry must have given his consent to this, because he was still intermittently *compos mentis* and capable of discussing affairs, but it is unlikely that he had any positive hand in it. Surrey was executed on 19th January, and Norfolk reprieved by the king's own death on the 28th. On 26th December the king approved a will giving the reforming party complete control over the executors who were to form Edward's council. He never signed it, and the stamp may have been applied after he had lost all awareness of his surroundings,[93] but it did represent his last conscious intention, and marked the end of a long and fluctuating faction struggle which had been going on since the early 1530s. It also brought to power in the new reign a party which had a number of clearly defined policies with a marked ideological content.

Within a few weeks the last important conservative on the council, the Lord Chancellor Wriothesley, had been dismissed, the Earl of Hertford had become Lord Protector, and the first indications of an openly Protestant religious settlement had appeared. The politics of the court had, however, moved a great deal faster than that of the country as a whole. A majority of the citizens of London, and a minority of university intellectuals and of the gentry of south-eastern England, supported the new orientation of policy. Otherwise its advocates were few and far between.[94] The political nation as a whole was either hostile or indifferent, and nothing demonstrates more clearly the ascendency which the court had achieved in national affairs than the failure of this hostility to become articulate and effective. One of the reasons for this was lack of leadership. Established magnates, like the Earls of Arundel, Shrewsbury and Derby, who were not members of the 'inner ring', nevertheless appeared at court and played their part in its ceremonies and formalities. This was partly because they had accepted the royal supremacy, and bought shares in it along with the monastic land; partly in the hope that there was more to come with the dissolution of the chantries; and partly because they had not grasped the radical implications of what was happening. For many months Stephen Gardiner was an isolated voice of protest; and when resistance did begin to appear in the summer of 1548, it was associated with agrarian discontent in a manner calculated to rally all men of property to the government.[95] Consequently the political strife of 1547–9 took place within the court, not between 'court' and 'country'; and between factions of the reforming party, not between reformers and conservatives. There were a number of reasons why the Lord Protector had become unpopular with his erstwhile supporters by 1549: he had failed in Scotland, with disastrous results for the Crown's finances; he had virtually appropriated the decision making functions of the council; and he had posed as a social reformer, in a manner more calculated to stir up strife than to appease or suppress it. First he was manoeuvred into ordering the execution of his delinquent brother Lord Seymour of Sudeley; and then his position was surreptitiously assailed by a coalition of interests led by the Earl of Warwick. In October 1549 Warwick brought down the Protector, very much as Cromwell had brought down Anne Boleyn, by allying with the conservatives and Marians.[96] Foreign observers thought that a religious reaction was likely, and that Mary would be named as Regent. However, in the power struggle which followed, Warwick gained control both of the council and the Privy Chamber, with results which we have already noticed. The Earls of Arundel and Southampton were expelled from the court and placed under house arrest; and far from initiating a reaction, Warwick allied himself with the most radical wing of the Protestant party.

However, his power base had by now became dangerously narrow. Instead of conciliating conservative, but basically tractable nobles such as Derby and Shrewsbury, he quarrelled with them, and by March 1551 they had entered into negotiations with the ex-Protector, by then released and restored to the council. As we have seen, Somerset's return to the court had created something of a siege mentality, and there were rumours of rebellion, and of an attempted *coup* throughout the summer.[97] Briefly, Warwick reconciled himself with the northern earls, and then in October, struck down Somerset a second time—this time finally. In December 1551 Warwick (by that time Duke of Northumberland) rallied his supporters and their retinues—'a gret muster of men of armes'—in Hyde Park. Present were the Marquises of Northampton and Winchester, the Earls of Bedford, Rutland, Huntingdon and Pembroke, and Lords Bray, Cobham and Darcy.[98] Of his allies, only the Marquis of

Dorset was absent from this display of strength—which was no doubt connected with the prosecution of Somerset, then going ahead. After Somerset's execution in January 1552, Northumberland appeared to be in complete command of the situation. Although Derby and Arundel remained aloof, the Earl of Shrewsbury was now drawn into the net, and was granted several valuable properties in London. Although some contemporaries thought he was being held at court against his will, there is no evidence of this, and he eventually became deeply involved in the proclamation of Jane Grey.[99] By the time that Edward's health reached crisis point in June 1553, it appeared that Northumberland had built up the narrow court faction which had backed him in the autumn of 1549 into an impressive political interest, with many ramifications beyond the confines of the court.

The king's death, as we have seen, exposed the limitations of this achievement, and brought about a confrontation between the 'country' and the 'court' of a kind which had not been seen since the mid-fifteenth century. Mary's earliest supporters were 'backwoods' peers, like John Bourchier, Earl of Bath, and East Anglian gentry, several of whom had connections with the fallen Howards.[100] However, the court was riddled with doubt and division. Apart from the three families of Dudley, Grey and Parr, Northumberland's support was far from solid. Not even the Protestants believed in the legitimacy of Jane Grey's claim, and many of those who signed the engagement of the council to support her had been bribed or bullied into line at the last moment, like Lord Paget and the Earl of Arundel. Confronted with the evidence of Mary's rapidly growing camp at Framlingham in the second and third weeks of July, this fragile and mutually suspicious coalition fell apart, and all those who could plausibly do so hastened to make their peace with the new queen. As a result, Mary picked up rather more debts of gratitude than she could conveniently handle, and was forced to assemble a large and heterogenous council. To the original core of her own household servants—men such as Sir Robert Rochester and Sir Edward Waldegrave—she added the more important of her early adherents as they joined her: John Bourchier, Earl of Bath, Henry Radcliffe, Earl of Sussex, and Sir Thomas Wharton.[101] However, until the first Edwardian councillors began to make their submissions, she could command very little political experience, and men such as Arundel, Paget and Bedford were indispensable. Eventually Mary recruited eleven out of the thirty-three members of Edward's last council onto her own board, and the presence of so many 'conspirators' caused considerable friction. On 16th August the Imperial ambassadors reported that there was great discontent among the queen's 'old servants', and that the Earl of Derby was grumbling vigorously.[102] Perhaps it was not a coincidence that Derby was sworn of the council the next day. Despite the queen's hopes for reconciliation, and an end to the strife which had been stirred up by the reforming factions, her own court and council were afflicted by similar divisions—less lethal in outcome, but motivated by the same mixture of personal and political disagreements.

Mary's lack of experience in dealing with such disputes was quickly exposed, and her natural diffidence encouraged her cousin, the Emperor Charles V, to intrude his influence and advice. On 23rd August he wrote to his ambassadors

> If you have an opportunity of speaking to her without her taking it in bad part, you might give her to understand that people are said to murmur because some of her ladies take advantage of their positions to obtain certain concessions for their own private interest and profit . . .[103]

Instead of being told to mind his own business, the resident ambassador, Simon Renard, was soon the queen's closest and most confidential adviser. Consequently, he was far too closely involved for his accounts of the politics of the court to be taken at their face value. For several weeks he feared the rivalry of the Courtenays, as he negotiated delicately for Mary's marriage to Philip, and they appear in his dispatches as a malign and disruptive influence.[104] On 27th August he reported that the Earl of Pembroke was seeking to advance himself by their means, and was consequently supporting the Earl of Devon's candidature for the queen's hand. In the event, the Courtenays turned out to be feeble antagonists, but opposition to the Spanish marriage was strong, particularly among the queen's household officers. The chief advocate of a domestic marriage was the Chancellor, Stephen Gardiner, and he was supported by a number of peers, such as the Earls of Derby and Pembroke, and by numerous members of the House of Commons. On the other side, supporting Renard's efforts, stood Lord Paget, a few other members of the council, and the Ladies of the privy Chamber. Once it became clear that the queen had made up her mind, Gardiner and most of his aristocratic allies accepted her decision with a good grace—but they did not like it. Moreover, the personal feud between Gardiner and Paget, which had existed for several years, had been greatly exacerbated by the marriage dispute, and continued to dominate the court until the early summer of 1554.

When Sir Thomas Wyatt's rebellion broke out in January, Paget tried to discredit the Chancellor by accusing him of half-heartedness in its suppression, and then got himself into difficulties by trying to protect Princess Elizabeth, who was widely suspected of involvement.[105] By the end of March, honours were more or less even, as Gardiner's religious interpretation of the revolt gained official credence, and Paget threw himself into the preparation of Philip's English household. This was naturally a contentious matter, and one which the English courtiers were determined to sort out for themselves. When the inquisitive Renard was fobbed off, he blamed his failure on the quarrelsomeness of the English.

> The disputes are so venemous at the moment that I am unable to discover who the officers are, or what posts they are to fill; for everyone tells me that the decision rests with the Earl of Arundel, Great Master of the Household, while Arundel sends me to other . . .[106]

When it finally emerged, Philip's English household can have contained few surprises. Under Sir John Williams as Chamberlain and Sir John Huddlestone as Vice Chamberlain were to serve the young Earl of Surrey (heir to the aged Duke of Norfolk), and the eldest sons of the Earls of Arundel, Derby, Shrewsbury, Pembroke, Sussex and Huntingdon, as Principal Gentlemen. Twenty-three gentlemen servants,[100] yeomen servants, and a guard of 100 archers were also named. There does not appear to have been anything particularly contentious about these appointments, but as the summer wore on and Philip did not come, several of his designated attendants took themselves off without permission, claiming that they could not afford to remain at court without fee or reward.[107] By the time that the Prince of Spain arrived, the main genuine feud of the court had been resolved. In April, acting in the interests of his imperial allies, and possibly on their instructions, Lord Paget sabotaged in the House of Lords the Chancellor's efforts to promote a religious settlement. The queen was furious. Paget was lucky to escape arrest, and withdrew to his estates, where he rapidly became another source of anxiety to the ever suspicious Renard. During June and July he reported that first one peer, and then another, was plotting with Paget at his country retreat; Arundel and Pembroke against Gardiner; Shrewsbury against Derby.[108]

There were, of course, personal and family quarrels at Mary's court, which went on throughout the reign, but the first major faction contest ended with the fall of Paget. Gardiner thereafter remained indisputably the queen's chief minister until his death in November 1555. However, Philip's arrival also changed a number of things. Renard was immediately eclipsed, and no longer featured in the inner circle of the court; squabbles between English courtiers paled into insignificance in the face of hostilities between English and Spaniards; and Philip himself became Mary's chief confidant. It was Philip who arranged Paget's gradual rehabilitation, and secured him the office of Lord Privy Seal after the death of the Earl of Bedford in March 1555. But the expectation that the king would build up a following among his English lords was never fulfilled, and there was never a 'king's party' (apart from Paget and a few soldiers) either during his residence in England or afterwards. Philip probably secured the release of the Dudley brothers from the Tower in January 1555, and, as we have seen, he made use of them in some tournaments,[109] but they did not return to court—presumably because of Mary's understandable hostility. After the king's departure in August 1555, the politics of the court seems to have been distinctly subdued. Gardiner's death and Paget's distance from the queen removed the two dominant personalities from the centre of events. Antoine de Noailles, the French ambassador, continued the intrigues which he had been conducting since the beginning of the reign, and continued to find informants among the minor courtiers, such as Sir John Leigh. It was rumoured that a party among the English peers, and particularly the Earls of Arundel, Derby, Shrewsbury and Pembroke, favoured Philip's coronation, and this caused some alarm, but it appears to have been without firm foundation.[110] The religious persecution, which has loomed so large in the subsequent historiography of the period, was scarcely an issue at court, although the fact that Cardinal Pole became Mary's closest adviser after Gardiner's death reduced the potential influence of his fellow councillors.

The two main issues of the latter part of the reign were the question of war with France, and the question of the succession. The majority of Mary's council were opposed to involvement in the war, but were eventually overridden by the king and queen. Once war was declared, the prospect of military service and reward brought a number of peers back to the court; the Earl of Shrewsbury found an honourable command on the Scottish border, and the Earl of Pembroke in the Low Countries; and the mobilisation of the fleet created many other opportunities. There seems to have been little social stress or contention during these years,[111] but the war was not popular outside the ranks of the military aristocracy, and a combination of harvest failure and disease produced an atmosphere of gloom which many observers commented upon. By the summer of 1558 the queen's health and spirits were failing rapidly. In early September Sir Edward Waldegrave and Sir Francis Engle-field had to be summoned to court 'for that presently, there wanteth councillors here . . .'.[112] Mary did not want Elizabeth to succeed, and clung desperately to the hope of children of her own; but by 1558 that hope had faded, and there was no plausible alternative except the Francophile Mary of Scotland, whose claim Philip would not countenance. Elizabeth had had friends and supporters in high places throughout the reign, particularly among her Howard kinsfolk, and in the late summer of 1558 this connection began to be quietly mobilised. Realising the situation, and being in no position to press a claim of his own, Philip sent his confidential envoy, the Conde de Feria, to see Elizabeth, and the result was, Feria reported, mutually satisfactory.[113] Fortunately, in the last weeks of her life, Mary accepted the inevitable, and there was no disputed succession when she died on the 17th November. An alternative court, and an alternative administration, existed at Hatfield and Ashridge in the autumn of 1558, and Elizabeth took over the reins of government more in the manner of an American president taking over the White House than in the manner of her father succeeding her grandfather, or of her brother succeeding her father. If there was an 'anti-court' party during Mary's reign, it was not a 'country' party in the normal sense, but a surreptitious link up between the princess's affinity and the remnants of the Dudley, Seymour and Parr connections, which were gradually rebuilding themselves after 1555.[114] Within the court, in addition to the feuds which we have noticed, there was a half concealed rift between the conservative politiques, who included Paget and most of the secular peers and administrators, and the committed papalists such as Pole, Gardiner, and the queen's 'old' servants. When he was incensed or threatened, Gardiner was in the habit of referring to these politiques as 'heretics'—a term which Renard also sometimes used. After Gardiner's death this rift was much less evident, but it did not go away, and many of the politiques were willing to serve Elizabeth after 1558, in a manner which contributed greatly to the stability of her regime.

According to Francis Naunton 'the principal note' of Elizabeth's reign was 'that she ruled much by faction and parties, which she herself both made, upheld and weakened as her own great judgement advised'.[115] Among modern scholars, Professor Lawrence Stone has disagreed strongly with this interpretation, suggesting instead that the queen's attitude towards factions was one of tolerance or timidity bordering on the supine; and as we have seen, she did little to curb aristocratic violence, even when it came dangerously close to the court.[116] More recently, Dr Simon Adams has suggested that the factiousness of Elizabeth's court has been both overstressed and oversimplified, and that factions in the late Henrician or Edwardian sense scarcely existed until the last decade of the reign, when the Earl of Essex and his affinity confronted the Cecils.[117] Unlike her father, Elizabeth bestowed her confidence consistently over a long period of time. However, that could not have been anticipated in 1558, and the dominant position of Sir William Cecil among her advisers was frequently assailed during the first decade of the reign, with every apparent likelihood of success. The dominant issues of that period were religion and the queen's marriage, and there was no consensus within the council upon either. Important councillors, such as Winchester and Shrewsbury, disapproved of the Protestant settlement just as strongly as Cecil and Bedford promoted it. The Earl of Sussex and the Duke of Norfolk strove to persuade the queen into marriage with the Catholic Archduke Charles, while Robert Dudley promoted his own cause as vigorously as possible, and fell out with Cecil in the process. The queen's principal concern during these years, and Cecil's also, was to avoid creating an ideological split between the men of the 'new learning'—the Protestants whom Elizabeth conspicuously favoured at court —and the more conservative Erastians. This division naturally tended to correspond to that between those who sought a Protestant marriage (and encouraged suitors such as Eric of Sweden) and those who supported the Archduke. However, Dudley was a maverick element in this contest, and Cecil tended to the conservative side, partly to confuse the ideology of the debate.[118]

There were numerous other issues of disagreement, such as intervention in Scotland and in France, and the personal feuds, like that between Sussex and Dudley which we have already noticed. Consequently the rivalry between Cecil and Dudley, although it was real enough, should not be overemphasised, or regarded as the sole key to court alignments. There were also some groups which were excluded from the court altogether by royal disfavour: extreme Protestants like Whitehead and Goodman, who might have expected major preferments after their years in exile; and the highly conservative Earls of Northumberland and Westmorland. These latter were probably no more 'Catholic' than many who remained at court, like Arundel and Shrewsbury, but they had never been courtiers, and Elizabeth gave them no encouragement. Indeed, by returning to her father's policy in the north, and depriving Northumberland of his recently recovered offices, she gave him one of the most potent of old-fashioned grievances. The critical year 1568 saw a series of events which rapidly sharpened all these conflicts. Negotiations with the Archduke Charles collapsed, removing the most promising candidate from the marriage stakes; Mary, Queen of Scots abandoned her throne and fled across the border; and Cecil requisitioned the Genoese ships bearing the cash to pay the Duke of Alba's troops in the Netherlands. This last move acutely alarmed the conservatives at court, who openly accused him of risking war with Spain, and secretly set up an intrigue to remove him, of which the main movers were the Earl of Arundel and Lord Lumley. Northumberland and Westmorland were also involved in this intrigue, but because of their remoteness from the court it is not at all clear how much they knew of what was going on. At the same time another group, led by the Earl of Leicester and Sir Nicholas Throgmorton, endeavoured to persuade the queen to neutralize Mary, Queen of Scots by marrying her to the Duke of Norfolk, who, if not a committed Protestant, was at least a conformist.[119] There was an overlap between these two groups, and Cecil's position (although he was not averse to the Norfolk marriage) appeared to be threatened on all sides. However, Elizabeth was less amenable to persuasion than her father, and in a celebrated scene in the Privy Chamber on 22 February 1569, she denounced the intrigues against her Secretary, and declared her full confidence in his judgement.[120] For a time Leicester bore the main brunt of the queen's displeasure, and carefully distanced himself from the attack upon Cecil, but as the summer wore on he discovered more about the wider implications of the conservative intrigues, and decided upon a bolder stroke to restore his fortunes. While the court was at Titchfield on the summer progress, he feigned illness, and persuaded the queen to visit him on his 'sickbed'. Having thus inveigled her into a private conversation he disclosed all that he knew, about the Norfolk marriage project and about the danger of Catholic disaffection.[121] His manoeuvre was completely successful. His own intimacy with Elizabeth was restored, and the queen rounded furiously on the Duke of Norfolk. Norfolk foolishly fled from the court in alarm, and there were immediate rumours that his affinity was in rebellion. Whether the Duke could have led a major revolt must remain an open question, because in the event he surrendered and was imprisoned in the Tower, leaving his northern allies (whose footwork was not sufficiently adroit), in an exposed state of semi-insurrection. The resulting crisis is outside the scope of this study, but it is quite clear that it was made at court. The only reason why the northern earls were trapped in open rebellion was that they were inadequately informed about what was happening at the centre—and particularly about the queen's real attitude to Cecil and Norfolk.

The 1569 rebellion, followed by the Bull *Regnans in Excelsis*, narrowed the political and religious options of the court sharply. Conservative positions which had been acceptable before 1569 now became indistinguishable from treason—a point emphasised by the Ridolphi plot and the execution of Norfolk. As a result the court became more homogeneous. More energetic Protestants were promoted: Sir Walter Mildmay, Sir Thomas Smith, the Earl of Warwick, Sir Henry Sidney and Sir Francis Walsingham. The conservative nobility withdrew to their estates—or in some cases, overseas. By 1580 recusancy was a serious problem, and although the queen typically reserved the right to protect (and even favour) individual Catholics, they ceased to be a significant presence. Significantly, this did not result in the development of a new and powerful 'country' party; and although the cause of Mary, Queen of Scots continued to have adherents, most of the Catholics, high and low, were only too anxious to deny all treasonable intent, and to make every possible demonstration of their loyalty.[122] After 1570 the political issues contested at court were somewhat different: the rise of puritanism (over which Leicester and Walsingham tended to be at odds with Burleigh and Hatton); the Anjou marriage; and above all, intervention in the Netherlands. In every case these were issues in which scope was given for conflict by the ambiguity of Elizabeth's own attitude.[123] Her own personality was completely dominant, and she dictated the limits within which her advisers might disagree. At the same time there were no factions in the proper sense, although the debate over the Netherlands tended to produce alignments, and the revived personal rivalry between Leicester and Sussex after 1580 correponded with their disagreement over policy.

This situation was changed by the deaths of Leicester (1588) and Walsingham (1590), which greatly increased the hold of the Cecils. Lord Burleigh and his second son, Robert, shared the queen's unenthusiastic attitude towards the war with Spain, and by 1595 had secured an ascendency in both court and council which neither they, nor any other group, had enjoyed earlier in the reign. As she became old, her old courtiers were naturally closest to her. Apart from Burleigh, these were Lord Howard of Effingham, who became Lord Steward and Earl of Nottingham in 1597, Lord Buckhurst, Sir Thomas Heneage (Vice Chamberlain from 1587) and Sir John Fortescue. The sons of earlier courtiers also tended to succeed their fathers; George, Lord Hunsdon, became Lord Chamberlain in 1597, and Sir William Knollys Comptroller in 1596.[124] Into this circle Robert Devereux, second Earl of Essex, intruded himself by a straightforward appeal to the queen's susceptibilities— as Dudley, Raleigh and Hatton had done before him. However, lacking their political intelligence, he presumed upon her favour too far. By 1600 he was firmly shut out of power by Robert Cecil, and found himself with an extensive clientage which he was increasingly unable to satisfy. Essex did not, in fact, have much of a faction. His only consistent ally among the older generation of courtiers was Lord North, and such unstable young men as the Earl of Southampton were liabilities rather than assets when it came to serious political in-fighting. As we have seen, it was desperation which drove him to revolt; but it was also a measure of the queen's deteriorating faculties that she had allowed such a situation to come about. Essex was the last, and perhaps the least admirable, manifestation of Elizabeth's consuming vanity. He succeeded only because he dazzled and flattered her; and although she had no opinion of his ability, and no intention of promoting him to office, she could not bear to dismiss him from the court. For the most part the political quarrels which divided Elizabeth's courtiers were affairs of state, usually tinged with religious ideology: her marriage, the succession, foreign policy. To a lesser extent they were personal quarrels between ambitious men promoting their careers. But there was also a third element which should be mentioned, because it emphasises the enhanced importance of the court as a national centre since the early part of our period. This was the tendency to resolve innumerable local quarrels by invoking the good offices of patrons at court. Usually informal arbitration by councillors or courtiers was the method used—or direct negotiations, if more than one patron was involved. Sometimes an intractable case might be referred to the more formal procedures of Star Chamber. Even more rarely, the queen herself might intervene. Sometimes, no doubt, patrons took up the quarrels of their clients, and made the situation worse rather than better; but the Earl of Leicester (who had plenty of experience in such affairs) described himself in terms of an honest broker.

> I have never been willing to make quarrels in this court nor to breed any. Mine own honour and poor credit always saved, I neither have nor will be a peace breaker but a peace maker.[126]

If Leicester is to be credited in this, Elizabeth's courtiers were more prone to settle the disputes of their countries at Westminster or Windsor than to take their courtly quarrels back to their estates. Perhaps that is why the decline in aristocratic habits of violence, noticed but not explained by Lawrence Stone, came about during this same period.

Resident ambassadors

The exchange of ambassadors had been a regular feature of the political life of western Europe for many centuries. Issues of war and peace, and of royal marriages particularly, required embassies to be despatched with great ceremony, and received with lavish entertainment and the exchange of gifts. When Edward IV decided to seek an alliance with Burgundy through the marriage of his sister Margaret to Charles of Charolais, protocol required that the bridegroom's father, in the guise of suitor, should make the first formal move.

> After that thys poynte was clerely resolved on, the Duke appoynted hys bastard sonne lord Anthony, commonly called the bastarde of Bourgoyne, chefe ambassadoure for this purpose; a man of great witte, corage, valiantnes and liberalitie, whiche beyng richely furnished of plate & apparel, necessary for his estate, having in his company gentlemen & other expert in all feates of chivalry, and merciall prowes, to ye number of cccc horses (as the Brabanters write) toke hys ship, and

with prosperous wynde arryved in Englande, where he was of the nobilitie receyved and with al honourable entertainement, conveyed to the kynges presence whiche like a prince, that knew what apperteined to his degre lovingly welcomed, and familiarlye inbrased the bastard & other nobles yt came with him. And after hys commission seene and hys message declared, the Kynge gave hym a gentell answere for that tyme, and so the ambassadours departed to their lodgynge, where they kept a great household, and made triumphant chere. . . .[127]

Anthony was entertained with jousts, and taken to the state opening of parliament. All the major nobility of England took part in the festivities, and the absence of the Chancellor, George Neville, Archbishop of York was a prelude to his dismissal from office.

Not all special missions were as grand, or as important, as this one. Envoys from Genoa, or Venice, or Danzig were frequent visitors on commercial business; England and France received each other's ambassadors over matters of piracy, or border tensions around Calais; Francesco Coppini, a papal nuncio, even became actively involved in the events leading up to Edward's accession.[128] By the middle of the fifteenth century, several of the Italian states, finding these constant exchanges troublesome and expensive between neighbours whose business and political relationships were permanent, began to accredit resident agents to each other's governments. From Italy the practice spread gradually into the rest of Europe, particularly via those powers which had most need of regular representation in the north Venice and the papacy.

The first resident ambassador accredited to the English court was the Venetian Bernado Bembo, who arrived in July 1483.[129] Thereafter, the sequence of Venetian ambassadors was very nearly continuous, and their numerous lengthy dispatches form one of the most valuable sources for the political and diplomatic history of Tudor England, as well as a storehouse of gossip and chitchat of every kind.[130] Venetian diplomacy was already highly developed by the end of the fifteenth century; they moved their agents round every three or four years as a matter of course, and a career diplomat, such as Giacomo Soranzo later in the sixteenth century, might have served in three or four courts over a dozen years before returning to domestic employment. The status of Venice as a power declined steadily after about 1520, and most of the business conducted by its resident agents was commercial and routine. However, because of their acknowledged expertise, the Venetians were often used as intermediaries, rather in the way that the embassies of 'non-aligned' states are used today. Occasionally they burned their fingers, and Soranzo was sharply rebuked by the Council of Ten in 1554 for meddling in English affairs, when he became too closely involved with the French in their efforts to frustrate Mary's marriage.[131]

The papacy never maintained a resident nuncio in England. At first the Curia used the Cardinal Protectors of England, and later the English ambassadors in Rome, the last of whom—Sir Edward Carne—was withdrawn in 1559. For more than half the Tudor period there were no diplomatic relations between England and Rome; and for two periods (1518–29 and 1554–7) the resident legate in England was a high-ranking English ecclesiastic. Henry VII actually maintained two ambassador-proctors in Rome, one English and one Italian, but was otherwise slow to join in the new diplomatic game. The only other English resident abroad in his reign was John Stile, who was sent to Spain in 1505. Ferdinand had maintained an ambassador in London since 1486, the ill-used and much maligned Dr Rodrigo de Puebla, who was kept at his post with only one break for twenty years. What de Puebla did not know about England by 1516 was not worth knowing, but more often than not his advice was ignored. France was even slower than England in developing a diplomatic service, and had no residents, except in Rome, before 1526. It was not until 1528 that Jean du Bellay became the first French ambassador to reside in London.[132]

Even when it came to involve all the major powers on a reciprocal basis, however, the new diplomacy supplemented the old, rather than replacing it. For example, it was the Imperial resident in England, Simon Renard, who negotiated Mary's marriage with Philip; but a grand embassy of the traditional kind, headed by the Count of Egmont, was sent across to sign the treaty in December 1553.[133] One of the reasons for this was that it was considered to be too expensive to maintain the estate of a nobleman as resident, and the permanent ambassadors tended to be career civil servants of middle rank. De Puebla (as his name suggests) was a commoner, and although a skilled lawyer and an excellent diplomat, was consistently disparaged by aristocratic critics, both in Spain and England. Du Bellay was a bishop, and the Venetians were nearly always minor nobles, but the Imperial ambassadors—Eustace Chapuys, Van der Delft, Jehan Scheyfve and Simon Renard, were, in the English terminology, 'mere' gentlemen. English ambassadors were mostly of the same status—men such as William Knight and Richard Pace—although as the century wore on it became more common to send men of knightly rank. Accommodation was provided for residents by the monarchs to whom they were accredited, but their own lords were supposed to finance them, and all ambassadors constantly complained of being short of funds. Sometimes these complaints were fully justified. The unfortunate de Puebla was allowed 350 crowns a year—between £70 and £80—which, even when it was paid, sufficed only for the most modest establishment. He had virtually no private income, and would have ended in a debtor's prison if Henry VII had not rescued him.[134] De Puebla was an extreme case. His successors, men of somewhat higher rank, were allowed over four times as much, and the first Spanish ambassador of Elizabeth's reign, Alvarez de Quadra, received the equivalent of about £600 a year. This level of remuneration ran to a household of twenty or so, a certain amount of entertaining, adequate horses, and a respectable appearance at court. All this was essential if an ambassador was to perform his functions properly, and to uphold the honour of his lord as well as do his business. As usual, economy and reputation pointed in opposite directions, and by the following century important residencies were often occupied by noblemen with lavish establishments. However, Don Diego Sarmiento de Acuña, Count of Gondomar, who had to keep up with the fast pace of James I's court, was owed over 33,000 crowns by the Spanish government, and, in spite of his private wealth, was almost as close to bankruptcy as de Puebla had been a century earlier.

Ambassadors went to court, of course, when summoned, either by the monarch or by the council. They were also frequently invited to participate in ceremonies or entertainments, although these were seldom provided specifically for their benefit. In that the residents differed markedly from the extraordinary ambassadors. They might also take the initiative, seeking audience, although they did not risk dishonourable rebuffs by turning up without warning. Occasionally an ambassador's presence at, or absence from, a particular ceremony might be of considerable significance—as, for instance, when Eustace Chapuys absented himself from the coronation of Anne Boleyn,[135] or when Antoine de Noailles did not turn up to greet Mary on her entry into London. Much depended upon the status of the power represented, and upon the relationship between the monarchs concerned at the moment in question. Resident agents of lesser powers, such as Mantua, or the Hanseatic League, were not accorded ambassadorial rank, and were summoned, or invited, much less frequently. Also, an ambassador who was particularly favoured might be accorded the *entré* to the monarch's presence without formal summons. Simon Renard apparently visited Mary secretly, and even in disguise, during the autumn of 1553 when the marriage negotiations were at a critical stage.[136] Such visits must have been arranged by the queen personally, and would have been known to the Ladies of her Privy Chamber, but were concealed from her council. Ease of access to the court was of immense importance to an ambassador. Not only did it facilitate routine business, such as negotiating the release of arrested ships or seeking compensation against pirates, it also enabled him to discharge one of his most important and delicate functions. Being *persona grata* meant friendly relationships with important courtiers, and endless opportunities to gather information. By the middle of the sixteenth century all monarchs depended heavily upon the reports of their resident agents or ambassadors for knowledge of each other's minds, and of the internal state of each other's kingdoms. In August 1528 the shrewd du Bellay informed Francis I that Wolsey was no longer high in the king's confidence and that Henry was conducting some of his business without the knowledge of his minister.[137] Similarly, in May 1532 Eustace Chapuys wrote to Charles V:

> The king has again applied to parliament for a subsidy in money to fortify the frontiers of Scotland. During the debate two worthy members of that assembly were bold enough to declare openly and in plain terms that ... Parliament ought at once to petition the King to take back his legitimate wife, and treat her kindly ...[138]

Everthing, from weighty affairs of state to the most trivial of court gossip, tended to go into such dispatches, partly because court gossip could hold important clues, and partly because the ambassador was always anxious to demonstrate his zeal and, if possible, his closeness to the centre of power.

In addition to, or, if necessary, instead of, information legitimately gained, all ambassadors ran intelligence networks, with paid informers, casual or regular. An ambassador who was not in favour, and whose access to the court was formal and limited, had no option if he was to discharge his duties. Chapuys under Henry VIII, Van der Delft under Edward VI, Noailles under Mary, and de Quadra or Mendoza under Elizabeth are all examples of diplomats working under that kind of disadvantage. Such ambassadors also had a natural tendency to attract the disaffected. Chapuys held many clandestine meetings with Catherine's supporters, whom he was instructed to encourage. Noailles openly wined and dined members of parliament who were critical of Mary's pro-Habsburg policies; and de Quadra was used as a semi-official intermediary between the English Catholics and the papacy.[139] Unless the ambassador was exceptionally wealthy, or exceptionally skilful, his paid informers were always too few, or too unreliable, to give him a full picture. On the other hand, the disaffected saw everything through coloured spectacles. Chapuys believed that aristocratic opposition to Henry's divorce was overwhelming, and that the Earls of Derby and Shrewsbury would lead a revolt. Noailles believed that Mary could be overthrown by the Protestants, and Mendoza that Elizabeth would succumb to a massive Catholic insurrection. The only monarch who was seriously misled by such partisan views was Philip II, and he also listened to the English Catholic exiles. However, there was no doubt that a monarch would be better informed about a friendly court than a hostile one. Poor Van der Delft seems to have learned virtually nothing of what went on around Edward VI, and when he was required in March 1550 to make direct representations about Mary's mass, he received only a sharp rebuke from the English council. Two months later was was recalled.[140]

It was but a short step from gathering information in a hostile land to active involvement in subversion. It was also a very risky step, because the later immunity of ambassadors from arrest and punishment was not clearly established. When Antoine de Noailles became deeply involved in the Dudley conspiracy in 1556, and his involvement was disclosed by the interrogation of the plotters, the English council debated whether they could proceed against him 'as a plotter and contriver against the state and person of the sovereign with whom he resides'.[141] The eventual decision not to do so was political rather than legal, because at that point neither side was ready for war. However, Henri II got the message and recalled him. Sixteen years later the same legal point was more fully tested in the case of John Leslie, Bishop of Ross and accredited representative of Mary, Queen of Scots, who became embroiled in the Ridolphi plot. Leslie's diplomatic status could be (and was) challenged on the ground that his mistress was no longer in possession of a throne. However, the same legal advice went on to answer the question 'whether ... an Ambassador be in confederacy with traytors, knowing his treason against the prince within the realm he pretendeth to be an Ambassador, is punishable by the laws of the realm of that Prince?'. The answer was an unequivocal 'Yes', and that decision brought de Spes, the Spanish ambassador, and later Mendoza, within the danger of the same law.[142] Leslie was arrested and interrogated, but in the event none of these men was proceeded against. All three were expelled. If the ambassador's person was not immune, then it followed that neither his servants, nor his residence, nor his correspondence, were immune either. In 1524 Wolsey intercepted the dispatches of Louis de Praet, the Imperial ambassador, which were found to contain derogatory remarks about Henry VIII, and warnings about his untrustworthiness

> ... and so he sent for Monsire Pratt, and declared to hym the matter, which answered him that he was counsailer and Ambassador to the Emperor, and that it was his parte to assertain the Emperor of every thyng that was or might sound prejudicial to his majestie, but howsoever that his aunswere was taken, he was not favoured with the Cardinall, but he saide openly that it was not well meant to the Emperour to stop his packet with letters and to open them, and the Spaniardes saide that the Emperor sent them not into Englande to slepe, but to do him service.[143]

Wolsey brought de Praet before the king's council, and he was ordered to be detained in England during the king's pleasure, as one who had forfeited his ambassadorial status. The matter was eventually resolved by negotiation, and de Praet departed with full honours, but the vulnerability of an ambassador in a hostile environment had been well demonstrated. Later in the century dispatches were not openly stopped, but were regularly intercepted, and the conveying of secret or confidential information in security provided constant exercise for diplomatic ingenuity. Ambassadorial residences and households enjoyed *de facto* a privileged status. Servants were not immune from prosecution, but could normally be rescued by the intercession of the ambassador. Houses were not the property, let alone the sovereign territory, of the ambassador's state, but their integrity was normally respected—and that respect enforced against local law officers by the royal authority.[144]

Ambassadors were an important fact of life at the Tudor court–centres of intrigue, and sometimes the setters of styles and fashions, in literature, music, or clothes. The residents did not have the glamour or the impact of the special embassies, but their continual presence broadened the horizons of the English courtiers, and created many extra opportunities for introductions to other courts. They were not numerous, and there were seldom more than three or four residents of ambassadorial rank in England at the same time, although the representation of Venice, the Empire and France was continuous from 1483, 1496 and 1528 respectively, except in times of war. In 1557–8 there were no ambassadors in England—the only year in the century, as far as I am aware, of which that was true. The French ambassador had withdrawn because of the war; Imperial representation was in abeyance; Spain and England were ruled by the same king; the papal legate had had his powers withdrawn and the Venetian was accredited to Philip rather than Mary, and was consequently in Brussels.[145] Coincidentally, 1557–8, for a variety of other reasons, was also one of the gloomiest years through which the Tudor court was fated to pass. Under normal circumstances the ambassadors added both to the interest and the variety of life.

Religion

The focus of the formal religious life of the court was the Chapel Royal. At the time of the *Liber Niger* the staff comprised the Dean, the Clerk of the Closet, the Sergeant of the Vestry, twenty-six chaplains and clerks, two Yeomen of the Chapel, eight children and a singing master, forming an entirely autonomous department,[146] financed directly from the Exchequer. Over the following century and a half, this establishment changed very little, although the terminology was modified from time to time. At the end of Henry VIII's reign the Dean was assisted by a Gospeller, an Epistoler, a Verger, two Yeomen and a Master of the Children. By that time there were ten choristers, and twenty Gentlemen of the Chapel Royal.[147] At Mary's coronation, six years later, there were thirty Gentlemen (ten of whom had featured on the earlier list), two Gospellers, six Epistolers, and ten choristers.[148] In the 1580s, besides the Dean, Sub-dean and Master of the Choristers, there were thirty-two Gentlemen and twelve choristers.[149] The Epistolers and Gospellers had apparently been subsumed into the general category of Gentlemen, and the servants, if they still existed, were no longer paid regular wages.

The duties of this sizeable staff do not seem to have been particularly exacting. In Elizabeth's reign the whole choir sang only on Sundays and Feast days, the ferial weekday services requiring only half the Gentlemen, who appeared on an alternating monthly basis. No services were sung on ferial weekdays between St Peter's day and Michaelmas, nor in the weeks following Epiphany, Candlemas, Easter, St George's Day and Advent. When the court was on progress the Chapel was stood down, and similarly if it was at a lesser residence without an adequate chapel—somewhere like Ampthill or Nonsuch. The main staff functioned only at Whitehall, Greenwich, Richmond and Hampton Court, because Windsor had its own staff, in St George's Chapel, which was entirely distinct from, and equal in status to, that of the main Chapel Royal.[150] The Windsor staff was not itinerant, and sang its services all the year round. Both chapels were royal peculiars, exempt from episcopal jurisdiction, and under the direct control of the sovereign. As was often the case with court posts, the formal remuneration of the Gentlemen was not generous—£11.8.1½ per annum in the later part of the sixteenth century—the same as that of a departmental Sergeant. However, recognised fees and allowances brought that figure up to about £30, and there were many opportunities for such skilled musicians to undertake lucrative commissions outside the court.[151] Both the Gentlemen and the choristers also frequently performed in entertainments of a secular nature, as we have seen, and were often separately rewarded for those appearances.

One man who did consider himself to have a grievance, however, was the Master of the Children. In November 1583 William Hunnis complained that the allowance of sixpence a day each was quite inadequate for the feeding of his charges;

> Also there is no allowance for the lodging of the said children, such time as they attend upon the court, but the Master to his great charge is driven to hire chambers both for himself, his usher, children and servants. Also there is no allowance for riding journeys when occasion serveth the Master to travel or send into sundry parts within this realm to take up and bring such children as be thought meet to be trained for the service of Her Majesty.[152]

Hunnis did not ask for an increase in his own stipend of £40 a year, but rather that the children be given bouge of court during their attendance, and that he be paid out-of-pocket expenses, lest he be left in the parlous predicament of some of his predecessors '. . . so deeply indebted that they have not scarcely left wherewith to bury them'. The result of his plea is unknown, but it gives an excellent insight into the nature of his responsibilities. The Children themselves, in spite of being 'requisitioned' from cathedral choirs and parish churches up and down the country, seldom seem to have been discontented, or to have presented a disciplinary problem. They were, on the whole, well trained and looked after. John Merbecke, who was brought up in the corresponding establishment at Windsor, complained that he

> . . . in a maner never tasted the swetnes of learned letters, but was altogether brought up in your Highnes college . . . in the study of musike and plaiying organs, wherein I consumed vainly the greatest parte of my life[153]

but that was a somewhat ungracious grouse from a man who owed his highly successful career to the thoroughness of the training which he had received. In spite of Hunnis's claim to the contrary, when the choristers' voices broke, adequate consideration was given to their future. Normally one of the Masters of Requests would arrange to place the boy in Oxford or Cambridge, if he were bookishly inclined, or otherwise in a suitable trade or profession. Several former choristers later rejoined the Chapel as Gentlemen, and since that seems to have been a common ambition, such places presumably competed successfully with other opportunities. They also provided jobs for life. Resignations for reasons other than old age and infirmity were uncommon, and dismissals for misconduct rarer still. One Solomon Compton was discharged for bigamy in 1588,[154] but usually a reprimand or a small fine was the worst sanction which a Gentleman faced. Even during the period of the most intense religious upheavals, between 1547 and 1561, there was no appreciable increase in the turnover of Chapel staff. At least five of the Gentlemen appointed under Henry VIII were still in post in 1560, and nineteen of Mary's coronation list served, happily or unhappily, well into Elizabeth's reign.[155] In this continuity they closely resembled the Gentlemen Pensioners, and for much the same reason; the high value which they placed upon their positions induced a ready conformity to the changing religious practices of the court. Some of them served for remarkably long periods. John Fisher, appointed before 1503, was still singing (or at least drawing his fee) in 1547; Williams Hychyns, appointed in 1520, died in 1566; and Robert Stone, who appeared at Mary's coronation, survived until 1613. Although no differentiation appears in the records, it seems probable that not all Gentlemen of the Chapel were equal in status or function. Some, like Robert Fayrfax and Richard Pygott, were distinguished musicians who performed many other functions, both inside the court and outside.[156] It seems unlikely that they were required to sing ferial weekday services, and there was probably a recognised distinction between those who were simply choirmen (some of whom were in holy orders) and those who were specialised musicians. Probably the monthly shift system took account of this difference, and some ordinary choirmen served almost continuously when the Chapel was functioning. Later in the century, when the music became more sophisticated, specialist organists were recognised—although not differently remunerated. Both Thomas Tallis and William Byrd described themselves as 'Organists of the Chapel Royal', and at the end of the century John Bull was so designated in the Check Book.[157] In earlier years the work seems to have been shared out among a number of Gentlemen. One of the qualifications for appointment laid down in the *Liber Niger* had been 'sufficiaunt in organes playying . . .'.

Down to 1547 there was little change in the seasonal routine of the Chapel Royal. The liturgy and music of the church was not significantly affected by the storms over the king's 'Great Matter', or the establishment of the royal supremacy. Only the appearance of Cranmer's English Litany in 1544 had given a taste of what was to come. Cranmer's own thinking on this matter is well revealed in a letter to the king, probably of October 1554:

> Concerning the *Salve festa dies*, the Latin note, as I think, is sober and distinct enough; wherefore I have travailed to make the verses in English, and have put the Latin note unto the same. Nevertheless they that be cunning in singing can make a much more solemn note thereto. I made them only for a proof, to see how English would do in song.[158]

In other words, he was taking the traditional music of the chant, and fitting the English words to it. However, in 1549 when the first English prayer book was introduced, that soon proved to be unsatisfactory. The vernacular was too easily disguised by those who had a mind to do so:

> . . . the mass priests, although they are compelled to discontinue the use of the Latin

language, yet most carefully observe the same tone and manner of chanting to which they were heretofor accustomed in the papacy.[159]

One answer to this was to devise new music for the new liturgy, and John Merbecke accomplished this with this *Boke of Common Praier noted* in 1550, a work which was devised, and first performed, in the context of the Chapel Royal. Merbecke's melodies derived from plainsong, but his settings were entirely syllabic, word for note, and emphasised the effective words by setting them to high notes. As a result the language emerged far more clearly. This was a matter of great importance to the reformers, and Merbecke's setting can thus be fairly described as the first Protestant church music in England. Up to this point, it could be argued that the reformation had enhanced, rather than damaged, the development of liturgical music; but the same could not be said of the radical changes which were made in the prayer book between 1549 and 1552. The second prayer book of the latter year was drastically simplified under the influence of Strasburg and Zurich theologians such as Martin Bucer and Heinrich Bullinger. The Zurich school, particularly, was hostile to liturgical music as distracting the mind of the worshipper from the Word of God, and under its influence church organs were frequently defaced or destroyed.[160]

No such fate overtook the Chapel Royal, but for a year or two it seems likely that musical activity was seriously curtailed, as the Duke of Northumberland could hardly allow such a show place of public worship to set an example different from that which it was his intention to enforce elsewhere. At the same time, the physical appearance of the chapel had been progressively modified in accordance with successive sets of injunctions. Our Lady of Pew had long since gone, to be followed by the other images of saints and martyrs, the elaborate sacramental furnishings, and finally the altar itself, which was replaced by a communion table.[161] The sermons which Edward VI was so fond of attending were not necessarily delivered in the chapel, or as part of a formal act of worship. Sometimes they were more in the nature of free-standing lectures; but by 1553 sermons had become a regular feature of morning and evening prayer, at least on Sundays and other major occasions. The calendar had also been drastically simplified, and many of the old services abrogated. Richard Sampson, who had been Dean since 1525 in addition to numerous other ecclesiastical preferments, had no doubt moved as slowly as prudence dictated. He was not in day-by-day control, but the whole establishment was as conservative as every other department of the court, and would have required a major effort to dismantle or transform. So beneath the veneer of conformity, the Chapel Royal continued its reduced functions in much the same spirit as before. With the return of the Catholic ritual under Mary, it seems to have speedily recovered its old luxuriance; the number of Gentlemen was increased from twenty to thirty, and several Epistolers and Gospellers were added. Although there are constant references to Mary's piety, and to her attendance at mass in the Chapel, little is known about this last upsurge of official Catholicism. Richard Sampson died in 1554, but whether he had been displaced as Dean before that is uncertain; at the time of Mary's death the Dean was a man called Hutchenson, who is only a name.[162] Whether the new splendour of vestments and ornaments, the traditional polyphonic masses, and the return of the elaborate pre-reformation calendar were matched by the quality of the music is not at all clear. Sermons retreated to the periphery of worship, and the sacrament of the altar returned to its central place. The Chapel Royal was required, as always, to demonstrate the nature of the monarch's religious convictions to the outside world, but it seems likely that both Philip and Mary depended for their main spiritual support upon their confessors and 'Chaplains of the closet', rather than upon the main chapel. To what extent attendance at the chapel was required of courtiers in any reign is impossible to say, and we have it on the testimony of Edward Underhill that there was no better place to 'shift the Easter time' than Queen Mary's court.[163]

With the accession of Elizabeth the liturgy of 1552 returned, and Hutchenson was promptly replaced by Dr George Carew, who had formerly been her domestic chaplain.[164] There was, however, no return to the bleakness of the second Edwardian rite. The queen enjoyed a certain amount of ceremony, and scandalised her more puritanically minded bishops by restoring the cross and candlesticks to her chapel in 1559. Ornaments and vestments were more controversial than music at this point, because the Genevan influence, which had largely superseded that of Zurich among the Protestant exiles, was much less hostile to the use of melody in worship. In 1563 John Day published *The whole psalms in foure parts*, which was a musical edition of the metrical psalms, and at about the same time Thomas Tallis produced settings for Archbishop Parker's metrical psalms.[165] These were both choral anthems and congregational songs, and although they seem to have been first introduced in St Paul's, were certainly used in the Chapel Royal. A brief eye-witness account by a Venetian visitor in 1575 gives a good idea of the nature of the services offered at that time:

> ... the Queen moved towards the chapel, where she remained about twenty minutes until the service ended. This service consisted, first of all, of certain psalms chanted in English by a double chorus of some thirty singers. A single voice then chanted the Epistle, and after this another the Gospel, and all the voices then sang the Creed.[166]

This was presumably a ferial weekday, with sixteen men and twelve boys on duty, and no sermon. A few years later the Lutheran Duke of Würtemberg attended a festal service at Windsor, and was deeply impressed by what he saw. His secretary later wrote

> In this church (St George's chapel) his highness listened for more than an hour to the beautiful music, the usual ceremonies, and the English sermon. The music, and especially the organ, was exquisite ... Their ceremonies indeed are very similar to those of the papists, with singing and so on ...[167]

It seems that on the first occasion the queen arrived after the service had begun, and on the second that the duke departed to his dinner before it was over—both, presumably, normal behaviour, not to be especially remarked upon. The Chapel Royal reflected the queen's own preference in worship, and both her deans, Carew and William Day, who succeeded him in 1572, were conformists without pronounced theological opinions. Once most of the former exile bishops had died, this ceased to cause serious friction, and the Anglican spirituality which was beginning to emerge by the end of the century accepted such liturgical expressions as right and proper. In the fifth book of *The Law of Ecclesiastical Polity*, Richard Hooker described 'musicall harmonie' as

> ... a thing which delighteth all ages and beseemeth all states; a thing as seasonable in griefe as in joy; as decent being added unto actions of greatest weight and solemnities ... The reason hereof is an admirable facilitie whiche musique hath to expresse and represent to the mind more inwardly than any other sensible meane ... the turnes and varieties of all passions whereunto the minde is subject.[168]

Hooker notwithstanding, there was very much more to the spiritual life of the court than the services in Chapel, however beautiful and uplifting. As we have already seen, the piety of a monarch and his (or her) consort was a matter of grave public concern, representing an essential channel of divine grace to the whole kingdom. Edward IV probably came as near as any responsible king of the time could to being indifferent to religion. His patronage was negligible, and not even his warmest admirers credited him with conspicuous zeal for the faith. Only St George's Chapel at Windsor benefited greatly from his interest, and that had more to do with Burgundian chivalry than with the salvation of souls. Henry VII could not afford to be quite so blasé, even if his mother had been disposed to allow it. In the first place he needed to squeeze what political advantage he could out of the supposed saintliness of Henry VI; secondly, he was badly in need of papal recognition and support, at least in the early part of his reign; and thirdly, he claimed that his victory at Bosworth had been a direct act of divine favour, in which he had been the instrument of God's vengeance upon a murderer and usurper.[169] All this created a fairly weighty obligation, which he discharged with rectitude rather than obvious enthusiasm. Henry gave alms generously, and made a regular charity from buying debtors out of prison.[170] He encouraged his mother's generous patronage, and in his will endowed no fewer than 30,000 masses for the repose of his soul, which he clearly expected to have a restless passage. He does not appear to have had any intellectual interest in theology, and was not personally involved in the upsurge of persecution against Lollardy which marked the middle and later years of his reign. On only one occasion is he reputed to have intervened in a case of heresy, and that was to exhort a condemned priest at Canterbury in 1498. According to the story, the man repented of his errors and 'died as a Christian', whereby the king gained great honour.[171] This may well be apocryphal, since it was not normal to burn the penitent, even if their repentance occurred at the last minute; but at least it demonstrates that the king was regarded as a model of orthodoxy, and one of whom such a tale was plausible. Little is known about the religious life of his court, beyond the fact that it was strictly orthodox, and almost untouched by scandal. Unlike most of his contemporaries, and most unlike his Burgundian exemplars, Henry's personal morality was never seriously called in question—in spite of his penchant for making large payments to mysterious dancing girls! Also, in an age when courtiers all over Europe were generally castigated for their vices by poets and preachers alike, the English court was regarded as sober and dignified. Perhaps Henry's generally good relations with the church gave him a 'good press' in this respect also, but it seems likely that neither Lollard nor libertine flourished under his watchful eye.

The younger Henry differed from his father in some respects, but by no means in all. As we have seen, he was an exceptionally vigorous youth, and in spite of his undoubted devotion to Catherine, had taken a number of mistresses before his fancy lighted upon Anne Boleyn in the waning days of his marriage. Only one, Elizabeth Blount, bore him an acknowledged child; which suggests that the king's virility was not as great as he might have wished, and may help to explain the strange mixture of passion and paranoia which surrounded his later relationships with women. Henry was not above being hypocritical about the sexual peccadiloes of others, as he demonstrated in lecturing his sister Margaret; but his court was certainly less strait-laced, and more normal in renaissance terms than that of his father. Perhaps the death of his grandmother at the very outset of his reign had something to do with the difference. Certainly the upbringing of Catherine Howard at court in the 1530s contributed to that ease of virtue which was to be her downfall.[172] In religious orthodoxy, on the other hand, Henry VIII yielded nothing. More intellectual than his father—or at least wishing to appear so—he showed an early interest in canon law, and particularly in issues of spiritual and temporal jurisdiction. There are some indications that as early as 1514 he was showing signs of that Caesaro-Papism which was to emerge eventually in the royal supremacy.[173] At that stage, however, he was well within the limits of orthodox debate, and his interest in the theological controversies stirred up by Martin Luther emerged in the form of a defence of the seven sacraments in 1521. It was probably Catherine, rather than the king himself, who set the religious tone and pace of the court in the early part of the reign. Her devotions were more frequent than his, her penances more rigorous. She undertook numerous small pilgrimages to local shrines—often while Henry was hunting—and left generous offerings, as happened at the obscure Oxfordshire shrine of Our Lady of Caversham in 1522.[174] Catherine had been brought up in the rigorous tradition of her mother, Isabella, and was tough and uncompromising, both in prosperity and adversity.

Both Henry and Catherine took a direct interest in the Observant Friars at Greenwich, a house which provided several royal confessors, in the Brigget-tines at Syon, and in the Carthusian houses at Sheen and London. These were all rigorous institutions of high spiritual standing, and the influence of the Carthusians, particularly, can be readily traced in court circles. It was the Carthusians at Sheen who shaped the spirituality of the young Reginald Pole, son of the Countess of Salisbury, and of Thomas More, who himself was to influence many others.[175] The fact that the king's chief minister during most of this time, and a dominating influence at court, was a Cardinal Archbishop seems to have made remarkably little difference. Wolsey was not noted for the high spiritual standards which he set, and his orthodoxy seems to have been more liberal than that of the king. He was not a persecutor by nature, and dealt leniently with the first Protestants who were denounced to him. But he had disappeared from the scene before religious controversy became inextricably entangled with politics by the king's 'Great Matter'. From about 1529 onwards Protestant influences began to infiltrate the court, partly through the encouragement of Anne Boleyn herself, and partly because they were generally available in London and south-east England in the form of printed books and pamphlets which episcopal censorship had totally failed to suppress. Tyndale's English New Testament (printed in Germany in 1526) was being imported in large numbers, and it would have been surprising indeed had none of these found their way to Westminster. In 1528 came the *Obedience of a Christian Man* and the *Parable of the Wicked Mammon*, both published in Antwerp.[176] The former of these is supposed to have impressed the king deeply by its political arguments, if not by its theology, and to have been brought to him by Anne Boleyn. Over the next decade, Henry developed his own unique brand of orthodoxy, to which his servants and courtiers were expected to conform; and much of the confusion of that period was caused by their attempts to follow—and occasionally to modify—the vagaries of the royal will. In spite of countenancing William Tyndale, and employing Robert Barnes, Henry never accepted, or allowed anyone else to accept with his knowledge, the central Lutheran tenets of *sola fide, sola scriptura* and consubstantiation.[177] On the doctrine of purgatory, he was ambiguous, but his actions speak louder than his words, and Hugh Latimer was right when he claimed that the dissolution of the monasteries '... argueth purgatory not to be'. Pilgrimages, shrines, relics and images were abandoned as superstitious—and of course the papal jurisdiction was repudiated, along with a fair part of the canon law. So by 1540 the English church had the king at its head, an official vernacular bible, no religious houses, and a greatly simplified calendar. On the other hand it still had the mass, transubstantiation, the full Latin rite, episcopal government, church courts, and a celibate clergy.

It was extremely easy to fall off such a delicate tight-rope, as was demonstrated by the simultaneous executions in 1540 of Robert Barnes for heresy and William Forrest for the treason of adhering to the pope. Political scores could also be settled by invoking religious misdemeanours, as was done when Thomas Cromwell was accused of sacramentarianism.[178] In the tense and crisis-laden atmosphere of the 1530s, the court began to divide: some emphasising the continuity of traditional doctrine, others the reforming humanism which had changed so much in the practice of the church. Some of the latter, although not Anne Boleyn or Thomas Cromwell, were already secret Protestants. Most were probably closer in their spirituality to Savonarola, or to Erasmus, and even Cranmer at this stage was orthodox upon such important matters as the sacrifice of the mass. It is, in any case, a mistake to attempt to pin down the fluid (and often puzzled) spirituality of the 1530s into doctrinal categories. What is important in terms of this study is to realise that the court, for a variety of reasons, had become a centre of the 'new learning' by 1540, and that the political groupings and affinities which always exist close to a prince had begun to acquire ideological overtones. This became even more pronounced after 1540, and particularly after 1543, when the conservatives lost their temporary ascendency, and tried to fight back by making charges of heresy against their rivals. The most celebrated example of this was the assault upon the queen organised by Stephen Gardiner in 1546. The actual victims were Anne Askew and John Lascelles.[179] Askew was not a member of the court, but was a Lincolnshire gentlewoman with many court connections; Lascelles was a lawyer, and also a Sewer of the King's Chamber. Both were Protestants of a radical kind; Lascelles was later described as having been a disciple of the German radical Andreas Carlstadt, and Anne Askew's own testimony puts her into the same category. Just how closely Anne was connected with the circle around the queen is not clear, because she refused, under torture, to incriminate anyone; but she seems to have been known to the Duchess of Suffolk (Catherine Willoughby, later a staunch Protestant herself), and the Countesses of Sussex and Hertford, as well as to Catherine Parr. Gardiner's attack was frustrated, partly by Anne Askew's courage, and partly by a timely and graceful submission by Catherine to the king.[180] As we have seen, it rebounded upon Gardiner's head, leaving the protagonists of the 'new learning' in complete command at the end of the reign. By then it appears that a number of important politicians, such as the Earl of Hertford and Sir Anthony Denny, had actually crossed the somewhat imprecise frontier between the 'new learning' and Protestantism; but whether the king appreciated that is another matter. Henry seems to have remained wedded to his own unique orthodoxy to the end.

The court of Edward VI was renowned neither for piety nor probity. Despite the lavish praise bestowed upon the king himself as a 'new Josias' by the Protestant preachers who began to appear there, they looked in vain for other encouraging signs of godliness. Sermons were not popular as a form of courtly entertainment, and those who could absent themselves upon one pretext or another commonly did so. Nor did the preachers much appreciate the continued secularisation of church property, which resulted in the drastic reduction of episcopal revenues, with no benefit either to poor livings, or education. As the bishops grew poorer, the courtiers grew fat. '. . . thy princes are wicked, and companions of thieves' thundered Latimer in 1549, 'they love rewards altogether.'[181] Presumably some derived a masochistic satisfaction from being denounced in this way, but there are few signs that the message was understood. In progressively dismantling the traditional pieties of the church, the government had not so far succeeded in putting much in their place. At the same time a literate, thoughtful Protestant spirituality was beginning to appear, as the upbringing of a young woman such as Jane Grey testifies, and it would be a mistake to see the court of Edward only through the eyes of its enemies, and of those whose extravagant expectations were bound to be disappointed. There were many young aristocrats, like Francis Russell, the son and heir of the Earl of Bedford, whose Protestantism was earnest and deep-seated; the Duke of Northumberland's own sons, Ambrose and Robert, appear to have been the same.[182] The inevitable suspicions of time-serving may have been justified in many cases, but by no means in all, as the events of the following reign were to demonstrate. At a lower level it seems clear that the court, like the city of London with which it rubbed shoulders, contained many converts to the new faith—from Edward Underhill who 'began to smell the Gospel' and turned against his boon companions, to those Yeomen of the Guard who expressed such strong resentment when Mary proposed to bury her brother with a requiem mass. There was no kind of a purge at any level, but probably those who at least professed Protestantism were preferred when vacancies were being filled—and where any freedom of choice existed. Edward's court may not have been godly, but it did prove to be a forcing ground for aristocratic Protestantism, the consequences of which were to reappear with enhanced vigour and importance after 1558.

Like her brother, Mary's personal reputation for piety stood very high, particularly among diplomats and other visitors who were favourable to the Habsburgs. 'She never took her eyes off the sacrament', commented one observer at her wedding, 'she is a saintly woman . . .'[183] Under pressure from Edward and the Duke of Northumberland, Mary had defied the law as it then stood, and insisted successfully upon her right to the sacrament in 1551. In that defiance she had been aided and abetted by her household officers, Rochester, Englefield and Waldegrave, who had spent some months in the Tower in consequence. When she came to the throne the mass was immediately restored in the Chapel, in all its splendour. However, beyond that point ambiguities began to appear. The Edwardian rite was banned by the end of 1553, and celibacy reimposed upon the clergy; churches were urged to restore their roods and patronal saints, and orthodox primers and Books of Hours began to reappear. On the other hand, the queen remained Supreme Head, there was no immediate attempt to restore the religious orders, and shrines and relics remained out of favour. In due course some of these anomalies were removed by political action. Both the papal authority and the religious orders returned in 1555—somewhat modified, and in the latter case on a very small scale.[184] Revived ecclesiastical jurisdiction resulted in religious persecution, and the fires of Smithfield were kindled anew. Nevertheless, many features of pre-reformation piety did not come back, and the queen made no attempt to reintroduce them. Mary never undertook a pilgrimage as queen, venerated a relic, or visited a shrine. No new editions of the once-popular lives of the saints were published, and the English bible, although often attacked, continued in authorised use. In spite of her conservatism, Mary was not as reactionary as she has sometimes been painted, and her piety was closer to that of Richard Whitford or John Colet than to Caesarius of Heisterbach, or the authors of the *Golden Legend*.[185] Mary employed no known Protestants in high office, or close to her person, and the majority of her courtiers happily followed her example in religious matters. However, as we have seen, she carried out no general purge, and even a notorious Protestant like Underhill continued to serve until he deemed it prudent to withdraw in 1555. Even after that, with the persecution in full swing, it is clear from Underhill's testimony that a considerable number of secret or crypto-Protestants remained in the court, even among the Gentlemen Pensioners. The same was true at a lower level, whence yeomen servants continued to get into trouble for their beliefs down to the end of the reign. Undoubtedly there were many Marian courtiers who 'never bowed the knee unto Baal'.

Philip brought his own confessors and chaplains with him, but the influence which may have been exercised outside the ranks of his Spanish-speaking servants is very hard to trace. These were men who, unlike most of their English counterparts, were thoroughly familiar with, and committed to, the latest continental theology. They were men of the counter reformation, but if they brought any of the new cults and pieties to England with them, they left no trace. There is no sign of Mary's courtiers practising the new meditational technique under expert spiritual guidance. Even so committed a Catholic as Jane Dormer seems to have discovered the joy of these practices only after leaving England with her Spanish husband.[186] It is perhaps not surprising that Philip found his English courtiers unsatisfactory from a religious point of view, and employed most of them as little as he decently could. It was not so much that they were heretical, but rather that that lacked the orthodox zeal and commitment which he expected of those close to him, and were ignorant of skills and attitudes which he took for granted among his fellow countrymen.

In spite of Mary's ultramontane and Habsburg associations, the restored Catholic church in England remained extremely insular. It was also of very short duration. Both of these facts greatly facilitated Elizabeth's task in turning the religious wheel another circle, and in encouraging insular Catholics to become conservative Anglicans in the decade after 1559. Elizabeth's personal piety is extremely hard to assess. As we have seen, she had been brought up in a learned reforming tradition which easily converted into Protestantism;[187] she surrounded herself upon her succession with men and women of similar background and mentality, and she encouraged open Protestant demonstrations by the citizens of London. On the other hand she loved colour and ceremony in her public worship, was hostile to puritanism, and seriously considered at least two Catholic marriages. In one sense, she obviously wanted to keep her options open, and to be able to welcome the service of all Englishmen, high or low, who were willing to accept her as their lawful queen. Before 1570 that included all but a tiny handful, who sought refuge in exile, and for that reason alone a sectarian approach to the religious life of the court would have been inappropriate. After 1570 the options were reduced, and there was much less incentive to accommodate the crypto-Catholic. So, although Elizabeth did not abandon her tastes, and the lavishness of her chapel continued to give offence, the piety of her household in the middle years of her reign became more distinctively Protestant. This was not due to any positive action on the queen's part, but rather to the fact that such leading courtiers as Leicester and Burleigh could vie with each other more openly and profitably in the promotion of godly and learned divines.[188] The queen herself did not like clergy, particularly if they were married, and seldom admitted even her archbishops to her closest councils. As a result, her court was probably more secular in spirit and culture than any which had preceded it; Deborah gave place to Astraea and Belphoebe, and the new Anglican spirituality of Richard Hooker and Richard Bancroft seems to have made no appreciable impact within its confines. Ironically, the woman who had been hailed as the new Constantine, and cast by some as the saviour of Protestant Christendom, a queen whose reign was characterised by the most complete and successful religious settlement in Europe, presided over a court whose glittering accomplishments included scarcely a nod in the direction of exemplary piety.

Further reading

S. Adams 'Eliza enthroned?' in *Elizabeth I*

G. W. Bernard *The Power of the Early Tudor Nobility*

S. B. Chrimes *Henry VII*

G. R. Elton *Reform and Reformation*

M. James 'English politics and the concept of honour, 1485–1640'

W. K. Jordan *Edward VI: the threshold of power*

W. K. Jordan *Edward VI: the young king*

D. M. Loades *The Reign of Mary Tudor*

W. MacCaffrey *Queen Elizabeth and the Making of Policy, 1572–1588*

W. MacCaffrey *The Shaping of the Elizabethan Regime*

C. Rawcliffe *The Staffords*

Conyers Read *Mr Secretary Cecil and Queen Elizabeth*

C. Ross *Edward IV*

J. Scarisbrick *Henry VIII*

Penry Williams *The Tudor Regime*

Derek Wilson *Sweet Robin*

5   CONCLUSION

The impact of the court

As Professor Elton observed not long ago, the Tudor court is a baffling institution.[1] Even when its slowly evolving structure has been analysed, and its personnel identified far more completely than I have been able to do in this brief study, certain aspects of its dynamics remain elusive. The main reason for this is that the capriciousness of individual monarchs could not be constrained. Experienced courtiers knew, for example, that Henry VII hated to hear doubt cast upon the loyalty of anyone he trusted, and was liable to rounded angrily upon the doubter. As Sir Hugh Conway pointed out,

> If you knew king Harry our master as I do, you would be wary how you broke to him any such matters, for he would take it that anything you said came out of envy, ill-will and malice, and you would have only blame and no thanks . . .[2]

At the same time he could be very suspicious, even of men whom he had appointed to high office, and it must have been extremely difficult to know which reaction a particular suggestion would produce. Knowing Henry VIII's volatile and dangerous temper, who could have anticipated his meek and embarrassed response to Sir George Throgmorton's accusation that he 'had to do' with both Mary Boleyn and her mother? Certainly not Thomas Cromwell, apparently, who felt obliged to issue a reproof on the king's behalf. Similarly, when Robert Carey, brother of the second Lord Hunsdon, committed the cardinal sin of deserting his post (at Berwick) and coming to court without permission, both Robert Cecil and his brother, then Lord Chamberlain, warned him not to draw attention to his fault by seeking access to the queen. However, by using the good offices of William Killigrew, an Usher of the Privy Chamber, he not only gained audience, but was favourably received—totally confounding the 'best informed sources'.[3] Rules could be made, customs established, and attitudes carefully observed, but all would count for nothing in the face of royal whim or fancy. This was no doubt why so many hopeful suitors kept up their attendance year after year in marginal and unremunerative posts, when any reasonable calculation of the odds would have sent them back to the often-praised delights of rustic obscurity. Edward Underhill had joined the band of Gentlemen at Arms about 1540, and had advanced no further when he finally gave up in 1563, echoing the bitter words which Shakespeare was to place in the mouth of the old lady who reproached Anne Boleyn with her success:

I have been begging sixteen years in court,
Am yet a courtier beggarly nor could
Come pat betwixt too early and too late
For any suit of pounds . . .[4]

At the beginning of Henry VIII's reign there were probably about 120 posts in the court which would have been 'worth a gentleman's having'. By the end of the reign, with the growth of the Privy Chamber and the establishment of the Gentlemen Pensioners, that number had risen to about 200. At the end of the century, after economies and the virtual demise of the Privy Chamber, Professor Stone has estimated it at 175.[5] Such figures indicate that at any given time about half the nobility and about a fifth of the major gentry families could expect to have one or more members serving at court. For lesser gentry families the proportion would have been much smaller—perhaps three to four per cent. Tentative approximations of this kind prove nothing, but they do tend to confirm what commonsense would in any case suggest: that the court played an important part in the lives of the majority of peers, and of a significant minority of the major gentry—the leading county families. As we have seen this meant the quest for, and often the achieving of, office or reward. It also meant the acquisition of expensive tastes and habits, in food, clothes, buildings and gambling particularly. Paradoxically, the most successful courtiers often accumulated the largest debts. When the third Earl of Sussex died in 1583, he owed £12,000 to the queen, and £4600 to fellow courtiers, servants and tradesmen. Sir Christopher Hatton owed a massive £42,000 to Elizabeth and £22,700 to individuals.[6] Debts on this scale, of course, made withdrawal from court impossible, because only the monarch had the resources to alleviate the problem, or pardon the consequences. They were a form of investment in the regime, and Elizabeth used them, much as her grandfather had used bonds and recognisances, as a means of ensuring continued service. There came point where the pardoning of debt became the most significant reward that a courtier could receive.

Consequently, the court came to shape the lifestyles of the aristocracy, just as it increasingly absorbed their political activities. Marriages still tended to be the subject of negotiated settlements between families, and in the case of major peerage families these were often worked out at court. In 1516, for example, the Duke of Buckingham, with Wolsey's assistance, proposed a double marriage settlement to the Earl of Shrewsbury, offering a cut-price deal on his daugher. As the Earl later wrote,

> It pleased him . . . to speake to me to have my lord his son, promysing that I should have him better chepe by a thousand marks than any other man. Howbeit when it came to the poynte that I desired to know what som he would aske it was so grete that I never durste speike of the mater sens . . .[7]

In this case the Cardinal's brokerage was unsuccessful, but in the changed circumstances of 1524, after Buckingham's fall, Mary Talbot was bestowed upon Henry Percy, the eldest son of the Earl of Northumberland, in a similar transaction. In view of the political importance of such families, it is not surprising that both Wolsey and the king wished to exercise a measure of control over dynastic marriages, or that a nobleman estranged from the court, as Shrewsbury largely was by 1524, should still have deemed it prudent to acquiesce in that control. When a wardship was involved, the king's interest was legal as well as political, and the transactions could become both complex and sordid. Wardships were commonly sold, and, as we have seen, could be a source of great profit both to the Crown and to the purchaser—although the ward was usually left to count the cost after attaining his majority. Heiresses were particularly prone to be treated like chattels, and examples could be picked from any part of the century. A particularly colourful fate awaited a young lady named Elizabeth Trussell, who became a ward of Henry VII in 1501. She was purchased by George, Earl of Kent, for £266, and when he died in 1503, bequeathed by will in marriage to his younger son, Henry. However, Henry's brother, the new Earl, disapproved of this arrangement, seized her by force and returned her to the king. There must have been some legal or financial pretext for this action, because the king accepted her, and promptly resold her to the Earl of Oxford for £1333.[8] The Earl shortly after married her himself, so perhaps the status of Countess of Oxford was some compensation for a troubled adolescence. The advantages to be gained from securing a strategic ward could be very great, as was demonstrated when the Duke of Norfolk secured control over the Dacre inheritance in 1566, so it is not surprising that both peers and substantial gentlemen used the court as a means of procuring suitable partners for their children. Even when the negotiations involved near neighbours, as was often the case, there were advantages in conducting them in London, where the best legal advice was to hand, and the brokerage services of Wolsey, Cromwell, Leicester or Burleigh could be called upon if necessary.

In this connection it is important to remember that the court was not a free-standing institution. It was seldom more than a short day's ride from the central law courts, the financial resources of the city of London, and the parliament houses, when they were in session. As Professor Stone observed of the early seventeenth century, 'No man of substance was without his quota of lawsuits with tenants, relatives or neighbours . . . to draw him up to London, term after term . . .'.[9] London was also the headquarters of trade and investment—and the only place where loans could be negotiated on the scale necessary to relieve a nobleman's debts. In other words, business of every conceivable kind drew the nobleman and gentleman to the capital, and within the orbit of the court—which meant in turn that the court influenced at second hand many who never actually set foot within the verge. By 1560 a row of noble houses fronted the Thames between Westminster and the city, and about thirty noblemen in all had London residences—residences which reproduced on a small scale the opulent life-style and intense intrigue of Whitehall or Greenwich. By the end of the century there was already a

14

15

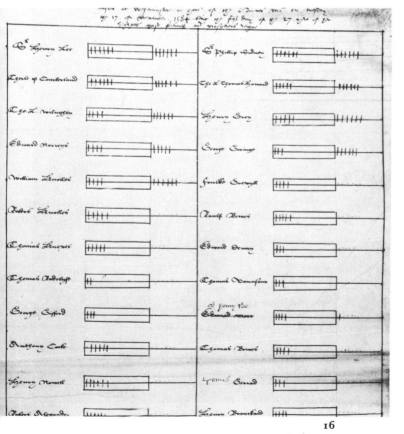

16

14 Renaissance triumph: Alphonsus the Great enters Naples in 1444. Detail of a sculpture over the entrance of Castelnuovo, Naples ('Photo Anderson')

15 The romantic idyll: *Allegory of Love* by an unknown artist, *c.*1560–70 (Louvre, Paris)

16 Score check for the Accession Day tilts, 1584, from the College of Arms MS Box 37 (Royal College of Arms)

17 Elizabeth I as icon: the 'Ditchley Portrait' by Marcus Gheeraerts, *c.*1590 (National Portrait Gallery)

18 Chivalric pageantry in a Renaissance setting: the procession of the Knights of the Garter, 1576 (British Museum)

19 Catherine Grey, Countess of Hertford: a rare example of the work of Levina Teerlinc (Victoria and Albert Museum)

20

Fitz Williams Earl of Southampton.

22

21

23

The monarch as healer: Mary I
ṇing for the King's Evil, by Levina
̣inc (?) (Westminster Cathedral
̣ary)

Nicholas Hilliard's 'approved style': the
̣an Portrait', 1572–6 (Walker Art
̣ry, Liverpool)

The faces of Henry VIII's court spring
̣ under the pen of Holbein: William
̣illiam, Earl of Southampton (Royal
̣ction)

The originator of the Accession Day
̣Sir Henry Lee, by 'Antonio Moro
̣onal Portrait Gallery)

The art of limning at its best: Henry
̣don, by Holbein (Royal Collection)

24

25 Visual propaganda of a crude kind: Edward VI and the
Pope, by an unknown artist (National Portrait Gallery)

26

27

28   29

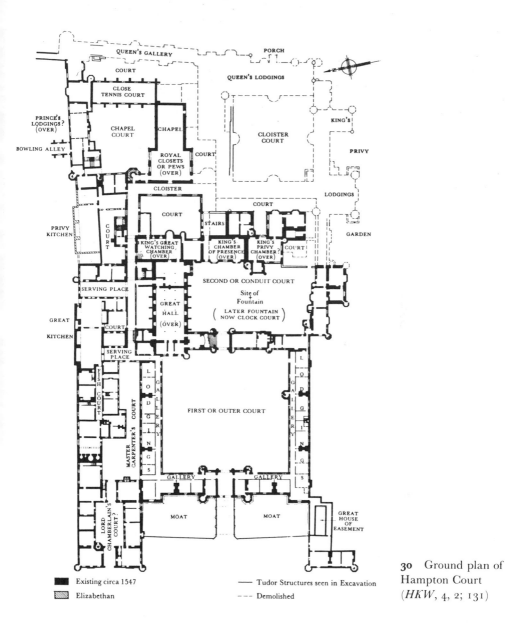

QUEEN'S GALLERY

PORCH

COURT

QUEEN'S LODGINGS

CLOSE
TENNIS COURT

PRINCE'S
LODGINGS?
(OVER)

CHAPEL
COURT

CHAPEL

KING'S

CLOISTER
COURT

BOWLING ALLEY

ROYAL
CLOSETS
OR PEWS
(OVER)

COURT

PRIVY

CLOISTER

LODGINGS

COURT

COURT

PRIVY
KITCHEN

COURT

STAIRS

GARDEN

KING'S GREAT
WATCHING
CHAMBER
(OVER)

KING'S
CHAMBER
OF PRESENCE
(OVER)

KING'S
PRIVY
CHAMBER?
(OVER)

COURT

SERVING PLACE

SECOND OR CONDUIT COURT

Site of
Fountain

GREAT

GREAT
HALL
(OVER)

LATER FOUNTAIN
NOW CLOCK COURT

KITCHEN

COURT

SERVING
PLACE

FISH
COURT

L
O
D
G
I
N
G
S

G
A
L
L
E
R
I
N
G
S

FIRST OR OUTER COURT

L
O
D
G
I
N
G
S

G
A
L
L
E
R
I
N
G
S

MASTER CARPENTER'S COURT

GALLERY

GALLERY

LORD
CHAMBERLAIN'S
COURT?

MOAT

MOAT

GREAT
HOUSE
OF
EASEMENT

■ Existing circa 1547

▨ Elizabethan

— Tudor Structures seen in Excavation

--- Demolished

30 Ground plan of
Hampton Court
(*HKW*, 4, 2; 131)

26 The image of power: Henry VIII, by Holbein (National Portrait Gallery)

27 Sober dignity: Mary I, by Hans Eworth (National Portrait Gallery)

28 Portrait as advertisement: Anne of Cleves, by Holbein (Louvre)

29 Warts and all: Mary I, the Lumley bust

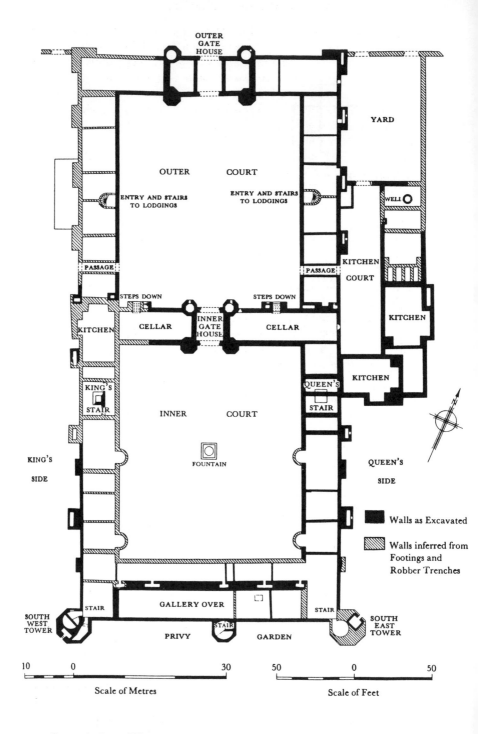

OUTER
GATE
HOUSE

YARD

OUTER   COURT

ENTRY AND STAIRS
TO LODGINGS

ENTRY AND STAIRS
TO LODGINGS

WELL

KITCHEN

PASSAGE

PASSAGE

COURT

KITCHEN

STEPS DOWN

STEPS DOWN

KITCHEN

CELLAR   INNER
GATE
HOUSE   CELLAR

KITCHEN

QUEEN'S

KING'S

STAIR

STAIR

INNER   COURT

KING'S

SIDE

QUEEN'S

SIDE

FOUNTAIN

■ Walls as Excavated

▨ Walls inferred from
Footings and
Robber Trenches

SOUTH
WEST
TOWER

STAIR

GALLERY OVER

STAIR

SOUTH
EAST
TOWER

PRIVY

STAIR

GARDEN

10   0   30   50   0   50

Scale of Metres   Scale of Feet

31 Ground plan of Nonsuch, as revealed by excavation (*HKW*, 4, 2; 197)

rudimentary London season, and Sir Robert Sidney could write to his wife in 1594 'there is no reason to leave you where you are at Penshurst without company in the winter . . .'.[10] An aristocracy which had been notorious for its rusticity in the early sixteenth century, for being interested in nothing but horses, hounds and coat-armour, had, by the end of Elizabeth's reign, begun to seek a metropolitan veneer. By 1605 Sir John Wynn of Gwydir, whose home in North Wales was as remote from London as could well be imagined (and who was by no means indifferent to his Welsh context), could still declare that he had 'resolved to spend the greatest part of the rest of my lyf for the wynter and spring quarter abowte London'.[11] Pleasure and curiosity also pointed in the same direction, and the complaints of those who, for one reason or another, were unable to join the throng echoed the lament of Sir John Harrington, who described himself as 'a private country knight that lives among clouted shoes in his frize jacket and galoshes'. The aristocratic bumpkins of Restoration comedy were already figures of fun by 1600.

The concentration of political business on the court was probably as much an effect as a cause of the enhanced attractiveness of London, which is clearly discernible from about 1540 onward. However, the steadily increasing importance of the Commission of the Peace tended to the same end. When the political affairs of a county were dominated by one or more noble families, they tended to settle their differences and make decisions on the spot. When that domination was eroded, or challenged by men newly promoted in the royal service, there were much greater opportunities for direct or indirect royal intervention. A classic example of this process is provided by the county of Norfolk after the attainder of the Duke in 1572. Before 1570 the Duke, and no doubt his father and grandfather before him, had exercised a controlling voice in the nomination of justices, in their order of precedence, and in the parliamentary representation of the county. Thereafter, there was extensive rivalry and intrigue, with successive bishops, Lords Lieutenant, and important royal servants resident in the county competing to demonstrate their influence.[12] In this latter category came a significant number of law officers— Sir Edward Coke, Sir Thomas Gawdy, Francis Wyndham, Sir Robert Bell, and others—who expected the Lord Keeper to listen to their advice, and were frequently justified in doing so. Influence which was based upon local knowledge could be beneficial to the royal service, and ensure the appointment of diligent and reliable men; but it could equally be used to promote the family or affinity of the person who exercised it. At the same time, suitors for office or promotion could bypass local patronage altogether, even official influence, and go straight to court. A very good example of this is provided by the appointment of Thomas Lovell to the Norfolk commission in 1599:

> The meanes that he camm in was by my Lord North (Treasurer of the Household). For after he had missed of his knighting for which he flewe such a pitch . . . he was contented at last of his meare humilitye to be made a justice of the peace . . . He made such a speache at my Lord North's boorde how he had long lyved in blindness

and that now God had opened his eyes so that he sawe his errors wherin he had lyved so long ... His speache in the ende tended to the good he ment to do his contry. Whereupon my lord upon meere zeale procured him to be in commyssion. And Sir Henry North (Lord North's younger son) for mere affection, was content to take £200 of him ...[13]

The account, admittedly, comes from Lovell's enemy, Philip Gawdy, but there is no reason to doubt its substantial accuracy, or to believe that it was an isolated case. North, as an important courtier, attracted hopeful suitors of Lovell's sort, and Lovell clearly seized a passing opportunity to turn a sympathetic hearing to account. Different, but equally orthodox in its way, was the rapid promotion of Robert Southwell in the same county. His great uncle, Sir Richard, had been an important royal servant, and a Privy Councillor under Mary, but Mary's favour was the kiss of death under Elizabeth, and the Southwells had fallen into obscurity until 1585, when the twenty-five-year-old Robert was suddenly knighted, appointed to a high position on the Bench, and made Vice-Admiral of Norfolk. The trick was that he had married, in 1584, Elizabeth, the daughter of Charles, Lord Howard of Effingham, Lord Chamberlain and Lord Admiral.[14] When James I succeeded to the throne the Lieutenancy of Norfolk was vacant, and a rumour that he intended to revive it set the lobbyists to work in earnest. Philip Gawdy, an indefatigable courtier, set about canvassing his brother Bassingbourne's claim:

I spake with my Lord Thomas, my Lord Henry and my Lord of Northumberland and besides I have now an especiall friend of the Councell; my Lord Souche, by whom I dare undertake at all tymes to do you a good turne ...[15]

Bassingbourne was not appointed, but that was not Philip's fault.

Not every county was as open as Norfolk to the tactics of courtly politics, but it was by no means unique, and probably became the norm as the number and wealth of the magnates declined, and as they themselves became more dependent upon office and court influence. Through rivalries and intrigues of this kind, the impact of the court was felt in every corner of the realm— wherever an ambitious family was trying to improve its status, or minor gentlemen scrambled for the last place on the Commission of the Peace. From the point of view of the common man, and in the whole perspective of the governance of the realm, much power remained in the counties. But the crucial question of who was to exercise that power in the monarch's name was being answered at the Lord Chamberlain's dining table, or in the casual-seeming conversations of courtiers passing the time of day in the Chamber, or on their way to chapel.

The impact of the court upon individual fortunes has been a recurrent theme of this study, and scarcely needs emphasis. Whether there were more losers than gainers in any given period is extremely difficult to ascertain, and can only be adjudged impressionistically. Before 1500 it seems unlikely that courtiers contracted substantial debts in the course of their service. Younger sons no doubt spent more lavishly than they would have been allowed to do at home, but the head of a substantial household would have found it almost as expensive to 'keep hospitality' in the country as to attend the king in London. The two things which did create major indebtedness in that period were unrewarded military service and excessive retaining. Both of these were aggravated by poor estate management—and the desperation with which Richard, Duke of York, sought to control the royal coffers in the 1450s was the most extreme example of the result. Neither Edward IV nor Henry VII allowed that situation to recur. Henry VII deliberately used 'debt dependence' as a political weapon, but there is no reason to suppose that he encouraged his courtiers to bankrupt themselves. Indeed, those who were particularly in favour tended to be protected, and although great fortunes were not made in Henry's court, there were fewer than usual complaints about the crippling expensiveness of attendance there. His son, as we have seen, adopted a much more extravagant style, but again there were few complaints from those who felt unable to stay the pace. Sir Henry Grey never claimed the Earldom of Kent, which he inherited in 1513, on the grounds of poverty,[16] and John Sutton de Dudley, the 'Lord Quondam', frittered his inheritance away, but neither of these exceptional cases had anything to do with the court. The main risk was political rather than financial in the ordinary sense. Several courtly families, great and small, were destroyed by attainder and forfeiture, and it could be argued that Henry's household resembled a great spider's web, in which a number of fat flies, from the Duke of Buckingham to the Duke of Norfolk, were ensnared to their doom. However, given the role of the court in the disposal of monastic land in the 1540s, it seems likely that substantially more was gained than was lost—despite the experience of the second Earl of Cumberland, who bit off more than he could chew when he married Lady Eleanor Brandon in 1537. Keeping his royal wife in the style to which she was accustomed forced him to alienate one of his richest possessions, Temedbury in Hereford. When Eleanor died in 1547 he retired to his estates, and successfully repaired his fortunes[17]—but his experience was far from typical in an otherwise profitable period.

Edward's minority, and the accession of Mary which followed it, were also politically hazardous, and a few great fortunes were made and lost again in less than a decade. However, those who absorbed inducements to collaborate with Northumberland were far more numerous than those who fell with him, and again we should conclude that Edward's reign was a profitable one for the courtiers. Unlike the previous century, the expense of the armed retinues which reappeared during these years was borne by the Crown, and apart from a few rather self-conscious revels, it was not a period of lavish spending on entertainments and hospitality. The same was true of Mary's reign, but a sharp brake had also been placed upon royal largesse, and although some men, such as Cornwallis, undoubtedly did well, we also hear for the first time of courtiers withdrawing for lack of means. These were, admittedly, members of Philip's English household who had been kept kicking their heels at

Southampton for weeks awaiting his arrival. Since he was to pay them, they could not expect any reward until he arrived, and understandably became bored and frustrated.[18] There is no general suggestion that Mary's court was an expensive place to be, and after Philip's departure in 1555 there were few occasions for personal extravagance. With the reign of Elizabeth, however, we begin to enter another world—a world in which the stakes were high, and the prizes uncertain. This was partly the result of inflation, partly of the increasing real wealth of the gentry, and partly of the style of competition which the queen fostered in her court. The spendthrift Robert Dudley was the early pace-setter, a man who, it was alleged, carried the price of several manors on his back, who spent £824 on apparel in less than a year, and upwards of £60,000 on enlargements and improvements at Kenilworth.[19] Such expenditure was, he alleged, necessary both for the queen's honour and his own, and his view was widely shared. Elizabeth cut a splendid figure herself, and expected her courtiers to do the same. Unlike her father, she was not in direct competition with them, and could therefore freely encourage them to compete with each other. Her vanity and sexual jealousy were equally evident in this attitude, because magnificent or powerful women—like Bess of Hardwick—were definitely not welcome. There could only be one queen-bee in the hive. As we have seen, the game of courtly love became a way of life, and one which encouraged conspicuous consumption, as the courtiers vied with one another to attract their mistress's attention. Enormous 'prodigy houses' were one result—places like Theobalds, Holdenby, Longleat and Kenilworth—partly designed to accommodate the court on progress, and partly just to demonstrate the wealth of their builders. Sir Christopher Hatton expressed the nature of these extravaganzas accurately when he described Holdenby as a 'shrine' for 'that holy saint (to) sit in ... to whom it is dedicated'.[20] Visits on progress could cost the hosts so honoured up to £300 a day, quite apart from the costs of building, and it is not surprising that the debts so acquired could take many years to discharge, given the modest nature of most of the favours which Elizabeth distributed.

Lavish expenditure on food was probably less common than it had been in the heyday of 'hospitality', when the Duke of Buckingham had entertained 500 guests at Thornbury castle in 1507; and indeed the decay of hospitality had been one of the great complaints of the 'commonwealth men' in the 1540s, but foreigners still commented upon the gargantuan meals to which the English treated themselves. Gambling, on the other hand, was beginning to get out of control by the 1580s, and the modest stakes on dice or cards which had characterised the courts of Henry VII or Mary, had given way to immoderate bets on horse racing, foot racing, cockfighting, bull baiting, bowling and shooting. In 1568 the Earl of Shrewsbury lost £100 at cards in the Privy Chamber; by the 1590s the Earl of Rutland was losing between £1000 and £1500 a year, which even his large income could not stand.[21] Again, the queen herself was partly to blame. She was such a bad loser that her courtiers regularly allowed her to take money off them in order to keep her in a good humour. Lord North is alleged to have sacrificed £40 a month in this way in the last years of the reign. Reckless gambling went along with the increasingly unscrupulous financial operations which characterised the workings of the government in the 1590s. As a result, instead of setting the fashion and the pace for the society of city and county to imitate, the *mores* of the court came to be looked upon with more than conventional disapproval. The anticourt literature of Robert Greene or Philip Massinger developed an edge which was lacking in the conventional images of Guevara. By the early seventeenth century aristocratic puritanism was beginning to set up an alternative lifestyle which was to have considerable political implications by the 1630s.

For most of the Tudor period, aristocratic households had followed the lead of the court without any moral or ideological qualms. Great halls went out of use, and private apartments multiplied, at Penshurst, Chatsworth or Compton Wynyates, no less than at Greenwich or Hampton Court.[22] The Earl of Leicester and Sir Francis Leek had their companies of players; the Marquis of Exeter had his chapel staff and musicians, not exactly in emulation of the court, but because they were part of the same noble style of housekeeping. New fashions in dress and music were first adopted at court, introduced particularly by the king's professional Italian and Flemish instrumentalists, and by young nobles and gentlewomen returning after periods of residence in the courts of France and the Low Countries. Family portraits and the long gallery first appeared at Richmond, as did the specially designated library.[23] Henry VIII set fashions in the encouragement of scholarship, no less than in chivalry or the breeding of horses. Most important of all, however, were influences which were not examples in the direct sense. After Nonsuch the Tudors set no fashions in building; yet, as we have seen, Elizabeth caused a whole new style of extravagant architecture to come into being. The court was no pace-setter when it came to streamlining household establishments, and diminishing the functions of manred; yet this was a consequence of frequent or prolonged visits, particularly after the middle of the century. A large retinue became a cripplingly expensive incumbrance in London, with its high cost of living, and the anti-social behaviour of underemployed servants was unacceptable to the authorities of court and city alike. The more frequently a nobleman or gentleman attended, or visited the capital on business, the less likely he was to come 'largely accompanied', with the result that status came to be differently measured. Instead of the 'tall fellows' who had attended the fourth Earl of Shrewsbury, and still attended Leicester and Sussex in the 1560s, by the 1590s we find expensive carriages and liveried pages being used to measure wealth and political influence alike. By the latter part of Elizabeth's reign we hear significantly less about the problem of 'superfluous' servants, not because the discipline of the court had been tightened from above, but because the pressure from the courtiers themselves had been relieved. The reduction of retinues, and sophistication of tastes which results from metropolitan and courtly influences, also tended to detach the aristocracy from their less wealthy or less ambitious country neighbours. This can be seen both in education and in entertainment. The gentleman's library, and his fashionable smattering of law, theology and the classics, set him apart from the *rustici* with whom his grandfather would have been completely at home, and stemmed from the demands of royal service and the influence of courtly humanists in the first half of the sixteenth century. Similarly the allegorical masques and witty comedies which were entertaining noblemen's and gentlemen's households in the early seventeenth century were much further from the crude burlesques and interludes of the inn yard and the market-place than the comparable plays and amusement which had been offered at Thornbury or Alnwick in the early years of Henry VIII. It could be argued that it was courtly influence in this sense which began to turn the aristocracy from a status group into a class—but the implications of such a rash thought go far beyond the limits of this study.

Nevertheless, it is a thought which forms a fitting postscript. The Tudor court was, as Professor Elton phrased it, a 'point of contact'—at the same time a political institution, a cultural centre, and a market-place of patronage and profit. It was to sixteenth-century England what the Agora had been to the Athens of the fifth century BC—the place where decisions were made and policies formed. Such policies frequently had to be implemented elsewhere, and that is a factor which must be constantly borne in mind; but the men responsible for that implementation shared the same point of contact. For all these reasons, it was essential that the court should be both open and attractive, and that the Tudors consistently succeeded in making it. As we have seen, their fifteenth-century predecessors had succeeded less well, with serious consequences for both their power and their prestige. Similarly, the early Stuarts were to fail, progressively isolating themselves, first by corruptions bordering on the grotesque, and later by a refinement and sophistication which made Charles I inaccessible and incomprehensible to all but a chosen few.[24] As a result, political opposition went 'out of court' in the 1630s, as it had in the 1440s, with consequences which provided the measure of the Tudor achievement.

Further reading

G. R. Elton 'Tudor government; Points of contact: the Court'
A. Hassell Smith *Court and County*

Appendix I

The King's houses

Ampthill, Bedfordshire
Acquired in 1524, probably by purchase. Frequently used by Henry VIII, and extensively repaired and improved between 1533 and 1540. Used by Catherine of Aragon between 1529 and 1533. The works continued until 1552. Partly demolished, and surveyed in 1567, there were plans to rebuild as late as 1605. These plans were never realised, and the house fell into ruin, and was totally demolished by 1649.

Ashridge, Hertfordshire
Originally the College of Bonhommes, retained by the Crown after the dissolution in 1539. In poor repair by 1564, when it was renovated in connection with a progress to Hertfordshire. Alienated in 1575 to Thomas, Lord Ellesmere.

Bagshot Lodge, Surrey
The original fourteenth-century lodge was demolished in 1539, and replaced. Repairs were carried out in 1572–3, but the house was very little used in the sixteenth century. Extensively renovated in 1609–10 and 1631–2.

Baynard's Castle, London
Part of the Yorkist inheritance acquired by Henry VII in 1485. Used and renovated by Henry VII on several occasions. Granted by Henry VIII successively to Catherine of Aragon, Anne Boleyn, the Duke of Richmond, Anne of Cleves, Catherine Howard and Catherine Parr. Repaired in 1549 and 1551. Subsequently the town house of the Earls of Pembroke. Largely destroyed in the Great Fire.

Beddington Manor, Surrey
Acquired in 1539 by the attainder of Sir Nicholas Carew. Used occasionally by Henry VIII, and granted to Thomas, Lord Darcy, in 1552.

Bridewell Palace, London
Built in 1515 on the basis of an earlier house owned by Wolsey, at a cost of over £20,000. Used in 1522 to accommodate the entourage of the

Emperor Charles V. For a few years Henry VIII's main London residence. Granted by Mary in 1556 for the establishment of a workhouse for the vagrant poor.

Byfleet, Surrey

Originally a possession of the Duchy of Cornwall; annexed in 1539 to the manor of Hampton Court. Used by successive Keepers, but visited only by Elizabeth in 1576.

Canterbury, Kent

Retained by the Crown after the suppression of St Augustine's in 1538, and extensively rebuilt. Used occasionally by Henry VIII and Elizabeth. Briefly granted to Cardinal Pole (1556–8), and finally to Edward, Lord Wootton, in 1612.

Charing Place, Kent

Obtained by Henry VIII from Archbishop Cranmer, by exchange, in 1545. Never used by a monarch, it fell into ruin, and was alienated in 1629.

Chelsea, Middlesex

Acquired from Lord Sandys by exchange in 1536. Occasionally used by the royal family, it was granted to Catherine Parr in 1544. Anne of Cleves died there in 1557. Alienated in 1639.

Chobham, Surrey

Purchased by Henry VIII in 1535, and extensively renovated. Used by the king occasionally, and sold in 1558 by Mary to Nicholas Heath, Archbishop of York.

Clarendon, Wiltshire

A possession of Edward IV, inherited by Henry VII, but never used by the Tudors. Some restoration was carried out in 1489–90, but the palace was in ruins by Elizabeth's reign.

Collyweston, Northamptonshire

Acquired by Edward IV on the attainder of the Duke of Clarence in 1478. Granted by Henry VII to his mother, and much used by her. Granted to Elizabeth in 1550, but visited by her only once as queen, in 1566. Alienated in 1625.

Dartford, Kent

Retained by the Crown after the dissolution of Dartford convent in 1539. Extensively rebuilt between 1540 and 1544. Granted to Anne of Cleves in

1547, and briefly restored to religious use, 1557–9. Repaired and visited occasionally by Elizabeth, it was granted to Robert Cecil in 1606.

Ditton, Buckinghamshire

Inherited by Henry VII from Edward IV, but not visited by members of the royal family until Henry VIII's reign. Kept in repair, but not visited thereafter, except by the Keepers, who lived there.

Dunstable, Bedfordshire

Retained by the Crown after the dissolution of the priory. Some repairs and renovations were carried out between 1540 and 1547, but the house does not appear to have been used, and was sold by Mary in 1554 for £300.

Durham House, London

Acquired by Henry VIII from Bishop Tunstall by exchange in 1536. Restored to Tunstall in 1553, and resumed by the Crown in 1559. Used by Elizabeth to house ambassadors and favoured courtiers, it was kept in repair until 1603, but demolished in the mid-seventeenth century.

Easthampstead, Berkshire

An ancient hunting seat in Windsor forest, it was frequently used by Henry VIII, and kept in repair during his reign. Thereafter it fell into decay, but had been renovated in 1607, and was visited frequently by James I on progress. Alienated by Charles I in 1628.

Eltham, Kent

A palace of Edward IV, it continued to be a principal royal residence throughout the reigns of Henry VII and Henry VIII, when substantial sums were regularly spent on repairs and modernisation. Thereafter it was less used, but continued to be kept in good repair, and was added to substantially in 1585–6. Further extensive work was carried out by James I, although there is no evidence that he used it much.

Enfield, Middlesex

Acquired by Henry VIII in 1539 by exchange from Thomas Manners, later Earl of Rutland. Repaired by Edward VI, it was granted to Elizabeth in 1550, and frequently visited by her after her accession. By the end of the century it was ruinous, and in danger of collapse.

Esher, Surrey

Acquired by purchase from the Bishop of Winchester in 1537, and added to the manor of Hampton Court. Restored to the diocese of Winchester by Mary in 1553.

Ewelme, Oxfordshire

A property of the De La Poles, it came to the Crown by the attainder of Edmund, Earl of Suffolk in 1504. Visited occasionally by Henry VIII, and held for about ten years (1525–35) by Charles Brandon, Duke of Suffolk. Greatly decayed by the beginning of Elizabeth's reign, it was patched up, and visited by her occasionally, on progress. Demolished early in James's reign.

Grafton, Northamptonshire

Acquired by exchange from Thomas, second Marquis of Dorset in 1526. Henry visited it frequently, and Wolsey had his last interview with the king there in 1529. Extensive repairs and renovations took place in 1541, and in 1542 it became the head of a new 'Honor'. Elizabeth visited Grafton occasionally, and it was kept in good repair, being described as a 'statlie manor house' in 1558. Destroyed during the Civil War.

Greenwich

This was a principal royal residence, and one of the great Tudor palaces. Altered and added to by Henry VII in 1499–1501, Henry VIII carried out building work there intermittently throughout his reign, and although nothing now survives, the layout of the buildings can be reconstructed from descriptions, drawings and building accounts. A further expensive overhaul was carried out between 1567 and 1570, and although Elizabeth added little to it, she kept the whole place in good repair. In the latter part of Elizabeth's reign it was one of her favourite residences, and large sums continued to be spent on it down to the Civil War.

Guildford, Surrey

Built in the 1530s in the precinct of the Greyfriars, the whole of which came to the king on the dissolution in 1539. A small house, it was kept in repair until Mary's reign, but little used. By the end of Elizabeth's reign it was completely ruinous, and had been pulled down by 1607.

Hackney, Middlesex

Formerly a part of the Percy estate, it was acquired by the king in 1535. Henry visited it occasionally, and was reconciled to his daughter Mary there in July 1536. Granted to Sir William Herbert, Gentleman of the Privy Chamber, early in the reign of Edward VI.

Halmaker House, Sussex

Obtained by exchange from Lord La Warr in 1539. Visited by Edward VI on progress in 1552.

Hampton Court, Middlesex

Built by Cardinal Wolsey between 1514 and 1525. Although it was obtained by the king on exchange in the latter year, Wolsey continued to use it until his fall in 1529. Between 1529 and 1538, extensive further building was carried out, costing in the region of £46,000. By 1547 it was the largest Tudor palace, except Whitehall, but much of Henry VIII's work was demolished in the late seventeenth century. Edward and Mary continued to use it, but undertook no additional building. Further alterations were carried out in 1565–70, and repairs and renovations from 1567–70. Elizabeth frequently lived there, and kept the whole building in repair, with occasional minor alterations, until the end of her reign.

Hanworth, Middlesex

Acquired late in Henry VIII's reign from the heirs of Sir John Crosby. Henry VIII often visited it, and kept the house and well-known gardens in good repair. It was granted to Anne Boleyn in 1532, and to Catherine Parr in 1544. In 1558 Mary bestowed it upon the Duchess of Somerset, who lived there until 1587, when it was leased, and later sold to Francis, Lord Cottingham.

Hatfield House, Hertfordshire

Obtained by exchange from the Bishop of Ely in 1538. It was used by Prince Edward, and in 1550 granted to the Princess Elizabeth, who made it her principal residence in 1555. As queen, she visited it occasionally, and kept it in repair, but did not live there..It was granted to Robert Cecil, Earl of Salisbury, in 1607.

Havering, Essex

Taken by Henry VII from the dowager Queen Elizabeth in 1487, it formed part of the jointure of Henry VIII's first three queens. The court was at Havering on a few occasions during Henry VIII's latter years, but no building work was done. Elizabeth visited it on progress, and it was extended in 1576–7. Used as a hunting lodge by James I.

Holdenby, Northamptonshire

Built by Sir Christopher Hatton in 1583, it did not come to the Crown until 1608.

Hunsdon House, Hertfordshire

Acquired from the Duke of Norfolk in 1525, it was considerably extended over the next nine years. Used by Princess Mary, and by Edward before his accession, it was granted to Mary for life in 1548. In 1559 Elizabeth granted it to her cousin, Lord Hunsdon.

Hyde Park
>The manor of Hyde was acquired from the Abbot of Westminster in 1536, and used mainly as a hunting ground. A banquetting house was built within the park by Sir Thomas Cawarden, the Master of the Revels, in 1551 for the entertainment of the French ambassadors. No further work was undertaken until the seventeenth century.

Langley, Oxfordshire
>Acquired by the Crown in 1478 on the attainder of the Duke of Clarence. A hunting lodge was built there by Henry VII, who visited it from Woodstock. Henry VIII visited it on a number of occasions, and undertook work there. In 1550 it was granted to John Dudley, Earl of Warwick, and passed from him via Anne Seymour and Sir Edward Unton, to the Earl of Leicester.

London, The Tower
>The royal apartments were used mainly in times of emergency, or during the preparations for a coronation. Maintenance and repair work was carried on throughout the period.

Lyndhurst, Hampshire: The King's House
>Residence of the Warden of the New Forest. Not used by the royal family in the sixteenth century.

The Royal Mews, Charing Cross
>Maintained by Henry VII, but burnt down in 1534, and not rebuilt until 1550–56. Periodically repaired under Elizabeth, and managed by Robert Dudley as Master of the Horse.

Minster Lovell, Oxfordshire
>Acquired by forfeiture from John, Lord Lovell in 1485. Not used, but kept in repair, and sold to Sir Edward Coke in 1603.

The More, Hertfordshire
>Obtained by exchange from the Abbot of St Albans in 1531, having been much embellished by Wolsey. Extended and repaired by Henry VIII, who made frequent use of it, the house fell into decay after 1547, and the estate was leased to the Earl of Bedford in 1576.

Mortlake, Surrey
>Obtained by exchange from Thomas Cranmer, Archbishop of Canterbury, in 1535–6. Building work was carried out between 1540 and 1545. In 1544 it was granted to Catherine Parr, and on her death in 1548, passed out of use.

The King's Manor, Newcastle upon Tyne
The house of the Austin Friars, retained after the dissolution for use by the Council of the North. Modest repairs were carried out to keep the house in use until 1570, and it was finally refurbished in 1595. Granted by James I to the Earl of Dunbar in 1605.

New Hall, Essex
Bought from Sir Thomas Boleyn in 1516. Extensive building was carried out over the next six years, at a cost of £17,000, but it was little used by the king, and in 1548 was granted to Princess Mary, who used it as her principal residence. Visited on progress by Elizabeth, but not kept in good repair, and granted to the Earl of Sussex in 1573.

Nonsuch, Surrey
A brand new palace, commenced by Henry VIII in 1538. Work was pressed on rapidly, regardless of expense, but was still incomplete on Henry's death in 1547. Extensive building accounts give a full picture of the buildings and their ornamentation, on which £24,536 was expended between 1538 and 1545. Edward VI visited Nonsuch only once, and in 1556 it was granted by Mary to Henry FitzAlan, Earl of Arundel. The house was demolished in the late seventeenth century, and the site excavated in 1959.

Oatlands, Surrey
Acquired by exchange from the heirs of Sir Bartholomew Reed in about 1536. Already a large house, it was added to considerably between 1537 and 1545, at cost of about £17,000, and regularly used by Henry VIII. Work was resumed in Elizabeth's reign, and continued spasmodically into the following century. The house continued in use, and was popular as a summer retreat from London. In 1603 Prince Henry was given an establishment, and took up residence there.

Otford and Knole, Kent
Two mansions acquired from Thomas Cranmer by exchange in 1537, and used occasionally by Henry VIII because of their allegedly healthy situation. Granted by Edward VI to John Dudley, Duke of Northumberland, they reverted to the Crown in 1553, and were alienated again by Mary.

Parlaunt Manor, Gloucestershire
Escheated to the Crown on the death of Sir Edward Stanley in 1523. Used as a Keeper's Lodge, and granted to Sir Anthony Denny in 1541.

Penshurst Place, Kent
>   Obtained through the attainder of the Duke of Buckingham in 1521.
>   Granted to Sir William Sidney in 1552.

Petworth, Sussex
>   Sold to Henry VIII by the Earl of Northumberland in 1535, and used
>   occasionally by both Henry and Edward. Kept in repair, but little used
>   thereafter.

Reading, Berkshire
>   The ex-monastic buildings of Reading Abbey were retained by the
>   Crown in 1539, and converted into a house, which was used occasionally
>   by Henry and each of his successors in turn. Not kept up after 1603, and
>   damaged during the siege of Reading in 1643.

Richmond, Surrey
>   Built on a lavish scale by Henry VII, as a replacement for the palace of
>   Sheen, burnt down in 1497. The work was substantially completed by
>   1501, at a cost of over £20,000. It was Henry's favourite residence, but
>   was much less used by his son, particularly after the acquisition of
>   Hampton Court. Anne of Cleves used it from 1540 to 1547, and it was
>   kept in repair, with extensive renovations in 1574–5. New building was
>   undertaken periodically throughout the later sixteenth century, and
>   Elizabeth, like her grandfather, died at Richmond. Both Henry and
>   Charles lived there as heirs apparent between 1610 and 1625.

Rochester, Kent
>   Buildings of Rochester cathedral priory, reserved by the Crown after the
>   dissolution. Largely rebuilt, but little used by Henry VIII, it was granted
>   to George Brooke, Lord Cobham, in 1548.

St Alban's, Hertfordshire
>   Building of St Alban's Abbey, retained by the Crown. It was kept in
>   repair, and visited on progress, but never used as a royal residence.

St James's Palace
>   Built by Henry VIII between 1531 and 1536, it was probably intended as
>   a London residence for the Duke of Richmond, who died there in 1536.
>   Used occasionally, and kept in repair by Elizabeth, it came into its own as
>   a major royal residence only in the seventeenth century.

Somerset House
>   Acquired by the attainder of Edward Seymour, Duke of Somerset, in
>   1551, it was Princess Elizabeth's London residence from 1553 to 1558.
>   Used occasionally by the court during her reign as queen, particularly for
>   the entertainment of important visitors. It was kept in repair, but no
>   major building work was undertaken until 1609.

Suffolk Place, Southwark
> Obtained by exchange from the Duke of Suffolk in 1536, it was used as
> an occasional royal residence until 1556, when Mary granted it to the
> Archbishop of York.

Sunninghill, Berkshire
> A lodge in Windsor Forest, rebuilt in 1511. It was visited frequently by
> Henry VIII and Elizabeth on hunting trips, and as a place of retreat.

Syon House
> Buildings of the former nunnery, retained after 1539. Catherine Howard
> was imprisoned there in 1541, and it appears to have been used as an
> ordnance factory between then and 1547. The house was held briefly,
> and reconstructed, by the Duke of Somerset. Under Mary the nuns
> returned for about three years, but in 1559 it reverted to use as an
> occasional royal residence, and place of entertainment. In 1594 it was
> leased to the Earl of Northumberland, but continued to be maintained by
> the Crown.

Tickenhill Manor, Worcestershire
> One of the manor houses used by the Council in the Marches of Wales.
> The building was renovated and extended in 1473-4, and was used by
> Prince Arthur as Prince of Wales. In 1525 it was repaired again for
> Mary, and kept in repair for the Council for the remainder of the
> sixteenth century. Important work was carried out by Sir Henry Sidney
> as Lord President in the early 1560s.

Tyttenhanger House, Hertfordshire
> A residence of the Abbot of St Albans, it was acquired by the Crown in
> the dissolution in 1539. In 1547 it was granted to Sir Thomas Pope.

Wanstead, Essex
> Purchased from Sir Ralph Hastings in about 1495, it was kept in repair,
> and visited occasionally, by Henry VII and Henry VIII. In 1549 it was
> granted to Lord Rich.

Westenhanger, Kent
> Obtained by exchange from Sir Thomas Poynings in 1540. It was kept in
> repair, but little used, being in and out of Crown possession until finally
> alienated in 1585. Elizabeth visited it once, on progress.

West Horsley Place, Surrey
> Obtained through the attainder of the Marquis of Exeter in 1538, it was
> kept in good repair, and granted to Sir Anthony Browne in 1547.

Westminster Palace

In 1485 Westminster was the king's principal residence, as well as the administrative centre, but by 1536 had been superseded by Whitehall and Hampton Court. In that year the old palace was annexed to the new palace of Whitehall, and thereafter used only for ceremonial purposes. Extensive building operations continued to be carried out, but for all practical purposes Westminster ceased to be a residence. Being only a few hundred yards from Whitehall, the distinction had little significance.

Whitehall Palace

Originally York House, Whitehall was the London residence of the Archbishop of York. It was rebuilt on a grand scale by Wolsey, commencing in 1514, and was appropriated by the king on his fall in 1529, being known thereafter both as 'the new palace of Westminster' and as 'Whitehall palace'. It was the principal royal residence for the remainder of the Tudor period, and was extensively and expensively rebuilt. More than any other place, Whitehall was the setting for the Tudor monarchy.

Windsor Castle

A principal royal residence in every reign, it was frequently repaired and refurbished. Alone among the royal palaces, it had its own independent chapel establishment, which was not part of the Chapel Royal. St George's was the home of the Knights of the Garter.

Windsor Manor, Berkshire

Originally a royal residence in the Great Park, it deteriorated to the status of a Keeper's Lodge by Elizabeth's reign, but was kept in good repair.

Woking, Surrey

Obtained in 1503 in exchange with Lady Margaret Beaufort. Considerably rebuilt by Henry VII, it was frequently visited by his son, who also extended and renovated it. After 1547 it was little used, but was periodically repaired. In 1620 James I granted it to Sir Edward Zouch.

Woodstock, Oxfordshire

An important residence of Henry VII, it was largely rebuilt and extended during his reign. Henry VIII visited it occasionally, and kept it in repair, but not at any great expense. Princess Elizabeth was confined there after the Wyatt revolt in 1554–5. As queen, she visited it from time to time on progress, and carried out building work regularly.

The King's Manor, York
   The former buildings of the Benedictine Abbey of St Mary's, which were
   retained for the use of the Council of the North after 1539. Visited by
   Henry VIII in 1541, it was extensively renovated at that time. By 1550
   several of the outlying buildings had been demolished, and the whole
   place was 'largely defaced' by 1562. Between then and 1570 it was
   renovated, and over the last twenty years of the century, largely rebuilt.
   It continued in use by the President of the Council until the Civil War.

Source: H. M. Colvin *The History of the King's Works* Vol. IV, 1485–1660, pt. II,
   1–367

Appendix II

The principal officers of the court

A. The Chamber

Lord Great Chamberlain
John de Vere, 13th Earl of Oxford	1462–1474
Vacant	1474–1485
John de Vere, Earl of Oxford	1485–1513
John de Vere, 14th Earl of Oxford	1513–1526
John de Vere, 15th Earl of Oxford	1526–1540
Thomas Cromwell, Earl of Essex	1540
Robert Radcliffe, Earl of Sussex	1540–1542
Edward Seymour, Earl of Hertford	1543–1549
John Dudley, Earl of Warwick	1549–1550
William Parr, Marquis of Northampton	1550–1553
John de Vere, 16th Earl of Oxford	1553–1562
Edward de Vere, 17th Earl of Oxford	1562–1604

Lord Chamberlain
William, Lord Hastings	1461–1470
Sir Richard Tunstall	1470–1471
William, Lord Hastings	1471–1483
Francis, Viscount Lovell	1483–1485
Sir William Stanley	1485–1495
Giles, Lord Daubeney	1496–1508
Charles Somerset, Earl of Worcester	1409–1526
William, Lord Sandys	1526–1540
Vacant	1540–1543
William Paulet, Lord St. John	1543–1546
Henry Fitz Alan, Earl of Arundel	1546–1550
Sir Thomas Darcy	1551–1553
Sir John Gage	1553–1556
Sir Edward Hastings	1556–1558
William, Lord Howard of Effingham	1558–1572
Thomas Radcliffe, Earl of Sussex	1572–1583
Charles, Lord Howard of Effingham	1584–1585
Henry Carey, Lord Hunsdon	1585–1596
William Brooke, Lord Cobham	1596–1597
George Carey, Lord Hunsdon	1597–1603

Vice Chamberlain

Sir Henry Marney	1509–1523
Sir William Morgan	1525(?)–1528
Sir John Gage	1528–1536
Sir William Kingston	1536–1539
Sir Anthony Wingfield	1539–1550
Sir Thomas Darcy	1550–1551
Sir John Gates	1551–1553
Sir Henry Jerningham	1553–1557
Sir Henry Bedingfield	1557–1558
Sir Edward Rogers	1558–1559
Sir Francis Knollys	1559–1570
Vacant	1570–1577
Sir Christopher Hatton	1577–1587
Sir Thomas Heneage	1589–1595

Treasurer of the Chamber

Sir Thomas Vaughn	1465–1483
Edward Chaderton	1483–1485
Thomas Lovell	1485–1492
Sir John Heron	1492–1521
John Mickslowe	1521–1522
Sir Henry Wyatt	1523–1528
Sir Brian Tuke	1528–1545
Sir Anthony Rowse	1545–1546
Sir William Cavendish	1546–1557
Sir John Mason	1558–1566
Sir Francis Knollys	1566–1570
Sir Thomas Heneage	1570–1595
Sir John Stanhope	1595–1617

B The Household

Lord Great Master

Charles Brandon, Duke of Suffolk	1540–1545
William Paulet, Lord St John	1545–1550
John Dudley, Earl of Warwick	1550–1553

Lord Steward

John Tiptoft, Earl of Worcester	1463–1467
Henry Bourchier, Earl of Essex	1467–1471
Thomas, Lord Stanley	1471–1483
Thomas Howard, Earl of Surrey	1483–1485
John Radcliffe, Lord Fitzwater	1486–1496
Robert Willoughby of Broke	1496–1502
George Talbot, Earl of Shrewsbury	1502–1538
Robert Radcliffe, Earl of Sussex	1538–1540
[Office discontinued; see Lord Great Master, above]	
Henry Fitz Alan, Earl of Arundel	1553–1564

Vacant	1564–1567
William Herbert, Earl of Pembroke	1567–1570
Vacant	1570–1572
Edward Fiennes, Earl of Lincoln	1572–1584
Robert Dudley, Earl of Leicester	1584–1588
Henry Stanley, Earl of Derby	1588–1593
Vacant	1593–1597
Charles Howard, Earl of Nottingham	1597–?

Treasurer of the Household

Sir John Fogge	1461–1467
Sir John Howard	1467–1474
Sir John Elrington	1474–1483
Sir William Hopton	1483–1484
Sir Richard Croft	1484–1502
Sir Thomas Lovell	1502–1522
Sir Thomas Boleyn	1522–1525
Sir William FitzWilliam	1525–1537
Sir William Paulet	1537–1539
Sir Thomas Cheney	1539–1558
Sir Thomas Parry	1559–1560
Vacant	1560–1570
Sir Francis Knollys	1570–1596
Roger, Lord North	1596–1600
Vacant	1600–1602
Sir William Knollys	1602–1616

Comptrollers

Sir John Scott	1461–1470
Sir William Parr	1470–1475
Sir Robert Wingfield	1475–1481
Sir William Parry	1481–1483
Sir Robert Percy	1483–1485
Sir Richard Edgecombe	1485–1489
Sir Roger Tocotes	1489–1494(?)
John Spelman	1494–1497(?)
Sir Richard Guildford	1497–1509
Sir Edward Poynings	1509–1516
Sir Henry Marney	1516–1520
Sir Thomas Boleyn	1520
Sir Henry Guildford	1520–1526
Sir William FitzWilliam	1526–1532
Sir William Paulet	1532–1537
Sir John Russell	1538–1539
Sir William Kingston	1539–1540
Sir John Gage	1540–1547
Sir William Paget	1547–1549
Sir Anthony Wingfield	1549–1552
Sir Richard Cotton	1552–1553
Sir Robert Rochester	1553–1556
Sir Robert Freston	1556–1558
Sir Thomas Parry	1558–1559

Sir Edward Rogers	1559–1568
Vacant	1568–1570
Sir James Croft	1570–1590
Vacant	1590–1596
Sir William Knollys	1596–1602
Sir Edward Wotton	1602–1616

Sources: Myers, *Household of Edward IV; Calendars of the Patent Rolls; Letters and Papers*. I am indebted to Dr Tighe for his help in compiling this list.

Appendix III

Illustrative documents

Document 1 Henry VIII's Privy Purse expenses

Itm	the xxij daye paied for a perwyke[1] for Sexten the kinges fole	xxs.
Itm	the xxiiij daye paied in rewarde to a s'vant of maister wodales for bringing a dog to the kinges grace	xxs.
Itm	the same daye paied to one peter Neghen in partie of payment of a more some by the kinges comaundement	iijli
Itm	the same daye paied to the prices grace[2] by the kinges comaundement for to disporte her w[t] this Cristemas	xxli.
Itm	the same daye paied to the Tresorer of Wolesnay And to Audito[r] of Wyn-Chest[r]. in rewarde by the kinges comaundemet	xiijli.vjs.viiid.
Itm	the xxviij daye paied to the subdean of the kinges Chapell for iiij scolars the whiche the king gyvith exhibicion in oxford	iiijli.
Itm	the last daye paied to John Wescote in rewarde for bringing a guelded dere unto the kinges grace	xiijs.iijd.
Itm	the laste daye delived by the kinges comaundement to my ladye Anne[3]	Cxli.
Itm	the same daye paied to the ferymannes wif for carying over the kinges horses at dives tymes at grenewich	vjs.viijd.
Itm	to S. Thomas Cheyney s'vant in rewarde for bringing a horse to the kinges grace	xxs.
Itm	to my lorde Chamberleyns s'vant in rewarde for bringing a wylde bore to the kinges grace	xls.

Sm̄ partes Clvjli.vjs. viijd.

Itm	delived to the kinges grace owne handes for to game therw[t] now at this tyme of Cristemas	Cli.
Itm	to the clerc of the kinges closet for his botehire for fetching of certen stuf fro grenewiche to yorke place	ijs.
Itm	the same laste daye of Decembr paied to the s'geant of the pantrye for certen trenchars for the king	xxiijs.iijd.
Itm	the same daye paied to marke and to the two guilliams by waye of the kinges rewarde[4]	xls.
Itm	a Northern man by way of rewarde, called John a Wylkinson	xls.

Itm	to wytham george lawson s'vent by waye of Rewarde	xls.
Itm	to william locke for certen stuf the whiche was solde unto the kinges grace As appereth by his bille	iiij.xix.li.xviij
Itm	to the pages of the kinges chambr by way of Rewarde	xls.
Itm	to the pages of the quenes chambr by way of Rewarde	xls.
Itm	to the Maister of the kinges beres by waye of Rewarde	xls.
Itm	to maister Bryan for so moche money by him gyven in rewarde to a straunge mynstrell at yorke place	xls.

Sm̃ partes CCxv li. xiijs. x d.

Summa totalis huius   M CCCCxlix li. ixs vjd.
mensis Decembris

HENRY R.

Source: N. H. Nicholas *The Privy Purse Expenses of King Henry the Eighth* (1827) 13–14, 'Yet paymentes in Decembre' [1529]

1. Wig or hair piece
2. Mary
3. Anne Boleyn
4. Musicians of the Chamber

Appendix IV

The Structure of the Court

Document 2   Notes for the reform of the household

Remembrance of chardgies that be not comprised in hir maiesties book of Ordinances, and cause the greater expenses.

1. Her majesties privy diet served every fish day throughout the year,
   (note in Cecil's hand) £646

2. Her majesties book of diets now daily served with the rest of her household, exceedeth muche her majesties book, signed with her owne hande, aswell in powle as by increase of prices.

3. Item that her majestie spendeth less in powle and nature yerely than her brother and sister did, and yet the money much increased as dothe appeare by recorde thereof.

4. Item the lodging of the white staves and others that be appointed ordinary tables without the Corte in the time of progress doth cause doble expense of beere ale and wine and other allowances.

5. Item the great number of noble personages lodged and being about the court, withe their great trains of servants much surmounting the auncient order of her house doth lykewyse cause great expensis of ale beer wine wood coles rushes etc.

6. Item eating and drinkinge in noble mens and womens chambers on the fish daies, whereby her majesties chamber is not onely unfurnysshed at meale tymes, and the same allowance unnecessarily spent but the meat appointed carried away by the gromes of the chamber, and eaten in places where there is a great number of their servants and others fedd, which causeth great and unorderly expenses.

7. Item late suppers and late serving of all night doth also cause great expenses.   (note in Cecil's hand) for the offices are open thereby.

8. Item the alteracion of removing, and daies not kept as they be appointed, doth not only cause great waste of provision laide in divers places, but also in expenses of purveyers and others in removing the same again.

9. Item if it might please her majestie to have her great service carried into her privy chamber, as it was in her father's day, it would greatly mynyshe the charges and expenses.

Item if all sweet wines to be spent for her highnes might be layde in privy cellars as heretofore they have been (except great feastes only) and to be kept by the gromes of the privy chamber by her majesties appointment would muche abate the expenses of the same.

Item for that her majesties diet is dressed in two severall kitchens doth doble the expenses of wood and coles.

Item meate dressed in divers places within the corte owte of her majesties owne ketchens, for divers and sundry persons doth not only cawse the greater expenses but also pestreth the corte with unfytt persons and hangers on by reason of the same.

Item the great numbers of hangers on the corte, and followers as artificers suters and launderers doth lykewise cause great expensis.

Item if noble men and women being lodged within the corte would be contented with suche allowance as is appointed unto them for their bouche of court and to keep no further number of persons then of olde tyme they were allowed, would lykewise abate the great expenses.

Memorandum prepared for Lord Burghley, *c.*1576
BL Lansdowne MS 21, no. 65, f.133

Document 3   On the ladies of Mary's Privy Chamber

My fame fanned onne me some what to see of yow
good ladyes all accepte my will this thing I only pray

Hawarde is not hawghte but of suche smylinge cheare
that wolde alure eche gentill harte hir love to hold full dere

Dacars is not dawngerus hir talk is nothinge coye
hir noble stature may compare with hectors wife of troye

Baynam is as bewtifull as nature canne devyse
stedfastenes posess her harte and chastitie her eyes

Arundell is auciaunte in thes her tender yeares
in harte in face in talke in deade a matrons wit appeares

Dormar is a darlinge and of suche lively hewe
that who so fedes his eyes one her may sone her bewte vue

Mancell is a merye one and is righte worthi love
whome nature wrowghte so setusly her coninge for to prove

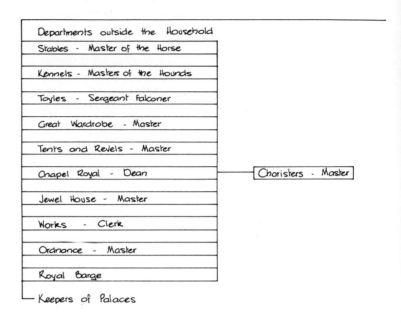

Departments outside the Household

Stables - Master of the Horse

Kennels - Masters of the Hounds

Toyles - Sergeant falconer

Great Wardrobe - Master

Tents and Revels - Master

Chapel Royal - Dean ———— Choristers - Master

Jewel House - Master

Works - Clerk

Ordnance - Master

Royal Barge

Keepers of Palaces

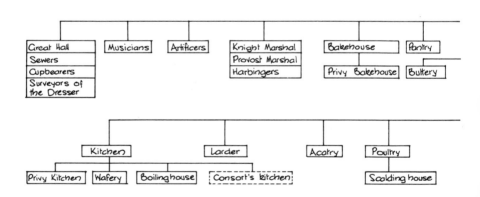

Great Hall / Sewers / Cupbearers / Surveyors of the Dresser

Musicians

Artificers

Knight Marshal / Provost Marshal / Harbingers

Bakehouse / Privy Bakehouse

Pantry / Buttery

Kitchen / Privy Kitchen / Wafery / Boilinghouse / Consort's kitchen

Larder

Acatry

Poultry / Scalding house

N.B. Solid lines indicate permanence or near permanence. Broken lines indicate non-permanence.

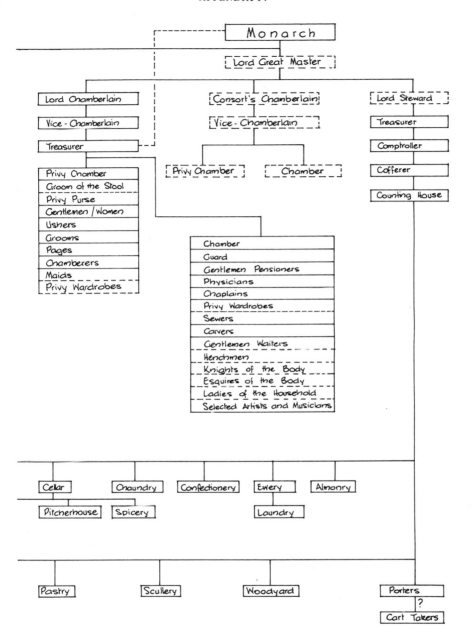

Appendix IV   *The Structure of the Court*

Coke is cumly and thereto in bookes sets all her care
in lerninge withe romayne dames of ryghte she may compare

Briges is a blessed wighte and praythe with harte and voise
which from her cradle hathe bene taughte in vertue to reioce

Thes eighte nowe serves one noble Quene but if powre were in me
for bewtise prayse and vertues sake eche one a Quene showld be

finis R.E.

BL Cotton MS, Titus A xxiv, f.83v

I am indebted to Dr W. J. Tighe for a transcript of these verses.

Note

Neither the identity of 'R.E.' nor the exact date of this document are known. The queen referred to must be Mary, but only three of these ladies can be positively identified as holders of positions in her Privy Chamber. Jane Dormer, the daughter of Sir William Dormer, and subsequently Duchess of Feria, is the best known. Ann Coke, although referred to here by her maiden name, had married Nicholas Bacon in February 1553, and served throughout Mary's reign despite the fact that her father was a notorious Protestant, and her husband a suspected one (*Cal.Pat.* Philip & Mary, II, 12; R. Tittler, *Nicholas Bacon*, 49–54). Katherine Bridges was a daughter of Sir Thomas Bridges, created Lord Chandos in 1554 (*Cal. Pat.* P&M, III, 35–8). 'Hawarde' may be Margaret, wife of William, later Lord Howard of Effingham. If so, she had ceased to serve by the end of the reign, and no Howard appears on Mary's funeral list (PRO LC2/4). 'Dacars' had similarly vanished by 1558, and may be identified with Elizabeth, wife of George Dacre Esq. of Warwickshire, who received a number of favours from the queen. 'Arundell' was probably either Dorothy or Jane, the young daughters of Sir Thomas Arundell, who had been attainted in 1552. A 'Mrs. Arundel' appeared among the queen's Maids in 1558. 'Baynam' could have been either the wife or daughter of Christopher Baynam Esq. of Gloucestershire, who, like George Dacre, received a number of favours, and may have been one of Mary's early supporters. 'Mancell' was probably the same person as the 'Lady Maunsell' of PRO LC2/4 and can be plausibly identified with Dorothy, wife of Sir Rees Maunsell, the Chamberlain of South Wales.

Notes and References

Chaper 1, pp. 1–37

1. 'Ballade to King Henry VI Upon his Coronation', *Early English Text Society*, no. 192, II, 627. In his 'Mumming at London', the same author associated magnanimity with both *fortitudo* and magnificence. M. Greaves, *The Blazon of Honour*, 19.
2. Charles had little trust in his son's ability as a military commander, and when he got his chance at St Quentin in 1557, he arrived too late for the battle, to his great annoyance.
3. 'Life of Alexander', *Early English Text Society*, no. 143, 23.
4. *The Order of Chivalry*, cited Greaves, op. cit., 49.
5. 'And they said to me "Lord, the game is not equal between us; for if it comes to flight, you are on horseback, while we are on foot; and the Saracens will kill us." And I said to them, "Lords, I swear to you that I will not fly, for I will remain with you on foot." So I dismounted and sent away my horse ...' *Histoire et Chronique du tres Chretien roi Saint-Louis*, trs. Marsials, 280.
6. These were normally sessions of *oyer et terminer*, administering the common law in the manner of a judicial Eyre of earlier times. For example, in January 1464 he went to Gloucestershire accompanied by the Chief Justices of both benches to deal with a local feud. Charles Ross, *Edward IV*, 401. He does not seem to have presided in sessions at King's Bench itself.
7. W. J. Jones, 'The Crown and the Courts in England, 1603–1625' in *The Reign of James VI and I*, ed. A. G. R. Smith, 189.
8. James Raine, *The Priory of Hexham*, I, ciii–iv.
9. Henry VI allowed himself to be controlled by the Beauforts, and latterly by Queen Margaret, so that the legitimate expectations of others were constantly disappointed. James I was indiscriminately generous; some of his beneficiaries (such as Robert Cecil) being hard working servants, others (such as Robert Carr) personal favourites of little worth.
10. M. St. Clare Byrne, *The Lisle Letters*, I, 15.
11. *The Book of the Courtier*, trs. Bull, 310.
12. D. M. Loades, *Politics and the Nation*, 304.
13. E.g. the Bowes, Tempests and Eures. M. James, *Family, Lineage and Civil Society*, 45.
14. J. A. F. Thomson, *The Transformation of Medieval England*, 278.
15. The Black Prince was created Duke of Cornwall. The first non-royal Duke was Robert de Vere, created Duke of Ireland in 1386, but there continued to be hostility to such creations well into the fifteenth century. J. E. Powell and K. Wallis, *The House of Lords in the Middle Ages*, 397–8, 418–9.
16. Edward Hall, *The Union of the two noble and illustre Famelies of Lancastre and Yorke*, ed. 1809, 591.
17. G. Mattingly, *Catherine of Aragon*, 109–110.
18. G. R. Elton, *Policy and Police*, 123 4. The government had to some extent asked

for this kind of criticism by urging that the good harvests and warm summers of the early 1530s were evidence of divine approval.

19. *Sermons and Remains of Bishop Ridley*, Parker Society (1845), 385.
20. E.g. the white falcon (Anne's symbol) descending upon a stock, or root, 'whereout sprang a multitude of red and white roses, curiously wrought'. *The noble and triumphant coronation of Queen Anne* (1533) repr. E. Arber, *An English Garner*, II, 43–60.
21. *Tractatus de Regimine Principum ad Henricum Sextum*, ed. J-P Genet, Camden Society, 4th series, 18, 53–169.
22. Ibid., 167.
23. This entry has been fully discussed and analysed in S. Anglo, *Spectacle Pageantry and Early Tudor Policy*, 56–98.
24. *Tres cartas de lo sucedido en el viaje de Su Alteza a Ingaterra*, La Sociedad de Bibliofilos Espanoles, (1877) Primera carta, 91.
25. *Calendar of State Papers, Spanish*, ed. Royall Tyler *et al.*, XIII, 58.
26. *Paston Letters and Papers of the Fifteenth Century*, ed. N. Davies, I, 539.
27. *Calendar of State Papers, Venetian*, ed. Rawdon Brown *et al.*, I, 795–6.
28. Ibid., II, 918.
29. Letter of a Spanish gentleman, 17 August 1554. *Cal. Span.*, XIII, 30–1.
30. *The works in verse and prose of Sir John Davies*, I, 189.
31. *The Household of Edward IV*, ed A. R. Myers, introduction, 1–13.
32. The household journal of Edward Stafford, 3rd Duke of Buckingham, from November 1508 to March 1509, is now in the Bagot Collection at the Staffordshire Record Office. For a full discussion of the household management of the 3rd Duke, see K. B. McFarlane, *The Nobility of later Medieval England*, 207–212; also Carole Rawcliffe, *The Staffords, Earls of Stafford and Dukes of Buckingham, 1394–1521*. For Percy management, see *The Northumberland Household Book*, ed. Bishop Percy (1770); also J. M. W. Bean, *The Estates of the Percy Family, 1416–1537*.
33. John Matthews, *Western Aristocracies and the Imperial Court, AD 364–425*, John Beckwith, *Early Christian and Byzantine Art*, 35–43. J. M. Hussey, 'The Christian Citadel; the Byzantine world of the ninth and tenth centuries', in D. Talbot Rice, *The Dark Ages*, 114–138.
34. W. Ullman, *The Growth of Papal Government in the Middle Ages*, and *Medieval Papalism*. The best account of the Avignon development is in B. Guillemain, *La Cour Pontificale d'Avignon*.
35. Guillemain, op. cit.
36. T. C. Van Cleve, *The Emperor Frederick II of Hohenstaufen*; A. G. Dickens, 'Monarchy and cultural revival' in *The Courts of Europe, 1400–1800*, 8–32.
37. M. H. Keen, *Chivalry*, 30. Keen provides the best general account of the origins and development of secular chivalry.
38. *De Arte Honeste Amandi*, trs. J. J. Parry (1941). The best short account of the development of courtly love is E. Salter, 'Courts and Courtly Love', in D. Daiches and A. Thorlby, *The Medieval World*.
39. Lines 2325–8, in Chaucer, *Works*, ed. F. N. Robinson. Cited R. F. Green, *Poets and Princepleasers*, 119.
40. Green, op. cit., 113. See also A. Kelly, 'Eleanor of Acquitaine and her Courts of Love', *Speculum*, xii, 1937.
41. 'Constitutio Domus Regis', in *Dialogus de Scaccario*, ed. C. Johnson, 128–35.
42. *Household Ordinances*, Society of Antiquaries (1790), 10.
43. Christine de Pisan, *Livre des fais et bonnes meurs du sage roy Charles V*, ed. S. Solente, I, 47. Cited and trans. Green, op. cit., 61.
44. G. Mathew, *The Court of Richard II*; J. A. Tuck, 'Richard II's system of patronage' in *The Reign of Richard II*, ed. F. R. H. Du Boulay and C. M. Barron, 1–20.

45. C. A. J. Armstrong, 'The Golden Age of Burgundy', in *The Courts of Europe*, 55–75.

46. R. Vaughan, *Philip the Good*. Anne was extremely popular in Paris, for her piety, energy and social panache.

47. O. Cartellieri, *The Court of Burgundy*, trs. M. Letts, 47. For a fuller consideration of the order, see M. Keen, *Chivalry*, 175 ff.

48. Cartellieri, loc. cit.

49. R. Vaughan, *Charles the Bold*.

50. Armstrong, art. cit. In the 1440s Philip's legitimate and illegitimate offspring were apparently taught together by a single tutor, Antoine Haneron, who was brought from Louvain for the purpose.

51. Cartellieri, 64–5. This was a notion of the courtier's role which Castiglione did his best to reject. *The Book of the Courtier*, 319–20 etc.

52. Otto Benesch, *The Art of the Renaissance in Northern Europe*.

53. Armstrong, art. cit.

54. Ibid. The French king promptly provided him with the heiress Helene de Chambres, and commanded his services thereafter.

55. Olivier de la Marche, *L'estat de la maison du duc Charles de Bourgoinge*, in *Memoires*, ed. H. Baune and J. d'Arbaumont, IV, 1–94.

56. Cartellieri, op. cit., 66–7.

57. *L'estat de la maison* . . .

58. Ibid. There appears to have been little practical distinction between the Duke's private expenses and those of the 'state'.

59. Cartellieri, 69.

60. Vaughan, *Charles the Bold*, Armstrong, art. cit.

61. Financial embarrassment caused the Burgundian court to be reduced or disbanded totally on six or seven occasions between 1404 and 1477. In 1454 Philip the Good departed secretly into Germany, leaving instructions with his chamberlains to carry out the disbandment.

62. Fastolf was suspended from the Order of the Garter for this offence, Keen, *Chivalry*, 175. E. de Monstrelet, *Chronique*, ed. L. Douet d'Arcq IV, 331–2.

63. Registres de la Toison d'Or, I, f2v. cit. Keen, 175. Armstrong, art. cit.

64. Ibid.

65. Benesch, op. cit.

66. Myers, *Household of Edward IV*, 69–75.

67. *Household Ordinances*, 16–24.

68. G. F. Beltz, *Memorials of the Order of the Garter* (London, 1841) clxii–clxvi.

69. A. B. Emden, *A Biographical Register of the University of Oxford to A.D. 1500*.

70. Myers, *Household of Edward IV*, 138. On the nature of 'noriture', see Green, *Poets and Princepleasers*, 85–91. There were a number of contemporary treatises on the subject, notably 'The Babees Book', in *Early English Meals and Manners* ed. F. J. Furnivall, *EETS* (OS, 1868).

71. Green, op. cit., 77–79. John Anwykyll was the first Master of Magdalen College School, Oxford.

72. Ross, *Edward IV*, 175.

73. Q. Skinner, *The Foundation of Modern Political Thought*, I, 117.

74. *The Great Chronicle of London*, ed. A. H. Thomas and I. D. Thornley, 215.

75. Myers, op. cit., 5.

76. *The Great Red Book of Bristol* ed. E. W. W. Veale, Bristol Record Society (18, 1953), 72–3.

77. R. H. Robbins, *Historical Poems of the Fourteenth and Fifteenth Centuries*, 221–6; cited Ross, *Edward IV*, 300.

78. *The Travels of Leo of Rozmital*, ed. and trs. M. Letts (Hakluyt Soc., 2nd. series, 108, 46–7).

79. PRO E404/74/1, n.35. Cited Ross, op. cit., 260.
80. Green, *Poets and Princepleasers*, 140–1, 144. Ross, 265.
81. *The Wardrobe Accounts of Edward IV*, ed. N. H. Nicholas, 124, 159, 162.
82. 'The Croyland Chronicle' in *Rerum Anglicarum Scriptores Veterum*, ed. W. Fulman, 559.
83. Ross, 421.
84. E. Hall, *The Union of the two noble and Illustre Fameles . . .*, 423.
85. Ibid.
86. *Great Chronicle*, 312–5. S. Anglo, *The Great Tournament Roll of Westminster*, 34–40. See also Anglo, 'Anglo-Burgundian feats of arms at Smithfield, June 1467', *Guildhall Miscellany*, ii, 7 (1965).
87. *York Civic Records*, ed. A. Raine, i. 155–9. Anglo, *Spectacle, Pageantry, and Early Tudor Policy*, 22–32.
88. S. B. Chrimes, *Henry VII*, 1.
89. S. Anglo, 'The British History in early Tudor propaganda', *Bulletin of the John Rylands Library*, 44 (1961), 17–48. Glanmor Williams, *Harri Tudur a Chymru/Henry Tudor and Wales*, 43–9.
90. Hence Dafydd Llwyd:
     'Arthur benadur ydoedd
     mawr draw, ac ymherodr . . .
     Bid Arthur, mae'r byd wrthaw-
     ym mrwydr, drom, ymherawdr.
     Gwylied am fuddugoliaeth
     ydd wyf, wrth yr enw ydd aeth.'
     (Arthur was a great leader of yore, and an Emperor . . . May Arthur—the world lies open to him—be a force in battle and an Emperor. I watch for his victories that go with the name.'). Williams, op. cit., 81.
91. Shakespeare, *Richard III*, V, v, 140–1.
92. *Anglica Historia*, ed. D. Hay (Camden Society, n.s. 74, 1950), 146.
93. College of Arms MS 1st. M 13, f.61v. G. Kipling, *The Triumph of Honour*, 3–5.
94. College of Arms MS 1st. M 13, f.62v. Kipling, op. cit., 59.
95. Kipling, 52 ff. and note. Maynard also painted 'Henry VII and his family with St. George and the dragon', now in the Royal Collection.
96. Kipling, 7.
97. For a full discussion of these pageants, see Anglo, *Spectacle . . .*, 56–97.
98. G. F. Warner and J. P. Gilson, *Catalogue of Western Manuscripts in the Old Royal and King's Collections in the British Museum*, II, 334–5.
99. BL Add MS 7099 (Craven Ord transcript, 1829) e.g. 'To Newark for making of a song . . . 20s' (5), 'To the young damsel that danceth . . . £30' (11). This latter very large sum might well arouse some speculation as to the nature of the entertainment provided!
100. *Calendar of State Papers, Spanish*, I, 238.
101. *Opus Epistolarum Des. Erasmi Roterodami*, ed P. S. and H. M. Allen, I, 214.
102. C. S. Goldingham, 'Warships of Henry VIII', *United Services Magazine*, 179 (1919), 453–62. C. J. Ffoulkes, *Gunfounders of England* (Cambridge, 1937).
103. This soon became apparent in the case of the Tournai campaign, C. G. Cruickshank, *Army Royal, passim*.
104. Hall, *Union . . .*, 565–6.
105. Cruickshank, op. cit. A. F. Pollard, *Wolsey*, 18–22.
106. Maximilian had commissioned a group of German artists to devise a lavishly illustrated triumph for publication, which never in fact took place. Benesch, op. cit.
107. *Cal. Ven.*, I, 918. Anglo, *Spectacle . . .*, 114.
108. J. J. Scarisbrick, *Henry VIII*, 33–4. J. W. McKenna, 'How God became an

Englishman' in *Tudor Rule and Revolution*, ed. DeLloyd Guth and J. W. McKenna, 25–43.

109. Andre Bossuat, 'La Formule "Le Roi est empereur en son royaume": son emploi au xve siècle devant le Parlement de Paris', *Revue historique du droit francais et etranger* (4 series, 39, 1961), 371–81.

110. F. Le Van Baumer, *Early Tudor Theory of Kingship*; G. R. Elton, *Policy and Police*.

111. The cartoon survives as National Portrait Gallery 4027, which is discussed in R. Strong, *Tudor and Jacobean Portraits*, I, 158–9.

112. Now in the Royal Collection; described in *Holbein and the Court of Henry VIII* (The Queen's Gallery, Buckingham Palace), 129–30.

113. S. Anglo, 'An Early Tudor programme for plays and other demonstrations against the Pope', *Journal of the Warburg and Courtauld Institutes*, 20 (1957), 176–9.

114. H. McCusker, *John Bale, Dramatist and antiquary*, 5. S. Anglo, *Spectacle . . .* 266–8.

115. C. Wriothesley, *A Chronicle of England*, ed. W. D. Hamilton (Camden Soc. n.s., I), 99–100.

116. For a full discussion of Henry's image and behaviour in the last decade of his life, see L. B. Smith, *The Mask of Royalty*.

117. From the portrait now in the National Gallery of Art, Washington, U.S.A. R. Strong, *Tudor and Jacobean Portraits*, I, 164; II, 91–2. This complex and mannered piece of Latin verse may be translated as follows: 'Little boy, take after your father and also inherit his virtues: the world in its immensity contains nothing greater. Heaven and nature can only with difficulty have produced in you an offspring to whom the honour of this your father, itself surpassed by you, will in its turn give honour. If you had merely equalled him in honour, men would have had this desire which would be difficult to fulfill: "You are to surpass the deeds of such a father"; and this is what you have done! Amongst all the Kings whom the world of old adores there will not be found one to surpass you.'

118. E.g. two portraits by William Scrots, one now in the Louvre and the other in the Royal Collection. Strong, op. cit., I, 172, 173; II, 93–4.

119. *Literary Remains of King Edward VI*, ed. J. G. Nichols, II, 209–10.

120. NPG 4165. Strong, I, 678; II, 344–5.

121. She had been the figurehead and symbol of religious conservatism since her mother's death in January 1536, and particularly at the time of the Pilgrimage of Grace. D. M. Loades, *The Reign of Mary Tudor*, 17–32.

122. *The Diary of Henry Machyn*, ed. J. G. Nichols (Camden Soc., 1848), 4–5.

123. *A newe balade of the Marigolde by William Forrest Preest.* Broadsheet 36 in the Library of the Society of Antiquaries

124. *Cal. Span.*, XIII, 30.

125. Albert Feuillerat, *Documents relating to Revels at Court in the time of King Edward VI and Queen Mary*. The entertainments themselves appear to have been relatively inexpensive, and were routine rather than spectacular, but the scale of the queen's housekeeping and wardrobe expenditure continued to be lavish until the fourth year of her reign. See below. For a discussion of themes, see Anglo, *Spectacle . . .*, 319–343.

126. Loades, *Mary Tudor*, 211–244. Anglo, *Spectacle . . .*, 324–339.

127. Both printed in Rome in 1554. There were numerous similar tracts in Italian, Spanish and German. Significantly, no English versions were printed at the time, although some were written, notably 'John Elder's letter describing the arrival and marriage of King Philip, his triumphal entry into London, the Legation of Cardinal Pole etc.' in *The Chronicle of Queen Jane and Queen Mary*, ed. J. G. Nichols (Camden Soc., 1850), App. X.

128. *Chronicle of Queen Jane and Queen Mary*, 146.

129. Philip's reputation for lechery appears to have been almost entirely fabricated

by English pamphleteers, such as John Bradford, although Federico Badoer, the Venetian envoy in Brussels, did report in the autumn of 1555 that news of the king's amusements was being kept from the queen 'as she is easily agitated'. *Cal. Ven.*, VI, 277–8.

130. On the Englishness of Mary's religious settlement see Loades 'The piety of the restored catholic church under Queen Mary' (forthcoming).

131. Thomas Dekker, 'Old Fortunatus', in *Works*, I, 83.

132. The Conde de Feria (Philip's envoy). *Cal. Span. Eliz.*, I, 7.

133. *The Passage of our most dread Sovereign Lady Queen Elizabeth through the City of London*, in E. Arber, *An English Garner*, IV, 239.

134. By William Birche; an adaptation of a traditional song. Broadsheet 47 in the Library of the Society of Antiquaries.

135. R. Strong, *The Cult of Elizabeth*, 129–163.

136. John Nichols, *The Progresses of Queen Elizabeth*, III, 652.

Chapter 2, pp. 38–83.

1. This patent was confirmed on 16 January 1554, when its terms were extended. *Calendar of the Patent Rolls, Mary*, I, 47. A liberty was a place exempt from normal jurisdiction, where the king's writ did not run save through the holder of the franchise.

2. Ibid. By the terms of this patent the officers of the City of London were specifically excluded from the liberty. On 22 December 1553 Waldegrave had had to write to the Lord Mayor, demanding the discharge of one of the Wardrobe servants, Richard Stoughton, who had been elected Constable of the parish 'by divers malicious persons' contrary to the ancient privileges of the Great Wardrobe—and this confirmation may well have been the result.

3. In 1593 the Master of the Horse had a staff of one Chief Avenor, 14 esquires, 6 riders and 16 footmen, all of which positions were within his gift. *Household Ordinances*, Society of Antiquaries, 1790, 256.

4. The Stables were always listed, with the Ordnance, the Armour, the Mint, and numerous departments, alongside the Household and the Chamber as accounting offices, e.g. PRO LC5/182. However, the Master of the Horse was allowed a bouge of two 'messes', and these were charged to the Board of Greencloth.

5. Myers, *Household of Edward VI*, 91–2.

6. G. W. Bernard, *The Power of the Early Tudor Nobility*.

7. *Calendar of State Papers, Spanish*, 13, 30–34. Earlier in the year the queen had ordered that her Gentlemen Ushers should 'appoint no lodging within the court ... but only to suche as be in ordinarie', but this would hardly have applied to the duchess, if there had actually been space.

8. *Household Ordinances*, 118.

9. 33 Henry VIII, c.12; 'An acte for murder and malicious bloodshed within the courte'.

10. Myers, 115.

11. The Eltham Ordinances complained of the 'seldom keeping of the kinges hall', and sought to impose a regular timetable of service. *HO*, 160, See also below.

12. R. C. Braddock, 'The royal household, 1540–1560' (Northwestern University, unpublished Ph.D. thesis, 1971). Braddock's evidence for this assertion is not very clear, and I have been unable to confirm it.

13. *HO*, 167–8.

14. D. Loades, *The Reign of Mary Tudor*, 213–5.

15. Ibid., 25–6.

16. 32 Henry VIII, c.39. For a full discussion of the implications of this change, see G. R. Elton, *The Tudor Revolution in Government*, 393–6.

17. 1 Mary st.3, c.4. PRO E101/428/17.

18. Braddock, op. cit., *passim*.

19. The fullest description of the functioning of these departments, although incomplete, is contained in the Black Book of Edward IV. Myers, 165–197. The Marian list, which may well have been connected with her coronation, is PRO E101/428/17.

20. For a full description of his activity in this connection, see C. G. Cruikshank, *Army Royal*.

21. *HO*, 239. The Almoner also received and distributed the goods of suicides.

22. *HO*, 250–3. In 1576 Lord Burghley had noted 'Officers in wages for ye hall not profitable'. BL Landsdowne MS 21/62 f.127.

23. Myers, 201.

24. D. Starkey, 'The development of the Privy Chamber, 1485–1547' (Cambridge University, unpublished Ph.D thesis, 1973) 3.

25. J. Dent, *The Quest for Nonsuch*, 247.

26. Myers, 199.

27. College of Arms MS Arundel XVII², cited by Starkey, 17. For the duties of the Esquires at an earlier date, see Myers, 11.

28. Arundel MS XVII², f.17v. Starkey, 24.

29. Starkey, 24–7.

30. Ibid.

31. It is not quite certain that these Knights had ever been discontinued, but there is no reference to them between the middle of Henry VII's reign and the early part of Henry VIII's. They were certainly not performing court service.

32. 7 Henry VIII, c.6.

33. Guildford's father, Sir Richard, had been Controller of the Household, and Brandon's father, Sir William, had been Henry VII's standard bearer.

34. Starkey, 97–103.

35. Hall, *Chronicle*, 598.

36. Ibid. Sir Richard Wingfield, Sir Richard Weston, Sir Richard Jerningham, Sir William Kingston.

37. Starkey, 116–7.

38. BL Cotton MS Vespasian C XIV, ff.257–94.

39. *Letters and Papers of the reign of Henry VIII*, II, ii, 3100.

40. *HO*, 137.

41. Ibid., 146–7, Hall, 707.

42. Hall, 707.

43. Starkey, 182.

44. The Ordinary of 1540 (sometime after 28 July) drawn up by William Dunch, the Cofferer's clerk, was partially published in *The Genealogist*, new series, 29, 12 ff, 94 ff, 144 ff, 238 ff; new series 30, 18 ff, 94 ff, 153 ff, 208 ff.

45. Starkey, 275–88. John Husee, Lord Lisle's agent, declared 'the Kinges Household shall be brought into the same order and state that the ffrench kings Cort is att ...' PRO SP1/114 ff.113–4. One pointer to what was intended can be seen in the fact that when the Earl of Oxford died in 1540, he was succeeded as Lord Great Chamberlain by Cromwell himself. The Lord Great Chamberlainship was an ornamental and occasional office which was supposed to be hereditary in the de Vere family, to which it eventually returned under Mary.

46. Hall, 512. Elton, *Revolution*, 382–5.

47. By 1547 there were 41 Gentlemen at Arms, and 12 Gentlemen Pensioners in reversion. PRO LC2/2.

48. *HO*, 165–6.

49. Starkey, 231. This arrangement was not consistently observed; the Eltham Ordinances allowed a special 'mess' to be served to the Gentlemen of the Privy Chamber in the event of the exigencies of the king's service making it impossible for them to keep regular mealtimes in the Chamber. *HO*, 158.

50. For a full discussion of the position of the Groom of the Stool, see Starkey, 241–5. For the political purges of 1536 and 1538, see below.

51. PRO LC2/2: 'The Lord Butler, the Lord Strange, Mr. Browne, Mr. Barnaby (FitzPatrick), Mr. Cotton'.

52. BL Royal MS 7 C XVI, f.92 'The names of such officers in ordinary of the chamber of the late King's majestie as be now discharged'; f.94 'Such gentlemen, Yeomen, Grooms and others that do remain unplaced and served the King's Majestie being Prince'; f.96 'The names of such of the King's Majesties servants as are newly placed in ordinary in the Chamber'.

53. Stanhope had become one of the Principal Gentlemen by 13 September 1547, and First Gentleman by August 1548. *Acts of the Privy Council*, II, 128; *Calendar of the Patent Rolls, Edward VI*, I, 391.

54. W. K. Jordan, *Edward VI; the Young King*. For a full discussion of Seymour's conspiracy, see D. E. Hoak, *The King's Council in the reign of Edward VI*.

55. D. E. Hoak, 'The King's Privy Chamber, 1547–1553' in DeLloyd J. Guth and J. W. McKenna (eds.) *Tudor Rule and Revolution*, 87–108.

56. *Acts of the Privy Council*, II, 344–5. The peers were: the Marquis of Northampton, the Earl of Arundel, Lord Wentworth, Lord St. John, Lord Russell, and the Earl of Warwick himself.

57. Hoak, art. cit.

58. W. K. Jordan (ed.) *The Chronicle and Political Papers of King Edward VI*, 26.

59. Ibid. Sir Richard Blount's detailed account of the office of Gentleman Usher of the Privy Chamber, written at this time, says that the Gentlemen of the Chamber 'saving those that be of the Bedd Chamber, ought to go noe further than the Privye Chamber unless they be called', but it is not clear that this meant any more than 'those on duty in the Bed Chamber'. Grose and Astle, *Antiquarian Repertory*, IV, 648; cited Hoak, 104.

60. Society of Antiquaries MS 125, f.31v; BL MS Stowe 571, f.32.

61. *Acts of the Privy Council*, III, 30; 11 May 1550.

62. R. C. Braddock, 'The character and composition of the Duke of Northumberland's army in 1553', *Albion*, 8 (1976), 342–56.

63. Braddock, 'Household', 81, notes only one, Thomas Ashley. Attempts to deprive Edward Underhill were unsuccessful.

64. PRO LC2/4, 2.

65. PRO LC2/4, 3.

66. Her son was Edward Courtenay, Earl of Devon, and briefly favoured by some as a candidate for Mary's hand—hence the interest aroused by his mother's position. Loades, *Mary Tudor*, 89. *Calendar of State Papers, Spanish*, XII, 39.

67. 'Underhill's narrative', in E. Arber, *An English Garner*, IV, 89.

68. PRO LC2/4, 2.

69. Loades, *Mary Tudor*, 89. Simon Renard considered it to be particularly important to gain her support for Mary's marriage with Philip. See below.

70. PRO LC2/4, 2. They were only three in number at the end of the reign. Elizabeth continued this custom, having six 'maids of honour' at her coronation, headed by Lady Jane Howard. LC2/4, 3.

71. List of Philip's English Household: *Cal. Span.* XII, 297.

72. This was Sir Anthony Browne, and the dismissal caused a furore because the English treated it as a demonstration of Spanish bad faith. *Calendar of State Papers, Spanish*, XIII, 49, 58.

73. Archivo General de Simancas, Estado Inglaterra, Legajo 811, f.121. *Cal. Span.*, XII, 158, 295; XIII, 45.
74. PRO LC2/4, 3.
75. Ibid.
76. Ibid.
77. None of the members of these ancillary groups was given livery, and therefore presumably did not belong to the Ordinary. PRO LC5/49.
78. S. Adams 'Eliza enthroned?' in C. Haigh (ed.) *The reign of Elizabeth I*, 60.
79. W. J. Tighe, 'The Gentlemen Pensioners in the reign of Elizabeth', (Cambridge University, unpublished Ph.D thesis, 1984).
80. Myers, 156.
81. *HO*, 140.
82. Myers, 71.
83. *HO*, 228–32. PRO E101/428/17. Braddock, 'Household', 87.
84. *HO*, 229.
85. *HO*, 211.
86. *HO*, 281.
87. See below.
88. *HO*, 281–2.
89. This division was introduced at some time between 1478, when it does not appear (Myers, 227), and 1526, when it does (*HO*, 142). In the later part of the sixteenth century the Hall kitchen was known as the Household, or Great kitchen.
90. Braddock, 'Household'. In 1554 the daily consumption was estimated at 80–100 sheep, 12 fat beeves, 18 calves, plus poultry, game, deer, boars and rabbits. *Cal. Span.* XIII, 30–31.
91. *HO*, 251–2.
92. BL MS Landsdowne 21, 65, f.133.
93. 'Item the taking of dysshes from her majesties borde is one of the greatest occasions of ther keping of ther servants for almost few or none in this howse that likes of ther ordinarye diet for that they ar growen in such delicacy that no meate will serve them but that whiche cometh from her majesties borde ...' BL MS Landsdowne 21, 67, f.140.
94. *HO*, 153. '... the first dynner in eating dayes to begin at tenne of the clock ... and the first supper at four of the clock on worke dayes ...' Ibid., 151.
95. 'Underhill's narrative', 95.
96. Braddock, 'Household'.
97. *HO*, 281–98, contains a schedule of these 'fees', as they existed at the end of the century. See also Braddock, 'Household', 196–8.
98. Braddock, 'Household', 138.
99. BL Add. MS 7099 f.16. *Letters and papers*, XIII, ii, 524–39.
100. *HO*, 164. Braddock, 'Household', 56.
101. Braddock, 'Household', Appendix. 'A general collection of the offices in England, with their fees, in her majesties gift' PRO LC5/182.
102. Braddock, 'Household', 82–5.
103. Ibid.
104. In 1513 and 1544. Henry also made a major expedition to France in 1520, to the Field of Cloth of Gold, on which the greater part of the Household also accompanied him, but that was warfare only in the psychological sense.
105. Braddock, 'Household', 127.
106. PRO LC2/2. For a fuller discussion of the matter of household careers, see Braddock, 'Household', 131–3.
107. Ibid., 119.
108. *HO*, 146. For the complaints which this produced, see above, and Hall, 707.

109. The commutation of diets into boardwages during sickness or absence on business was a well-established practice by 1526. By 1540 it seems to have been a common practice for household servants to 'live out', and draw their board-wages in cash during their normal service. Most of the staff of the Stables were also paid boardwages in cash. This was probably a result of the chronic shortage of accommodation, particularly for married men. *HO*, 208–214; 202–205.

110. PRO E101/426/2.

111. Each palace had a Keeper, whose task it was to maintain the fabric and cleanliness of the building when it was not in use. He was paid a fee by direct warrant, and was responsible for his own staff. A list of these keepers, and an inventory of the stocks for which they were responsible, exists in BL MS Harleian 1419, pt.2.

112. Braddock, 'Household', 59.

113. BL MS Lansdowne 21, 65, f.133.

114. Myers, 67.

115. Myers, 68. It was not until the statute of 1555 that there was any specific requirement for the commission to be in English.

116. *Rotuli Parliamentorum*, V, 154.

117. Awareness of these problems is apparent from the rules devised for the purveyors, but there was little chance of remedy until the accounting system was changed. Myers, 221–2.

118. Ibid., 221.

119. Ibid., 222. *HO*, 138–9.

120. P. L. Hughes and J. F. Larkin, *Tudor Royal Proclamations*, I, 135.

121. *HO*, 217–227.

122. Ibid.

123. Statute 2 & 3 Philip and Mary, c.6, 4. *Statutes of the Realm*, IV, i, 282.

124. *HO*, 228.

125. Allegra Woodworth, *Purveyance for the Royal Household in the reign of Queen Elizabeth*, Transactions of the American Philosophical Society, 1945.

126. PRO SP12/127/46. Woodworth, 77.

127. PRO E351/1795; E351/541 f.40; BL MS Lansdowne 4, vi, f.17.

128. *Rotuli Parliamentorum*, V, 157.

129. Ibid., 61–2.

130. Ibid.

131. *Rotuli Parliamentorum*, V, 247, 330.

132. *RP*, VI, 198.

133. Statute 1 Henry VII, c.31. *RP*, VI, 299. In the following year the accounts of the Treasurer of the Household show receipts of £14,480, all on assignments from the Exchequer, PRO E101/412/19.

134. *RP*, VI, 497. PRO E101/414/14.

135. PRO E101/415/8.

136. Ibid. It seems likely that these 'foreign' receipts at this time were internal departmental credits, since no source is ever recorded.

137. PRO E101/414/6, under 13 November. Such transactions appear to have been frequent, if not regular. BL Add. MS 7099, f.31. The largest which I have been able to trace amounted to £12,000.

138. This was certainly the case at a later date. See below, and Elton, *Tudor Revolution in Government*, 404–8.

139. PRO E101/416/8. It seems likely that the uncertainty about the payment of household wages arises from the fact that they were simply subsumed under the weekly departmental diets. If any Chamber wages were being paid in the

Countinghouse at this time, it is difficult to see how they could have been similarly concealed.

140. W. C. Richardson, *Tudor Chamber Administration*, 410n.
141. PRO E361/8 mm. 37–44. Cited Elton, *op. cit.*, 400n.
142. Elton, 407.
143. Ibid., 410.
144. BL Arundel MS 97, f.120; cited Elton, 404.
145. BL MS Lansdowne 4, vii, f.19; PRO E351/1795.
146. PRO E351/3027.
147. PRO E351/1795. The Cofferer's expenditure rose enormously between 1549 and 1550—from £20,474 to £38,804—and this can only be accounted for by the re-allocation of spending, not by straightforward increase.
148. BL MS Stowe 571, ff.3–76.
149. BL MS Lansdowne 4, vii, f.19; PRO E351/1795. SP11/1/14; 'The debt of the household in Mr. Ryder's time, £13,574. The debt of the household in Mr. Weldon's time, £7,451'. John Ryther had died in 1552. His executors had accounted for 6/7 Edward VI, and Thomas Weldon's first year of account had been 7 Edward VI/1 Mary. PRO E351/1795.
150. PRO SP11/1/14.
151. PRO E101/427/20.
152. BL MS Cotton Titus B IV, f.133. PRO E101/428/8.
153. PRO E101/428/9.
154. PRO E351/1795.
155. For a list of these accounts, see PRO LC5/182. The Revels spent £3209 between 5 April and 20 September 1561. BL MS Lansdowne 5, i, f.1.
156. BL Add. MS 7099 f.12 etc.
157. PRO E101/414/16.
158. W. C. Richardson, *Tudor Chamber Administration*, 414–442.
159. PRO E101/424/9 'Certificate of the Accounts of Sir William Cavendish, Treasurer of the Chamber'.
160. Ibid.
161. Ibid., f.61.
162. PRO E101/424/10.
163. PRO SP11/1/14.
164. PRO E101/424/10.
165. PRO E351/541 f.21.
166. PRO E351/541 f.7.
167. PRO E351/3027, Statutes I. Henry VIII c.17, 4 Henry VIII c.17.
168. PRO E351/3033 et seq.
169. Elton, op. cit., 38. Richardson, *Tudor Chamber Administration*, 228 and n.
170. N. H. Nicholas (ed.) *The Privy Purse Expenses of King Henry the Eighth*, London, 1827.
171. Richardson, op. cit., 422.
172. Brodyman is known to have handled Philip's payments to the Cofferer for his Yeomen's wages, and can therefore be plausibly identified as the Keeper of the Privy Purse. PRO E101/429/9. Susan Clarencius handled plate for the Queen's use. PRO E101/520/14.
173. The Privy Purse under Edward is again something of a mystery. Edward himself controlled no money, but Peter Osbourne, Clerk to the four Principal Gentlemen, handled at least £40,000 between January 1552 and May 1553, without presenting any accounts. Whether this fund should be described as the Privy Purse is a matter for debate. D. E. Hoak, 'The King's Privy Chamber, 1547–153', 107. Tamworth's accounts are in PRO E351/2701.

Chapter 3, pp. 84–132

1. Earl of Rutland to the Earl of Arundel (Lord Steward), 2 July 1554. Rutland MSS; calendared in the *Reports of the Historical Manuscripts Commission*, 24, 1.
2. G. W. Bernard, *The Power of the Early Tudor Nobility*, 85.
3. Petyt MS 538, vol. 47 f.315; calendared in the *Reports of the Historical Manuscripts Commission*, 2, App., 154. *Chronicle of Queen Jane* (ed. J. G. Nicholas, Camden Society, 38, 1850), 63; PRO SP11/3, 21.
4. A servant of Edward Stafford, Duke of Buckingham, was paid for bearing his master's New Year gift to court in 1518, which suggests that Buckingham himself was not there. C. Rawcliffe, *The Staffords*, 186.
5. *Crisis of the Aristocracy*, 463.
6. Ibid., 232.
7. *Household Ordinances*, 155.
8. Ibid., 149.
9. BL. Lansdowne MS 2, 12, f.36.
10. Ibid. This list differs in many ways from the schedule of 'Horses' and 'Bedds' contained in the Household Ordinances, which gives a Duke or an Archbishop 24 and 9 respectively, and does not specify any number for a Cardinal. *HO*, 198.
11. 1533. Hughes and Larkin, *Tudor Royal Proclamations*, I, 211–2.
12. *HO*, 239.
13. Hall, *Chronicle*, 750.
14. *Letters and Papers*, IV, 4649.
15. Hughes and Larkin, I, 229, 319–20.
16. *HO*, 146, 148, 154.
17. Hughes and Larkin, I, 405.
18. Hughes and Larkin, II, 318–20; III, 111, 121.
19. Hall, 697.
20. Stone, *Crisis of the Aristocracy*, 226.
21. Ibid., 233–4.
22. *HO*, 150.
23. Statute 33 Henry VIII, c.12; 'An acte for murder and malicious bloodshed within the Courte.' The Chief Surgeon who was to carry out the amputation was one of three surgeons who assisted the royal physicians. Their status was that of yeomen servants of the Chamber.
24. The school was established at Blackfriars by Rocco Bonetti. For a discussion of this matter, see Stone, 242–50. For the earlier history of the London 'masters of defence', who taught broadsword and buckler, see J. P. Auglin, 'The schools of defense in Elizabethan London, *Renaissance Quarterly*, xxxvii, 393–411.
25. 'Nuestro Señor nos guarde! creo que seriamos ya todos muertos, porque estos ingleses, como gente barbara e muy heretica, no tienen cuenta en sus animas e consciencias, ni temen a dios y a sus sanctos.' *Tres Cartas de lo sucedido en el viaje de Su Alteza a Inglaterra* (La Sociedad de Bibliofilos Espanoles, 1877), Tercera Carta, 102.
26. Francis Yaxley to Sir William Cecil, 12 October 1554. BL Lansdowne MS 3, f.92.
27. Memorandum for the commission. PRO SP 11/4, f.10.
28. I am indebted to Dr David Starkey for this suggestion. On Stanley's treason, see S. B. Chrimes, *Henry VII*, 85 and n.
29. *Acts of the Privy Council*, III, 29–30. BL Stowe MS 571, f.32.
30. *APC*, III, 354, Warrant of 6 September 1551.
31. 'The narrative of Edward Underhill' in E. Arber, *An English Garner* (1882), IV, 72–100.
32. *Chronicle of Queen Jane*, 39. D. M. Loades, *Two Tudor Conspiracies*, 61–3.
33. A full list of the weapons issued was drawn up in 1559. PRO SP12/1, f.53.
34. Underhill, 'Narrative', 81.

35. *APC*, VI, 137, 1 August 1557. PRO KB27/1184, r. Rex 12d.
36. *HO*, 277; Braddock, 'Household', 115. BL Cotton MS Vespasian C. XIV, f.438.
37. Hall, 597.
38. *HO*, 145.
39. The laundresses appear to have been the only female servants 'below stairs'. There were a few musicians of yeoman status attached to the Chamber. Braddock, 'Household', *passim*. See also below.
40. *HO*, 150.
41. D. E. Hoak, 'The King's Privy Chamber, 1547–1553', 105–107; Starkey, 'The King's Privy Chamber', 262; BL Add. MS 43563 ff. 1–5.
42. BL Add., MS 43563 ff. 1–5. A book of appointments and warrants, 1557–8.
43. BL Add. MS 7099, *passim*. N. H. Nicholas, *Privy Purse Expenses of Henry VIII*.
44. Frederick Madden, *Privy Purse Expenses of Princess Mary* (London, 1829).
45. F. E. Emmison, *Tudor Food and Pastimes* (London, 1964), 81. Most of this book is based on the Petre household accounts at Ingatestone, and is not individually referenced.
46. Ibid.
47. *HO*, 157.
48. Underhill, 'Narrative', 87.
49. Statute 33 Henry VIII c.9. Emmison, op. cit. 80.
50. Quoted in John Stevens, *Music and Poetry in the Early Tudor Court*, 172-3.
51. BL Add. MS 7099, f.72; *Privy Purse Expenses of Henry VIII*, 81.
52. Emmison, op. cit., 79.
53. Henry VIII's MS, no. 33. Printed in Stevens, *Music and Poetry*, App., 386–428.
54. Stevens, *Music and Poetry*, 208–226; Kenneth Muir, *Life and Letters of Sir Thomas Wyatt*.
55. Kenneth Muir, 'Unpublished Poems in the Devonshire MS', *Proceedings of the Leeds Philosophical Society*, vi, 1947, no. 9. H. A. Mason, *Humanism and Poetry in the Early Tudor period* (London, 1959), 167–9.
56. Stevens, *Music and Poetry*, 179–185.
57. Hall, 513.
58. Baldesar Castiglione, *The Book of the Courtier*, trs. George Bull, 63–4. Castiglione thought that tennis was an excellent game to show off the strength and grace of a courtier.
59. For an earlier reference to Henry wrestling and 'castinge of the barre', see Hall, 515.
60. *Privy Purse Expenses of Henry VIII*, 218.
61. BL MS Add. 7099, ff. 18, 19, 36, 41.
62. Jean Wilson, *Entertainments for Elizabeth I* (London, 1980), 114.
63. *Calendar of State Papers, Spanish*, Elizabeth, I, 314. D. Wilson, *Sweet Robin* (London, 1981), 91.
64. PRO E351/2791.
65. Emmison, 78.
66. *HO*, 262.
67. BL. Add. MS 7099, f.67.
68. Madden, *Privy Purse Expenses of Princess Mary*, 107.
69. Hall, 517.
70. Ibid., 533–4.
71. Ibid., 689–90.
72. In 1502 he paid 100 marks 'to the challengers at the jousts', and another 100 to the 'defenders'; BL Add. MS 7099, f.20.
73. R. C. McCoy, 'From the Tower to the Tiltyard; Robert Dudley's return to glory', *Historical Journal*, 27 (1984), 425. S. Anglo, 'Archives of the English tournament; score checks and lists', *Journal of the Society of Archivists*, 2 (1960), 160.

74. McCoy, loc. cit.
75. *Calendar of State Papers, Spanish*, xiii 126; *Calendar of State Papers, Venetian*, vi, 1.
76. On College of Arms MS 6, see S. Anglo, 'Financial and heraldic records of English tournaments', *Journal of the Society of Archivists*, 2 (1962), 192.
77. For a discussion of the Accession Day tilts, see R. Strong, *The Cult of Elizabeth*, 129–163.
78. *Faerie Queene*, book 2, 2, xlii.
79. Strong, *Cult of Elizabeth*, 129–134.
80. 'Journey through England and Scotland made by Lupold von Wedel in the years 1584 and 1585', *Transactions of the Royal Historical Society*, new series, 9 (1895), 258–9.
81. '. . . one of his servants in pompous attire of a special pattern mounted the steps and addressed the Queen in well-composed verses or with a ludicrous speech, making her and her ladies laugh . . .' Ibid.
82. The descriptions of several such masks, given by Hall, are discussed by S. Anglo in *Spectacle, Pageantry and Early Tudor Policy, passim*.
83. P. Reyher, *Les Masques Anglais*, 500; cited by Stevens, 250–1.
84. BL Add. MS 7099, f.54.
85. Hall, 518–9.
86. Ibid., 513.
87. Hall, 631–2; Anglo, *Spectacle*, 120–1.
88. Anglo, *Spectacle*, 235–7. Rightwise was also a noted Latinist.
89. A. W. Reed, *Early Tudor Drama*, 1–29.
90. *Calendar of State Papers, Venetian*, II, 328.
91. PRO E351/2791; Accounts of John Tamworth.
92. John Leland, *De Rebus Britannicis Collectanea* (ed. T. Hearne, 1770), IV, 284–5.
93. Stevens, op. cit., 278.
94. BL Add. MS 31922; published and discussed by Stevens, 386 ff.
95. *Bowge of Courte*, in *The Poetical Works of John Skelton* (ed. A. Dyce, 1843), 1, 40, lines 256–9.
96. See below. Several skilled musicians are also known to have come with Philip.
97. *Psalms, sonnets and songs of Sadness and Piety* (London, 1588).
98. Myers, *Household of Edward IV*, 132.
99. BL Add. MS 7099 f.24 etc. There are also rewards to 'the princess's stringminstrels' and 'the princes organ player'.
100. Stevens, 301–3; 'The king's book of payments, 1538', *Letters and Papers* XIII, 2, 524–539.
101. Rawdon Brown, *Four Years at the Court of Henry VIII* (1854), 1, 296; 2, 97. Stevens, 265–6.
102. Ibid., 266.
103. BL Lansdowne MS 2, 13, f.38.
104. N. H. Nicholas, *Privy Purse Expenses*, 25, 26, etc. J. Pulver, *A Biographical Dictionary of Old English Music* (1927); Stevens, 319.
105. *HO*, 256; this list is of 1576–8, but is simply a copy of Society of Antiquaries MS 125, which is the list of 1552.
106. PRO LC5/182. A general cost estimate of about 1565 budgets only £541 for the musicians, but there is no other evidence to suggest such a drastic reduction, and this is probably the result of different accounting practices. BL Cotton MS Tiberius B III.
107. Wilson, *Entertainments*, 115–6.
108. BL MS RP 294; New Year's Gifts, 1557.
109. BL Add. MS 7099 *passim*; there are a number of other similar references. Visits by groups of players seem to have occurred every few weeks.
110. A. W. Reed, *Early Tudor Drama*, 62.

111. Reed, 94–100 (on Medwell). Heywood had a very long career; he was born in 1497, joined the court sometime before 1519, and retired in 1558.
112. PRO SP1/45 f.36; BL Egerton MS 2605 f.37; Anglo, *Spectacle*, 232–4.
113. Report by Gasparo Spinelli; *Calendar of State Papers*, Venetian, IV, 225; 8 January, 1528.
114. *HO*, 256. PRO LC5/182.
115. Reed, 62–5.
116. Albert Feuillerat, *Documents relating to the revel at court in the time of Edward VI and Queen Mary* (1914), 215–7. See also *Reports of the Historical Manuscripts Commission*, 6 (More Molyneux MS) App., 611, 613.
117. Towards the end of Henry's reign the house of the dissolved Blackfriars was devoted to this purpose. 'Annis xxxvii & xxxviii Henry 8—Primo et secundo Edward VI—The Repairing off the Blackefriars in London being a storehouse for the Kinges Maiesties Tentes, Pavilions & Revells.' Cited E. K. Chambers, *Tudor Revels*, 14.
118. In earlier generations these had sometimes appeared as 'Lords' or 'Abbots' of Misrule—both forms are found under Henry VII. BL MS Add. 7099.
119. The Duke of Northumberland seems to have been responsible for resurrecting the Lord of Misrule in 1551, allegedly to distract the king's attention from the trial of the Duke of Somerset. However, the decision may have been the king's own. At the end of November, Northumberland wrote to Cawarden

   '. . . I understand by Mr. vicechamberleyn that the kinges maiesties plesser ys for his highness better recreation the tym of theis hollydayes to have a Lorde of Mysrule and hathe apoyntyd apon this berer Mr. fferrys. wherfor the tyme beinge so nere at hand that he can not prepare soche thinges for the furnishynge of that offyce as he wold have done yf he had some knoledge of his highness plesser. . .'

   which does not suggest a deep laid plot. Feuillerat, *Revels*, 56. For Ferrers' expenses, and 'devices', see Ibid., 77–81.
120. Feuillerat, *Revels*, xii–xiii.
121. E. B. Fryde, 'Lorenzo de' Medici; high finance and the patronage of art and learning', in A. G. Dickens, *The Courts of Europe*, 77–97.
122. G. Kipling, *The Triumph of Honour*, 19; Armstrong, 'The golden age of Burgundy'.
123. Ross, *Edward IV*, 268.
124. Samuel Bentley, *Excerpta Historica*, (1831), 9.
125. Myers, *Household*, 126–7.
126. Ibid., 137–8.
127. S. B. Chrimes, *Henry VII*, 16.
128. G. Williams, *Harri Tudor, passim*. For a brief summary of Henry's attitude to Wales, see also W. S. K. Thomas, *Tudor Wales*, 33–42. Throughout his reign Henry gave the Welshmen in his court 40/- every year to celebrate St. David's day (1 March), and retained at least one Welsh harper.
129. Green, *Poets and Princepleasers*, 193.
130. Desiderius Erasmus, *Opus Epistolarum* (ed. P. S. and H. M. Allen, Oxford, 1906–58), 1, no. 1.
131. BL MS Royal 16 G VIII; Royal 15 D VI; and Royal 17 F IV. Kipling, 19.
132. Scarisbrick, *Henry VIII*, 5–6.
133. *The Antiquarian Repertory* (ed. F. Grose and T. Astle) (London, 1807–9), 2, 320.
134. Garrett Mattingly, *Catherine of Aragon*.
135. Scarisbrick, 15. Croke was later tutor to the Duke of Richmond.
136. *Opus Epistolarum*, 5, 241.
137. *DNB*.
138. Mattingly, *Catherine of Aragon*, 103–4.

139. Ibid., 138–9. J. K. McConica, *English Humanists and Reformation Politics*, 53–4.
140. J. W. McKenna, 'How God became an Englishman', in *Tudor Rule and Revolution*, 25–44.
141. McConica, *English Humanists*, 106–149.
142. For a full study of this programme, see G. R. Elton, *Reform and Renewal, Thomas Cromwell and the Commonweal*, (1973) and *Reform and Reformation* (1977).
143. *Letters and Papers*, VIII, 957; 14, i, 285; McConica, 152–3.
144. McConica, 153.
145. Strype, *Cranmer*, I, 107; McConica, 213–4.
146. J. G. Nichols, *Literary Remains of King Edward VI* (1857), 1.
147. See below. On this point I am indebted to the advice of Dr Maria Dowling and Miss Elizabeth Culling.
148. *The first tome or volume of the Paraphrase of Erasmus upon the newe testament* (1548); preface to the Gospel of St. John. *STC* 2854.
149. This conclusion should, I think, be drawn from the words of her well-known submission to the king.
150. Nichols, *Literary Remains*, 1, xxix. McConica, 215.
151. McConica, 216.
152. Ibid., 217–8.
153. McConica, 203–4; W. K. Jordan, *Edward VI; the threshold of power*, 405–7.
154. PRO SP6/12 ff.14–35. McConica describes Cooke as one of Edward's tutors, but this is challenged by Jordan, op. cit., 406 n.4.
155. See below.
156. The best independent assessment of Edward's abilities at this stage is provided by an Italian visitor, Hieronymous Cardano. Nichols, *Literary Remains*, 1, ccviii–ccxii. The fullest discussion of Edward's involvement with public affairs is Jordan, 403–423.
157. Hooper and Knox were the most outspoken of that group who blamed the 'carnal gospellers' (including Northumberland) for the judgement which fell on the Church in Mary's reign. D. M. Loades, *The Oxford Martyrs*, 96–100. See also, Richard Cox to Bullinger, 5 October, 1552; *Original Letters relative to the English Reformation* (1856), 1, 123; and H. Latimer, *Sermons* (1844), 203.
158. M. McKisak, *Medieval History in the Tudor Age*, 1–25. Leland received some minor ecclesiastical preferments from the Crown in recognition of his Latin scholarship, and in 1533 authority to search monastic libraries in pursuit of his historical researches, but no assistance in his salvage work. See also A. Wood, *Athenae Oxonienses*, (ed. P. Bliss, 1813–20), I, 197.
159. F. Madden, *Privy Purse Expenses*, *passim*.
160. *STC* 18076; Loades, *Reign of Mary*, 343.
161. J. I. Tellechea Idigoras, *Fray Bartolomé Carranza y el Cardenal Pole* (1977).
162. Loades, *Reign of Mary*, 168–75. Gardiner was anxious to bring about the reconciliation with Rome before Philip's arrival, but was frustrated by Imperial policy.
163. D. B. Fenlon, *Heresy and Obedience in Tridentine Italy* (1972); Loades, *Reign of Mary*, 428–52.
164. *Reign of Mary*, 473–4.
165. There is some doubt about the date at which Ascham assumed responsibility for Elizabeth's studies. He was in correspondence with Cheke, and with Elizabeth herself, before the end of 1545, but was still based in Cambridge in 1547. McConica, 212–13, 263. I am here assuming that he began to direct the Princess's studies some time in 1545, but did not take up a position at court until several months after Edward's accession.
166. McConica, 231.
167. *Calendar of the Patent Rolls, Edward VI*, II, 328.

168. Wallace McCaffrey, *The Shaping of the Elizabethan Regime* (1969), 35–6.
169. W. P. Haugaard, 'Elizabeth Tudor's *Book of Devotions*; a neglected clue to the Queen's life and character', *Sixteenth Century Journal*, 12/2 (1981), 79–106.
170. Strong, *The Cult of Elizabeth*, 129 ff. F. A. Yates, *Astraea*, 88–111.
171. E.g. 'For making the king's scholar at Oxon. to be master of arts ... £4 ..' BL Add. MS 7099, f.23; 'To Thomas Preston, student at Cambridge, for his entertainment of five years. ... £20 ...' PRO E351/2791.
172. McKisack, *Mediaeval History*, 26–49.
173. F. A. Yates, *Astraea*; Wilson, *Sweet Robin*, 151.
174. G. Pettie, *The Civile Conversation of S. Guazzo* (1586), sig. Av.
175. BL Harleian MS 2252 f.147, 'Colyn Clout', lines 621–5. Cited in M. Pollet, *John Skelton, poet of Tudor England* (1971), 128.
176. E. Auerbach, *Tudor Artists* (1954), 185.
177. This work was dedicated to Prince Arthur, and embellished with a portrait of the Prince. Kipling, *Triumph of Honour*, 43 and n.8.
178. Kipling, 52–6. Henry employed other painters, such as Robert Fyll, who are also occasionally described in the accounts as 'king's painters', but 'Meynnart' or Maynard is consistently so described, and undertook all the most important assignments.
179. Kipling, 65. Roy Strong, *Tudor and Jacobean Portraits*, 1, 20–21.
180. Kipling, 69–70. BL Add. MS 7099, f.52.
181. Roy Strong, *The English Renaissance Miniature* (1983), 14.
182. *Letters and Papers*, III, i, 826. J. G. Russell, *The Field of Cloth of Gold*, (1969), 39–40.
183. Auerbach, *Tudor Artists*, 187–8. A certain John Brown had been King's Painter since 1511, receiving £20 a year. He did much decorative work but is not known to have painted portraits. Vincent Volpe, a Neapolitan, had also been employed on a regular basis; Strong, *Renaissance Miniature*, 28–9.
184. Strong, *Renaissance Miniature*, 8.
185. Ibid., 11.
186. PRO E351/340 f.23. Susanna Horenbout married twice in England; first John Parker, Yeoman of the Robes, and second John Gylmyn, Sergeant of the Woodyard. She was never paid separately for her work. Strong, *Renaissance Miniature*, 38, 44.
187. Ibid., 42.
188. *Holbein and the Court of Henry VIII* (Queen's Gallery, 1978/9), 7–9. Paul Ganz, *The Paintings of Hans Holbein* (1950).
189. Strong, *Renaissance Miniature*, 45–53.
190. *Holbein and the Court of Henry VIII*, 11.
191. John Dent, *The Quest for Nonsuch*, (1962), 49–50, 108–9.
192. Kipling, 49–52; Strong, *Renaissance Miniature*, 54–64.
193. Auerbach, *Tudor Artists*, 75–6.
194. Ibid., 104. Early in Elizabeth's reign 'George Tarlynke, alien' was included in the household subsidy assessment at £26.13s.4d., the lowest rate of any Gentleman Pensioner. Levina was not mentioned. BL Lansdowne MS 3, 103.
195. Strong, *Renaissance Miniature*, 55–59.
196. On the evidence for the connection between Teerlinc and Hilliard, see Strong, *Renaissance Miniature*, 66–69.
197. Ibid., 54. Strong, *Tudor and Jacobean Portraiture*, 1, 88–94.
198. R. Strong, *The English Icon: Elizabethan and Jacobean Portraiture* (1969) 8–10, 83–106, 342–5.
199. Strong, *Renaissance Miniature*, 66.
200. Hughes and Larkin, II, 240. Strong, *Renaissance Miniature*, 66.
201. Edward Horsey to Don John of Austria, 22 March 1577; Kervyn de Lettehove,

Relations Politique des Pays Bas et de l'Angleterre (1890), 9, 250. See also Roy Strong, *Nicholas Hilliard* (1975).

202. E. Auerbach, *Nicholas Hilliard*, 28–31; N. Blakiston, 'Nicholas Hilliard, some unpublished documents', *Burlington Magazine*, 89 (1947), 188–9.

203. R. Strong, *Portraits of Queen Elizabeth* (1963); Strong, *Tudor and Jacobean Portraiture*, 1, 99–112. The great 'Darnley' portrait is attributed to Zuccaro.

Chapter 4, pp. 133–183

1. *Paston Letters, 1422–1509* ed. J. Gairdner, I, 259.
2. This was during one of his not infrequent periods of mild disfavour. D. Wilson, *Sweet Robin*, 186–7. P. Williams, *The Tudor Regime*, 26. On Bedell, see PRO SP11/7/57.
3. A. L. Brown, 'The Authorisation of Letters under the Great Seal', *Bulletin of the Institute of Historical Research*, 37 (1964), 152–5; PRO SP10/14/45. Williams, 22–3.
4. Stone, *The Crisis of the Aristocracy*, 403.
5. *Calendar of State Papers, Domestic*, 1595–7, 532–4.
6. *The Papers of George Wyatt*, ed. D. Loades, Camden Society, 4th series, 5 (1968), 5.
7. For this information concerning Brandon, I am indebted to Dr Stephen Gunn of Merton College, Oxford.
8. There are many discussions of the impact of the dissolution of the monasteries. The most succinct and informative is that by Joyce Youings, *The Dissolution of the Monasteries* (1971).
9. Wilson, 292.
10. Williams, 97–8. 'English politics and the concept of honour, 1485–1642', *Past and Present* Supplement 3 (1978).
11. Stone, *Crisis*, Appendix VI. Between 1487 and 1603 the total fluctuated from 43 to 62, but a proportion of these were always minors.
12. James, 'Concept of Honour', 28–9, 38–9, etc.
13. J. G. Bellamy, *Crime and Public Order in England during the later Middle Ages* (1973), 196–8.
14. Ross, *Edward IV*, 335, 424.
15. S. B. Chrimes, *Henry VII, passim.* K. B. McFarlane, *The nobility of later medieval England* (1973), 157–8, 149–50.
16. Chrimes, 140 and n.
17. Ibid., 102. G. W. Bernard, *The Power of the Early Tudor Nobility* (1985), 1–6.
18. Chrimes, 57 and n. C. Rawcliffe, *The Staffords, Earls of Stafford and Dukes of Buckingham* (1978), 35–6. M. Jones and M. Underwood, 'Margaret Beaufort Countess of Richmond', *History Today*, 35 (1985) 23–31.
19. Rawcliffe, 36.
20. Bernard, 5.
21. J. R. Lander 'Bonds, coercion and fear' in *Florilegium Historiale; Essays presented to W. K. Ferguson*, ed. J. G. Rowe and W. H. Stockdale (1971). Williams, 394.
22. F. M. Powicke (ed.) *Handbook of British Chronology* (1939), 289–338. Courtenay was the husband of Catherine, the 2nd daughter of Edward IV, and Margaret was the daughter of George, Duke of Clarence.
23. G. E. Cockayne (ed.) *The Complete Peerage of England*, rev. V. Gibbs etc. (1910–59).
24. De la Pole surrendered the dukedom in 1493, agreeing to be known only as Earl. He was attainted in 1504, and eventually executed in 1513. After 1513, his brother Richard, an exile in France, styled himself Duke of Suffolk. He was killed at Pavia in 1525.

25. The *Letters and Papers . . . of the reign of Henry VIII* contains scores of examples, and others may be found in *The Lisle Letters*, ed. M. St. Clare Byrne (1981).

26. James, 'Concept of Honour', 28–9. The king's view was that, since Aske was a traitor, Darcy was absolved of his promise.

27. C. S. L. Davies, 'The Pilgrimage of Grace reconsidered', *Past and Present*, 41 (1968); R. B. Smith, *Land and Politics in the reign of Henry VIII* (1970); Williams, 317–325. Bernard, 30–54.

28. G. R. Elton, *Reform and Reformation* (1977), 233–7 etc. Cromwell, of course, presided over the very early stages of the sale, but the pattern of petition and grant was well established by the time of his fall.

29. PRO SP1/152, 242 (*Letters and Papers*, XIV, i, 1338).

30. This became obvious when the question of restoring the Papal jurisdiction was raised in Queen Mary's reign, and resulted in prolonged and difficult negotiations on the status of the former monastic property. D. Loades, *Reign of Mary Tudor*, 321–9.

31. W. K. Jordan, *Edward VI: the young king* 51–64. B. L. Beer, *Northumberland*, 43–50.

32. Beer, 92–124. W. K. Jordan, *Edward VI; the threshold of power, passim*. For a somewhat different view, see D. E. Hoak, 'Rehabilitating the Duke of Northumberland; politics and political control, 1549–53' in J. Loach and R. Tittler (eds.) *The Mid-Tudor Polity* (1980), 29–51.

33. For a full discussion of this crisis, see Jordan, *Threshold*, 494–532.

34. Loades, *Reign of Mary*, 187. The total value of the lands restored to these two families was approaching £5500 per annum.

35. PRO SP12/1/64. *Calendar of State Papers, Spanish*, XI, 183–93.

36. For a full discussion of the restoration of the Percy Earldom and its implications, see P. Bosher, 'The Anglo-Scottish Border, 1550–1560' (Unpublished Durham Ph.D. thesis, 1985).

37. PRO SP12/1/64.

38. R. C. Braddock, 'The rewards of office holding in Tudor England', *Journal of British Studies*, 14 (1975), 29–47.

39. Archivo General de Simancas, Secretaria de Estado, Estado Inglaterra, Legajo 811, f.119 etc. *Cal. Span.*, XII, 315.

40. Loades, *Reign of Mary*; W. T. MacCaffrey, *The Shaping of the Elizabethan Regime* (1968). Winchester and Shrewsbury were among those who dissented from the Bill of Uniformity in April 1559; Bernard, 91.

41. Loades, *Reign of Mary*; Appendix.

42. In October 1561 he received an annuity of £1000 from the customs of the Port of London, but this was an isolated and exceptional instance. Wilson, *Sweet Robin*, 132–3.

43. PRO SP12/24/10. Stone, 416, 405.

44. Wilson, 168.

45. Ibid., 167.

46. Longleat, Dudley Papers, Box III, no. 52. In his will, Dudley confessed 'I . . . have lived always above any living I had . . .' Wilson, 144.

47. For a full discussion of Robert Cecil's manipulations, see Lawrence Stone, *Family and Fortune* (1973), 3–115.

48. S. Adams 'Eliza enthroned?' in C. Haigh (ed.) *The Reign of Elizabeth I* (1984), 55–79.

49. Stone, *Crisis*, Appendices, VI, VIII.

50. Helen Miller, 'The Early Tudor Peerage, 1485–1547', *BIHR*, 24 (1951), 88; Stone, Appendix VIII.

51. Stone, Appendix III. W. A. Shaw, *The Knights of England* (1906).

52. James, 'Concept of honour', 22–28. Stone, Appendix II.

53. G. R. Elton, *England under the Tudors* (1974), 469–73.

54. L. L. Peck, *Northampton; patronage and policy at the court of James I* (1982) provides a good recent account of the Jacobean situation. See also L. Stone, *Crisis of the Aristocracy* and *Family and Fortune*.

55. *Rotuli Parliamentorum*, V, 216.

56. 'The queen is a great and strong laboured woman, for she spareth no pain to sue her things to an intent and conclusion to her power', *Paston Letters*, III, 75. See also *An English Chronicle of the reigns of Richard II, Henry IV, Henry V and Henry VI* ed. J. S. Davies (Camden Society 1856), 79. R. A. Griffiths, *King Henry VI* (1980).

57. Ross, *Edward IV*, 93–103.

58. Clarence had no obvious grounds for discontent beyond his own 'ambition and instability'; Ross, 117 and notes, 129–31.

59. Cook, a former Lord Mayor of London, was falsely accused of treason, imprisoned and heavily fined at the instance of Earl Rivers in 1468; *The Great Chronicle of London*, ed. A. H. Thomas and I. D. Thornley (1938), 204–8.

60. Ross, 101–2.

61. Richard was named as Protector in Edward IV's will, altering a former verbal instruction. C. T. Wood, 'The deposition of Edward V', *Traditio*, 31 (1975). See also Charles Ross, *Richard III* (1981), 67, 75.

62. *Materials for a history of the reign of Henry VII*, ed. W. Campbell (1873–77), II. 148. There is no reason to suppose that this was connected with any particular conspiracy, but it effectively removed her from the political scene. Chrimes, *Henry VII*, 76 and n.

63. Chrimes, 76–7.

64. *Calendar of State Papers, Spanish*, I, 439; A. F. Pollard, *The Reign of Henry VII from contemporary sources* (1913), I, 240–50. This latter document is a report by John Flamank of a conversation which took place at Calais between 1502 and 1506.

65. Pollard, *Reign of Henry VII*, III, 187–9.

66. Of the major peers, the Earl of Derby at about 30 was the youngest; Arundel was 59, and Oxford and Surrey both over 60. Cockayne, *The Complete Peerage*.

68. Hall, *Chronicle*, 511 etc. See also above.

69. M. Levine, 'The fall of Edward, Duke of Buckingham', in A. J. Slavin (ed.) *Tudor Men and Institutions* (1972), 31–48; Rawcliffe, 42–4; see also above.

70. Rawcliffe, 36–9; J. H. Round, *Peerage and Pedigree* (1910), I, 147–66.

71. *The Anglica Historia of Polydore Vergil* ed. D. Hay, Camden Society, 3rd series, 74 (1950), 265; Rawcliffe, 42.

72. *Calendar of State Papers, Venetian*, III, 213.

73. Rawcliffe, 44.

74. BL Add. MS 19398, f.644.

75. On Shrewsbury's estrangement from Wolsey, see Bernard, 24–5. Any peer who remained within the court circle after 1518 had to be able to accommodate himself to Wolsey's ascendency.

76. Elton, *Reform and Reformation*, 98.

77. See above.

78. The articles against Wolsey are listed in *Letters and Papers*, III, 6075. See also 'A chronicle and defence of the English Reformation' in D. Loades, (ed.) *The Papers of George Wyatt*, Camden Society, 4th series, 5, (1968) 144–5.

79. Elton, *Reform and Reformation*, 135–6.

80. John Foxe, in the 1570 edition of his *Acts and Monuments* (I, 1234), described Anne as an active promoter of Protestantism. Modern opinion is more cautious, and she certainly died professing orthodoxy.

81. G. R Elton, 'Politics and the Pilgrimage of Grace', in *Studies in Tudor and Stuart Politics and Government*, III, 183–215, almost certainly overstates the case for factional involvement in the Pilgrimage, but provides a useful corrective to the traditional 'spontaneous' view.

82. Shrewsbury's son, Francis, Lord Talbot, was present at the coronation, in which he took a leading part. Bernard, 50.

83. G. R. Elton, *Policy and Police* (1972), *passim*.

84. G. R. Elton, 'Tudor Government: the points of contact; III: the Court' *Studies*, III, 38–57; E. W. Ives, 'Faction at the court of Henry VIII; the fall of Anne Boleyn', *History*, 57 (1972), 169 ff.

85. Chapuys to the Emperor, 19 May 1536; *Calendar of State Papers, Spanish*, V, 122–31.

86. Loades, *Reign of Mary*, 17–9.

87. M. E. James, 'Obedience and dissent in Henrician England; the Lincolnshire rebellion of 1536', *Past and Present*, 48 (1970), 61. Elton, 'Politics and the Pilgrimage of Grace', 210–11.

88. See above.

89. Elton, 'Politics and the Pilgrimage of Grace'; for a different view which indicates the on-going debate, see J. J. Scarisbrick, *The Reformation and the English People* (1984), 72–3.

90. On Cranmer's position during the last years of the reign, see A. G. Dickens *The English Reformation* (1964), 182–4.

91. John Foxe, *Acts and Monuments*, ed. G. Townshend (1843–9), V, 544–5. See also below.

92. Elton, *Reform and Reformation*, 331–2 and n.

93. Elton, loc. cit.; Scarisbrick, *Henry VIII*, 488; L. B. Smith, 'The last will and testament of Henry VIII: a question of perspective', *Journal of British Studies*, II, (1962) 20 ff.

94. Scarisbrick, *The Reformation and the English People, passim*, which errs on the side of caution in estimating support for the Reformation. For a more optimistic and traditional view, see C. Cross, *Church and People 1450–1660* (1976).

95. D. Loades, *The Oxford Martyrs* (1970), 75–79; B. L. Beer, *Rebellion and Riot* (1982) *passim*.

96. W. K. Jordan, *Edward VI; the young king*; 494–523.

97. D. E. Hoak, 'The king's Privy Chamber, 1547–1553', 93–4; see above.

98. J. G. Nichols, *The Diary of Henry Machyn*, Camden Society, 42 (1848), 13.

99. Bernard, 72–3.

100. Loades, *Reign of Mary*, 7–74. D. MacCulloch, 'The Vitae Mariae Angliae Reginae of Robert Wingfield of Brantham', *Camden Miscellany*, 28 (1984), 182–301.

101. Loades, loc. cit.

102. Ambassadors to the Emperor, 16 August 1553; *Calendar of State Papers, Spanish*, XI, 172.

103. *Cal. Span.*, XI, 180.

104. For example that of 4 November, in which he reported that Courtenay was trying to win Pembroke to his cause. *Cal. Span.*, XI, 332.

105. D. Loades, *Two Tudor Conspiracies* (1965), 238.

106. Renard to the Emperor, 22 March 1554; *Cal. Span.*, XII, 170.

107. *Cal Span.*, XII, 289. For a full list of Philip's English Household, see *Cal. Span.*, XII, 297.

108. *Cal. Span.*, XII, 231; XIII, 23.

109. See above, 103. On Philip's willingness to pardon and employ former opponents see Loades, *Reign of Mary*, 255 and n.

110. Loades, op. cit., 254. Bernard, 87–8.

111. The tensions of the late 1540s caused little concern during Mary's reign, and religious tensions arising from the persecution, although acute, were localised in London and the south-east. It is also probable that the onset of the influenza epidemic had an anaesthetising effect upon potential disorders.

112. *Acts of the Privy Council*, VI, 390, 1 September 1558.

113. *Cal. Span.*, XIII, 399–400. For a further discussion of Feria's knowledge of English affairs in this period, see S. Adams and M. Rodriguez Salgado, 'The Count of Feria's despatch to Philip II of 14 November 1558', *Camden Miscellany* 28, (1984), 302–345.

114. R. C. McCoy, 'From the Tower to the tiltyard; Robert Dudley's return to glory', *Historical Journal* 27 (1984), 425 ff.; S. Adams, 'Faction, clientage and party; English politics, 1550–1603', *History Today*, 32 (1982); Wilson, *Sweet Robin*, 48–78.

115. D. Loades, *Politics and the Nation, 1450–1660* (1974), 475.

116. Stone, *Crisis of the Aristocracy*, 223–234.

117. S. Adams, 'Eliza Enthroned?' in C. Haigh, ed., *The Reign of Elizabeth I* (1984), 55–78.

118. W. McCaffrey, *The Shaping of the Elizabethan Regime* (1955), 105–148.

119. N. Williams, *Thomas Howard, fourth Duke of Norfolk* (1964), 116 ff, 146 ff. James, 'Concept of Honour', 41–2.

120. Conyers Read, *Mr. Secretary Cecil and Queen Elizabeth* (1955), 442–3.

121. Wilson, 213.

122. P. McGrath, *Papists and Puritans under Elizabeth I* (1967); A. Morey, *The catholic subjects of Elizabeth I* (1978); A. Dures, *English Catholicism, 1558–1642* (1983).

123. W. T. MacCaffrey, *Queen Elizabeth and the making of policy, 1572–1588* (1981).

124. Son of Henry Carey, 1st Baron Hunsdon; son of Sir Francis Knollys.

125. Adams, 'Eliza Enthroned?', 69.

126. PRO SP12/126/20–21.

127. Hall, *Chronicle*, 267.

128. C. Head, 'Pope Pius II and the Wars of the Roses', *Archivum Historiae Pontificae*, VIII, (1970), 139–78.

129. *Calendar of State Papers, Venetian*, I, 484.

130. Retiring Venetian ambassadors developed the practice of sending lengthy 'narratives', or descriptions of the countries in which they had served to the Council of Ten. Although these tend to be repetitive, and full of general topographical information, they also contain much shrewd political and social comment. See, for example, that by Giacomo Soranzo in 1554; *Cal. Ven.* V, 532–564.

131. Loades, *Two Tudor Conspiracies*, 57; E. H. Harbison, *Rival Ambassadors at the Court of Queen Mary* (1938), 161 and n.

132. *Letters and Papers*, IV, 4649.

133. *Cal. Span.*, XI, 428–31; Harbison, 100.

134. Garrett Mattingly, *Renaissance Diplomacy* (1955), 224.

135. Chapuys is conspicuous by his absence from the list of supporters given in the government propaganda account *The Noble Triumphant Coronation of Queene Anne*, reprinted in E. Arber, *An English Garner* (1870) II, 46.

136. Harbison, 86–7; Loades, *Reign of Mary*, 75–6. Renard's confidential relationship with the queen is reflected in the gift of 1,223 ozs of plate on his departure in September 1555. This was far more than a diplomat of his relatively humble status would normally have received. BL Cotton MS Titus B II.

137. *Letters and Papers*, IV, 4649.

138. *Cal. Span.*, IV, 440–41.

139. Harbison, 276–7; Loades 'Relations between the Anglican and Roman Catholic Churches in the 16th and 17th centuries', in *Rome and the Anglicans* (1982), 1–53.

140. Jordan, *Threshold of power*, 256–7. Van der Delft's ignorance was not the result of any inadequacy on his part; whereas his successor, Jehan Scheyfve, was simply not up to the job.

141. *Cal. Ven.*, VI, i, 460; Harbison, 288–92.

142. L. J. Ward, 'The Elizabethan Law of Treason, 1558–1588' (Unpublished Cambridge Ph.D thesis, 1985).

143. Hall, *Chronicle*, 691–2; Mattingly, 262 and n.

144. Mattingly, 256–268.

145. Michel Surian came to England with Philip, and departed with him. *Cal. Ven.*, VI, 991, 1195.

146. Myers, *Household*, 133–9.

147. *Household Ordinances*, 169–70; P. Le Huray, *Music and the Reformation in England* (1967), 68.

148. C. C. Stopes, 'William Hunnis and the Revels of the Chapel Royal' in *Materialen zur Kunde des alteren Englischen Dramas* (1910), 21–2.

149. *HO*, 253.

150. Le Huray, 79–80. Eltham and St James had substantial chapels, rebuilt during Henry's reign, but it is not clear that they were ever used for the full establishment.

151. *HO*, 253; John Stow, *Chronicles of England* (1631), I, 890.

152. H. M. Hillerbrand, 'The early history of the Chapel Royal', *Modern Philology*, 18 (1920), 80–81.

153. J. Stevens, *Music and Poetry at the Early Tudor Court*, 304.

154. Le Huray, 71.

155. Ibid., 68–9.

156. W. H. Gratton Flood, *Early Tudor Composers* (1925), 34, 37.

157. Le Huray, 65–6.

158. Thomas Cranmer, *Miscellaneous writings and letters*, ed. J. E. Cox, Parker Society (1846), 412.

159. John Hooper to Henry Bullinger, 27 December 1549; *Original Letters relative to the English Reformation*, ed. H. Robinson, Parker Society (1846) i, 72.

160. For an unsympathetic assessment of Zurich influence upon the English Church, see P. Hughes, *The Reformation in England*, (1950), II.

161. First Royal Injunctions of Henry VIII (1536); Royal Injunctions for St. George's, Windsor (1547); Ridley's Injunctions for London Diocese; W. H. Frere and W. M. Kennedy, *Visitation Articles and Injunctions* (1910), II, 1-11, 160–5, 241–5.

162. *Calendar of State Papers, Venetian*, VII, 2–3; this merely records his replacement by George Carew. A chapel list of 1554 is headed by the Bishop of Norwich (Thomas Thirlby) as Dean. Whether this is a mistake for 'Lichfield' (i.e. Sampson), or whether Thirlby did hold the position briefly, is not clear. W. H. Gratton Flood, 'Queen Mary's Chapel Royal' *EHR*, 33 (1918) 83–89.

163. See above.

164. Carew was clearly a conformist, since he had held livings in plurality throughout Edward's and Mary's reigns, in addition to being Elizabeth's chaplain. He died as Dean of Exeter in 1583. P. Le Huray, 58.

165. Stevens, 87–8.

166. *Calendar of State Papers, Venetian*, VIII, 525.

167. W. B. Rye, *England as seen by foreigners* (1865), 16.

168. Hooker, *Laws of Ecclesiastical Polity*, Book V, sect. xxxviii (i). Stevens, 90.

169. Chrimes, 50–2; Hall, *Chronicle*, 422–3.

170. BL Add. MS 7099, f.56 etc.

171. Chrimes, 240.

172. For a lengthy discussion of Henry's sexual psychology in the later years of his life, see L. B. Smith, *The Mask of Royalty* (1971), *passim*. On Catherine Howard, see Smith, *A Tudor Tragedy* (1961).

173. Elton, *Reform and Reformation*, 54–6.

174. D. Loades and C. Haigh, 'The Shrine of Our Lady of Caversham', *Oxoniensis*, 45 (1981), 62–72.

175. W. Schenk, *Reginald Pole, Cardinal of England* (1950), 19; R. Marius, *Thomas More* (1984), 34–5.

176. A. W. Pollard and G. R. Redgrave, *Short Title Catalogue* (1926 rev. 1976), 24446, 24454.

177. Justification by faith alone, the exclusive authority of the scriptures, and the transmutation of the Eucharistic elements, while retaining the substance of bread and wine. On Henry's theology, see Scarisbrick, *Henry VIII*, 384–423.

178. Elton, *Reform and Reformation*, 292–4.

179. A. G. Dickens, *The English Reformation* (1964), 183, 194. John Merbecke and Robert Testwood of the Chapel Royal were also condemned at this stage for holding heretical views. Merbecke was pardoned, but Testwood was subsequently executed. Hall, *Chronicle*, 858–9.

180. Elton, *Reform and Reformation*, 329–30.

181. *Sermons and Remains of Bishop Latimer*, ed. G. E. Gorrie, Parker Society (1844), 41.

182. C. H. Garrett, *The Marian Exiles* (1938), 275–7; Wilson, 24–5.

183. Letter of a Spanish gentleman, August 1554; *Cal. Span.*, XIII, 7–13.

184. Loades, *Reign of Mary*, 321–355.

185. D. Loades, 'The piety of the restored catholic church under Queen Mary' (forthcoming).

186. Henry Clifford, *The Life of Jane Dormer, Duchess of Feria*, ed. J. Stevenson (1887).

187. See above.

188. P. Lake, *Moderate Puritans and the Elizabethan Church* (1982); B. W. Beckingsale, *Lord Burghley* (1967); Wilson; on Dudley's religious position see Wilson, 105.

Chapter 5, pp. 184–192

1. 'Tudor Government: the points of contact. III; the Court' in *Studies*, III, 38–57.

2. *Letters and Papers*, I, 231–40; Chrimes, *Henry VII*, 308.

3. *The Memoirs of Robert Carey*, ed. F. H. Mears (1972), 29–31, 43–4. Elton, 'The Court', 47.

4. *Henry VIII*, Act II, scene 3.

5. Stone, *Crisis*, 467.

6. Ibid., 542.

7. Talbot Papers, P 11, 27; Bernard, 13.

8. Stone, 600.

9. Ibid., 386.

10. F. J. Fisher, 'The Development of London as a centre of conspicuous consumption in the sixteenth and seventeenth centuries', *Transactions of the Royal Historical Society*, 4th series, 30 (1948), 43.

11. Stone, 388.

12. A. Hassell-Smith, *County and Court; government and politics in Norfolk*, 1558–1603 (1974).

13. Hassell-Smith, 64–5.

14. Ibid., 65–6.

15. I. H. Jeayes, *Letters of Philip Gawdy of West Harling*, Roxburghe Club (1906), 131.

16. Powicke, *Handbook*, 313.

17. Stone, 451.

18. *Cal. Span.*, XII, 289.

19. Wilson, 14, 148.

20. Stone, 551.
21. Ibid., 567–572. In the following century stakes went still higher, as much as £2500 being wagered on a single tennis match.
22. M. Girouard, *Life in the English Country House* (1978), 57–60.
23. See above.
24. 'Charles I of England; the tragedy of absolutism', by P. W. Thomas in *The Courts of Europe*, 191–211.

Bibliography

Manuscript sources

Archivo General de Simancas: Estado Inglaterra, Legajo 811
British Library:
   Cotton MSS: Tiberius B III, Titus B IV, Vespasian C XIV
   Egerton MSS: 2605
   Harleian MSS: 1419
   Lansdowne MSS: 1, 2 (xii), 3, 4 (vi), 4 (vii), 21 (lxii), 21 (lxv), 21 (lxvii)
   Royal MSS: 7 C XVI
   Stowe MSS: 571
   Additional MSS: 19398, 43563, 7099 (Craven Ord Transcript)
Public Records Office:
   Exchequer: E101/414, 415, 416, 424, 426, 427, 428
           E351/340, 429, 520, 541, 1795, 2701, 3027, 3033, 31922
   King's Bench: KB27/1184
   Lord Chamberlain's Office: LC2/2, 4
                   LC5/49, 182
   State Papers: SP1/45, 114, 152, 242
            SP6/12
            SP10/14
            SP11/1, 4, 7
            SP12/1, 24, 126, 127
Society of Antiquaries: MS 125
                   Broadsheets

Calendars and printed sources:

Acts of the Privy Council, ed. J. R. Dasent (London, 1890–1907)
Adams, S. and Rodriguez Salgado, M. eds. 'The Count of Feria's despatch to Philip II of 14 November 1558' in *Camden Miscellany*, 28, (1984), 302–345
Allen, P. S. and H. M. *Opus Epistolarum Des. Erasmi Roterdami* (Oxford, 1906–58)
Arnold, Janet (ed.), *Queen Elizabeth's Wardrobe unlock'd; the inventories of the Wardrobe of Robes prepared in July 1600* (Leeds, 1988)
'Ballade to King Henry VI upon his Coronation', *Early English Text Society*, 192, 2, 627
Bentley, S. *Excerpta Historica*; Extracts from the Privy Purse expenses of King Henry VII (London, 1831)
Byrne, M. St Clare *The Lisle Letters* (London, Chiacgo, 1981)
Calendar of State Papers, Spanish, ed. Royall Tyler *et al.* (London, 1862–1964)
Calendar of State Papers, Venetian, ed. Rawdon Brown *et al.* (London, 1864–1898)
Calendar of the Patent Rolls; Henry VII (London, 1914–16); Edward VI (London, 1924–9); Philip and Mary (London, 1936–9). Elizabeth (London, 1939–)
Campbell, W. *Materials for a history of the reign of Henry VII* (London, 1873–1877)
Castiglione, B. *The Book of the Courtier*, trs. George Bull (London, 1967)

Clifford, H. *The Life of Jane Dormer, Duchess of Feria*, ed. J. Stevenson (London, 1846)

Cranmer, T. *Miscellaneous writings and letters* ed. J. E. Cox, Parker Society (London, 1846)

Davies, J. S., ed. *An English Chronicle of the reigns of Richard II, Henry IV, Henry V and Henry VI*, Camden Society, 64 (1856)

Dictionary of National Biography

Dyce, A., ed. *The Poetical Works of John Skelton* (London, 1843)

Emden, A. B. *A Biographical register of the University of Oxford* (Oxford, 1974)

Feuillerat, A. *Documents relating to the office of the revels*, 2 vols. (Louvain, 1908–14)

Fox, J. *The Acts and Monuments of the English Martyrs*, ed. G. Townshend (London, 1843–9)

Frere, W. H. and Kennedy, W. M. *Visitation Articles and Injunctions*, 3 vols., Alcuin Club (London, 1910)

Furnivall, F. J. *Early English Meals and Manners*, Early English Text Society, 32 (1868)

Gairdner, J. *et al.*, eds. *Letters and Papers, Foreign and Domestic, of the reign of Henry VIII* (London, 1862–1932)

Gairdner, J., ed. *The Paston Letters, 1422–1509* (London, 1904)

Genet, J-P., ed. *Tractus de Regimine Principum ad Henricum Sextum*, Camden Society, 4th Series, 18 (1977)

Gibbs, V., ed. *The Complete Peerage of England* by G. E. Cockayne (London, 1910–1959)

Hall, E. *The Union of the two noble and illustre famelies of Lancastre and York* (London, 1809)

Household Ordinances, Society of Antiquaries (London, 1790)

Hughes, P. L. and Larkin, J. F. *Tudor Royal Proclamations*, 3 vols. (New Haven, Conn., 1964, 1969)

Johnson, C., ed. 'Constitutio domus regis' in *Dialogus de Scaccario*, 128–135 (London, 1950)

Jeayes, I. H., ed. *The Letters of Philip Gawdy of West Harling*, Roxburghe Club, 1906

Latimer, H., *Sermons*, ed. G. E. Gorrie, Parker Society, 1844

Letts, M., ed. *The Travels of Leo of Rozmital*, Hakluyt Society, 2nd Series, 108 (London, 1957)

Life of Alexander ed. J. Westlake, Early English Text Society, 143 (London, 1913)

Loades, D. M., ed. *The Papers of George Wyatt*, Camden Society, 4th series, 5, 1968

MacCulloch, D., ed. 'The Vitae Mariae Reginae of Robert Wingfield of Brantham', *Camden Miscellany*, 28, 1984, 182–301

Madden, F. *The Privy Purse Expenses of Princess Mary* (London, 1829)

Mears, F.H., ed. *The Memoirs of Robert Carey* (London, 1972)

Myers, A. R. *The Household of Edward IV* (Manchester, 1959)

Nicholas, N. H. *The Privy Purse Expenses of King Henry the Eighth* (London, 1827)

Nicholas, N. H. *The Privy Purse Expenses of Elizabeth of York and the Wardrobe Accounts of Edward the Fourth* (London, 1830)

Nichols, J. G. *Literary Remains of King Edward VI*, Roxburghe Club, 1857

Nichols, J. G. *The Chronicle of Queen Jane, and of two years of Queen Mary*, Camden Society, 48, 1850

Nichols, J. G. *The Diary of Henry Machyn*, Camden Society, 42, 1848

Original Letters relating to the English Reformation, ed. H. Robinson, Parker Society, 1856

Palmer, J. *A biographical dictionary of old English music* (London, 1927)

Parry, J. J., ed. and trs. *De Arte Honeste Amandi* (London, 1941)

Perry, Maria, *The Word of a Prince* (London, 1990)

Pollard, A. F. *The Reign of Henry VII from contemporary sources* (London, 1913)

Pollard, A. W. and Redgrave, G. R. *A short title catalogue of books printed in England, Scotland and Ireland, and of English books printed abroad, 1475–1640*; rev. W. A. Jackson and F. S. Ferguson (London, 1976)

Powicke, F. M. *The Handbook of English Chronology* (London, 1939)

Raine, A. *York Civic Records*, Yorkshire Archaeological Society Record Series, 1939–1953

Reports of the Historical Manuscripts Commission, 2 (Petyt MSS), 7 (More-Molyneux MSS), 12, 17 (Rutland MSS)

Rotuli Parliamentorum

Sermons and Remains of Bishop Ridley, ed. H. Christmas, Parker Society, 1841

Shaw, W. A. *The Knights of England* (London, 1906)

Statutes of the Realm ed. A. Luders *et al.*, Record Commission (London, 1810–28)

Stow, J. *Chronicles of England* (London, 1631)

'The narrative of Edward Underhill' in E. Arber, *An English Garner*, IV, 72–100 (London, 1879–1882)

'The noble and triumphant coronation of Queen Anne' in E. Arber, *An English Garner*, II, 43–60

'The passage of our most dread Sovereign Lady Queen Elizabeth through London to her coronation' in E. Arber, *An English Garner*, IV, 217–248

Thomas, A. H. and Thornley, I. D. *The Great Chronicle of London* (London, 1938)

Tres cartas de lo sucedido en el viaje de Su Alteza a Inglaterra, Sociedad de los Bibliofilos Espanoles (Madrid, 1877)

Vergil, Polydor *Anglica Historia*, ed. D. Hay, Camden Society, 3rd. series, 74, 1950

Wilson, Jean *Entertainments for Elizabeth I* (London, 1980)

Wood, A. *Athenae Oxoniensis*, ed. P. Bliss (London, 1813–20)

Wriothesley, C. *A Chronicle of England*, ed. W. D. Hamilton, Camden Society, New series, 11, 1875

Secondary works

Adams, S. 'Eliza enthroned?' in C. Haigh, *The Reign of Elizabeth I* (London, 1984)

Adams, S. 'Faction, clientage and party; English politics, 1550–1603' *History Today*, 32, 1982

Anglo, S. 'An early Tudor programme for plays and other demonstrations against the Pope', *Journal of the Warburg and Courtauld Institutes*, 20, 1957

Anglo, S. 'Anglo-Burgundian feats of arms at Smithfield, June 1467', *Guildhall Miscellany*, ii, 7, 1965

Anglo, S. 'Archives of the English tournament; score checks and lists', *Journal of the Society of Archivists*, 2, 1960

Anglo, S. 'Financial and Heraldic records of English tournaments', *Journal of the Society of Archivists*, 2, 1962

Anglo, S. *Spectacle, Pageantry and Early Tudor Policy* (Oxford, 1969)

Anglo, S. 'The British History in early Tudor propaganda', *Bulletin of the John Rylands Library*, 44, 1961

Anglo, S. *The Great Tournament Roll of Westminster* (London, 1968)

Anglo, S. *Images of Tudor Kingship* (London, 1992) (also RS, p. 37)

Armstrong, C. J. A. 'The Golden Age of Burgundy in *The Courts of Europe, 1400–1800*, ed. A. G. Dickens (London, 1977)

Auerbach, E. *Tudor Artists* (London, 1954)

Baumer, F. le van *The Early Tudor Theory of Kingship* (New Haven, Conn., 1940)

Bean, J. M. W. *The Estates of the Percy family* (Oxford, 1958)

Beer, B. L. *Northumberland* (Kent State U.P. 1973)

Beer, B. L. *Rebellion and Riot* (Kent State U.P. 1982)

Bellamy, J. G. *Crime and Public Order in England during the later Middle Ages* (London, 1973)

Benecsh, O. *The Art of the Renaissance in Northern Europe* (London, 1965)

Bernard, G. W. *The Power of the Early Tudor Nobility* (London, 1984)

Bernard, G. W. 'The rise of Sir William Compton, early Tudor courtier', *English Historical Review*, 96, 1981.

Bernard, G. W. *The English Nobility in the Sixteenth Century* (London, 1989)

Bossuat, A. 'La Formula "Le roi est empereur en son royaulme"; son emploi au xve siècle devant le Parlement de Paris', *Revue Historique de droit Français et etranger*, 4th series, 39, 1951

Braddock, R. C. 'The character and composition of the Duke of Northumberland's army in 1553', *Albion*, 8, 1976

Braddock, R. C. 'The rewards of office holding in Tudor England', *Journal of British Studies*, 14, 1975

Brown, A. L. 'The authorisation of letters under the Great Seal', *Bulletin of the Institute of Historical Research*, 37, 1964

Cartellieri, O. *The Court of Burgundy*, trs. M. Letts (London, 1929)

Chambers, E. K. *The Elizabethan Stage* (Oxford, 1923) Vol. I

Chrimes, S. B. *Henry VII* (London, 1972)

Colvin, H. M. *The History of the King's Works*, Vol. IV, ii (London, 1982)

Condon, Margaret, 'Ruling elites in the reign of Henry VII', in *Patronage pedigree and power in late medieval England*, ed. C. Ross (London, 1979) (also RS, p. 183)

Cruikshank, C. G. *Army Royal* (Oxford, 1969)

Davies, C. S. L. 'The Pilgrimage of Grace reconsidered', *Past and Present*, 41, 1968

Dickens, A. G. 'Monarchy and cultural revival' in *The Courts of Europe, 1400–1800*

Dickens, A. G. *The English Reformation* (London, 1964)

Dowling, Maria, *Humanism in the Age of Henry VIII* (London, 1986) (also RS, p. 132)

Dowling, Maria, 'The gospel and the court; reformation under Henry VIII', in *Protestantism and the National Church in Sixteenth Century England*, ed. P. Lake and M. Dowling (London, 1987) (also RS, p. 183)

Dunlop, Ian, *Palaces and Progresses of Elizabeth I* (London, 1961)

Dures, A. *English catholicism 1558–1642* (London, 1983)

Elton, G. R. *Policy and Police: the enforcement of the Reformation in the time of Thomas Cromwell* (Cambridge, 1972)

Elton, G. R. 'Politics and the Pilgrimage of Grace' in *Studies in Tudor and Stuart Politics and Government*, III (Cambridge, 1983)

Elton, G. R. *Reform and Reformation* (London, 1977)

Elton, G. R. *Reform and Renewal; Thomas Cromwell and the Commonwealth* (London, 1973)

Elton, G. R. *The Tudor Revolution in Government* (Cambridge, 1953)

Elton, G. R. 'Tudor Government: the points of contact; III, the Court' *Studies*, III

Elton, G. R. 'Tudor Government' (Review article), *Historical Journal*, 31, 1988.

Elton, G. R. *Thomas Cromwell* (Bangor, 1991)

Emmison, F. E. *Tudor Food and Pastimes* (London, 1964)

Fenlon, D. B. *Heresy and Obedience in Tridentine Italy* (Cambridge, 1972)

Fisher, F. J. 'The development of London as a centre of conspicuous consumption in the sixteenth and seventeenth centuries' *Transactions of the Royal Historical Society*, 4th series, 30, 1948

Fox, A. *Politics and Literature in the reigns of Henry VII and Henry VIII* (Oxford, 1989) (also RS, p. 132)

Fryde, E. B. 'Lorenzo de' Medici; high finance and the patronage of art and learning' in *The Courts of Europe, 1400–1800*

Ganz, P. *The paintings of Hans Holbein* (London, 1950)

Garrett, C. H. *The Marian Exiles* (Cambridge, 1938)

Gratton Flood, W. H. 'Queen Mary's Chapel Royal', *English Historical Review*, 33, 1918

Greaves, M. *The Blazon of Honour* (London, 1964)

Green, R. F. *Poets and Princepleasers* (Toronto, 1980)

Griffiths, R. A. *King Henry VI* (London, 1980)

Griffiths, R. A. *The making of the Tudor dynasty* (Cardiff, 1989)

Guillemain, B. *La Cour Pontificale d'Avignon* (Paris, 1962)

Gunn, S. J. *Charles Brandon, Duke of Suffolk* (Oxford, 1988)

Gunn, S. J. and Lindley, P. G. *Cardinal Wolsey; church, state, and art* (Cambridge, 1991) (also RS, p. 132)

Guy, J. A. 'The king's council and political participation' in *Reassessing the Henrician Age*, ed. J. Guy and A. Fox (London, 1986) (also RS, p. 83)

Guy, J. A. *Tudor England* (Oxford, 1988)

Gwynn, P. J. *The King's Cardinal* (London, 1990)

Haigh, C. *Elizabeth I* (London, 1988)

Harbison, E. H. *Rival Ambassadors at the court of Queen Mary* (Princeton, 1940)

Hassell Smith, A. *County and Court; government and politics in Norfolk, 1558–1603* (Oxford, 1974)

Haugaard, W. P. 'Elizabeth Tudor's Book of Devotions, a neglected clue to the Queen's life and character', *Sixteenth Century Journal*, 12/2, 1981

Hillerbrand, H. M. 'The early history of the Chapel Royal', *Modern Philology*, 18, 1920

Hoak, D. E. 'Rehabilitating the Duke of Northumberland; politics and political control, 1549–1553' in J. Loach and R. Tittler, eds. *The Mid-Tudor Polity* (London, 1980)

Hoak, D. E. *The King's Council in the reign of Edward VI* (Cambridge, 1976)

Hoak, D. E. 'The King's Privy Chamber, 1547–1553' in DeLloyd Guth and J. W. McKenna, eds. *Tudor Rule and Revolution* (Cambridge, 1982)

Hoak, D. E. 'The Secret History of the Tudor Court; the King's Coffers and the King's Purse, 1542–1553', *Journal of British Studies*, 26, 1987 (also RS, p. 83)

Holbein and the Court of Henry VIII; the Queen's Gallery, Buckingham Palace (1978–9)

Hopkins, Lisa, *Elizabeth I and her Court* (London, 1990)

Hughes, P. *The Reformation in England*, 3 vols. (London, 1950)

Hussey, J. M. 'The Christian Citadel; the Byzantine world of the ninth and tenth centuries', in D. Talbot Rice *The Dark Ages* (London, 1965)

Ives, E. W. 'Faction at the court of Henry VIII; the fall of Anne Boleyn', *History*, 57, 1972

Ives, E. W. *Anne Boleyn* (Oxford, 1987)

James, M. E. 'English politics and the concept of honour, 1485–1642' *Past and Present*, Supplement 3, 1978

James, M. E. *Family, lineage and civil society* (Oxford, 1970)

James, M. E. 'Obedience and dissent in Henrician England; the Lincolnshire rebellion of 1536' *Past and Present*, 48, 1970

Jones, M. and Underwood, M. 'Margaret Beaufort, Countess of Richmond', *History Today*, 35, 1985

Jones, W. J. 'The Crown and the courts in England, 1603–1625' in *The reign of James VI and I*, ed. A. G. R. Smith (London, 1973)

Jordan, W. K. *Edward VI; the threshold of power* (London, 1970)

Jordan, W. K. *Edward VI; the young king* (London, 1968)

Jordan, W. K. *The Chronicle and Political Papers of Edward VI* (London, 1966)

Keen, M. H. *Chivalry* (New Haven, Conn., 1984)

Kelly, A. 'Eleanor of Acquitaine and her courts of love', *Speculum*, 12, 1937

Kipling, G. *The Triumph of Honour* (Leyden, 1977)

Lake, P. *Moderate puritans and the Elizabethan church* (Cambridge, 1982)

Le Huray, P. *Music and the Reformation in England* (Oxford, 1967)

Levine, M. 'The fall of Edward, Duke of Buckingham' in A. J. Slavin, ed. *Tudor Men and Institutions* (Baton Rouge, 1972)

Loades, D. M. *Politics and the Nation, 1450–1660*, 3rd ed. (London, 1986)

Loades, D. M. *The Oxford Martyrs* (London, 1970)

Loades, D. M. *The Reign of Mary Tudor* (London, 1979)

Loades, D. M. *Two Tudor Conspiracies* (Cambridge, 1965)

Loades, D. M. *Mary Tudor; a life* (Oxford, 1989)

MacCaffrey, W. T. *Queen Elizabeth and the shaping of policy, 1572–1588* (Princeton, 1981)

MacCaffrey, W. T. *The shaping of the Elizabethan regime* (Princeton, 1968)

McConica, J. K. *English Humanists and Reformation Politics* (Oxford, 1965)

McCoy, R. C. 'From the Tower to the Tiltyard; Robert Dudley's return to glory', *Historical Journal*, 27, 1984

McFarlane, K. B. *The nobility of later Medieval England* (Oxford, 1973)

McKenna, J. W. 'How God became an Englishman' in *Tudor Rule and Revolution*.

McKisack, M. *Medieval History in the Tudor Age* (Oxford, 1971)

Marius, R. *Thomas More* (London, 1984)

Mason, H. A. *Humanism and Poetry in the Early Tudor period* (London, 1959)

Mathew, G. *The Court of Richard II* (London, 1968)

Mattingly, G. *Catherine of Aragon* (London, 1963)

Mattingly. G. *Renaissance Diplomacy* (London, 1955)

Miller, Helen, *Henry VIII and the English nobility* (Oxford, 1986)

Miller, H. 'The Early Tudor peerage, 1485–1547', *Bulletin of the Institute of Historical Research*, 24, 1951

Muir, K. *The Life and Letters of Sir Thomas Wyatt* (Liverpool, 1963)

Muir, K. 'Unpublished poems in the Devonshire MSS', *Proceedings of the Leeds Philosophical Society*, 6, 1947

Murphy, J. A. 'Popinjays or professionals; officers and ministers of the mid-Tudor household', in *Exeter Studies in History* (Exeter, 1981)

Murphy, J. A. 'The illusion of decline; the Privy Chamber, 1547–1558', in *The English Court from the Wars of the Roses to the Civil War*, ed. D. Starkey (London, 1987) (also RS, p. 83)

Nichols, J. *The Progresses of Queen Elizabeth*, 3 vols. (London, 1823)

Osborne, June, *Entertaining Elizabeth I; the progresses and great houses of her time* (London, 1989)

Peck, L. L. *Northampton; patronage and policy at the court of James I.* (London, 1982)

Pollard, A. F. *Wolsey* (London, 1929)

Pollet, M. *John Skelton; poet of Tudor England* (London, 1971)

Powell, J. E. and Wallis, K. *The House of Lords in the Middle Ages* (London, 1968)

Rawcliffe, C. *The Staffords, Earls of Stafford and Dukes of Buckingham* (Cambridge, 1978)

Read, C. *Mr. Secretary Cecil and Queen Elizabeth* (London, 1955)

Reed, A. W. *Early Tudor Drama* (London, 1926)

Richardson, W. C. *Tudor Chamber Administration* (Baton Rouge, 1952)

Ross, C. *Edward IV* (London, 1974)

Ross, C. *Richard III* (London, 1981)

Russell, J. G. *The Field of Cloth of Gold* (London, 1969)

Rye, W. B. *England as seen by foreigners* (London, 1865)

Salter, E. 'Courts and courtly love' in D. Daiches and A. Thorlby, eds. *The Medieval World* (London, 1973)

Scarisbrick, J. J. *Henry VIII* (London, 1968)

Scarisbrick, J. J. *The Reformation and the English People* (Oxford, 1984)

Smith, L. B. *A Tudor Tragedy* (London, 1961)

Smith, L. B. 'The last will and testament of Henry VIII; a question of perspective', *Journal of British Studies*, 2, 1962

Smith, L. B. *The Mask of Royalty* (London, 1971)

Starkey, D. 'The age of the household: politics, society and the arts *c.* 1350–*c.* 1500' in S. Medcalf, ed. *The Later Middle Ages* (London, 1981)

Starkey, D. 'The court: Castiglione's ideal and Tudor reality: being a discussion of Sir Thomas Wyatt's *Satire addressed to Sir Francis Bryan*', *Journal of the Warburg and Courtauld Institutes*, 45, 1982

Starkey, D. 'Representation through intimacy', in *Symbols and Sentiments*, ed. Ioan Lewis (London, 1977)

Starkey, D. 'From feud to faction; English politics, *c.* 1450–1550', *History Today*, 32, 1982

Starkey, D. 'Intimacy and Innovation; the rise of the Privy Chamber, 1485–1547', in *The English Court* (also RS, p. 83)

Starkey, D. 'Court and Government', in *Revolution Reassessed*, ed. C. Coleman and D. Starkey (London, 1986) (also RS, p. 83)

Starkey, D. 'Tudor government; the facts', *Historical Journal*, 31, 1988

Starkey, D. 'Castiglione at the court of Henry VIII; was there a renaissance court after all?', in T. Schochet (ed.), *Reformation, Humanism and 'revolution'; Proceedings of the Folger Institute for British Political Thought* (Washington D.C., 1990)

Stevens, J. *Music and Poetry in the Early Tudor Court* (London, 1961)

Stone, L. *Family and Fortune* (Oxford, 1973)

Stone, L. *The Crisis of the Aristocracy, 1558–1640* (Oxford, 1964)

Strong, R. *Holbein and Henry VIII* (London, 1967)

Strong, R. *Nicholas Hilliard* (London, 1975)

Strong, R. *Portraits of Queen Elizabeth* (London, 1963)

Strong, R. *Splendour at Court* (London, 1973)

Strong, R. *The Cult of Elizabeth* (London, 1977)

Strong, R. *The English Renaissance Miniature* (London, 1983)

Strong, R. *Tudor and Jacobean Portraiture* 2 vols. (London, 1969)

Thomas, W. S. K. *Tudor Wales* (Llandysul, 1983)

Thomson, J. A. F. *The Transformation of Medieval England, 1370–1529* (London, 1983)

Tighe, W. J. 'Courtiers and politics in Elizabethan Herefordshire; James Croft, his friends and foes', *Historical Journal*, 32, 1989

Ullman, W. *Medieval Papalism* (London, 1949)

Vaughan, R. *Philip the Good* (London, 1970)

Vaughan, R. *Charles the Bold* (London, 1973)

Walker, Greg, 'The expulsion of the minions of 1519 reconsidered', *Historical Journal*, 32, 1989

Williams, G. *Harri Tudor a Chymru/Henry Tudor and Wales* (Cardiff, 1985)

Williams, N. *All the Queen's Men* (London, 1972)

Williams, N. *Thomas Howard, Fourth Duke of Norfolk* (London, 1964)

Williams, N. *Henry VIII and his court* (London, 1971)

Williams, P. *The Tudor Regime* (Oxford, 1979)

Wilson, D. *Sweet Robin; a biography of Robert Dudley, Earl of Leicester* (London, 1981)

Woodworth, A. *Purveyance for the Royal Household in the reign of Queen Elizabeth*, Transactions of the American Philosophical Society, 1945

Wright, Pamela, 'A change of direction; the ramifications of a female household', in *The English Court* (also RS, p. 183)

Yates, F. A. *Astraea; the Imperial theme in the sixteenth century* (London, 1975)

Youings, J. *The Dissolution of the Monasteries* (London, 1971)

Young, Alan, *Tudor and Jacobean Tournaments* (London, 1987) (also RS, p. 132)

Unpublished theses

Boscher, P. 'The Anglo-Scottish Border, 1550–1560' (Durham, 1985)

Braddock, R. C. 'The Royal Household, 1540–1560' (Northwestern, 1971)

Starkey, D. R. 'The development of the Privy Chamber, 1485–1547' (Cambridge, 1973)

Thurley, Simon, 'English Royal Palaces, 1450–1550' (Cambridge, 1989)

Tighe, W. J. 'The Gentlemen Pensioners in the reign of Elizabeth I' (Cambridge, 1984)

Ward, L. J. 'The Elizabethan Laws of Treason, 1558–1588' (Cambridge, 1985)

INDEX

Almoner 28, 43, 44, 121
Ampthill, Bedfordshire 172
Andre, Bernard 24, 116, 127
Arthur, Prince of Wales 6, 24, 26, 106, 109, 116, 118, 150, 201
Ascham, Roger 124–5, 126
Ashley, Catherine 58, 124
Ashridge, Hertfordshire 162
Aske, Robert 139
Askew, Anne 157, 180
Audley, Thomas 156

Bacon, Francis 26, 125, 145
Bacon, Nicholas 145
Bagnall, Ralph 97
Baldwin, William 113
Bale, John 31, 123
Baynards Castle, London 38
Beauchamp, Sir John 4
Beaufort, Edmund, Duke of Somerset 147
Beaufort, Margaret, Countess of Richmond and Derby 116, 127, 137, 150, 202
Bedingfield, Sir Henry 67, 95
Bell, Sir Robert 187
Bellay, Jean du 168–9
Berwick 73, 184
Blount, Edward 97
Blount, Elizabeth 178
Blount, William, Lord Mountjoy 27, 116, 117, 118
Boleyn, family of 125, 139
Boleyn, Anne 5, 29, 30, 109, 119, 129, 139, 153–4, 158, 169, 178, 180, 184, 193, 197
Boleyn, Mary 155, 184
Boleyn, Thomas, Earl of Wiltshire 139, 146, 153, 154–5, 199
Bosworth 24
Bourchier, Henry, 2nd Earl of Essex 151
Bourchier, John, Earl of Bath 159
Brandon, Charles, Duke of Suffolk 28, 47, 102, 103, 111, 120, 130, 134, 135, 140, 145, 146, 152–3, 155, 157, 196, 200
Brandon, Lady Eleanor 189
Brandon, Henry, Duke of Suffolk 121, 138–9, 153
Brereton, William 155

Brooke, George, Lord Cobham 200
Browne, Sir Anthony 155, 201
Browne, Anthony, Viscount Montague 143
Brown, Sir George 133
Bryan, Francis 3, 47, 48, 50, 53, 94, 97
Bryan, Margaret 120
Bucer, Martin 175
Bulmer, Sir William 151
Byrd, William 109, 111, 174

Cambridge 68, 116, 120, 121, 125
Camoys, Sir Thomas 4
Canterbury, Kent 109, 177
Carew, Nicholas 47, 48, 94, 155, 193
Carey, Henry, 1st Lord Hunsdon 197
Carey, Robert 184
Carey, William 88
Carwarden, Sir Thomas 113, 129, 198
Castiglione, Baldesar 3, 12, 99–100
Catherine of Aragon 4, 5, 6, 26, 56, 67, 98, 103, 106, 117–20, 123, 139, 151, 154–5, 170, 193
Cavendish, Sir William 80–81
Caxton, William 2, 21, 114
Cecil, Robert, Earl of Salisbury 146, 165, 195, 197
Cecil, William, Lord Burghley 63, 68, 72, 79, 125, 126, 144–5, 163–5, 183, 186
Chamber, Treasury of 48, 49, 73–7, 79
Chamberlain, Lord 40, 41, 45–7, 51, 53, 59, 60, 87, 91, 92, 111, 118, 120, 135, 149, 161, 165, 188
Chancellor Lord 2, 11, 16, 52, 154, 160, 161, 167
Chapel Royal 9, 33, 41, 106, 107, 109–12, 115, 123, 172, 174–6
Chapuys, Eustace 154–5, 168, 169–70
Charles I 192, 195, 200
Charles the Bold, Duke of Burgundy 7, 14, 15, 18, 22
Charles V, Emperor and King of Castile and Aragon 6, 29, 160, 169, 193
Charles V (of France) 18
Charles VI (of France) 13
Charles VII (of France) 13, 18
Chaucer, Geoffrey 2, 11

Cheke, John 121, 122, 123, 125
Cheney, Sir Thomas 155
Clarence, George, Duke of 136, 148, 194, 198
Cleves, Anne of 67, 193, 194, 200
Clifford, family of 139
Clifford, Henry, Earl of Cumberland 138
Clinton, Edward Fiennes de, Baron and Earl of Lincoln 91, 145
Clouet, Jean 128-9
Cobham, Thomas 92
Cofferer of household 42-3, 60-2, 73-82
Coke, Sir Edward 2, 187, 198
Colet, John 116, 118, 182
Compton, William 47-9, 82, 88, 151, 153
Controller (of household) 42, 59, 60-2, 66, 74, 78, 165
Conway, Sir Hugh 184
Cooke, Sir Anthony 122
Cook, Sir Thomas 148
Cope, Sir Anthony 67
Cope, William 74-5
Cornish, William 107, 112
Cornwall 72
Cornwallis, family of 144
Cornwallis, Sir Thomas 142-3, 189
Cottingham, Francis Lord 197
Courtenay, family of 135, 139, 142, 160
Courtenay, Edward, Earl of Devon 142, 160
Courtenay, Henry, Earl of Devon and Marquis of Exeter 49, 108, 111, 138, 155-6, 191, 201
Courtenay, William, Earl of Devonshire 102
Coxe, Dr. Richard 120-1, 123, 125
Crane, Sir Edward 167
Cranmer, Thomas, Archbishop of Canterbury 119, 120-23, 131, 154, 156, 157, 174, 180, 194, 198, 199
Croft, Sir James 59
Croke, Richard 117
Cromwell, Thomas 5, 30, 42, 51, 53, 60, 65, 70-1, 97, 107, 112, 119-20, 133-4, 139-40, 154-8, 179-80, 184, 186
Crosby, Sir John 197

Darcy, Thomas, Lord 135, 139, 156, 193
Darrel, Stephen 64
Delft, Van der 168, 170
Denny, Sir Anthony 82-3, 122, 157, 180, 199
Denys, Hugh 82
Devereux, Robert, 2nd Earl of Essex 85, 134, 145-7, 165
Devereux, Walter, Earl of Essex 145
Dormer, Jane 182
Douglas, Margaret, Lady 98
Dudley, family of 104, 143-4
Dudley, Ambrose, Earl of Warwick 103, 145, 165, 181
Dudley, Edmund 149

Dudley, Henry 133, 170
Dudley, John, Earl of Warwick, Duke of Northumberland 53-5, 68, 91-2, 103, 122-3, 141-2, 158-9, 175, 181, 189, 198, 199, 201
Dudley, Robert, Earl of Leicester 54, 86, 89, 103-4, 121, 126, 132, 134-5, 144-5, 163-6, 181, 183, 186, 190, 191, 198
Dürer, Abrecht 18
Durham Place 39

Edward III 12, 44
Edward IV 2, 5, 7-9, 15, 18-27, 44-5, 62, 74, 79, 109, 114-15, 127, 133, 134, 136, 146, 148-9, 166-7, 189, 194, 195
Edward VI 8, 30, 31, 32, 42, 51-6, 58, 62, 65, 66-7, 77, 78, 81-3, 88-9, 91, 95-7, 108, 113, 120-1, 123-4, 129, 131, 134, 146, 156-7, 159, 170, 175, 177, 180-1, 189, 195, 196, 197, 199
Eleanor of Aquitaine 11, 14
Elevetham 101, 111
Elizabeth I 5, 7, 8, 31, 35-6, 42-4, 57-9, 61-4, 68, 73, 78, 82-3, 85-6, 88-9, 92, 96, 100-1, 104-5, 107-9, 111-13, 124-6, 130-2, 134, 143-6, 160, 162, 168, 172, 182-3, 185, 188, 190-91, 194-7, 199-202
Elizabeth of York 5, 21, 23, 109, 150
Eltham, Kent 88, 100
Eltham Ordinances 44, 51, 59, 60, 63, 86, 89, 94, 97, 101, 153
Elyot, Sir Thomas 129
Empson, Richard 149
Englefield, family of 144
Englefield, Sir Francis 142, 162, 181
Erasmus, Desiderius 27, 116-21, 123-4, 126, 129, 180
Eric of Sweden 163
Essex 72
Eure, Sir William 139
Eworth, Hans 33, 131
Exchequer 16, 38, 48-9, 73-8, 80-81, 83
   Clerk of 9
Eyck, Jan Van 15, 17

Fane, Sir Ralph 55
Fastolf, Sir John 17
Felton, Edmund 81
Ferdinand of Spain 28
Ferrers, George 113
Field of Cloth of Gold 28, 100, 127, 152
Fisher, John 116, 119, 151, 174
Fitzalan, Henry, 12th Earl of Arundel 51, 54, 57, 85, 96, 143, 159, 160, 163, 164, 199
Fitzalan, William, 11th Earl of Arundel 158
Fitzpatrick, Barnaby 54, 121
Fitzroy, Henry, Duke of Richmond 121, 138, 152, 193, 200

Fitzwilliam, William, Earl of
     Southampton 155, 157–8
Fleet Street 89
Flodden, battle of 28, 138
Fortescue, Sir John 22
Fowler, John 53
Fox, Richard, Bishop of Winchester 137, 151
Framlingham 159
Francis I 1, 6, 18, 28, 48, 52, 100, 110, 117,
     128, 169
Freston, Richard 78

Gage, James 66
Gage, Sir John 66, 92
Gardiner, Stephen 30, 119, 120, 124, 133,
     154, 156–8, 160–61, 180, 195
Gawdy, Sir Thomas 187
Gheeraerts, Marcus 132
Gibson, Richard 107
Goodman, Christopher 163
Great Master, Lord 42, 51, 55, 60–61, 66,
     160
Greencloth, Board of 41, 43, 60, 62, 64,
     66–7, 69, 70–71
   Clerk of 61, 64, 65
Greenwich 68, 95, 100, 103, 104, 113, 172,
     178, 186
Grenville, Sir Richard 140
Gresham, Sir Thomas 83
Grey, family of 143, 159
Grey, George, Earl of Kent 186
Grey, Henry, Marquis of Dorset and Duke of
     Suffolk 141, 158–9
Grey, Sir Henry 189
Grey, Thomas, 1st Marquis of Dorset 148–9
Grey, Thomas, 2nd Marquis of Dorset 47,
     196
Grindal, William 121
Guevara, Antonio de 97, 191
Guildford, Sir Henry 47, 107, 129, 151
Guildford, Richard 74

Hall, Edward 50, 87, 106
Hall, Great 18, 44–5, 52, 62–4, 92
Hampton Court 45, 68, 100, 130, 172, 191,
     200–1
Hastings, Edward, Lord 95
Hastings, Francis, 2nd Earl of
     Huntingdon 121, 158
Hastings, George, 1st Earl of
     Huntingdon 154
Hastings, Lord Henry 143
Hastings, Sir Ralph 201
Hastings, William, Lord 136, 148–9
Hatfield, Hertfordshire 163
Hatton, Sir Christopher 109, 145, 165, 185,
     190, 197
Heath, Nicholas, Archbishop of York 194
Heneage, Sir Thomas (d 1553) 81

Heneage, Sir Thomas (d 1595) 145, 165
Henry II 9, 12
Henry II (of France) 89, 170
Henry III 10
Henry IV 13, 133
Henry V 13, 31, 114
Henry VI 1, 3, 5, 13, 18, 20–1, 26–7, 73–4,
     114, 135, 147–8, 177
Henry VII 5, 7, 8, 9, 20–1, 23–4, 25–8, 41,
     45–6, 50, 62, 65, 74, 79, 80, 82, 91,
     95–7, 100–1, 103, 106, 109, 113, 115–17,
     127, 134, 136–8, 140, 149–50, 168, 177,
     184, 189–90, 193–8, 200–2
Henry VIII 1, 3–8, 27–32, 41–2, 45, 47,
     52–3, 57–8, 60, 63, 65, 68, 71, 75–7,
     81–3, 86–9, 95–103, 106–8, 110, 113,
     115–18, 121–3, 125–7, 129, 130, 132,
     134–5, 138–42, 145–6, 150–57, 170–72,
     174, 178, 184–5, 191–202
Henry, Prince of Wales 199, 200
Herbert, William, Earl of Pembroke 85, 143,
     145, 158, 160–62, 196
Herbert, William, Lord 115, 136
Heron, John 79
Heywood, John 112–13
Hill, Richard 65
Hilliard, Nicholas 130–2
Holbein, Hans (the younger) 30–31, 129–30,
     132
Holcrofte, Sir Thomas 40, 91
Hooker, Richard 177, 183
Hopton, Sir Ralph 92
Horenbout, Lucas 128–31
Horenbout, Susanna 128
Howard, family of 125, 135, 139–40, 142,
     155–7, 159, 162
Howard, Catherine 156, 178, 193, 201
Howard, Charles, Lord Howard of
     Effingham and Earl of Nottingham 145,
     165, 188
Howard, Edward Sir 151
Howard, Elizabeth, Duchess of Norfolk 58
Howard, Sir George 104
Howard, Henry, Earl of Surrey 94, 98, 133,
     139, 157
Howard, Thomas, Lord 98
Howard, Thomas, 2nd Duke of Norfolk 28,
     136, 138, 152, 189
Howard, Thomas, 3rd Duke of Norfolk 92,
     142, 153, 157, 197
Howard, Thomas, 4th Duke of Norfolk 85,
     142, 144, 161, 163–4, 186, 187
Huddlestone, Sir John 161
Hussey, Anne, Lady 155
Hussey, John, Lord 135, 156
Hyde Park 158

Ingatestone Hall 68
Isabella, Queen of Castile 117, 125

James I 2, 3, 62, 147, 169, 188, 195–8, 202
James IV of Scotland 28, 106, 117, 127
Jane, Queen 55, 121, 156, 159
Jane, the fool 56, 113
Jerningham, Richard 49
Jewel House 16, 41, 78, 81
  Master of 75
John I 29
Jonson, Ben 108
Jones, Inigo 108
Julius II (Pope) 29

Kenilworth 190
Killigrew, William 184
Knevett, Charles 151
Knight of the Body 9, 22, 45–8, 151
Knight, William 168
Knollys, Sir Francis 57, 66, 81, 125
Knollys, Robert 48
Knollys, Sir William 165
Knox, John 123
Knyvett, Sir Thomas 47, 102

Langdale, George 109
Lascelles, John 180
Latimer, Hugh 5, 179, 180
Lee, Sir Henry 104
Leek, Sir Francis 191
Leigh, Sir John 161
Leland, John 123
Leslie, John, Bishop of Ross 170–71
'Liber Niger' 8, 18, 39, 41–2, 59–60, 62, 74,
  115, 172, 174
Lily, William 121
Linacre, Thomas 116, 118, 123
London 4, 33, 72, 92, 129, 139, 148, 152–3,
  157, 169, 178, 179, 186–7
  Tower of 92, 155, 161
Louis XI, of France 18
Louis XII, of France 28
Lovell, John, Lord 198
Lovell, Thomas 187–8
Lovett, George 79
Ludlow 114, 119
Lumley, John, Baron 164
Lumley, Lord 121
Luther, Martin 29, 119

Machiavelli, Niccolo 27, 120
Manners, Roger 57
Manners, Thomas, Earl of Rutland 139, 195
Manners, Henry, Earl of Rutland 85, 158
Margaret of Austria, Regent of the
  Netherlands 128
Margaret of Parma 131
Margaret, Queen (of Scotland) 178
Mary I 7–8, 32, 34, 42–3, 51, 55–9, 62, 64,
  65, 67, 71–2, 77–8, 80–3, 85, 88–9, 93,
  96/7, 101/2, 104, 108–9, 111–14, 118–21,
  123–4, 130–31, 135, 142–4, 146, 154–6,
  158–62, 168–70, 172, 174–6, 181–2, 188,
  189–90, 194–7, 199–201
Mary, Queen of Scots 162, 164–5, 170
Mason, Sir John 73, 81
Master of the Horse 38, 56, 101, 104, 144
Maximilian, Emperor 28
Medici, Lorenzo de 20, 114
Medwell, Henry 112
Memo, Dionisius 110
Mildmay, Sir Walter 80, 164
Mody, Edmond 89
More, Thomas 116, 118–19, 123, 129, 134,
  139, 154, 179
More, The Hertfordshire 198
Moro, Antonio 33, 131
Morton, John, Cardinal 112, 137
Moryson, Richard 30
Mowbray, Ann 22
Moyle, Sir Thomas 80
Muñatones, Brivesca de 40, 90

Naunton, Francis 163
Neville, Charles, Earl of Westmorland 85,
  135, 163–4
Neville, Edward 50, 102, 151
Neville, George, Archbishop of York 167
Neville, George, Lord Burgavenny 152
Neville, Henry, Earl of Westmorland 143
Neville, Ralph, Earl of Westmorland 152
Neville, Richard, Earl of Warwick 136, 148
New Romney 109
Noailles, Antoine de 161, 169–70
Nonsuch, Surrey 45, 63, 68, 130, 172
Norfolk 187–8
Norris, Henry 155
Norris, John 56
North, Roger, Lord 89, 165, 187–8, 191

Oldenhall, William 93
Oliver, Isaac 132
Opitiis, Benedictus de 110
Otford (Kent) 3
Oxford 19, 94, 118

Pace, Richard 118, 126, 168
Page, Sir Richard 120
Paget, William, Lord 65, 143, 156–7, 159–61
Paris 13
Parker, Henry, Lord Morley 120
Parker, Matthew, Archbishop 126
Parr, family of 139, 143–4
Parr, Catherine 65, 67, 89, 120–2, 125, 156,
  180, 193/4, 197–8
Parr, William, Earl of Essex, Marquis of
  Northampton 58, 139, 141, 144, 157–8
Parry, Blanche 133
Parry, Sir Thomas 57
Partridge, Miles 97

Paston, John 7, 133
Paulet, William, Marquis of Winchester 141, 143, 145–6, 158, 163
Peckham, Sir Edmund 77–8
Penshurst, Kent 39, 187
Percy, family of 135, 139, 156
Percy, Henry, 4th Earl of Northumberland 150
Percy, Henry, 5th Earl of Northumberland 152–4, 186
Percy, Henry, 6th Earl of Northumberland 152, 186
Percy, Thomas, 7th Earl of Northumberland 85, 135, 142, 163–4
Petre, John 96
Petre, Sir William 68, 96, 98
Philip II 6–8, 33–4, 40–41, 57, 67, 71, 78, 90, 93, 95, 103, 123, 131, 143, 160–62, 168, 172, 176, 189–90
Philip the Fair, Duke of Burgundy 127
Plantagenet, Arthur, Lord Lisle 3
Pole, Edmund, Earl of Suffolk 139, 196
Pole, Henry, Lord Montague 156
Pole, John de la, Earl of Lincoln 149
Pole, Margaret, Countess of Salisbury 157, 179
Pole, Reginald, Cardinal 95, 120, 124, 162, 179, 194
Pole, William de la, Duke of Suffolk 147
Pope, Sir Thomas 201
Poynings, Sir Thomas 201
Privy Chamber 3, 41, 44–59, 65, 76–7, 80, 83, 86, 88, 90, 91, 95–6, 98, 107, 111, 130, 133, 141, 150, 153, 155–8, 160, 164, 169, 184, 190, 196
Privy Seal 15, 78, 120, 145
  Clerk of 12
Praet, Louis de 171
Puebla, Rodrigo de 149, 168–9

Radcliffe, Henry, 2nd Earl of Sussex 159
Radcliffe, Robert, 1st Earl of Sussex 154
Radcliffe, Thomas, 3rd Earl of Sussex 86, 89, 104, 131, 145, 163, 165, 191, 199
Raleigh, Walter 145, 165
Randolf, Colonel Edward 143
Rastell, John 112
Ratcliff, Sir James 133
Ray, Sir Roger 45
Reed, Sir Bartholomew 199
Renard, Simon 160–1, 168
Rich, Sir Richard 140, 156, 201
Richard II 9, 13, 22, 26
Richard III 23, 33, 134, 136
Richmond, Surrey 25, 26, 127, 172
Rochester, Sir Robert 55, 159, 181
Rochford, George, Lord 155
Russell, Francis, 2nd Earl of Bedford 181, 198

Russell, John, Earl of Bedford 141, 158–9, 161

Sackford, Henry 58
Sackville, Thomas, Lord Buckhurst 165
Sadler, Ralph 133
Sampson, Richard 175–6
Sandys, Lord William 51, 194
Saxton, Christopher 126
Scrots, William 131
Seymour, family of 139, 157
Seymour, Anne 198
Seymour, Edward, Duke of Somerset and Lord Protector 54–5, 65, 72, 81, 91, 122, 133–4, 156–9, 180, 200–1
Seymour, Edward, Earl of Hertford 139–41, 144
Seymour, Jane 89, 119, 155
Seymour, Sir Thomas 67, 83
Seymour, Thomas, Lord S. of Sudeley 53–4, 156, 158
Sheen 178, 179
Sidney, Sir Henry 145, 165, 201
Sidney, Philip 2, 125
Sidney, Sir Robert 3, 187
Sidney, Sir William 120, 199
Simnel, Lambert 149
Skelton, John 98, 108, 112, 116, 126, 153
Smeaton, Mark 110, 155
Smith, Sir Thomas 164
Somers, William 56, 113
Somerset, Charles, Earl of Worcester 47–8, 138
Southwark 92, 127
Southwell, Sir Richard 92, 188
Southwell, Robert 188
Stafford, Edward, 3rd Duke of Buckingham 85, 136–7, 139, 146, 150–53, 185, 189, 190, 199
Stafford, Henry, Earl of Wiltshire 137–8, 150–2
Stafford, Henry, Duke of Buckingham 149
Stanhope, Sir Michael 53–4, 141
Stanley, Sir Edward 199
Stanley, Edward, 3rd Earl of Derby 142–3, 146, 152, 158, 161, 170
Stanley, Thomas, 1st Earl of Derby 136
Stanley, Sir William 91, 138, 149
Starkey, Thomas 119
Steward, Lord 4, 39–42, 50–51, 53, 57, 60–61, 66, 67, 85, 90–91, 138, 145, 153, 165
St Albans, Hertfordshire 147
St Low, Sir William 57
le Strange, Sir Nicholas 133

Talbot, Francis, 5th Earl of Shrewsbury 143, 158–9, 161–3

Talbot, George, 4th Earl of Shrewsbury 137, 142, 153–4, 156–7, 170, 185–6, 191
Talbot, George, 6th Earl of Shrewsbury 190
Talbot, Gilbert, 7th Earl of Shrewsbury 146
Talbot, Mary 185
Tallis, Thomas 109, 111, 174, 176
Teerlinc, Levina 130–2
Thornbury Castle 152
Throgmorton, Sir Nicholas 164, 184
Tiptoft, John, Earl of Worcester 114
Titchfield 164
Tonge, Susan, *alias* Clarencius 56, 58, 95, 133
Torrigiano 127, 130
Treasurer, Lord 19, 20, 78, 81, 148
Treasurer (of Household) 40, 42, 61, 73, 75, 187
Treasorer, William 109
Tudor, Jasper, Duke of Bedford 115, 136, 150
Tuke, Sir Brian 80, 82
Tunstall, Cuthbert, Bishop of Durham 52, 194
Tyler, William 47
Tyndale, William 119, 179
Tyrwhyt, Sir Thomas 67

Udall, Nicholas 32, 113, 120
Underhill, Edward 56, 64, 92–3, 97, 176, 181, 182, 184
Unton, Sir Edward 198

Vere, Edward de, Earl of Oxford 89
Vere, John de, Earl of Oxford 186
Vere, Robert de 4
Vergil, Polydore 25, 115
Vice-Chamberlain 50, 53, 57, 66, 95, 120, 161, 165

Vives, Juan Luis 118, 121, 123

Waldegrave, Sir Edward 38, 159, 162, 181
Waldegrave, William 55
Walsingham, Sir Francis 125, 145, 165
Warbeck, Perkin 137, 149
Warham, William, Archbishop 129, 151
Warton, Sir Thomas 159
Weldon, Thomas 73, 79
Wentworth, Lord Thomas 154
Westminster Palace 4, 105, 113, 166, 186
Weston, Sir Francis 155
Whitehall 30, 68, 92, 129, 172, 186
Williams, Sir John 161
Willoughby, Catherine (Duchess of Suffolk) 122, 180
Winchester 64
Windsor Manor, Berkshire 22, 68, 166, 172, 173, 176–7
Wolsey, Thomas 4, 28, 44, 48–51, 53, 70, 75–6, 79–80, 82, 86, 88, 94–6, 107, 112, 118, 128, 133–5, 139, 151–4, 169, 171, 179, 185–6, 193, 196–8, 202
Woodstock, Oxfordshire 68
Woodville, family of 134, 148–9
Woodville, Anthony, Earl Rivers 114, 136
Woodville, Elizabeth 149
Woodville, Richard, Earl Rivers 148
Wotton, Edward, Lord 194
Wriothesley, Thomas, Lord Chancellor 52, 141, 157
Wyatt, Sir Henry 134
Wyatt, Sir Thomas 92–3, 160
Wyatt, Thomas (the elder) 98
Wyndham, Francis 187

York Place 39

Zouch, Sir Edward 202